DESPERATE MAGIC

VALERIE KIVELSON

DESPERATE MAGIC

The Moral Economy of Witchcraft in Seventeenth-Century Russia

CORNELL UNIVERSITY PRESS ITHACA AND LONDON

First published 2013 by Cornell University Press
First printing, Cornell Paperbacks, 2013

Printed in the United States of America

Library of Congress Cataloging-in-Publication Data

Kivelson, Valerie A. (Valerie Ann), author.
Desperate magic: the moral economy of witchcraft in seventeenth-century Russia / Valerie Kivelson.
pages cm
Includes bibliographical references and index.
ISBN 978-0-8014-5146-1 (cloth : alk. paper)
ISBN 978-0-8014-7916-8 (pbk. : alk. paper)
1. Witchcraft—Russia—History—17th century. 2. Magic—Social aspects—Russia—History—17th century. 3. Trials (Witchcraft)—Russia—History—17th century. 4. Russia—Social conditions—17th century. I. Title.
BF1584.R9K58 2013
133.4'3094709032—dc23 2013016811

Cornell University Press strives to use environmentally responsible suppliers and materials to the fullest extent possible in the publishing of its books. Such materials include vegetable-based, low-VOC inks and acid-free papers that are recycled, totally chlorine-free, or partly composed of nonwood fibers. For further information, visit our website at www.cornellpress.cornell.edu.

Cloth printing 10 9 8 7 6 5 4 3 2 1
Paperback printing 10 9 8 7 6 5 4 3 2 1

With love and gratitude,

I dedicate this book to

Myron and Lynne Hofer

and to my aunts, Nina Auerbach and Ellie Palais

Contents

Maps and Figures

MAPS

FIGURES

Acknowledgments

WHEN A PROJECT takes as long to come to fruition as this one, debts of gratitude mount up and memory dims. I fear omitting recognition of people and institutions that have been critical to the completion of this book and to whatever degree of success it manages to achieve.

My thinking about Russian witchcraft began when I was in Moscow doing research for my dissertation, and has perked along as a side project in the intervening decades. My thanks therefore have to stretch back to the inspiration and guidance of my Stanford friends and mentors, above all Nancy Shields Kollmann, who continues to inspire and guide my thinking.

In Russia, I need to thank the indefatigable Olga Kosheleva, for her strenuous efforts in locating and scanning documents, offering advice, references, and her help with difficult translations. To the staff at RGADA, and particularly Andrei Bulychev, my thanks for filling my many archival requests. I have benefited from the intellectual community of the lively circle of scholars of Russian witchcraft in Moscow, E. B. Smilianskaia, A. L. Toporkov, and A. V. Chernetsov, who have become dear friends.

The small group of scholars interested in Russian witchcraft extends beyond the borders of Russia, and I am grateful to have extended my world by getting to know many of them. I want to extend a special thanks to the ever generous and admirably learned Will Ryan. For an unforgettable workshop devoted to Russian witchcraft, held in Paris in the summer of 2009, I thank our host, Aleksandr Lavrov, who not only organized the workshop but also shared his archival notes, his insights, and his suggestions unstintingly. Many hours spent disputing, debating, and discussing with him and others interested in Russian magic, including Kateryna Dysa, Eve Levin, Elena Smilianskaia, and Christine

Worobec, are reflected in this book. To Christine Worobec, I owe deep gratitude for her close and careful reading of the entire manuscript.

Other colleagues also have read the manuscript in part or in whole, some repeatedly. For their generous readings, good humor, and sometimes pointed criticism I thank Hussein Fancy, David Goldfrank, Bob Greene, Sueann Caulfield, Sue Juster, Nancy Kollmann, Leslie Pincus, Helmut Puff, Michael MacDonald, Gary Marker, Paolo Squatriti, and Elise Wirtschafter.

The number of people who have offered valuable ideas and productive suggestions in conversation or in response to my various presentations are too many to list here, but I will mention a few in particular: Brian and Elena Boeck, Jane Burbank, Paul Bushkovitch, Nikos Chrissidis, Stuart Clark, Michael Flier, Michael David-Fox, Sean Hanretta, Jean Hébrard, Dan Kaiser, Carol Karlsen, Webb Keane, Michael Khodarkovsky, Richard Kieckhefer, Erik Midlefort, Claudio Ingerflom-Nun, Michael Ostling, Don Ostrowski, Dan Rowland, Rebecca Scott, Dan Smail, Laura Stokes, Charles Zika. Brian Levack welcomed me into the field when I first ventured into witchcraft studies. I've been lucky enough to teach all aspects of witchcraft over the years, and I want to thank collectively the students in my courses and the graduate student instructors who have taught with me. Among them I should single out Jon Shaheen, whose philosophical insight provided the basis for our coauthored article, and Leann Wilson, always a sharp interlocutor. Joan Neuberger, as always, has been with the project at every step of the way, from greasy Moscow apartments to beignets and inspiration in New Orleans. Ron Suny has suffered through more conversations about witchcraft than anyone, especially someone with interests in political science, would ever want to hear.

John Hill and Karl Longstreth put many long hours into generating the maps for this project. Resident statistical and computer consultant Tim Hofer walked me through the perils of databases and Rebecca Hofer produced the chart of trial dates with finesse. John Ackerman at Cornell University Press responded to my initial proposal with his signature acumen and clarity. I am grateful for his support through the publication process.

For making this research and travel possible, I need to acknowledge the generous support of the National Endowment for the Humanities and IREX, as well as numerous branches of the University of Michigan: the Office for the Vice President for Research, the College of LS&A, the Department of History, the Center for Russian, East European, and Eurasian Research, and especially the Institute for the Humanities, where I was privileged to spend one of the most intellectually exciting years of my career in the company of a varied group of dynamic scholars.

To my amazing family, my dynamic and delightful aunts, Nina Auerbach and Ellie Palais; my brilliant in-laws, Lynne and Myron Hofer; my girls, Rebecca, Leila, and Tamar, who have grown up while I was staring at my notes and computer screen; my brother Steve, who gamely listens; my space-physicist mother Margaret Kivelson, who takes the time to read whatever I send her, I send my love and thanks. For Tim, always and ever, I thank my lucky stars.

PORTIONS OF THE FOLLOWING ARTICLES appear in this book in reworked form, with permission of the publishers: "Caught in the Act: An Illustration of Erotic Magic at Work," in *Dubitando: Studies in History and Culture in Honor of Donald Ostrowski*, edited by Brian Boeck, Russell E. Martin, and Daniel Rowland, 285–300. Bloomington, IN: Slavica Publishers, 2012. "Lethal Convictions: The Power of a Satanic Paradigm in Russian and European Witch Trials," *Magic, Ritual, and Witchcraft* 6, no.1 (2011): 34–61. ©2011 University of Pennsylvania Press. "Torture, Truth, and Embodying the Intangible in Muscovite Witchcraft Trials," in *Everyday Life in Russian History: Quotidian Studies in Honor of Daniel Kaiser*, edited by Gary Marker, Joan Neuberger, Marshall Poe, and Susan Rupp, 359–73. Bloomington, IN: Slavica Publishers, 2010. "Coerced Confessions, or If Tituba had been enslaved in Muscovy," in *The New Muscovite Cultural History: A Collection in Honor of Daniel B. Rowland*, edited by Valerie Kivelson, Karen Petrone, Nancy Shields Kollmann, and Michael Flier, 171–84. Bloomington, IN: Slavica Publishers, 2009. "What was *Chernoknizhestvo*? Black Books and Foreign Writings in Muscovite Magic," in *Rude and Barbarous Kingdom Revisited: A Festschrift for Robert O. Crummey*, edited by Chester S. L. Dunning, Russell E. Martin, and Daniel Rowland, 1–15. Bloomington, IN: Slavica Publishers, 2008.

Abbreviations

ARCHIVAL ABBREVIATIONS

RGADA	Rossiiskii gosudarstvennyi arkhiv drevnikh aktov (Russian State Archive of Ancient Documents), Moscow
RNB	Rossiiskaia natsional'naia biblioteka (Russian National Library), St. Petersburg
SPbII(RAN)	Arkhiv Sankt-Peterburgskogo instituta istorii Rossiikoi akademii nauk (Archive of the St. Petersburg Institute of History of the Russian Academy of Sciences), St. Petersburg

Within archival citations:

ch.	*chast'* (part)
d.	*delo* (document)
ed. khr.	*edinitsa khraneniia* (document)
l.	*list* (folio, plural *ll.*) When a single trial occupies an entire document, the number precedes the *ll.* (thus, a 208 page document appears as 208 *ll.*)
ob.	*oborot* (verso)
stol	bureau
stlb.	*stolbets* (file, stack of papers stored as a unit)
stolpik	small stack, part of a subdivided file

Publications

AAE	*Akty, sobrannye v bibliotekakh i arkhivakh rossiiskoi imperii arkheograficheskoiu ekspeditsieiu.*

AI	*Akty istoricheskie*
AIu	*Akty iuridicheskie*
ChOIDR	*Chteniia v imperatorskom obshchestve istorii i drevnostei rossiiskikh, pri Moskovskom universitete.* 264 vols. Moscow: Universitetskaia tipografiia, 1846–1918.
ODiB	*Opisanie dokumentov i bumag, khraniashchikhsia v Moskovskom arkhive Ministerstva iustitsii.* 21 vols. Moscow: Tipo-lit. T-va I. N. Kushnerev, 1869.
PLDR	*Pamiatniki literatury Drevnei Rusi.* 12 vols. Edited by D. S. Likhachev and L. A. Dmitriev. Moscow: Khudozhestvennaia literature, 1978–1994.
PRP	*Pamiatniki russkogo prava.* Edited by S. V. Iushkov and L. V. Cherepnin. 8 vols. Moscow: Gosudarstvennoe izd. Iuridicheskoi literatury, 1952–1963.
PSRL	*Polnoe sobranie russkikh letopisei.* 43 vols. as of 2004. St. Petersburg and Moscow: various publishers, 1841– .
PSZ	*Polnoe sobranie zakonov rossiiskoi imperii.* Series 1, 1649–1825, 45 vols. St. Petersburg: Otdelenie sobstvennoi Ego Imperatorskago Velichestva kantseliarii, 1830.
RIB	*Russkaia Istoricheskaia Biblioteka.* 39 vols. St. Petersburg: Petrograd, Leningrad: various publishers, 1872–1927.
SKKDR	Likhachev, Dmitrii Sergeevich, ed. *Slovar' knizhnikov i knizhnosti Drevnei Rusi.* 3 in 8 vols. Leningrad: "Nauka," Leningradskoe otd-nie, 1987.
TODRL	*Trudy Otdela drevnerusskoi literatury.* Leningrad-St. Petersburg, Nauka, 1934– .

Note on Names and Transliteration

IN THE SEVENTEENTH CENTURY, only highly placed elites enjoyed the privilege of using patronymics as we know them today, adding *-ovich or -evich*, for men and *-ovna* or *-evna*, for women, onto the father's first name. The rest of the population used two-word familial indicators, such as *Andreev syn* (Andrei's son), Ivanova *doch'* (Ivan's daughter), or *Maksimova zhena* (Maksim's wife). I have tried to preserve that distinction, while working not to weigh down the text with unwieldy names.

Transliteration from Russian conforms to the Modified Library of Congress system. I have followed the original spellings for most names, but have chosen a single spelling when the documents are inconsistent. Spelling can be haphazard in the original texts. When using names or titles in the English text, I have dropped some soft and hard sign indicators, but have left them where I provide the Russian terminology. Certain names have been modified for ease of English readers.

Arkhangel'sk
Iarensk
Tot'ma
Belozersk
Sokol
Vologda
Chukhloma
Galich
Gdov
Novgorod
Kostroma
Kineshma
Iaroslavl'
Bezhetskii Verkh

Map of European Russia showing locations of witchcraft trials.

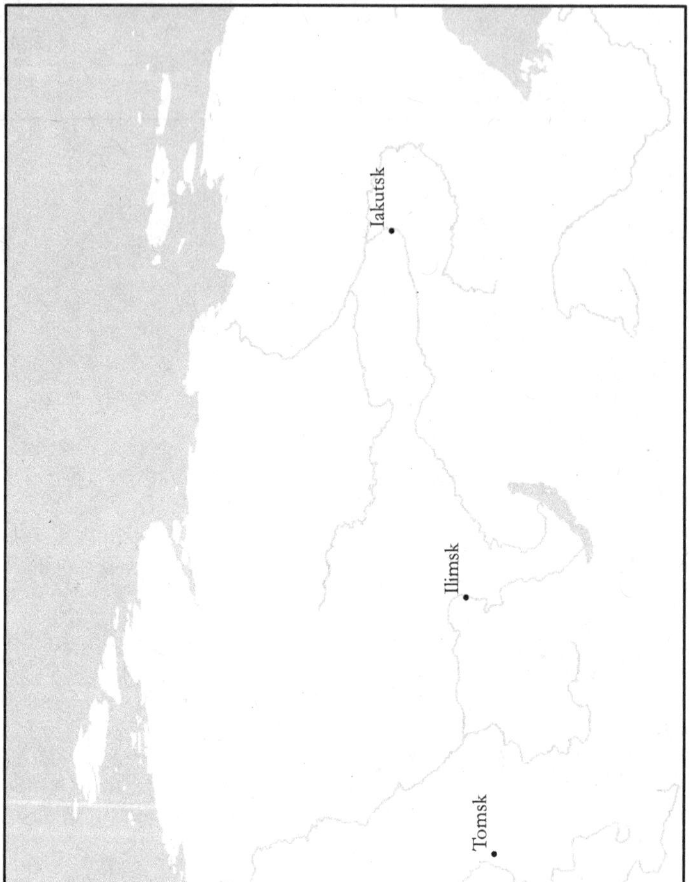

Map of Siberia and Eurasia showing locations of witchcraft trials.

DESPERATE MAGIC

Introduction

The Moral Economy of Desperation in Seventeenth-Century Russia

IN 1626 THE GOVERNOR OF DEDILOV, a provincial center not far from Kursk in the south of Russia, found himself responsible for trying a local low-ranking military servitor, Iakushko Shchurov, on charges of practicing magic. The charge was based on the telltale evidence of a root, found tucked under his belt. Possession of a root was more than enough to land Iakushko in court, facing serious consequences. Confronted with such incriminating evidence, Iakushko admitted to possessing the root, but insisted that he had not used it to work any harm. In fact, the root was so innocuous that he ate it in the presence of the judge, and "nothing happened to him." In spite of the drama of his courtroom performance, Iakushko was subjected to two rounds of torture, during which he elaborated on his story. When he had spent time in the town of Novosil, in the southern frontier region, a man called Vesela (Cheerful) Neustroika gave the root to him, but he knew nothing further about who the man was or whose bondsman he might be. Having obtained the root, he admitted as he endured first one and then a second round of unspecified torture, he put it to use as a magical aphrodisiac when "he went for illicit reasons to the wife of his fellow Kursk military servitor, Sidorko Kostiantinov. And in the past year, that military servitor Sidorko caught him with his wife and beat him and robbed him." It was when Iakushko took the angry husband to court over the beating and robbery that the court officials spotted his root and the real trouble began for him. "But other than that root," he explained "he doesn't know anything about roots and has worked no evil against anyone."[1] The report on this case, involving low-level soldiers, heard before a provincial governor in a distant part of Russia, was sent directly to the tsar, or at least the representatives who acted in his name at the Ministry of Military Affairs in Moscow, and the resolution was sent back to the regional officials. Iakushko was to be released from jail and restored to his previous station, but he was to be held to a firm guarantee "not to use witchcraft (*vedovstvo*) or to engage in criminal behavior (*vorovat'*) or conspire or use grasses or roots or keep anything evil on his person."[2]

Twenty years later, in 1647, another man faced charges of witchcraft, this time after being seen in possession not of a root but of "improper" writing (*neistovye pis'ma*)." Iuri Shestakov, clerk of the Zemskii Prikaz (tax office), reported to his superiors in the chancellery that on the riverbank behind the Savior Monastery in Kozlov, in the militarized southern frontier region, he had come across a monastic servitor reading those "improper writings." Tearing them out of the man's hands, Iuri dutifully turned them in to the chancellery under his own seal, "but he didn't say the name of the servitor so that the servitor, having heard of this denunciation, wouldn't conceal himself." The court record reports that the monastic servitor was found and said his name was Garasimko Kostiantinov. The case immediately reached the attention of the highest authorities, and within days, Garasimko found himself in Moscow, facing interrogation by top ranking nobles of the land. A panel of mighty officials questioned him to discover "whether those heretical notebooks were his and whether he wrote them and who taught him such criminality (*vorovstvo*), and from whom he copied them." The notebooks, when examined by the court, were found to contain the formulaic words "slave of God Garasimko," written over and over again. Garasimko also confessed to possessing a spell for protection against gunshot wounds. While these jottings might sound harmless, they did not appear so to the company of noble officials. Assembling in the torture chamber, they interrogated Garasimko as he stood alongside the instruments of torture. Subsequently, he was "tortured harshly. He was raised on the strappado twice and he was given forty-two blows, and his head was shaved, and water was poured on his head, and he was burned hard with fire." His ill-considered notes were not taken lightly. Nonetheless, the case took a surprising turn at the end: On October 2, after a four-month ordeal, "the sovereign favored Garasimko and ordered him released on firm surety for good behavior."[3]

Throughout Christian Europe, ecclesiastical and secular courts oversaw the interrogation, conviction, and execution of tens of thousands of supposed witches in the late sixteenth and seventeenth centuries. Orthodox Russia, slightly late to enter the fray, jumped into the general mêlée with some enthusiasm by the early 1600s, and tried its fair share of witches and practitioners of magic.[4] Records survive for about 230 seventeenth-century trials conducted in secular courts. The cases involved about 500 people accused in one way or another of practicing or using magic.[5] About an equal number of court cases survive for the following century.[6]

When compared with the better-known and far more sensational trials that held much of continental Europe spellbound from the fifteenth through the early eighteenth century, Iakushko's and Garasimko's stories seem quite modest. Their trials display none of the key narrative elements that someone even glancingly familiar with Western witch trials might expect to encounter, particularly given the fact that their confessions were extracted through the repeated application of torture. In European trials, torture could reliably elicit ornate confessions of sexual encounters with devils, flight to distant locations through the use of unguents or airborne beasts or brooms, participation at black Sabbaths, pacts with the Devil, and, frequently, lurid descriptions of infanticide, cannibalism, and orgies. Iakushko, by contrast, had a root in his pocket and occasionally made illicit visits to his married lady-friend. Garasimko's infraction consisted of carrying scraps of paper in his purse, and hoping for improving his odds in battle. Ultimately, both of these men were released, despite clear, material evidence of their guilt in the particular crimes of which they stood accused. Not all Russian witches received such lenient sentences; close to 15 percent of those for whom sentences can be documented were executed, almost 40 percent were exiled, and the same percentage were released, like Iakushko and Garasimko, with "firm sureties," that is, bound to good behavior by a document signed by themselves and their neighbors and enforced through collective oversight. The remainder suffered a variety of fates: some died during torture, some escaped from prison and disappeared, and a few were sent to monasteries or convents where they were sentenced to prayer, repentance, and hard labor.[7] Moreover, in sharp contrast to the prototypical European witch, Iakushko and Garasimko were men. Unlike the vast majority of European witches, who were so overwhelmingly female that the term itself carries female associations in most languages, our subjects, as men, were typical of those tried as witches in Russian courts. Far more men than women faced formal charges of witchcraft during the period of the trials, but women too were brought before the courts, and their stories followed similar, usually unspectacular, lines.

A third example, one involving female witches and charges of malevolent magic, rounds out this brief introduction of Russian witchcraft trials. This one began in 1682 in Putivl', in the south, with a complaint filed by the governor himself, Prince Ivan Nikiforovich Bol'shoi Beloselskoi, against a local widow, Natalia Iatsyna, and her household slave woman, Nastasia. The governor charged that the slave woman came to his house, took a potion (*zel'e*) out from a cloth, and sprinkled it on the threshold between the entry hall and the visiting chamber. "At that moment," he continued, "my household boys, Garaska and the Tatar Sereshka, who live with me in my chambers, grabbed that slave woman Nast'ka with that potion, and brought her to the governor's office, and I, your slave,[8] ordered the secretary (*d'iak*) Ilia Kolpakov to question [her]." In the first round of questioning, Nast'ka admitted that she had sprinkled the potion on the threshold of the governor's house. During her second interrogation, she added that she had done so at the behest of her mistress, so that the governor and his wife and children "would die a painful, miserable death." The magic was evidently effective, as the governor added that he and his wife and children all were critically ill at the time of his writing. This case surfaces in the archives only thanks to a suit that revisited the circumstances eight years later, when a local clerk sued about the governor's improper procedures in the earlier case. The clerk claimed that the witchcraft charges had been part of what he revealed to be a larger, intra-familial dispute over property: various estates were contested among various branches of the intermarried Iatsyn and Beloselskoi families, and these intricate tensions pitted the governor against his own stepmother, the widow Iatsyna. This post hoc petition illuminates the familial hostility that underlay the governor's original suspicions: he knew that Iatsyna had good reason to harbor animosity against him, since his property claims conflicted with those of her son. The documentary record trails off without any satisfactory resolution or clarification.[9]

These brief examples raise the pressing question of terminology. Since translation is required to fit Russian categories into European ones, one can ask whether "witch" and "witchcraft" accurately convey the kind of people and practices, the understandings of magic and its workings, that characterize the Russian evidence. Anthropologists have long attempted to distinguish among various manifestations of the supernatural through carefully defined terminology. Magic is generally loosely differentiated from religion in that the efficacy of the former derives from the mechanical performance of particular rites and rituals, whereas religion (prayer) involves supplication to higher forces and achieves its ends only to the extent that the deities respond. E. E. Evans-Pritchard established a widely adopted taxonomy when he distinguished witchcraft from sorcery. In his terminology, the witch exercises innate supernatural powers (such as the evil eye), whereas sorcery is a learned craft.[10] Useful though they are, these neat distinctions do not hold up well in exploring the dynamics of either European or Russian witchcraft. Russian suspects usually described their skills as learned from others, self-taught, or acquired in a vision. Occasionally, however, they were credited with a more innate power to curse through the evil eye, which shows that the internal versus learned distinction, like other efforts at delineation and definition, falls flat.[11] Historians have generally adopted more pragmatic definitions: witchcraft is often defined loosely as "the practice of *maleficium* [harm inflicted through supernatural means], which often (but not always) involved an imagined liaison between the witch and the Devil, or a demonic being such as a familiar," or simply "the attribution of misfortune to occult human agency."[12] Russian witchcraft conforms to the latter, more hands-on definition. Witches were thought to inflict harm through manipulation of supernatural forces. In this study, I have chosen to maintain the distinctions evident in the sources themselves. I translate any of the spectrum of terms applied to Russian, Christian practitioners of magic (*koldovstvo, vedovstvo, volshebstvo, chernoknizhestvo, charodeistvo*) as witchcraft. The terms *volkhovstvo* or *volkhovanie*, which the sources generally reserve for non-Russian, non-Christian practitioners, I translate as "sorcery."[13]

Healers who muttered spells over their medicaments or fortunetellers who cast bones or dice to predict the future might be accused of witchcraft, but for the most part they were not. Muscovy was a society rife with practices that could, under the right circumstances, earn the label of magic, but under other circumstances might be accepted as perfectly appropriate. Without any kind of professional or "scientific" medical establishment to pose a more respectable alternative, in times of need Muscovites had no choice but to turn to the rituals of the church, to seek home remedies, or to employ the services of passing healers.[14] The pervasiveness of magical healing, using roots and spells, raises the puzzling questions of why so few cases reached the courts and how Muscovites decided what should pass unremarked and what, by contrast, constituted a grievous supernatural crime. The evidence of court testimony points to particularly dire outcomes, intense personal vendettas, or, most particularly, perceived moral violations as the triggers that propelled cases from the unexceptional to the horrific.

Russian witch trials remain largely unexplored in scholarly literature, while the literature on European and North American witchcraft in the early modern era is vast and ever expanding. Studies of witchcraft from Germany to Salem, produced since the 1970s, offer exciting insights into the lives, experiences, and mentalities of people whose worlds were framed by particular belief systems, gender regimes, and material constraints. More recently, a newer line of research has begun to tap the sources on witch trials and witch belief in the European peripheries, particularly of eastern and northern Europe. This exceptionally rich European historiography is alluring, but also daunting. How can yet another investigation of witchcraft make its mark in a field so densely populated with brilliant scholars and dazzling books? Rolf Schulte mentions in passing that for his study of male witches in central Europe he analyzed data from eighty-two monographs published prior to 2007, each of which focused on territories within the Holy Roman Empire and met his standards of scholarly rigor.[15] If one expands the field to include studies outside of this geographic area (or with less quantitative rigor), the numbers soar. One more niche study—the witch trials in yet another distant periphery of Europe—seems hardly necessary.

And yet, as already intimated here, Russia witchcraft offers novel twists that make it particularly intriguing, both as a test case or controlled study of witchcraft itself as a cross-cultural phenomenon and as a route to new insights into the otherwise all-but-inaccessible lives of ordinary Russians in a largely illiterate society. With *Desperate Magic*, I hope to speak to the central puzzles of Muscovite history as well as to the transnational issues of comparative witchcraft.

What features characterized the Russian difference? First, and most strikingly, where throughout the rest of the Christian West, from Poland to New England, with only small pockets of exception, the overwhelming majority of those accused of witchcraft were female, in Russia the gender ratio was reversed. It was males who comprised 75 percent of the accused. Second, where by the sixteenth century in most of Western and central Europe, and by the second half of the seventeenth century in the Scandinavian and Baltic lands of the north and in New England, the link between witchcraft and Satan had established itself as an incontrovertible presumption, an overarching explanatory model for understanding the eerie efficacy of magic, in Russia that connection remained blurry, undeveloped, and little invoked. And third, perhaps most revealing of all, the particular issues of anxiety and concern that impelled people to turn to magic differed in significant ways from those that have been identified at the core of Western European witchcraft.

In Russia, where the whole enterprise of rational theology was somewhat lethargic, little intellectual energy was directed toward understanding or theorizing the phenomenon of witchcraft. Its links to demons or to the satanic remained undeveloped. As in other regions, infertility, illness, death, and sustenance all figure in as important foci of magical intervention, for good or for ill. Significantly, however, another layer of concerns surfaces again and again as a key element in Russian cases, a strand little remarked in the Western literature. The central concern, the desperation that pushed people to seek magical solutions to their problems, stemmed from the arbitrary and cruel exactions of hierarchy. Magic offered a language for understanding and a tool for ameliorating the harsh conditions of abusively enforced patriarchy, bondage, and social inequality. Such concerns appear in the annals of Western witchcraft trials as well, but with far less frequency, as an occasional note rather than a constant dirge.

Not only those at the bottom of the social heap—poor beggars, abused wives, or oppressed serfs and slaves—but literally every degree of person turned to magic with the fervent hope that it might rid them of a cruel superior or stay his or her hand, whether through benign or malignant means. From the slave woman tormented by her master to the boyar-prince seeking favor with the tsar, magical intervention aimed toward evoking mercy and mitigating punishment from those more powerful: may my husband be kind to me and stop beating me, may my in-laws love me, may my master and mistress not torment me with fire and chains, may my military commander not send me to die at the front, may the judge rule in my favor, may my patron at court assist me in time of extremity, may the tsaritsa favor my cause, may the tsar look kindly on me. Such are the bread and butter of Muscovite magic, the nexus of fantasy intermingled with the harsh, physical realities and social structures and strictures of daily life. The life-or-death need to sway the otherwise unchallengeable will of a social superior subsumed everyone in society from top to bottom of the social pyramid. Magic was bred of desperation, a desperation endemic to the social order.

This particular cast of Muscovite magic emerged within the increasingly entrenched and oppressive structures of hierarchy, dependence, and serfdom that characterized the seventeenth century. In making sense of the ways in which witchcraft was a product of and response to that overarching context, the notion of a "moral economy" provides a useful conceptual tool. The term made its scholarly debut in E. P. Thompson's influential 1971 article, "The Moral Economy of the English Crowd," and has gained traction as an enormously productive model in history and in other disciplines in the intervening decades. Drawing his evidence from interactions between protesters and authorities during the English grain riots of the eighteenth century, Thompson formulated a culturally inflected model, by which "grievances operated within a popular consensus as to what were legitimate and what were illegitimate practices. . . . An outrage to these moral assumptions, quite as much as actual deprivation, was the usual occasion for direct action."[16] Although new notions of capitalist commodity exchange were circulating and were available to justify pricing according to market demand, "the form of much economic argument remained (on all sides) moralistic: it validated itself at most points with reference to moral imperatives (what obligations the state, or the landowners, or the dealers *ought* to obey)."[17] Those in power "referred back to [the protectionist, paternalistic] model whenever emergency arose. In this they were in part the prisoners of the people, who adopted parts of the model as their right and heritage."[18] In Thompson's view, the food rioters' goal was not to topple the system but rather to set it to rights, to recall those in power to their rightful duties and to set tolerable limits on exploitation and resistance.

The notion of a moral economy offers a framework for understanding why Muscovite magic so frequently operated at the junctures of hierarchy where the exercise of authority met its moral limits. In the Muscovite case, economic relations (and political/power relations) were configured through personal bonds of patronage and dependency. Subjects of the tsar were classified and understood as dependents under the protection of identifiable patrons or masters. Highly individualized, personalized relations of dependency created opportunities for invoking the mercy and protection of one's superiors. Subjects of the tsar addressed him as his "slaves" and "orphans" to remind him, in their humble supplications, of his obligation to defend and protect them, and this language of abject dependency was replicated in appeals to masters and protectors all the way down the social scale. During the seventeenth century, human beings were being gradually transformed into property as serfdom became a legal and practical reality, and slavery was still widely practiced.[19] Although the terminology of ownership was not yet applied to human beings, establishing "under whose authority" (*za kem*) a person lived was already an essential aspect in determining a person's identity.[20] Blurring any public/private distinction to the point of meaninglessness, the intimacy of dependency encouraged exploitation and hideous violence within the dangerous closeness of patronage, kinship, and household.

In the intimate hostilities engendered by inequitable relationships, assumptions about the moral, the merciful, the fair come into sharp focus.[21] Muscovite magical spells reflect the fervent effort to survive in a world where power and politics were built entirely out of personalized human relations. Spells, which survive in the hundreds, in spell books, on scraps of paper presented as evidence, and in transcripts of courtroom confessions, take aim at the affective ties that could support or ensnare. With startling poetic, affective language and imagery, incantations activated the power of charged emotion to win the desired ends. Here too, desperation characterizes Muscovite magic, as motivator and as agent.

The evidence of witchcraft trials demonstrates that by the seventeenth century, Russian society was remarkably integrated into a widely shared, homogeneous culture with beliefs, norms, and expectations held in common. However, and this is important to emphasize, the homogeneity in question was not marked by the organic harmony imagined and projected back onto the Muscovite past by later Slavophiles and other Russophiles of a romantic bent. Rather the commonalities drew on a shared recognition of the pervasive hierarchical relations of abuse that tied society together into a single coercive and cohesive whole. Ideas about witchcraft grew, in large measure, out of a consensual understanding of where the limits to abuse resided, where violence or physical torment or exploitation was acceptable, and where it strayed into excess. Magic, as imagined and exercised from below and as suspected and feared from above, erupted at precisely those points of trespass. In its latent or active threat, witchcraft served to patrol those norms and obligations, to mitigate the harshness, and to some small degree rein in the arbitrary exactions of a fiercely tiered system.

This finding, the heart of my study, illuminates both strands of this investigation. It opens a new way of understanding witchcraft itself in a broad, comparative sense, and simultaneously, it allows us a rare glimpse into the workings of Muscovite society at an on-the-ground, intimate level. Within Muscovite studies, much of the energy of the last century or so of historical research has revolved around the painful and persistent questions of Russia's proclivity toward harsh, untrammeled despotism, replicated at all levels of society from the tsar in Moscow to the provincial serf owner on his estate. Witchcraft cases provide disturbing reinforcement for some of these old saws about the pervasiveness and oppressiveness of Russian autocratic absolutism and vicious patriarchy, but also offer fruitful angles for exploring the ways in which these hierarchical structures were questioned, undermined, and defended by actors implicated in their cruel logic and, at some level, aware of its iniquity.

Muscovite witchcraft served as an implement for acknowledging the excesses of hierarchy, and its effects were as actively invoked by those it targeted as by those who utilized it. This assessment shares some elements with the proposition that magic, along with mockery, malingering, and flight, served as a "weapon of the weak," as a part, however imaginary or ineffectual, of the arsenal of the downtrodden against the powerful.[22] Rather than view spells and curses as subversive acts of resistance, however, I argue in the following chapters that witchcraft is more fruitfully viewed as a shared language and conceptual tool with which the pressure points in the moral economy were assessed and negotiated, *not only from below but also from above.* Witchcraft served as what Lila Abu-Lughod calls "a diagnostic of power," which allowed Muscovites of all walks of life, and us as retrospective investigators, to comprehend "forms of power and how people are caught up in them."[23] The accusations lodged by masters, patrons, and tsars against those beneath them suggest that those situated toward the top of the social chain shared an uneasy sense that their privileges entailed certain responsibilities. Their suspicions of magical foul play betray a disquieting anxiety that their menials might have grounds to fight back through whatever underhanded, natural, or supernatural means available to them. The recurrent pattern of accusations by social superiors against their subordinates lets us hear the whisperings of unease, and of outright fear resonating beneath the ugly surface of an abusive hierarchy.[24]

Magic was not the purview of the poor, the ignorant, the untutored: no one in Muscovy had the luxury afforded to skeptical elites in other societies of distancing themselves from the possibility of suffering witchcraft's power. No Muscovite in the seventeenth century advanced doubts about the reality of magic, although witnesses in numerous cases questioned particular practitioners' command of the supernatural or contested attributions of particular deaths to magic. "His stepson Mishka put a root in the cradle with Davyd's grandson, the baby Ivan, so that he would die, but whether the baby died from that or not, he doesn't know."[25] One would search in vain, however, for trenchant critiques of the entire enterprise of witch-hunting or of the ludicrous conduct of witch trials such as were voiced by some European skeptics.[26] Priests and peasants, boyars and foot soldiers, men and women, educated and illiterate, all engaged in a world in which witchcraft was always a viable possibility, as explanation for misfortune or as a means to an end.

Within this peculiarly uniform inequality or homogeneous stratification, magic could be unleashed to avenge perceived wrongs or out of envy, malice, or spite, but it could also serve as moral agent to correct a system that had fallen out of kilter. People on all ends of the process—its users, its victims, and its judges—turned to it for that purpose. Muscovites looked to magic to reassert the reciprocal obligations and entitlements that stabilized a cruelly structured social order. The stress fractures that arose between levels of hierarchy created sites of particular vulnerability to magical intervention.

This study concentrates on seventeenth-century material. The pre-history of Muscovite witchcraft dates back to the late fifteenth century, when the young bride of Ivan III, the grand prince of Moscow, died a terrible death attributed to the machinations of evil witches. As her corpse lay in public view on her catafalque, an eyewitness reported, it swelled to monstrous size, confirming the diagnosis of witchcraft. Ivan was no luckier with his estranged second wife, Sofia, who contracted with some old witch women in Moscow to bewitch her husband with their potions. When he discovered the plot, Ivan ordered the witches thrown into the river and drowned, and, the chronicle tells us with characteristic understatement, "he lived with his wife in great vigilance."[27] Whispers of witchcraft persisted throughout the sixteenth century, haunting both the bedchambers and council chambers of the grand princes and tsars. Witchcraft felled beloved tsaritsas and offered hope to barren ones, and charges of witchcraft flew back and forth among the intimate advisers of grand princes and tsars. Riots broke out in Moscow in 1547, triggered in part by rumors that the Ivan IV's maternal grandmother had sprinkled a potion made of human hearts throughout Moscow, causing the city to burn.[28] Anxieties about magical plots and bewitchment plagued Ivan and his advisers throughout his reign. The Time of Troubles, the aptly titled episode of warfare, invasion, and rebellion that tore the realm apart in the opening years of the seventeenth century, witnessed an acceleration of such accusations. The Tsar-Pretender Dmitrii himself bore the stigma of sorcery after his violent (though temporary) death in 1606. His serial return from the dead can only have fueled such rumors. It is only in the seventeenth century, however, that actual formal trials of witches took place and left their traces in the documentary record. Only at that point did the state develop sufficient administrative mechanisms to penetrate society and to claim, with any degree of plausibility, the ability to adjudicate such crimes. A great fire that swept through the central chancelleries of the Kremlin in 1626 destroyed countless documents and robbed us of all but the scantest traces of trials from the early part of the century, but it is likely that few such trials took place during the disrupted years of the troubles.[29] With the growth of the tsarist court system in the years after the consolidation of Romanov rule and the concomitant creation of a usable, surviving source base, the 1620s mark a clear starting point for this study.

The decision to stop at the end of the seventeenth century rests on less neat or satisfying grounds. Imperial Russian courts continued to hear and prosecute witchcraft cases until the 1760s, when Catherine the Great finally brought the proceedings to a close. In a series of decrees, she declared matters of witchcraft and "superstition" to be minor infractions and relegated them to the purview of low-level courts, where they continued to be heard into the early twentieth century. Through the eighteenth century the nature of the charges, the gender distribution of the accused, and the form and numbers of the hearings remained largely unchanged, with only a few marked deviations from earlier patterns. A number of important studies of the eighteenth century and beyond by Russian and Western scholars have already appeared, and they chart a compelling picture of the conception, practice, and prosecution of witchcraft in the Petrine period and beyond.[30]

My choice of endpoint derives not only from taking the easy road and relying on the fruits of my colleagues' hard work. The sustained, consistent focus on the seventeenth century facilitates rigorously historical attention to both the continuities and the distinctive practices of the time. Presumptions about the timeless persistence of belief and practice are endemic in even some of the best studies of peasant cultures and magical thinking, where stasis, tradition, and lack of innovation are often taken as defining attributes. But, historically speaking, nothing stays still, not even magic, and a focused study of the seventeenth century makes visible the magical beliefs of that era, unencumbered by later encrustations. What then to do with the wealth of material on folk belief and practice documented among Russians in the three centuries since 1700? Methodologically, my approach in this book is to start from the evidence of the documents, in order to avoid what Gary Marker calls "ethnographic seduction." If a motif or ritual does not appear in the seventeenth-century sources, then, while I cannot rule out the possibility, I do not assume it was prevalent at the time. If, however, a document mentions a particular practice, then the evidence of later centuries can be useful in parsing the meaning of the reference in the text. Agrarian magic, for instance, is well documented in the nineteenth century, and all but invisible in the seventeenth.[31] Techniques of casting bones, reading fortunes in pails of water or platters of salt, making teas and poultices from roots and herbs, and tying talismanic roots to pendant crosses, however, all make appearances in seventeenth-century sources and can be better understood by studying their survivals into the twentieth century.

The chapters that follow explore the uses, meanings, and brutal prosecution of practices of magic and suspicions of witchcraft in the period between 1600 and 1700, and situate their findings in the particular context of Muscovy under the early Romanovs. In this same period, the tsarist administration extended its ambitions and its oversight into the smallest and most distant recesses of the realm, and the political theology of rulership became more fully sacralized at the same time that the practice of governance grew more bureaucratic and depersonalized. This was the time when serfdom tightened its hold on the population. Movement, both social and spatial, was increasingly limited by law, but vast new frontiers opened up and beckoned ambitious men (and exiled witches) to staff the frontier garrisons, farm the rich southern lands, or cull the profits of the Siberian taiga. Military and administrative service assumed new forms, and the culture of patronage, obligation, and reciprocity faced the first serious challenges posed by expectations from above and from below of impersonal norms of fairness and procedural equity.[32] Against this dynamic backdrop, individual men and women of the Muscovite realm confronted the charges of witchcraft leveled against them by their neighbors and relatives, their masters and officers, and prosecuted by governors in the courthouse, dignitaries in the Moscow chancelleries, and executioners in the torture chamber.

The voices of the accused and their accusers, the officials, judges, and witnesses, express a remarkably uniform vision of witchcraft, and collectively demonstrate that expectations imported from Western studies may mislead as much as they illuminate. Witchcraft made sense to Muscovites without any developed explanatory framework, diabolic, pagan, or other, and along with that conceptual openness, they were flexible in conceiving of evil without association with any particular gender. While magic pervaded Muscovite society and was practiced everywhere, by people of all levels, it was perceptions of magically induced harm that brought suspects to court. Men and women were most likely to be seen to work harm when they undermined established social hierarchies and threatened, whether through magic, insubordination, or excessive brutality, to upend the fragile consensus that held the tsardom together. When expectations of a moral compact collided with harsh manifestations of excess, Muscovites looked to magic as a desperate measure to restore the cracked edifice of firm but merciful rule from above and submissive humility from below.

1

Witchcraft Historiography

Russia's Divergence

THE LITERATURE ON WITCHCRAFT in other parts of the world offers a rich smorgasbord of sophisticated models for understanding the essence of the phenomenon. The Russian case, intriguingly, fits none but the most general of these. The disjuncture between the Russian material and those of its Western neighbors allows me an opportunity in the following historiographic review to celebrate the accomplishments of what is truly an exciting literature on witchcraft throughout Europe and the world, while at the same time foregrounding the ways in which the models on offer elsewhere have little relevance for Russia. The disparities provide useful insights into what did and did not constitute the core of Russian witchcraft thought and practice.

The study of witchcraft traces its origins back to the earliest records of writing in the ancient world and, in the Christian West, enjoyed a boom in the form of demonological treatises beginning in the late Middle Ages.[1] Works written from a skeptical vantage point made early appearances in Western Europe already in the second half of the sixteenth century. Early modern critics, both Catholic and Protestant, generally accepted the theoretical possibility of witchcraft, which was incontrovertibly attested in the Bible, but they questioned the notion that "toothles, old, and unwieldie" women might alter the course of nature as established by God, and they doubted the outlandish content of both accusations and confessions.[2] Enlightenment-era thinkers pushed their critique further, contending contemptuously that the fear and persecution of witches flared into a deadly combustion when the salacious fanaticism of self-serving clerics was loosed on ignorant and superstitious women. Voltaire, for instance, characterized witch trials as "judicial murders which tyranny, fanaticism, or even error or weakness, have committed with the sword of justice. . . . France was one vast theatre of judicial carnage."[3] Such critical thinkers established the outlines of historical scholarship on witchcraft in its earliest manifestations, and simultaneously set forth the first set of shibboleths that modern revisionists determined to overthrow. Early revisionists included Jules Michelet, who asserted, on the basis of no evidence but a great deal of enthusiasm, that the accused witches were indeed guilty, in a heroic vein, of sedition against the oppressive feudal and ecclesiastical order. The witch was "the offspring of despair," and the crusade launched against her wild nature cult he labeled "the terrorism of the Middle Ages."[4] Michelet's romantic vision of actual pagan cults meeting in rebellious collective rites stirred the imaginations of early twentieth-century researchers and fantasists, including the much-maligned Margaret Murray, an Egyptologist who strayed into the field of witchcraft studies, claiming reality for the collective practices of witches whom she cast as adepts of "the Old Faith" or "the Old Religion." The response to Murray's claims came rapidly, and except among ardent fans of the concept of a surviving submerged paganism, it was unrelentingly dismissive. Until Carlo Ginzburg's examination of surviving pre-Christian belief systems in the Friuli region of northern Italy, the entire notion of vestigial paganism and "actual" witch cults was set aside to gather dust.[5] New approaches had to be developed.

First and foremost, scholars revisited questions of chronology and threw out the simple and self-congratulatory explanatory frameworks erected by Enlightenment rationalists. Where Voltaire and his followers derided witch-hunting as a symptom of superstitious medieval ignorance and fanaticism, twentieth-century researchers concluded that witch-hunting, and even the familiar concept of witchcraft and the witch herself, were not medieval at all. Rather, although magic and witchcraft traced their lineages back to antiquity, the particular ideas and practices condemned during the witch-hunts were developed in the late Middle Ages and assumed new forms and practical reality only in the early modern era. Nor, it turned out on further investigation, were ideas of witchcraft the fruit of primitivism or ignorance. Questioning the linkage of witch belief with ignorance, scholars began to notice that demonological ideas originated not from the huts of unkempt peasants but rather from the treatises of the best educated men in Europe. In fact, the earliest scholarly research on witchcraft in Europe was carried out in the centuries prior to and contemporaneous with the trials by erudite theologians and other serious thinkers concerned with matters metaphysical. Although ideas about witchcraft developed from a wide variety of starting points and incorporated a range of local mythic and practical idioms, the initial drive to consolidate a functional understanding of witchcraft and to extirpate its practitioners grew out of an ecclesiastical crack down on heresy and on heretics as identifiable collectives.[6] The melding of multiple elements—heresy, Satanism, and *maleficium*—into a single, heinous vision of witchcraft was an on-going process. By the late fifteenth or early sixteenth century, the preeminent voices in European writings on the subject had converged on a single interpretive line that defined witchcraft as the inflicting of harm on people, animals, or the environment utilizing magic obtained through a pact with the Devil. The pact, often sealed through a carnal union, ensured the subjugation of the foresworn witch to the Devil, and her willing participation in a dark anti-world of inverted behavior and values, the mirror image of all that was good, orderly, and Christian. Interest in late medieval and early modern demonological writings spawned many of the interpretations advanced during the fruitful decades of witchcraft scholarship from the 1970s through the early 2000s, a great, extended boom period for witchcraft studies that continues to today.

In these exciting years, a good number of theories have been advanced, each purporting if not to explain the totality of the phenomenon, then at least to identify the core issues involved in witch belief, anxiety, and persecution. One important line of analysis has focused on the striking fact that the vast majority of those accused of and persecuted for witchcraft were female. Astonishingly, the gender dimensions of the witch-hunts were long overlooked in the literature, but the late twentieth century made up for that lag. Barbara Ehrenreich and Deirdre English published a powerful opening salvo in this direction with their influential pamphlet, *Witches, Midwives, and Nurses* (1973). They argued that the assault on purported witches reflected a concerted attack by male professionals, particularly physicians, on women whom they viewed as competitors: wise women, healers, and midwives. Although later studies revealed that the data failed to support this claim, nonetheless the midwife theory crossed over into popular awareness, where it has taken firm root.[7] It is, indeed, a grand theory, even if it does not stand up to scrutiny.

Other scholars, though, have taken up the banner, seeking to explain the evident and irrefutable fact that witch-hunts devoured women preferentially and in far greater proportion than men. With various degrees of subtlety, these studies have pointed to a range of factors that could set women more at risk than men to such charges. Feminist theologian Mary Daly sharply satirized the inherent misogyny of oppressive patriarchy. She laid the blame for the witch burnings on the Catholic Church, describing the "androcratic time/space regime of the Patriarchal Church of God-the-Father and Jesus Christ the Son," which launched a sustained, "gynocidal" attack on women outside the control of the patriarchal family, "women who presented an option, an option of eccentricity, and indigestibility." Andrea Dworkin, Marianne Hester, Deborah Willis, and Anne Barstow all made important contributions to exploring the deadly dimensions of patriarchy and misogyny at work in early modern Europe.[8]

A persistent line of argument points to the origins of the most virulent misogyny in the witch-hunting treatises penned by celibate monks, most notoriously Heinrich Kramer (Institoris), the Dominican inquisitor who authored the vile *Malleus Maleficarum*, or *Hammer of Witches*. Hans Broedel's rich monograph on the *Malleus* demonstrates that Institoris's determined attack on women as witches led him to downplay the significance of the satanic Sabbath, a gathering that could enmesh men as well as women in the nefarious business of witchcraft, and instead to play up the lurid sexuality of women, whom he viewed as a collective cesspool of sin and temptation.[9]

On the Protestant side, scholars of gender note that the Reformation's somewhat less negative assessment of the human body, marital sex, and the gendering of salvation spawned modifications of Catholic views of women and witchcraft. Yet historians of New England have demonstrated that Puritan communities remained committed to upholding patriarchal order, and women in New England might suffer the taint of witchcraft accusations if their neighbors sensed they had violated that order in any way. As Jane Kamensky notes, women were judged witchlike whether they displayed in excess traits considered female (such as envy, jealousy, or lasciviousness) or those coded male (such as aggression or assertiveness). Damned either way, women benefited little from the concessions made to them by Puritan theology, which, as Elizabeth Reis demonstrates, allowed for equality in divine grace and even gendered the soul female.[10]

Protestant patriarchy participated with gusto in condemning the daughters of Eve as repositories of sin. Exploring the roots of hostility toward older women, John Putnam Demos's experiment in psychohistory locates the roots of New England witchcraft accusations in the traumatic moment when young Puritan boys were removed from the tender world of their mothers and set adrift in the harsh male sphere. He argues that boys experienced that rough transfer as abandonment by their mother and that those same boys avenged that betrayal later in life when, as middle-aged men, they hurled accusations against women of their mothers' generation.[11]

Examining the flip side of the coin, the distaff side of the psyche, much productive gender analysis has delved into the psychologies of the women, both accused witches and their putative victims, those possessed by demons. These studies suggest that repressed desires and ambitions operated as a motivating and explanatory force not only among frustrated, celibate clerics but also among women, whose desires and ambitions were routinely and severely squelched by early modern norms and attributed to the sinful promptings of the Devil. The psychology of repression and projection proves a useful lens for viewing many cases, particularly possession cases, where the Devil permitted women and girls to voice the resentments, to act out the rebellion, and to vent the anger in words and actions otherwise denied to them.[12]

In the 1970s and 1980s, social historians, particularly of England and New England, took gender studies in a somewhat different direction and documented the economic status of women within particular societies and the way that structural impediments to female wealth or property holding, in combination with particular cultural and religious norms, might render women especially vulnerable to suspicions of witchcraft. Keith Thomas and Alan Macfarlane showed that in early modern England, elderly women and women alone in the world were disproportionately represented among the poor, having few resources for generating income independently. Carol Karlsen shows that in New England, by contrast, it was the possession of any modicum of property, particularly landed property, that put females particularly at risk for accusations. Female inheritance, which violated presumptive expectations that land and inheritance would pass in the male line, signaled something so amiss in the given order of things that ambient suspicions might land on the female legatee.[13]

A third line of gender analysis points to ideas about female carnality and sexuality, of the female body and its porosity and weakness, that circulated in theological and medical treatises of the time and may even have gained purchase in the broader popular imagination. Early modern writers, influenced by both medical and religious notions, maintained that women were characterized by insatiable desire. When paired with their innate vanity, tendency toward envy, and weakness of will and intellect, their inherent lust drove them to sin. Unable to satiate their desire with mortal men, they succumbed readily to the blandishments of demon lovers, sealing their hellish pacts on the material canvas of their bodies. Walter Stephens has provocatively and convincingly argued that the demonologists' obsessive interest in the specter of physical copulation between mortal women and immaterial devils was "not pornographic, but metaphysical." Their interest stemmed not from prurience, but rather from a burning need to quell their own terrifying doubts about the actuality of the spiritual realm and the ability of the two worlds to touch each other. They assured themselves and others that the physical testimony of women's bodies, bearing the corporeal imprint of the supernatural, bore witness to the reality of the immaterial world. Whether their fascination with demonic intercourse grew from doubt or conviction, whether the stakes were libidinous or theological, the unwavering certainty that it was women who served as the receptacles of satanic penetration and manipulation drew on powerful ideas about gender, bodies, and power in early modern European society.[14]

Still maintaining the focus on gender but altering the explanatory mechanism, a fourth avenue of interpretation explores the implications of witchcraft cases that concerned matters arising among women. Spearheaded by Lyndal Roper and Diane Purkiss, this cluster of scholars has noted the extent to which witchcraft trials, though adjudicated by men, were initiated by women and reflected anxieties generated within an exclusively female sphere. The charges brought against suspected witches in hundreds of cases stemmed not from male preoccupations with maintaining gender dominance or protecting their manhood, but rather from women's defensive need to protect their families, their homes, their possessions, and their sustenance from the invasive glances, importunate demands, or even lavish praise or excessive generosity of other women. Testimony revolved around the health of children and livestock, the production of milk and cheese, the baking of bread or puddings, the carding, spinning, and weaving of wool. Concerned with preserving the boundaries of home and of the familial body from unwanted penetration or depredation, women voiced their most urgent fantasies when they charged other women with invasion and violation of hearth and home.[15]

Each of these four lines of analysis advances an understanding of witchcraft as a Western and central European phenomenon and helps to explain the predominance of females among the accused. Still more elements—the power of stereotype, of folklore, of biblical and classical texts, of widely circulating visual images, and of the use of gendered nouns designating witches in most European languages—confirmed the femaleness of the category of "witch," an equation that was actively reinforced by the widely publicized trials and executions of female witches. These multiple strands of explanation complement each other, providing a persuasive, layered understanding of the many forces that conspired to make witchcraft the particularly female horror that it was, with different facets emerging most perniciously in different places or particular cases across Christian Europe.[16]

Of course, not all of the individuals who suffered in the European witch trials were female; men constituted about 20 percent of those charged with witchcraft across Europe, slightly fewer of those convicted and executed. Men even made up the majority in small pockets—in Normandy, for instance—in the European landscape.[17] Even if only 20 percent of the victims of the witch-hunts were male, and even if we take the low-end number of roughly fifty thousand for Europe-wide executions, that would still mean that ten thousand men died as witches, not an insignificant number.[18] The presence of male witches has been noted in the literature for a long time, and has generally been explained, quite satisfactorily, as primarily due to a coattail effect, that is, men became vulnerable to witchcraft charges only after the women closest to them, their mothers or wives, were branded with that infamy. Erik Midelfort refined this idea with his observation that witch panics displayed a life cycle of their own: men fell victim to accusations mainly during major panics, when stereotypes broke down. The panics were brought to a halt when the resultant "social chaos" threatened the core values of society, leading to a "crisis of confidence" in the legal system and an end to the trials.[19]

In the last decade, a number of scholars have turned their attention more actively to trying to explain the phenomenon of male witchcraft. Several studies have addressed the problem of identifying the characteristics that made particular men vulnerable to witchcraft charges within a culture in which the normative witch was gendered female. Lara Apps and Andrew Gow, for instance, examine several of the best-known trials of male witches, and suggest that these men somehow fell short in their performance of masculinity Their behavior was somehow effeminate, and reminiscent of the unruly female witches. More satisfyingly, E. J. Kent, in her article on male witches in England and New England, finds on the contrary that the characteristics that made individual men susceptible to witchcraft charges were those associated specifically with masculinity itself, such as literacy and litigation, activity in the public sphere. Male witches, she finds, matched a very different profile than female witches. Eva Labouvie takes this argument in a slightly different direction, exploring the distinctive kinds of magic employed by or attributed to male and female witches, with women more prone to accusations of malevolent magic. Rolf Schulte's study of male witches in the Holy Roman Empire finds distinctive patterns in each region of the empire. He gives close consideration to the nuances of the experts on demonology in each region, and finds that these intellectual leaders exerted significant influence on the shape of the witch-hunt as it unfurled locally. His local studies reveal slight differences in gender patterns according to religious affiliation: Catholic authorities proved somewhat more willing than Protestant ones to entertain the idea of male witches.[20]

Alison Rowlands' edited collection, *Witchcraft and Masculinities in Early Modern Europe* (2009), provides the most insightful work to date on the topic, with a set of superb essays by top-notch scholars, each essay addressing a different place in Europe and raising its own interesting questions. Returning to some of the hypotheses raised by earlier scholarship on male witches, these essays test several of the central propositions circulating in the field. Robin Briggs confirms the importance of prior family history of witchcraft in incriminating men but challenges the idea that men were accused primarily during large-scale panics. Willem de Blécourt finds evidence in support of Labouvie's notion of separate spheres of magic, particularly in the gendered divisions of occupation and in the more common attribution of harmful magic to female practitioners, but he also illustrates important blurring of those lines in actual application. In a related finding, a number of the authors investigate the influence of theology on the gender profile of the accused, and confirm Broedel's argument that emphasis on the black Sabbath allowed for more male participation than did an emphasis on maleficium. The authors pursue the question posed by Apps and Gow and by Kent about whether men who displayed particular character traits deemed inappropriate to their gender placed themselves at risk for accusation as male witches. On this point, the essays draw a variety of contradictory findings from their different regional samples. Malcolm Gaskill, with his work on familiars, and Willem de Blécourt, with his discussion of werewolves, remind the reader that the male–female binary was not the only troublesome one for early modern imaginations: human-beast separation might also stir anxious fantasy.[21]

Rowlands herself makes the valuable suggestion that we should attempt to understand both male and female witchcraft through a single lens, setting aside our current preoccupation with finding "gender-specific spheres of influence within early modern society and culture that immediately exclude men from any analysis." The core anxieties involved in witchcraft accusations may not have been strongly gendered ones ("such as housewifery or motherhood"), but instead "coalesced especially around the practices of parenthood, neighbourliness, and Christianity—categories that included both men and women, even if they were clearly inflected in different ways according to gender."[22] This formulation serves well as a blueprint for my study of Russia, although the specific core elements require a little tweaking to fit the Muscovite material.

In aggregate, this literature forces a welcome rethinking of the notion of European witches as an exclusive sorority. Ideas about gender must be flexibly broadened and deftly reconsidered in order to take adequate account of the thousands of male victims of the trials. Yet the kinds of investigations and explanations that the scholarship has produced in the context of European culture have been shaped by ingrained underlying assumptions about witches' gender, and presume the male witch to be the exception in need of explanation. This entirely reasonable baseline, drawn from European reality, makes the new insights on male witches impossible to translate directly into a Russian context. With no female majority and no such working stereotype to push against, gender will figure altogether differently in the Russian case. The evidence of Muscovite trials and tales suggest that male and female witches conformed to very similar patterns of behavior and that gender played only a secondary role in determining who would suffer from accusations.

Another literature has been animating the field of witchcraft studies with surprising findings about male witches, and that is the literature on Europe's peripheries, particularly the northern margins. Russia was not unique in its line-up of majority male witches. Some of its neighbors along the northern tier, in Scandinavia and the Baltic regions, shared its gender skew. Since the 1990 publication by Bengt Ankarloo and Gustav Henningsen of their brilliantly conceived collection of witchcraft "centres and peripheries," the margins of Europe have insistently entered the general discussion. With chapters on Iceland, Finland, and Estonia, all of which targeted primarily men, the collection forced Europeanists to take these alternative scenarios into account. Iceland with its tradition of seers who sang their spells and engraved them in runes on magical staffs, Finland with an active tradition of shamanic paganism and bookish magic, and Estonia with its werewolf lore, all challenge witchcraft specialists to broaden their definitions and their expected demographics.[23]

These Scandinavian and Baltic regions, with their majority male witches, appear at first glance to have much in common with Russia and to offer an appropriate comparison group. Late to convert to Christianity, these regions remained closer to their pagan traditions than much of Western and Southern Europe, where an additional millennium had deepened the roots of Christianity. Medieval Russia (or, more accurately, Rus') shared with its northern neighbors a pre-Christian tradition of shamanic religion. Its priests were known as *volkhvy*, sorcerers, seers, or pagan priests, the same word used to translate the biblical Magi. The nature of Russia's male witches by early modern times, however, was so distinct from that of its near neighbors that it is more revealing of contrast and difference than of productive similarity. What the contrast highlights is the limits of the shamanic model for explaining the origins or meaning of witchcraft in society. The shamanic model has enjoyed significant currency in witchcraft studies since the publication of Carlo Ginzburg's influential *Ecstasies: Deciphering the Witches' Sabbath* in 1989 (English translation, 1991). Ginzburg's dazzling trek across millennia of Eurasian history and prehistory popularized the notion that witches—real, actual, practicing witches—were the heirs to a grand tradition of shamanic mediation between two worlds, the worlds of the living and the dead, the material and the immaterial. Like Ginzburg's shamanic witches, Finnish and Icelandic seers possessed arcane knowledge and effected results through invoking the powers of a metaphysical realm. Lapp shamans were known to bang on drums to invoke the spirits while chanting, falling into a trance state, or flying off in the forms of animals or birds. Estonian werewolves displayed the telltale trait of shape shifting, a signal characteristic of shamanic ability to move between worlds. Éva Pócs documents similar patterns of shape shifting and communicating with the spirit realm in Hungarian witch trials.[24]

But Russia, again, marched to a different drummer. Neither shamanism nor paganism makes the least detectable appearance in Muscovite magical practices. The sole exceptions to this rule arise in cases involving non-Christian, non-Russian practitioners, that is, Cheremis (now called Mari, Finnic inhabitants of the middle Volga region), Chuvash (a Turkic people resident from the middle

Volga region into Siberia), and Mordvin (speakers of a Uralic language, from the same middle-Volga region).[25] These non-Russian subjects of the tsardom were probably animists, although occasionally a Muslim Tatar shows up among the accused. The striking disparity in the magic attributed to Russian Christians and non-Russian, non-Christians underscores the extent to which Russian magic derived from its own traditions, not the shamanic ones of Inner Asia or Lapland. As documented in trial materials, saints' lives, and material culture, Russian magic had nothing to do with shape shifting or inter-worldly transport, and only a few of the magical practitioners claimed to receive visions. An occasional confession records spectral visions. One fortune-teller explained that she gained her insights from the behavior of "little men" who laughed or cried as they ran about on a tray of salt. A male fortune-teller said that he inherited his craft from his mother but initially did not understand how to utilize his gift. "And later, two years ago, he lay down to sleep in a haystack at midday and in a dream there appeared to him an old man with red hair, and his dress was like a priest's chasuble (*riza*), and he told him to tell fortunes with bones and thereby feed himself. And from that time on, [he knows the answers to questions whenever] someone asks the bones about something . . . , because the faces of the people involved in the matter appear before him on the bones and they tell him about this." In two separate cases, a decade apart and in different regions, a man and a woman each confessed to receiving a vision of a "shaggy (*kosmatyi*) man," who instructed them in various matters.[26] More commonly, Muscovite seers left the realms of the spirits or of the dead to fend for themselves. So, appealing as the shamanic model may be, particularly for Russia, geographically nestled within a surrounding arc of clearly documented shamanic practice, it turns out to have little utility in explaining Russian witchcraft.

APPLICABLE APPROACHES: RUSSIAN WITCHCRAFT AND WESTERN HISTORIOGRAPHIC MODELS

If the specific gender models derived from European cases do not apply and the shamanic archetype finds no support in Russian material, what other interpretive frameworks might be tested in the Russian case? Theories and models attempting to explain the European trials of course abound. It would be impossible (and tedious) to address all of them in detail, but quite a few are important and interesting in their own right and merit brief consideration for the commonalities and differences they reveal in comparison with Russia. Among the most compelling in the European context are those that highlight the specifics of the historical conjuncture at which witch persecution accelerated, a time dominated by the Reformation and Catholic Reformation, characterized by fierce and bloody religious warfare, the exuberant growth of print culture, and overseas encounters and colonization.[27] In Russia, untouched by either Reformation or Counter Reformation theology, relatively free from religious warfare, and insulated from the effects of the print revolution by the complete monopoly on print held by the Orthodox Church and tsarist regime, none of these factors translates effectively. Russian witch trials were not fueled by the circulation of texts and images, nor were witchcraft ideas and anxieties ignited by fiery preachers: sermons were frowned on by the Orthodox establishment and were accepted only at the highest levels of society toward the end of the seventeenth century. Overseas encounters had no direct counterpart, but one could argue that Muscovite conquest and settlement of Siberia and inroads into the southern steppe regions stood as a close equivalent. Nonetheless, since Russians had always been in close contact with people of other faiths and cultures, Muscovy experienced none of the shock of encounter that reverberated so powerfully in Western European culture. Caliban's mother, the blue-eyed North African witch, Sycorax, spawned no offspring and inspired no equivalent soul-searching or demonizing among Russians.[28] Nor does the association between the Indian Wars and the New England witch trials documented so intriguingly by James E. Kenses and further developed by Mary Beth Norton find an echo in the Russian material, despite the ongoing wars in the south and east against people of different faiths and ethnicities. Perhaps because the Russian battles risked nothing comparable to the total eradication that the New England colonists envisioned, the wars along the peripheries did not exercise an equivalent impact on their domestic nightmares.[29]

The linkage between burning witches and burning heretics, explicitly articulated in Western Christian teaching, appears slightly more promising than the previous theories when transferred to Russian soil. The seventeenth century, after all, witnessed both the first inklings of the Old Belief, the first major schism in the Russian Orthodox Church, and the first formal trials of witches. It is indeed possible that concern about the schism heightened anxieties regarding other forms of heterodoxy and heteropraxy in the second half of the century, and recast the previously innocuous practices of village healers and fortune-tellers as suspicious and dangerous deviations. This idea has some plausibility and would help to explain an increasingly fraught ideological environment in which low-level sorcery came to be seen as necessitating severe punitive action. The theory suffers, however, from a nearly complete absence of substantiating evidence. Records of witchcraft trials survive from the early 1600s; the first protests of the prophets of the Old Belief were raised only in the 1660s, and the disparate voices did not coalesce into a single, more or less coherent movement until the early eighteenth century.[30] Moreover, accusations of schismatic activity and accusations of witchcraft remained entirely distinct, with only a very few isolated cases invoking both sets of terms. The term "heresy" does enter into witchcraft accusations, as discussed in chapter 8, but more as a free-floating negative signifier than as a specific religious or anti-religious attribute.

The drive to crush heresy and idolatry was closely related in the early modern European context to a powerful current of apocalyptic thinking that was expressed in every possible medium, from architecture, painting, and furniture making to rituals, sermons, and diaries.[31] The impending battle with the Antichrist endowed the struggle for each Christian soul with cosmic intensity, and the prevalence of witches at large among honest folk assumed the added threat of augmenting the ranks of the enemy. Awareness of the imminence of End Times was alive and well in sixteenth- and seventeenth-century Russia too, and its imprint is felt in a similarly wide array of forms and media. In its official guise, however, it took on a far different valence from that familiar in the West. Far from a horrific vision of apocalyptic terror, with rivers of blood and monsters loosed in the world, official Muscovite eschatology looked ahead eagerly to the Last Days, when the Orthodox tsar would lead his pious flock to salvation.[32] Apocalyptic thinking, therefore, offers an interesting avenue for comparative examination, but Russian witchcraft thought betrays no imprint of its influence.

Much of the horror that European authors attributed to the vile sin of witchcraft was its inversion of all that was good and proper and holy, enacted most vehemently in the satanic mass, the dark mirror image of the divine Catholic mass, but expressed in every aspect of witchy "anti-behavior." If a good Catholic attended mass, venerated Jesus and the Host, and abjured the Devil, a witch attended a black Sabbath, adulated Satan, desecrated the Host, and renounced all that was good and holy. Witches did everything backwards, upside down, and inside out. They kissed the Devil's anus, they copulated back to front or with women on top, and occasionally they rode backward to their Sabbath orgies and parked their mounts upside down in the corner while they enjoyed their obscene romps. As Deborah Willis and Diane Purkiss so powerfully argue, where a good mother nurtured her rosy-cheeked babies and nursed them at her breast, a bad mother caused babies to wither with her look or touch, enjoyed them as midnight snacks and party food at sabbaths, and suckled demon-familiars at her unnatural teats instead.[33] The power of binary models in the European context has been most clearly elucidated in the work of Stuart Clark on English and European ways of "thinking with demons." Parallel modes of binary thinking have also been identified in a Russian context. In fact, the pervasiveness of binary models in Russian culture has been widely accepted in the wake arguments set forth by the Tartu School semioticians, Yuri Lotman and Boris Uspenskij.[34] Following their lead, scholars of Russian witchcraft and sorcery in the nineteenth and early twentieth centuries have documented comparable inversions in their subjects' taxonomies of the world. Will Ryan and Christine Worobec find documented beliefs in anti-behaviors in the late nineteenth and early twentieth century, particularly in Ukrainian areas to the south.[35] For instance, witches reportedly indulged in "anti-behaviors" such as donning their clothing back to front. To some limited extent, this model fits the Muscovite evidence as well. One accused witch purportedly wore his cross "behind his back," and many surviving spells explicitly employ the language of inversion and negation: "I rise without crossing myself; I leave through the window, not through the door"; or, "I deny father, mother, sister, brother, clan, and tribe."[36] On the whole, early modern Russians appear not to have elaborated a picture of witches as the negation of society or culture. Rather, as this book will argue, witchcraft figured in the Muscovite imagination as a continuation of routine practices by other means. Adding a root to a curative tea extended the healer's pharmacopeia, but did not invert it. Muttering a spell for successful hunting augmented the power of prayer in the situation, but did not negate it. Even casting spells on one's in-laws or masters to ameliorate or avenge ill-treatment extended the more acceptable means of petition, supplication, and invocation of divine protection. Spells often shared space with more standard prayers in Muscovite herbals and spell books, and magical roots or amulets were deemed particularly effective if worn with a cross. In general those individuals suspected of witchcraft were not accused of sacrilege, or of religious or sexual perversity. Some were unsavory types, with records of drunkenness, violence, arrogance, criminality, or rape, but no one appears to have fantasized about their engaging in parodic inversions of normative conduct.

Nor will another, more anthropological, category—liminality—do much toward explaining the profile of Russian witches.[37] "Liminality" is a wonderful concept, and has been put to work with marvelous results, particularly in anthropological and folklore studies of witchcraft. Liminal times are magical times in most cultures, including Russia's. Magic works most powerfully at dusk, midnight, or dawn, times of transition. Its effects are most dangerous at transitional times of life: at birth, in the risky period before baptism, on the eve of marriage, at the deathbed. All of this applies nicely to Russian magic as elsewhere. However, when one moves past the qualities of magic itself to those of its practitioners, liminality ceases to function as an effective mode for understanding the profile of Russian witches. In many cultures, not only the magic but also the witches themselves occupy a categorical gray zone, outside of the human social norm yet of the mortal realm. They may be transgendered or celibate, or occupy a third gender category, as in some Native American cultures. They often occupy a spatial medium, between settlement and wilderness, or at the outskirts of town, at the edge of the forest. Muscovite witches do not markedly display any of these characteristics. As far as the documents illuminate the social composition of the pool of suspects, it looks much like everyone else. Russian witches could be itinerants (approximately 15 percent) and some were ethnically non-Russian (less than 15 percent can be identified as such), but most of them were neighbors of their accusers, fellow members of a military regiment or household, even kin. Geographically and socially, they fit squarely in the middle of things. Magical disputes broke out at taverns and kitchen tables, over shared drinks and food. They broke out at weddings and feasts, during the festivities. They erupted over exchanges of insults on the street or at the well, or in conjunction with the sharing of spells among gunners or musketeers on assignment. To the extent that they are identified in the sources, the sexual partners of the accused were uniformly of the opposite sex. The only distinguishing physical trait that the sources note among those accused in Muscovy is blindness. Three cases involving female witches mention the fact that the women were blind, a disability that perhaps enhanced their ability to see beyond the limits of the here and now.[38] Like inversion, then, the concept of "liminality" has limited resonance in the Russian instance.

Also appealing is the concept of "limited good," applied by Michael Ostling in his study of Polish witchcraft. Taking his inspiration from an impressive line-up of anthropologists, George Foster, Ralph Austen, Michael Taussig, and Raymond Kelly, Ostling remarks a strongly articulated sense of a zero-sum economy in his sources, such that one person's (illicit, magical) gain results directly in another person's loss. Ostling explains: "there is only so much fortune, or prosperity, or fertility to go around, and one cannot acquire more than one's share except by stealing it from others. The image of the limited good may be treated as the key metaphor of the 'common language' of Polish witchcraft, while milk—its lack or overabundance, its theft and preservation—stands as the central synecdoche for the imagined activities of witches and the real practices of those who would protect themselves from witchcraft."[39] In a Russian context, in occasional cases tavern keepers accused their rivals of bewitching customers into patronizing their establishments, thereby appropriating an unfair share of clientele, another limited good.[40] In general, however, Russian cases display little of this logic. Neither beauty, nor health, nor milk is transferred from victim to recipient. Health or ill-health, love or hostility, fertility or infertility were invoked or inflicted, but not purloined from another. Only in the most general sense, articulated effectively by A.L. Toporkov in his study of love spells, was magic seen as manipulating a limited good. The good in question was, in Toporkov's analysis, the general collective good of the community. Magic served the individual, therefore by definition the selfish, self-serving, and antisocial goals of the user, and thereby undermined the collective in the interests of the one.[41]

James Siegel, in his study of witch-killings in contemporary Indonesia, offers a useful typography of approaches to the topic of witchcraft. Anthropologists and sociologists, he notes, generally view witchcraft accusations as a useful tool for societies in consolidating and policing norms and encouraging stability. Historians, by contrast, have tended to focus on the dysfunction, the violence, and the ruptures caused by witch trials. For some historians, he writes:

> the witch hunt shows how some individuals and even groups can be placed outside the community, and how therefore they can be slain with the consent and the participation of the community to which they had belonged. By contrast, anthropologists have tended to minimize the violence of witchcraft, instead focusing on social tensions and their resolution through witchcraft accusations.[42]

Siegel himself takes seriously the hideous violence entailed in witch-killings, while still embedding them in the social, "as an example of the inability of socially determined thinking . . . to comprehend certain situations."[43] His study reveals the subtle and dangerous interplay between the unspeakable, the unknowable, and what, once named, must be eliminated.

In keeping with Siegel's typology of historical and anthropological/sociological approaches, the historical sociologist Kai Eriksen, in his important *Wayward Puritans*, argues that "deviant forms of behavior are often a valuable resource in society, providing a point of contrast, which is necessary for the maintenance of a coherent social order."[44] Operating as both a safety valve, releasing pent up social, legal, and religious tensions, and as a moral reinforcement of Puritan norms, the trials ostensibly contributed to the enduring strength of the New England community.

While punishments of witches often did serve to mark the boundaries of acceptable behavior, the costs in terms of social disruption, unchecked hostilities, ruined lives, and unquestioned executions surely must undermine any sanguine assessment of the contribution of witchcraft trials to the social order. Witchcraft suspicions developed over time in local communities. Rumors swirled around particular individuals for decades, sentencing them to a hundred small deaths and a lifetime of fear even if the gossip never turned into formal charges. Moreover, once loosed in the world, whispered innuendos clung not only to the immediate suspect, but also to her children and grandchildren. The historian Robin Briggs describes with chilling immediacy the dread felt by the daughters of accused witches when talk of witchcraft would arise in French villages. Lyndal Roper describes the sad fate of children orphaned by the execution of their mothers as witches, children who subsequently found themselves suspected of the same infractions or, even more devastatingly, concocted charges of witchcraft against themselves.[45] Seeing either functional or redemptive qualities in such a dark picture requires rosy-tinted spectacles indeed.

In keeping with Eriksen's line of argument, the findings of this book confirm that that magic itself, both its practice and its lurking threat, played a part in identifying and to some extent policing Muscovy's moral boundaries. My reading parts company with his sociological explanation, however, where it suggests that victimizing the occasional deviant might serve a positive and constructive function in maintaining community values and reifying norms. Such a view requires firmly shutting one's eyes to the violence of the courts' reprisals, the pall of fear and resentment cast over the survivors, and the glaring gaps left in families and lives when suspects were tortured, exiled, and executed. Witchcraft provided grounds for negotiations within oppressive webs of power. Even the trials allowed for some exchanges of viewpoints, construction of narratives and counter-narratives. But the routine application of torture, punitive violence, and harsh sentences of exile and execution served a far more disciplinary function, less productive of social cohesion and internal harmony than Eriksen's view allows.

Another set of explanatory mechanisms arising from the particular historical circumstance of early modern Europe revolves around the growth and development of the law, of judicial and administrative institutions and practices of investigation, surveillance, enforcement.[46] These strands of analysis resonate loudly in the Russian material. In the processes of state formation and institution building, Muscovy followed closely on the heels of its European counterparts. The late sixteenth and seventeenth centuries were periods of explosive growth in the apparatus of both church and state. Witchcraft cases fell almost exclusively under the purview of secular rather than religious courts, so it is the expansion of the state apparatus that is most pertinent. Promulgating a series of increasingly long and ambitious law codes, the state laid claim to jurisdiction over every aspect of the life of its subjects, from guaranteeing regular payment of taxes and performance of mandatory service to rounding up brigands, highwaymen, and murderers; from regulating property and inheritance to tying peasants and townspeople to the land. The law incrementally extended its reach, encompassing violations of morality, propriety, and religious conformity. Shifting from a passive role as arbiter of suits brought to their attention, the tsar's courts increasingly assumed an active and even proactive stance, participating in surveilling the population, seeking out malefactors, and bringing wrongdoers to justice. All of this surveillance and enforcement required a vast machinery of administration and enforcement, which had to be created more or less de novo in short order. By the end of the seventeenth century, armies of administrators staffed dozens of bureaus and chancelleries, surveyors mapped the territories and recorded the population in situ, making it possible to adjudicate not only property disputes but also disputes over which human beings belonged on which pieces of land, as dependents of which landlords. In tandem with the burgeoning of the central administration, the provinces received their own phalanxes of officials and bureaucrats. Provincial governors (*voevody*) were appointed from Moscow, and their local offices were staffed with a combination of clerks (*pod'iachie*) from the central chancelleries and local men. No distinction was made between executive and judicial functions, so the governors and their staffs served as judges of the first instance in local hearings. Just about all decisions, however petty, were referred back to Moscow for resolution. The explosive growth of the state was a necessary precondition to witch trials, in Russia as elsewhere. Without outreach and penetration of society, no state, however ambitious, could hope to dredge up the remote village fortune-tellers and itinerant healers that filled the witchcraft docket. Here, at last, Russia falls squarely within the fold, marching in step with the consolidating European monarchies.[47]

An interesting branch of discussion in the European literature concerns the various merits of centralized versus fragmented or localized nodes of judicial authority. While most of the literature concurs that an extensive, developed judicial apparatus was a sine qua non of witch trials, a good deal of evidence suggests that the trials grew to enormous proportions only when power was localized, usually in the hands of a local bishop or prince with a particular stake (so to speak) in prosecuting witches, or when authority temporarily broke down or grew hazy. This kind of breakdown accompanied the peaks in witchcraft trials in England during the civil war, and in New England, where the absence of a royal charter disrupted the normal processes of litigation on the eve of the Salem events.[48] In Russia, there were no huge witch panics where large numbers of witches were tried or executed, so in this regard it supports the proposition that centralized judiciaries impeded snowballing witch panics. The tsarist state worked hard to prevent the emergence of pockets of local judicial or administrative autonomy, and for the most part enjoyed remarkable success in this effort. Throughout the seventeenth century, provincial courts and administrators referred even the pettiest decisions back to Moscow, and the tsars oversaw a far more centralized judicial system than most of their more Western contemporaries. Although witchcraft trials did peak during times of general unrest, the explanation does not seem to rest in the same kind of breakdown of central judicial authority or institutional control that scholars have noted elsewhere.

Not only periods of social unrest or political disorder but also crises of other kinds have featured in a number of major studies tracking patterns and timing of witch-hunting in Europe. Wolfgang Behringer and other specialists on German witchcraft have correlated the intensification of witch-hunting with particularly harsh weather, crop failure, and subsistence crises. In the European context, severe environmental conditions coincided with periods of political upheaval and religious ferment, creating a perfect storm of deprivation, uncertainty, and insecurity in which suspicions of witchcraft proliferated. In Bavaria in particular, Behringer shows, the years 1586–1630 witnessed intense religious debates, political unrest, the worst famines of the early modern mini-ice age, and, not coincidentally, the high-water mark for witchcraft executions.[49] In Muscovite historiography, the concept of crisis has also found its advocates, both as an extension of the idea of "the general crisis of the seventeenth century" and, more specifically, in the context of witchcraft.[50] A graph of the incidence of trials in the seventeenth century lends some credence to the idea that times of political crisis and social unrest produced greater anxiety about witchcraft. A large peak spikes up around the time of the wave of urban uprisings, 1648–1650, and a smaller rise is noticeable in the years when the Razin rebellion swept across much of the country and threatened the stability of the regime, 1670–1671. Witchcraft anxiety appears to have risen during the periods of instability and revolt accompanying the early years of Peter's reign, 1682 and following, when charges of politically motivated magical assaults on the tsar and his family surged. For the century as a whole, however, the crisis explanation shares the inherent weakness of any post-hoc explanatory model: some of the years we would label crisis years show spikes in trials, but other obvious candidates do not. The years of devastating plague (1654), for instance, or of the great copper riots (1662), appear as troughs rather than peaks on the chart. Connections between grand political events and the petty actors involved in local trials are indirect at best and impossible to document. If a case out in the sticks happened to coincide temporally with a riot in Moscow but has no explicit connection with those events, should it be classified as a product of that distant political upheaval? My inclination is to acknowledge a possibility of heightened ambient anxiety in crisis years but not to presume a causal connection unless the sources indicate such a link.

More useful than cataloging specific crises is Adam Ashforth's notion of a society living in a state of chronic "spiritual insecurity," in which everyone must be ever vigilant lest the ill will of neighbors, relatives, and even those considered close friends might at any moment condense into a powerfully destructive force of malice. In a world like Soweto, where Ashforth conducted his fieldwork in the 1990s, fear of bewitchment surfaced not as a paroxysm in time of crisis, but rather as a ubiquitous, free-floating anxiety. Ashforth found that "the sense that life is continually exposed

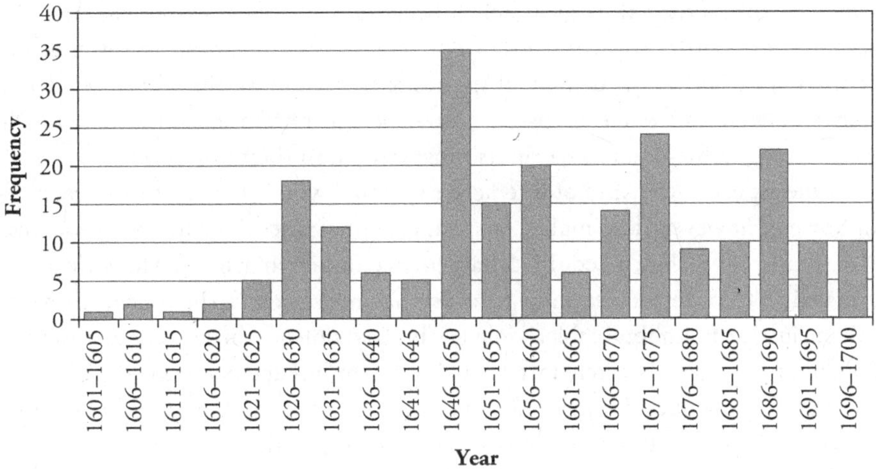

Frequency of witchcraft trials in five-year intervals, 1601–1700.

to people deploying evil forces to harm and kill is palpable, the fear of occult assault is real, and the enterprise of healing devoted to protection from evil forces is enormous." "Most of the time, this possibility that people harboring malice can do anything exists merely as a background fact of life in a place like Soweto—no cause for undue worry. Sometimes, however, when suffering and misfortune become acute and demand action, the possibility that they have been deliberately inflicted by malicious others is cause for serious alarm." In the cultures of early modern Europe, where words, thoughts, or looks, hidden desires and unspoken resentments were understood as empowered actors, capable of working material effects on others, a similar sense of perpetual vulnerability to unseen threats kept people on their guard against supernatural assault. Practically speaking, most of the time everyday life was "lived more in a mode of suspicion and fear of occult assault rather than open accusation and persecution of witches," but the chronic spiritual insecurity engendered by a world understood as populated by active malice served as tinder for the smallest spark.[51] Testimony from trials indicates that Muscovites too lived with the burden of inchoate anxiety about potential occult attacks.

In each of these very different cultural spheres, the common denominator was belief, a notoriously difficult subject to document. It seems undeniable that Muscovites, like their counterparts elsewhere, believed in a dynamic supernatural sphere that penetrated and manipulated earthly beings in the natural world. Muscovites understood their world as a crowded one, densely populated by supernatural beings and forces. In the chapters that follow, we will touch little on questions of belief or of the rich world of spirits and sprites who probably activated magical belief, because they appear extremely rarely in seventeenth-century sources. Aside from rare, passing mentions in seventeenth century spell books, the delightful species of household spirits (*domovye*), wood spirits (*leshye*), and water devils (*vodianye cherty*) are familiar only from much later ethnographies, and so by rights must remain in their purview.[52]

One aspect of the kind of interactive spiritual world that Ashforth describes in Soweto, however, does make conspicuous appearances in Muscovite sources: "In a world of witches, all conflicts have an occult dimension. . . . Many weapons are available to persons seeking to cause harm or protect themselves from it. When justice is unobtainable, violence breeds violence in a cycle of revenge: witchcraft also breeds witchcraft."[53] A significant linkage between suspicions of witchcraft and a quest for justice where justice was not forthcoming turns out to be a defining characteristic of Muscovite magical practice.

This sweeping run across the surface of the Western witchcraft literature has surveyed a good number of models, with multiple subvariants, models emphasizing the explanatory power of ignorance, fanaticism, religious conflict, gender, psychology, sociology, theology, institution building and power, law, and ideology. Few of these analytical frameworks have proven immediately applicable in interpreting the phenomenon of witchcraft in early modern Russia, at least not in the forms developed in the European context. Yet the analytical frameworks developed in regard to other parts of the globe provide models for fruitful thinking and rethinking in the Russian context. Surely gender, ideology, and religion contributed in fundamental ways to the formation of Russian ideas about witches, even if they did not assume precisely the same shape as elsewhere. The perceptive analyses emerging in other contexts serve as vital inspiration for this study.

A review of the literature is a necessary part and important foundation for any historical study, but in the case of Russian witchcraft, that literature must be addressed with a carefully calibrated mix of enthusiasm and caution. The enthusiasm derives from the high caliber and extraordinary inventiveness of scholarship on witchcraft in other parts of the world, and particularly in early modern Europe. The caution, however, is necessary to guide our interpretation away from overly glib assumptions about what witchcraft signified and how it was imagined. Imported ideas and expectations have distorted understandings of the Russian case to the point that the entry on "Woman" in the *Entsiklopedicheskii slovar'* (*Encyclopedic Dictionary*) of 1894 asserted that "the ratio of witches to wizards punished by law in medieval Russia has been estimated at 10,000 to 1." Along the same lines, the classic though now dated work on Russian witchcraft, "Baby bogomerzkiia (Impious/Heinous Women)," by S. Smirnov (1909), maintained confidently that in Muscovy women were more prone to practice witchcraft than men. Smirnov even provided a logical explanation for this female proclivity: women's work in the kitchen exposed them to the idea of stirring ingredients and their delicate little fingers predisposed them to tying intricate magical knots and fashioning spells.[54] Of course, in early modern Russia, women were *not* more prone to practice magic than men, or at least were not more likely to face charges, regardless of these imported European expectations. Approaching the sources with a receptive mind, setting aside deeply ingrained assumptions about the sources of magic, the gender of evil, and the religious framing of witchcraft, we can embark on an examination of the often surprising, unexpected twists and turns of witchcraft in a Muscovite guise.

RUSSIAN WITCHCRAFT SCHOLARSHIP

For many decades, a widespread impression that Russia escaped the episode of witch-hunting prevailed in Western historiography. Placing responsibility for the European witch craze squarely on the shoulders of the Catholic Church and the refined demonology its theologians developed, Hugh Trevor-Roper asserted: "the Greek Orthodox Church built up no systematic demonology and launched no witch-craze. By the schism of 1054 the Slavonic countries of Europe—with the exception of Catholic Poland, the exception which proves the rule—escaped participation in one of the most disreputable episodes in Christian history."[55] If this proposition were entirely correct, this book would serve no purpose. As it turns out, Trevor-Roper's declarative assessment does not align with the historical record, and significant scholarly energy has been directed to penetrating the mysteries of witchcraft in its Russian guise. With his pioneering 1977 article, Russell Zguta was the first to reopen serious scholarly engagement with witch trials in Russia for English-language audiences, but he built on what was already a sizable literature produced in Russia.[56]

Interestingly, perhaps the first major author to devote attention to the role and reception of magic in Russian culture was none other than Catherine the Great (reigned 1762–1796), who penned a satirical play entitled *The Siberian Shaman*. In the full bloom of Enlightenment rationalism, the empress mercilessly lampooned the ignorance, superstition, and gullibility of people who fell into the snares set by mountebanks and con artists.[57] Later, in the early nineteenth century, with a boom of interest in the ethnography of the "folk," of Russian and Ukrainian peasantry, interest shifted increasingly toward the study of what came to be seen as Russian national tradition. Seized on by both Slavophiles, those with an interest in vaunting the simple piety of the Russian people, and Westernizers, eager to acknowledge Russia's backwardness as a first step toward propelling their nation along the path of Westernizing and rationalization, folk belief became a touchstone in polemics and debates about Russian national character. What the modernizers denigrated as "backwardness" and "superstition," the Slavophiles and nationalists celebrated as "folk tradition."[58] Caught in the spotlight of these highly charged debates, witchcraft and folk practice attracted a good deal of scholarly attention throughout the late nineteenth and early twentieth century. The most important contributions of this era were collections of source materials, particularly N. Ia. Novombergskii's compendia of seventeenth-century trial records, V. B. Antonovych's eighteenth-century Ukrainian trials, and ethnographic data published by A. N. Afanasiev and V. I. Dal', although major analytical studies appeared as well.[59]

The Revolution and the difficult period ensuing put an understandable damper on academic pursuits, and in the Stalin years, research on religion and folk belief fell under a cloud of suspicion as retrograde and even counter-revolutionary topics. Soviet scholars almost universally avoided it until the late Brezhnev era.[60] In the waning years of the Soviet Union, however, discussion of folk belief, and with it, witchcraft, resumed. Brave forays into this risky terrain were sometimes made palatable by titles such as *Russian Popular Social-Utopian Legends*, which cast folk beliefs as somehow progressive and proto-revolutionary, or *Critique of Religious Sectarianism*, published under the auspices of the Institute of Scientific Atheism of the Academy of Sciences.[61] Gaining momentum toward the end of the Soviet era, witchcraft studies have accelerated dramatically in the decades since the collapse of the Soviet Union.

One resilient thread in the study of witchcraft and folk religion more generally in Russia and abroad has been the concept of *dvoeverie*, dual faith, which posited a double allegiance on the part of the peasantry. Writing in the 1930s in emigration, Georges Florovsky composed one of the most compelling presentations of the idea. He identified two concurrent, fundamentally distinct religious lives lived by the people of medieval and early modern Russia, the "day life" being the clean, pure life of Orthodox Christianity, the "night life," the suppressed yet lingering paganism of pre-Christian Rus': "This second life flowed underground and frequently broke through to history's surface. Yet one always detects its hidden presence as a boiling and stormy lava." He maintained that "paganism did not die, nor was it rendered powerless." Its traces were preserved, faintly but sometimes quite visibly, "in the popular mind and customs and style."[62] The binary paradigm was later amplified by Lotman and Uspenskij in their famous essay on the dualism of Russian culture. They concentrated on the antithetical relationship between the old and new systems, explaining that Rus' culture did not simply remake itself on new principles with the introduction of Christianity, but actually turned the old culture "'inside out,' by rearranging what [had] previously existed but with a change of signs."[63] The notion of *dvoeverie* continued to attract partisans throughout the Soviet era, with B. A. Rybakov, a specialist on the early centuries of Rus', as the leading spokesman.[64]

At the same time that Rybakov defended the concept, opposition to the *dvoeverie* model began to emerge. An ever growing number of scholars have dismissed the utility of the *dvoeverie* conceit, particularly for the periods after Rus' settled into the more profoundly Christianized early modern era and beyond. According to V. Ia. Petrukhin, the term "dual belief" may have had some relevance from the point of view of religious purists, but had no purchase in the world of traditional culture "which saw itself as Christian."[65] At present, a general consensus in the field supports this position. While Orthodoxy, like all forms of Christianity, had its syncretic elements, the valence of religious practice was distinctly and self-consciously Christian by the early modern period. Stella Rock elegantly labels the persistent dual-belief model an "academic myth."[66] E. B. Smilianskaia underscores the insufficiencies of a schema in which two cultural systems ran parallel to each other with occasional eruptions of one into the other. Rather, she argues, the two (or multiple) levels of culture constituted each other in very fundamental ways. Russian Christianity developed its own magic, and those "magical beliefs" worked in "lively interaction with Christianity."[67] The evidence of witch trials in the seventeenth century present an even stronger case: magical practices were viewed as an aspect of an integrated, seamless, single culture that combined explicitly Christian with folk innovations and the pious with the impious. No identifiable paganism is to be found.[68]

The amalgam of Orthodox Christianity and folk traditions characterized Muscovite religious practice at every level. Except for a thin layer of highly literate individuals, high and low cultural distinctions have little meaning in Muscovite society, and in particular when it comes to witchcraft. Belief, practice, and fear united all ranks. Nonetheless, Novombergskii argues strongly that the trials were very much the project of the authorities, conducted from above and foisted on the population: "In our view there remains no doubt that the struggle with witchcraft was carried out by the agency of the organs of power."[69] Muscovite laws set increasingly harsh penalties for the practice of witchcraft, and tsarist decrees mandated that the new laws be broadcast far and wide by heralds and town criers. Still, accusations flowed in from below. Muscovy had no equivalent of an inquisitor who would comb the countryside for spiritual violators; rather, a member of the broader community had to lodge a complaint before a court would initiate an investigation. Thus, tempting though it is to posit that the seventeenth-century crackdown on witchcraft represents yet another piece of the Romanov regime's attempt to secure a monopoly on all power and authority, spiritual or otherwise, the evidence militates in another direction: concern about witchcraft was shared by the entire population and its prosecution resulted from the joint efforts of the regime and its subjects.

Another area in which the Russian historiography has been strongly shaped by comparative questions is in the matter of comparative numbers and severity. Were Russian trials as numerous as their Western counterparts, or as harsh in their punishments? Advocates line up on both sides of the divide. Following Trevor-Roper, Zguta explains what he considers the relatively mild persecution of witches in Russia as an outgrowth of the flexible and tolerant traditions of a system steeped in *dvoeverie*. "Not only were a comparatively small number of victims tried and burned, but the witch persecutions in seventeenth-century Russia demonstrated a sense of measure and restraint largely absent in the West. . . . What carries the label 'witch craze' in the West might more accurately be termed only a 'witch scare' in Muscovite Russia."[70] W. F. Ryan, in his comprehensive survey of Russian magic through the ages, states that although the tsarist regime did occasionally prosecute and even execute witches, it did so with far less intensity than its Western counterparts.[71] This school of thought has the force of numbers to back its position. At a stretch, one may count in surviving records between 450 and 500 trials, involving perhaps 900 people, for the entire period 1600–1760s. Across those two centuries, under 15 percent suffered the ultimate penalty, execution, while the rest were left to live their lives, either in their home communities or registered into service units in Siberia or along the Ukrainian frontier. Particularly when the target of comparison for the Western trials was understood at the vastly inflated many millions of victims burned in a great conflagration of witches, Russia's numbers seemed almost absurdly modest. Even now that scholarship has radically revised the numbers of convicted witches executed overall during the European witch-hunts, bringing them down from millions to tens of thousands, Russia's scant collection of cases remains strikingly small.[72]

Given the highly charged question of Russia's standing relative to an abstracted "West," a question that always lurks in the background if not pushing to the fore in Russian studies, the matter of comparison assumes not only factual but also moral weight. The low numbers have provided support for a claim that Russia was generally a more humane place than the rest of Europe, more tolerant of difference, less prone to extremes of cruelty, and generally better able to keep focused on the things that mattered, the simple piety and faith of the Russian people, rather than quibbling over details around the edges.[73] In the opposing camp were those eager to see Russia as Europe's equal in witchcraft persecution as in all other aspects of statecraft and development. Novombergskii wrote, in the introduction to his publication of trial materials, "This struggle [against witchcraft] was [carried out] with no less cruelty than in Western Europe: in the struggle with witches Muscovite Rus' suffered the same general terrorizing investigation, torture, and public burning of those convicted of witchcraft."[74] Partisans of this approach advance a twofold argument to support their case. First, while it is true that the number of surviving case records is relatively small, those that do survive reveal a court system just as zealous in its drive to find and eliminate witches as any in the heart of Europe. With a series of increasingly harsh decrees prescribing the lavish application of torture and the burning of witches along with the implements of their craft, Muscovite courts demonstrated a fierce commitment to the cause. Second, in a move betraying somewhat perverse optimism, adherents of the "just as bad as Europe" school dwell on the incompleteness of the documentary record, which allows them to presume that a vast subterranean pool of cases remains untapped, either lost forever or awaiting discovery in the recesses of the archives.

My own position on this question falls somewhere between these poles. The numbers of trials and particularly the numbers executed do seem to have remained relatively low, because of the absence of a consistent demonological vision of witchcraft, a lack of alternatives to folk healing practices, a blurry sense of division between acceptable and unacceptable practices, and the difficulties in policing an empire of this scale. On the other hand, after reading transcript after transcript describing the application of torture "without mercy," it is hard to disagree with Novombergskii's conclusion that Muscovite authorities did indeed engaged in a struggle against witchcraft with as much cruelty as any European court. The following chapter examines those transcripts to outline standard court procedures and to assess their promise and pitfalls as records of Muscovy's struggle against witchcraft.

2

"Report on This Matter to Us in Moscow, Fully and in Truth"

Documentation and Procedure

WITCHCRAFT TRIALS FELL, for the most part, under the jurisdiction of the tsar's secular courts. Like other Muscovite trials, they began with a denunciation, filed in the form of a supplicatory petition addressed to the tsar himself. As a general rule, such petitions were initially presented to the local governor (*voevoda*) of the town or province in which the petitioner resided, and were processed by the administrative staff (*pod'iachie*) of his office (*s'ezzhaia izba; prikaznaia izba*). The procedure was substantially the same for all kinds of offenses, from name-calling and insults to honor, to arson, theft, assault, and murder. After conducting a cursory preliminary investigation into the matter, the governor would refer the matter up, to Moscow. Sometimes, in an intermediary move, a local official would transfer the case to the governor of the major administrative center of the region, for instance, from the relatively small Briansk to the larger administrative unit in Sevsk, and from there it would be sent to Moscow. If a complainant initially addressed someone other than the governor, for instance an estate bailiff, a town elder, an abbot of a local monastery, or a representative of a bishop's court, then it was up to that official to bring the matter to the attention of the governor. Petitions generally open by recounting the chain through which the grievance reached the proper authorities. For instance, in 1659, the governor of the town of Lukh reported to Tsar Aleksei Mikhailovich that the town elders (*zemskie starosty*), a smith and a shoemaker, petitioned him in his office and submitted a petition signed by all the townspeople of Lukh, complaining of an outbreak of possession among the women of the town. "They petitioned you, Sovereign, and me, your slave, in the governor's office and gave me another petition signed by [two] townspeople . . ., and I have attached the petition and sent it to you to Moscow."[1] Governors normally directed their summaries to the Chancellery of Military Affairs, the *Razriad,* with a request for instructions of how to proceed.[2]

The record of a trial for bewitchment that began in December 1648 exemplifies the administrative flow and the juridical process. The documentation opens with a report, in the form of a petition, from the governor of Kozlov, a fortress town on the southern frontier, to Moscow. Employing the standard self-effacing language of servility and identifying himself with a belittling diminutive form of his name, the *stolnik* governor Vasilii Semyonovich Volynskoi sent a communiqué to Moscow, reporting on the denunciation of one Kozlov military servitor, Ivashka Gubanov, by another, Kuzemka Podolskoi: "To Sovereign Tsar Aleksei Mikhailovich, Autocrat of all Great, Small, and White Russia! Your slave, Vaska Volynskoi, petitions. In this year 1648, on December 22, . . . Kuzemka Podolskoi informed me [orally in the Kozlov governor's office] and accused Ivashka Gubanov, saying that Ivashka had bewitched many people." In response to this accusation, the governor took immediate action to determine the nature and extent of the problem: "I, your slave, questioned Kuzemka to find out whom, by name, Ivashka bewitched, and by what means, and in what years. And following up on Kuzemka's denunciation, I questioned Ivashka Gubanov and those people whom, according to Kuzemka, Ivashko bewitched." In support of his claim, Kuzemka turned to "the entire village of Lezhaisk, saying that all the military servitors of that village know that Ivashka bewitched many people." Taking the next logical step, the governor brought a number of villagers "to the governor's office and questioned them each separately." A court scribe transcribed their testimony at length, and the governor explained: "I sent those reports to you, Sovereign, with [a] Kozlov military servitor." With these steps, the governor reached the limits of his sanctioned autonomy, and he dutifully turned to Moscow for direction.[3] He closed his report by noting that he had ordered the accused witch, Ivashka Gubanov, "placed under guard until your sovereign order arrives." Accompanying the governor's cover letter were twenty pages of testimony, handwritten by the court scribe, recording what kinds of bewitchment Ivashka purportedly had or had not worked and whom he had or had not bewitched. Some witnesses claimed he had boasted of his knowledge of witchcraft, had caused illness, impotence, and even death, and that he had stolen a goose and extorted payment from his victims. Ivashka himself pleaded innocence, and asserted that he had not stolen the goose, but rather had taken it in exchange for some peas.[4]

The next step would take the form of a return missive from Moscow. Generally the document emanating from the Razriad would open with a copy of all the previous documentation: "On December 22nd 1647, you, our *stolnik* and governor in Kozlov, Vasilii Semyonovich Volynskoi, wrote to us and in your petition you said. . . ."[5] A verbatim copy of the earlier report would follow, and only after this tedious repetition would the Moscow authorities indicate what the next step should be. Usually, they ordered "a full, truthful investigation" with all witnesses being interrogated independently. Often they also ordered an "eye-to-eye" or direct confrontation between the accuser and accused, to see if the accusation held up under personal contact. After the provincial branch or the special investigators assigned from Moscow had completed this next round, another repetitive report, complete with more exact copies of the ever-mounting mutual summaries of previous exchanges, would wend its way to Moscow, and eventually the boyars and secretaries of the Razriad might order the governor to administer "harsh" or "merciless" torture to anyone plausibly implicated in criminal witchcraft. The governor would be instructed to send the "torture speeches," that is, the reports of testimony taken during torture, to Moscow. Alternatively, or subsequently, the chancellery officials in the central office might require that the suspects and witnesses be transported under close guard to Moscow for questioning and torture in the prison of the Razriad under their own supervision. The accumulating documents, written on the long, thin sheets of thick paper that were standard issue at the time, would be collected in a stack, a *stolbets*, or glued into a long, continuous ribbon and folded up, accordion style, and filed away on the shelves of the relevant Razriad bureaus in Moscow, where they still reside today.[6] Ultimately, it was the Razriad officials who sentenced the accused and issued orders to their provincial agents or to their underlings in Moscow to carry out the sentences, which ranged from release under surety bond to exile and a life of mandatory service, to corporal punishment or mutilation followed by exile, to execution. Execution was the fate of a minority of convicted witches, about 14 percent in the seventeenth century, and took various forms. Men were generally beheaded or possibly hanged. A few women were given the special distinction of burial alive, the prescribed punishment for women who killed their husbands.[7] Nine or ten male and female witches received the sentence of burning, not at the stake, but in a boxy wooden structure or cage, as illustrated in figure 2.1.[8]

A profound methodological and ethical challenge haunts the transcripts from witchcraft trials: almost without exception, the testimony reported by court scribes was elicited through the administration of torture. Recognition of this stark reality, that the words of the accused come to us indelibly marked and distorted by cruel physical violence, casts into doubt any claims that court records report what "really happened," or even what the litigants and witnesses believed to have transpired. How can one take seriously narratives produced by coercive interrogation or testimony molded in a crucible of pain?

Sadly, the problems posed by this circumstance are not unique to Muscovy or to the seventeenth century or even to witchcraft trials, and scholars have

Burning v srube. *Executions by burning were relatively rare in witchcraft cases, but when they did occur, the condemned were burned alive inside a small wooden structure rather than at the stake. Here is depicted the execution of the Judaizers, condemned as heretics at the Council of 1504. Seated in judgment, from right to left, are Metropolitan Simon, Grand Prince Ivan III Vasil'evich, and his son, Vasilii Ivanovich. Miniature from the great illustrated chronicle compilation overseen by Metropolitan Makarii during the reign of Ivan IV, the* Illustrated Chronicle Compilation Listevoi letopisnyi svod, *1570s (RNB. f. 4. 232. l. 644).* Litsevoi letopisnyi svod XVI veka: Russkaia letopisnaia istoriia. *Bk. 18, 1503–1527 (Moscow: Akteon, 2010), 43. (See also plate 1)*

had ample opportunities to consider the analytical implications. The most sophisticated responses approach torture testimony with the same caution they would bring to any other text.[9] All texts are constructions, recording impressions mediated through various screens of cultural, personal, and structural perception. Victims of torture generally respond to leading questions posed by the inquisitors. At the very least, then, torture transcripts represent the preoccupations of the torturers, and thus reflect some of the ideas and preconceptions available in the society.

In formulating their responses, the tortured drew not only on the clues provided by their interrogators' questions, but also on their own sense of the possible. If only to end the ordeal, they would deliberately or unconsciously structure narratives that they thought would satisfy their tormentors. Their testimony had to meet criteria of plausibility, again reflecting the framing beliefs and expectations of the society, and they had to derive from ideas, vocabulary, and motifs available in the world that they knew. Testimony, whether provided spontaneously in preliminary questioning or ripped from the suspect through torture, could not venture beyond the limits of the imaginable.

Following methods developed in studies of medieval and early modern inquisition material and of witchcraft and treason trials elsewhere in Europe, the approach taken in this book is to accept that the documentary record preserves something akin to the actual testimony given in court. As Walter Stephens suggests, the whole point of exacting testimony through torture was to have the examinees convince the interrogators that they were telling the truth. It would not have served their purpose to force their subjects to confess according to a script; rather confessions had to "be laboriously extracted through a 'cat-and-mouse' dialogue."[10] This position assumes that court officials and scribes had no particular investment in fabricating the words of their prisoners, but rather in shaping them as they were uttered. The variety of testimonial reports, ranging from compliant to defiant, supports this presumption. Even while enduring bitter torment, the tortured set some limits beyond which they would not confess or incriminate. Although constrained by the demands and expectations of their tormentors, they spoke from their own experience and imagination and expressed, through a miasma of coercion, their own commitments and their own anguish. As Michael Ostling observes, "Painful though it is to hear these voices, we ought to listen to what they say."[11]

In examining the evidence, I have by and large set aside the next piece of the question, the relation of testimony to some more fundamental reality. Their testimony may have drawn on their cultural imaginary and on their experience, while not reflecting their actions in any literal way. Whether or not the men and women on trial actually committed the crimes to which they confessed, the dialogue of the courtroom illuminates a great deal about the ways in which Muscovites could think about witchcraft and the anxieties that provoked them to do so. In places, the particular concatenation of evidence—the patterns in accusations, confessions, and witness testimony, the sequence of unforced and coerced testimony, the presence of material evidence—encourages me to think a glimpse of someone's experience glimmers through a chink in time. The prosaic nature of the crimes attributed to Russian witches makes their confessions, concocted with or without torture, easier to believe than those of European witches, who confessed to night flying, Satan worship, and cannibalism. The concurrence between the concerns of ordinary subjects who leveled accusations and the officials who conducted the trials similarly supports an argument that coerced interrogation exerted less of a distorting effect on Muscovite witch trials than has been documented in the demonologically inflected trials in other parts of Europe.

Questions of reality remain to some extent secondary to the beliefs and fears that led some people to tremble in fear of a witch's curse and sentenced others to suffer and die at the hands of torturers or executioners. In order to try to answer the ethical demands of exploiting this material and writing analytically about the agonies of people in the past, I have made a deliberate choice of foregrounding the uses of violence and the application of physical torment at every juncture. In the course of writing this book, I, along with the rest of the world, have come to realize how immediately present such practices remain in the world today. As an acknowledgment of the role of torture in distorting the human record of the past and the present, I try not to let that brutal routine slip out of view.

QUESTIONS OF SOURCES

While the question of how to read testimony produced through torture poses unique ethical as well as methodological dilemmas, a host of other barbed questions encircle the source base. Russian scholars have been assiduous in publishing witchcraft material, either in dedicated collections or as individual findings.[12] Novombergskii identified and published about fifty of these already in the early years of the last century. All but a few of the rest of the seventeenth-century cases can be tracked through the scrupulous listings in the obsessively complete pre-revolutionary catalogue of the holdings of the archives of the Imperial Ministry of Justice, the collection currently housed in the Russian State Archive of Ancient Documents in Moscow.[13] The nineteenth- and early twentieth-century compilers appear to have taken particular note of all matters bizarre or sensational, thus where a file full of tax registers may be listed in the catalogue simply as "tax registers," legal cases involving spectacular violence, incest, rape, or, fortunately for the purposes of this study, witchcraft, drew special notice. Thus, for example, an entry in the archival catalogue may list a set of documents generically as "cases from Alatyr, 1628–32" or "cases from Kostroma from the years 1670–72," but will further specify, for the reader's delectation: "On fols. 617–638: investigation of the death of Iv. Fed. Levashov's wife from grasses, given to her to cure possession by a peasant of the Nizhegorod Pecherskii monastery, Maks. Ivanov"; or "On folios 1–54, investigation of Iv. Leont. Laptev's denunciation of his brother, Os. Leont. Laptev, along with a bailiff and the peasant of Andr. Il. Bezobrazov for the bewitchment of people, heresy, and composing written spells."[14] Witchcraft studies, therefore, are the direct beneficiaries of the piqued curiosity of earlier generations of archivists.

On the other hand, the sense of completeness conveyed by the twenty-six-volume catalogue may be severely misleading, for several reasons. Researchers may have been lulled into confidently assuming that the cataloguers identified all witchcraft cases, when in fact many more remain unnoted and therefore invisible. Witchcraft specialists have repeatedly culled through the collection of the Military Chancellery (*Razriadnyi prikaz*) that directly or indirectly oversaw most judicial matters throughout the seventeenth century. It is possible, though, that the holdings of other chancelleries, such as the Armory (*Oruzheinaia palata*) or the Secret Chancellery (*Prikaz velikogo gosudaria tainykh del*), still contain untapped resources.[15] However, both the holdings of the archives themselves and the progressive concentration of judicial authority within the Razriad suggest that most witchcraft cases were heard and recorded in the Military Chancellery. Suits involving the highest levels of society and even magical attacks on the tsar and his relatives were heard in the Razriad, indicating that the special courts and chancelleries that served the tsar and his elite servitors deferred to the Razriad in witchcraft cases. Other, regional, chancelleries with potentially competing juridical authority, such as those along the militarized southern line, ultimately referred back to the Razriad for authorization and instruction in the course of their investigations. Several of the cases preserved in the archive of the Razriad note their initial hearing in other branches of the administration, the regional authority of the *Chetvert'* in one case, the *Prikaznye dela starykh let* in another, but transcripts were sent to and stored in the Razriad as well.[16] Several cases survive in the collections of both local and central bureaus, lending support to the idea that communication with the center made for duplication rather than dispersion of records.[17]

Sometimes litigants would initiate their suits in a chancellery with direct pertinence to their lives: for instance in 1647 a clerk of the *Zemskii prikaz* (Tax office) stationed in Kozlov, in the south, addressed his complaint against a monastic servitor to the administrators of his own chancellery, but the defendant landed in the prison and torture chamber of the Razriad and faced harsh interrogation by the lofty boyars arrayed on the judicial panel of that chancellery. Similarly, in 1650 a gunner from Ostashkov submitted a complaint to the Chancellery of Gunners (*Pushkarskii prikaz*), but the officials there immediately forwarded the case to the governor of Ostashkov with instructions that he should conduct the investigation in consultation with the Razriad.[18] The same sequence was followed in a 1683 case from Efremov, which originated in the Musketeers' Chancellery (*Streletskii prikaz*), but was remitted to the Razriad.[19] Of course, there is some possible circularity in the claim that all cases eventually fell under the purview of the Razriad, since the primary archival cache of witchcraft trials extant today is that of the Razriad. Still, given the survival of internal evidence of the back-and-forth communication among various chancelleries, one might expect the survival of some cases that remained outside of the Razriad, if such cases there were.

The fact that attentive eyes, alert to all traces of magic, have passed over the documents for well over a century, lends some credence to the idea that there are not huge caches of witchcraft trials lying unnoticed in a dusty corner of the archive. There may well be some lurking undiscovered, but the treats in store will probably prove quite limited. On the other hand, there are doubtless numerous cases that I have missed in my investigations, even ones that have been discussed in the published literature. I can make no claim to having succeeded in making a truly exhaustive compilation of witchcraft cases, and I continue to encounter new documents and unfamiliar cases in the literature and to be delighted by references sent to me by generous friends and colleagues, even now, as my research draws to a close.[20] Nonetheless, at this point I am coming across very few new cases, and, so far, those few conform to the general outlines of witchcraft cases described in this book.

The second problem is more substantive. Were there hundreds, thousands, of trials that took place outside the tsar's court system, in ecclesiastical courts, for which archival records are sparse, or in local, or even manorial, courts? Were there episodes of unofficial justice or even lynchings that took place off the record, beyond the purview of the state, and therefore never made it into the central documentary record? Church courts certainly did hear some magic cases, at least as the courts of first instance, and minor infractions involving low-level magic could sometimes be addressed through fasting, penance, and prayer. Ecclesiastical texts claimed jurisdiction over the crime of witchcraft. Penitential guides advised confessors to be on the lookout for "anyone who brings sacrifices to devils and heals the sick with charms and wax," and "anyone who prays to devils for harm to people." Penitentials noted that "anyone who believes in charms brings pleasure to devils," and mandated that "whoever prays to Satan or to his names should be sentenced to five years on bread and water."[21]

The fingerprints of clerical jurisdiction are evident in a handful of full-blown witchcraft cases that survive in the archives of the secular courts, but only because the cases were ultimately wrested out of church control and transferred to the secular chancelleries, where the law decreed they belonged. Sometimes tensions ensued, as in a case in the 1680s where a village priest refused to relinquish another priest charged with witchcraft to the secular authorities without an order from the patriarch himself.[22] In other cases the authorities negotiated the transfer more smoothly, with the secular courts triumphing in the end, even in cases involving ecclesiastical personnel. Charges exchanged among monastic servitors or monastic peasants were heard in secular courts.[23] In principle, members of the clergy were supposed to be tried in church courts. A decree issued in January 1669 specified that "if ecclesiastical people are accused of theft from church or secular people, or of forging money (*denezhnye dela*) or banditry or murder or witchcraft (*vedovsto*), and are caught and brought to town to the investigator (*syshchik*), they should be turned over to ecclesiastical courts." The same division of jurisdiction was articulated in the "Newly Ordered Articles (*Novoukaznye stat'i*)" of that same year: "For clerical people and people of ecclesiastical ranks, do not take testimony from them because clerical people are supposed to be questioned by clerical courts and state investigators (*syshchiki*) are not allowed in clerical courts."[24] Despite these prescriptions, in witchcraft cases from the 1630s right through the end of the century, priests and deacons appeared frequently in Razriad courts as defendants and "sat under guard at the Razriad," awaiting interrogation and sentence. A fascinating petition from 1679/80 demonstrates that clerical personnel were aware of the legal principle that assigned them to ecclesiastical rather than secular courts, but that they had to battle to enforce it. In this case, a certain Ivan, priest of a rural church in Vologda province, wrote from Vologda, where he was being held prisoner and was under investigation by the governor and the Chancellery of Criminal Investigation (*Sysknoi prikaz*) on charges of purveying healing grasses. The priest petitioned the archbishop of Vologda and Beloozero to order him transferred from the jurisdiction of the chancellery to that of the archbishop, "by law and by reason of [my priestly] rank." What ultimately happened in this case, which survives in only this fragment, is unknown, but he and his brother (and accuser), a church deacon, both languished in secular detention at the time the petition was written.[25] Their presence in the secular courts reveals that the principle of ecclesiastical jurisdiction, so dear to historians, was "more what you'd call 'guidelines' than actual rules" (to purloin a phrase from *The Pirates of the Caribbean*).[26]

With or without guidelines protecting spiritual jurisdiction, the tsar's courts at times aggressively proclaimed their power over ecclesiastical ranks. The single most forceful assertion of secular control to arise in the course of a trial appears in the record of a trial that pitted Fedor Dalmatov, a Zemliansk serviceman, against his daughter-in-law, whom he accused of bewitching his wife and daughters. Perhaps because the accusation named a local priest as a co-conspirator in the bewitchment, the matter was initially heard by the Spiritual Chancellery in the nearby provincial center, Voronezh, but the plaintiff petitioned to have the case transferred "from the Spiritual Chancellery to the sovereign's chancellery and the city court (*k gradtskomu sudu*) for truthful investigation." He provided two reasons to justify the switch of jurisdictions. First, he complained, the case was being unfairly held up because the staff of the Spiritual Chancellery favored their friend, the priest Timofei. More substantively, Fedor noted, "by your sovereign decree it is ordered that matters of poison should be adjudicated in the great sovereign's chancelleries and not in spiritual chancelleries. Merciful great sovereign. . . . Favor me, your slave. Order that suit against my daughter-in-law Marfa transferred to the judicial chancellery."[27] Investigating relevant legal precedents, the spiritual authorities returned a ruling on this matter of procedure: "By the order of the sovereigns and by a decree [sent] to the most holy bishop in 1689/90, clerics and people of priestly and monastic ranks are not to be sent to the city court for investigations and direct confrontations with prisoners being interrogated; instead it is ordered that such prisoners/witnesses should be sent for confrontation to the Spiritual Chancellery and [only] if people from the clerical ranks are implicated in such matters, . . . they should be sent to the city court."[28] The transfer to secular courts was denied.

The position of the Spiritual Chancellery, however, did not stand. A countermanding order arrived from Moscow. The boyars "ruled that the case of bewitchment of Fedor's wife and daughter by his daughter-in-law Marfa . . . should be transferred from the Voronezh Spiritual Chancellery to the Razriad because that matter is a criminal investigation (*delo rozysknoe*) and not spiritual, and the people who have been implicated should be sent for interrogation to the Razriad in Moscow under guard and with signed security documents."[29] Lest any uncertainty remain, the case record repeats the order in unambiguous terms: "Send to Moscow to the Military Chancellery because this is a *criminal investigation and not spiritual* (Vyslat' k Moskve v Rozriad dlia togo chto to delo *rozysknoe a ne dukhovnoe*)." The patriarch himself was enlisted to write to the bishop in Voronezh, binding him to comply with the order.[30] This ruling appears to settle the question once and for all, establishing witchcraft as a secular and not a spiritual infraction, but of course in Muscovy, nothing was ever so clear-cut. Muscovite chancelleries were fully capable of changing their minds or issuing contradictory decrees.

The internal evidence of jurisdictional competition and cooperation between the chancelleries and religious institutions suggests that Moscow authorities kept abreast of witchcraft cases being heard in clerical venues and required full reports, if not the transfer to the secular court system. Numerous witchcraft cases were investigated jointly by secular and ecclesiastical agencies, as, for instance, in a case tried by the Razriad where a priestly witness was questioned in the Patriarchal Chancellery, or where the patriarch worked in conjunction with the *Dvortsovoi prikaz,* the Court Chancellery.[31] In complex cases involving multiple offenses, jurisdiction was sometimes divided between the Patriarchal Chancellery and the Razriad. Interestingly, the witchcraft charges always ended up under the secular agency in such divisions of labor. For example, in 1690 the boyars in the Razriad heard charges and countercharges in two related cases: one involving witchcraft; the other defiling the Host. The boyars remanded the desecration case to the Patriarchal Chancellery but chose to resolve the witchcraft case themselves.[32] Similarly, another complex case that shuttled back and forth between spiritual and secular jurisdiction was ultimately divided between the two, with the spiritual authority responsible for dealing with accusations of fornication while the Razriad, again, retained the witchcraft charges under its own aegis.[33] Aleksandr Lavrov has carefully combed the archives of the bishops' palaces of Vologda and Velikii Ustiug, collections that survive more or less intact though now scattered among several repositories. He reports that these eparchial courts rarely adjudicated witchcraft cases, although they enjoyed broad competence in spiritual and moral crimes, including rape.[34] His finding thus parallels the division of responsibility seen in the cases noted above, where defiling the host and fornication fell under ecclesiastical jurisdiction, while hearing witchcraft cases remained a secular prerogative. Collectively, all of this evidence strongly suggests that even cases heard in clerical courts would have left traces in the records of the Razriad, but there is once again some circularity in this reasoning: cases heard in ecclesiastical courts show up only when they were mentioned in Razriad records, leaving a shadow of doubt hanging over the issue of completeness.

The same uncertainty clouds the question of whether or not all of those cases tried in local governors' courts left traces in the central administrative archives. Occasionally trial records refer to earlier stints in a local prison on healing or fortune-telling charges resulting from a trial otherwise unregistered in surviving records. For example, in one of the anecdotes recounted in the Introduction, the case involving the Putivl' governor's accusations against a widowed relative and her serving woman, no trace of the original trial survives. We know of it only from a later suit that referred to the earlier proceedings. Similarly, when an elderly fortune-teller in the Suzdal' region was named as a witness for the prosecution in an unrelated case in 1647, she described a long history of run-ins with the law. Years earlier, she had made the mistake of using her skills as a seer to identify the thief who had stolen a book from the governor. He repaid her efforts by having her incarcerated in a convent on charges of fortune-telling and condemning her to a harsh regime of fasting and prayer. Evidently she was resistant to such forced re-education, because as soon as she was released, she returned to her previous habits. Her testimony reveals that fortune-telling landed her in hot water again in subsequent years, but still prior to the surviving case record. Tortured to identify her accomplices, Daritsa named another fortune-teller, Olenka. She explained that she knew Olenka well from the time they had spent together "in chains" in the Suzdal' prison, where they both had done time for fortune-telling. Daritsa added, a bit snidely, that the local chancellery official had freed Olenka from irons in exchange for a bribe, but that "he freed her (Daritsa) from irons without a bribe."[35]

This incidental revelation of a cascade of cases otherwise undocumented in archival records necessitates a sober assessment of the completeness of the sample that survives. The two women's hostile acquaintance in the Suzdal' prison, along with Daritsa's earlier incarceration in a convent, suggests that witchcraft charges such as these, which involved no victim and no tangible harm, might be prosecuted locally, with significant flexibility in sentencing. On the other hand, the fact that the elderly Daritsa was already imprisoned in Moscow when the new investigation began in Suzdal' reminds us that even low-level infractions drew the ire of Moscow and pulled suspects into the courtrooms and torture chambers of the Razriad. Daritsa's testimony cautions us not to presume completeness of the surviving archival trove, but it also offers encouragement as to the representativeness of the surviving sample. The charges that brought Daritsa and Olenka to the attention of the authorities in the 1647 extant case were no more heinous, in fact, were in no way different, than those that had landed them in prison in the earlier, unrecorded trials.

We cannot know for certain whether reports on Daritsa's and Olenka's earlier trials in Suzdal' were ever sent to Moscow, that is, whether there was a class of infraction considered trivial enough to fall below Moscow's supervision. Given the phenomenal level of minutia that was routinely communicated to the center—reports on low supplies of paper and ink, reports on missing horses, drunken brawls, or exchanges of insults—it seems probable that reports on the women's activities indeed had to be submitted to Moscow at some point, but were somehow lost in the intervening centuries. In other words, although it is possible that cases of low-level witchcraft were routinely adjudicated locally, without recourse to Moscow's supervision, this scenario seems unlikely. Surveys of provincial administrative records support the contention that, with rare exceptions like the ones identified here, the vast majority of cases documented in provincial offices also left traces in central chancellery archives.[36]

The question of local or manorial courts is perhaps an even trickier one to resolve. Few records survive for the estate courts of the seventeenth century, and for the eighteenth century the archives are still poorly catalogued. It is indeed possible that landlords or their bailiffs adjudicated witchcraft charges on the spot, but because they left no documentation, the weight of those cases vanished from the record. Once again, it is possible, but unlikely. The Muscovite state, and the Petrine state after it, disliked sharing authority, particularly in issues of real import. Actively stretching its tentacles into every pore of society, regulating, adjudicating, and supervising every interaction, movement, or exchange that it could possibly claim, the tsarist regime was unlikely easily to shrug off an arena of crime that it took seriously enough to classify with treason, rebellion, and aggravated murder. Furthermore, a number of cases reveal in the course of their documentation that complaints were initially lodged with estate agents, who conducted preliminary investigations and then turned the matter over to state authorities.[37] At least twelve cases survive of masters or bailiffs dragging their own serfs or slaves before the authorities to face witchcraft charges.[38] These dramas suggest that witchcraft cases were too hot to handle within the confines of the serf- or slave-owning estate. Both because of the danger of exposing oneself to magical assault and because of the risk of incurring the tsar's wrath, masters preferred to air their concerns about witchcraft in the courts.

Extra-legal justice, called *samosud* or "self-administered justice" in Russian, provided a much-used mode of retribution in the nineteenth century, and, as Stephen Frank and Christine Worobec have demonstrated, suspected witches became prime targets for gruesome vigilante assaults. The legal situation, however, had fundamentally altered between the early modern and modern periods. The law reclassified what had once been a serious crime as a minor irritant, a matter of fraud or ignorant superstition, and judges and educated elites no longer had any interest in prosecuting it. People who deemed themselves the victims of supernatural attack had no recourse but to take matters in their own hands.[39] Until the late eighteenth century, however, the courts readily credited the efficacy of magic, and the illegality of witchcraft was beyond doubt. Mob justice was unnecessary, since grievances could be aired in sympathetic courts. Vigilante action was also dangerous; unsanctioned killing would certainly bring down the wrath of the tsar, however justified the assault. In her extensive study of Muscovite legal practice, Nancy Kollmann finds negligible numbers of lynchings noted in court records, and the few that did draw the attention of the state precipitated full-throttled investigations by the central authorities. Given the state's strong interest in squelching unauthorized killings and protecting its control over criminal justice, Kollmann's finding supports the notion that vigilante justice was successfully suppressed or even obviated by the activity of the tsar's courts.[40]

Even state officials risked severe punishment if they carried out executions without first securing the proper authorization. Missives from Moscow routinely warned local officials that they were not to take any significant action without the sovereign's order, and instances where people were imprisoned, tortured, or executed without such orders offered grounds for successful suits against the officials.[41] A case from the Ukrainian lands reached the attention of the authorities in Moscow, and hence found its way into the archive, only because an informant denounced the hetman of the Zaporozhian Cossack host for taking the law into his own hands: "Boyar and hetman Ivan Martynovich ordered five women witches (*baby ved'my*) and a sixth, the wife of a Gadiach lieutenant (*polkovnik*), burned" on his own initiative, without the tsar's imprimatur.[42] In another case also from the southern frontier, a group of Cherkassian weavers suspected of using stolen Eucharistic bread for magical purposes pointed in self-defense to the torture they had endured at the hands of the archpriest who, with the help of an army officer, had held them in chains and tortured them "without the sovereign's order." "At the lieutenant's house Vaska and Sidorko were chained to a cannon for three days, and he, the archpriest, came to the lieutenant on the third day, . . . and the archpriest told the lieutenant to command the guards to beat them with whips, and on the street in front of the lieutenant's house, the guards beat those weavers, Vaska and Sidorka, with whips." The archpriest's excuse was that "he never wrote to Belgorod to boyar and voevoda Prince Boris Aleksandrovich [Repnin] and comrades, and never informed [any other officials] . . . because he didn't know about the sovereign's order in this matter. He carried out this punishment following ancient Cherkassian custom, and even today in their Cherkassian towns they act this way in such cases."[43] In this case, the archpriest's explanation warded off official reprisals, but his unauthorized actions merited notice in the record. Since Muscovites of all social standings were in the habit of turning to the tsar's courts to settle the most petty of disputes, over street brawls or misspellings, there is no reason to doubt that as the first course of action in a matter of witchcraft, people turned to the courts.

If the logic of these suppositions is correct, then the relatively small collection of cases that makes up the source base for this study represents a substantial fraction of the witchcraft trials from the seventeenth century. While inevitably some must have escaped detection in the archives, and others undoubtedly have been lost over the centuries or were never properly recorded or filed in the Moscow chancelleries, it appears that what survives must give a strong sense of the whole. To that whole, and to the beliefs that inspired Muscovites to practice and to punish witchcraft, we now turn.

3

Muscovite Prosaic Magic and the Devil's Pale Shadow

IN MARCH 1676 TIMOFEI KARAULOV, the governor of the southern frontier town of Dobroe, reported to the tsar the details of a complaint filed by a local clergyman, Priest Davyd of the town church of the Mother of God, against his hired man, Mishka Kireev, and Kireev's wife, Arinka. In his denunciation, Priest Davyd wrote:

> In past years and in this current year on various dates, roots and dirt appeared in the upper chamber (*gornitsa*) of his house under the ceiling and stuck in the corner. Davyd and his wife also saw those roots in their drinks, in home brew (*braga*) and kvas, and Arinka, the wife of the hired man Mishka, brought those drinks to them. And from those poisonous roots his wife and children are dying. And his suspicion in this matter fell on his hired man Mishka and his wife Arinka.

"Merciful sovereign, tsar, and grand prince Fedor Alekseeich!" the priest implored, ". . . order my hired man Mishka and his wife questioned in Dobroe about the roots and bewitchment, [about] who gave them the roots, and who instructed them to bewitch me and my little wife and children, so that those heretics do not cause me, your pilgrim, to perish along with my family and with my little children for no reason."[1]

If there is such a thing as a typical witchcraft case, this is it. As the case unfolds, it conforms to all the tacit conventions of Muscovite witch belief and persecution. The demographic profile of the suspects, the relationship between accuser and accused, the prosaic techniques, the earthy pharmacopeia, and the immediate goals of the imputed magic, all match the general patterns evident in trials from the period. The steps in the judicial process too follow the Muscovite norm. In this chapter, what is particularly relevant, however, is what is absent from the record, the questions that remain unasked throughout the trial and that no one, from the tsar in Moscow to the accused in the torture chamber, saw fit to address. Stupendous in his glaring absence is Satan, the missing malevolent center, at least if one bears in mind the European example.

FORGETTING SATAN

Robert Mathiesen, in an article on "Magic in Slavia Orthodoxia," underscores the crucial importance of this absence:

> In western Europe during the high middle ages, the theory became dominant that all magic involved a pact with demonic powers or allegiance to them, and hence could be seen as the ethical and moral equivalent to treason to God. . . .
>
> It cannot be too much emphasized that such a theory is not universal, even within Christendom. Rather its dominance is the result of quite specific developments within western European Christianity.

After this observation, he concludes, significantly, "There is no reason to expect comparable events in the history of the eastern Orthodox churches, and they did not take place there."[2] He is right on both counts. Centuries of careful intellectual and cultural work pulled together a single great and terrifying vision of satanic witchcraft across Catholic and Protestant Europe. There is no reason to expect that particular concatenation of ideas to reproduce itself in other cultural settings. Rather, the reverse would hold true: it would be extraordinary if, in the absence of direct borrowing, the same rather perverse mythic complex coalesced elsewhere. As Brian Levack underscores, "It is the diabolical component of early modern European witchcraft that distinguishes it most clearly. . . . [No society outside of the late medieval and early modern Christian West] has developed a set of beliefs that duplicates or even approximates those of late medieval demonologists, and none of them has nurtured the belief that a large sect of flying magicians worships demons secretly in orgies characterized by cannibalistic infanticide."[3]

The Devil, of course, was not an unknown quantity in Russian Orthodox thought, and he made memorable appearances in tales and hagiographic works from time to time. O. D. Zhuravel' establishes that the theme of the pact with the Devil, of humans selling their souls to the Devil, arrived in Russia no later than the twelfth century, brought over in translations from the Greek "Life of Vasilii (Basil) the Great" and in an apocryphal tale about Adam's pact with Satan.[4] From the twelfth century forward, the theme circulated in translated

Greek texts but was little developed by Russian authors. Its circulation in Muscovite ecclesiastical circles is witnessed by a surviving miniature icon from the sixteenth century, depicting a demon guiding the hand of a sinner (who failed to protect himself by making the sign of the cross) signing away his soul to the Devil.[5] From a later period, a lively fresco from 1716 from the Church of St. Ilia in Iaroslavl shows the monk Theofilus at the very moment of selling his soul to the Devil.[6] The story maintains that Theofilus was saved from his satanic bargain by the Mother of God, who intervened on his behalf, wiped clean the text of the pact, and returned the lost sheep to the fold. With his pact, Theofilus sought career advancement and the favor of his superior, the bishop, themes familiar in Muscovite spells, though usually without recourse to the Devil. Similar motifs run through the literary "Tale of Savva Grudtsyn," a seventeenth-century story about a young man who sells his soul to the Devil in order to gain the sexual favors of his benefactor's wife. Savva too is saved by the intervention of the Mother of God.[7]

These allusions to the biblical Satan are, overall, rare in Muscovite textual and iconographic sources. As scholars have noted, more common than depictions of a full-blown Devil are the petty demons (*besy*) invoked in magical spells, and the small, black, pointy headed and winged devils whose nearly featureless silhouettes appear on icons if and only if they are necessary for the story line. If St. Nicholas exorcises a devil from a well, then a scene from his life will illustrate that episode.[8] Satan himself appears mainly in Last Judgment icons, usually equally dark and featureless. He appears safely chained inside the maw of Hell, signaling the triumph of God over the Devil.

Connections between magical practice and the devil were not unknown in prescriptive or literary texts, but this satanic motif made up only one thin strand among many threads of meaning that constituted Muscovite understandings of magic. Those many threads intertwined and unraveled in the complicated, messy, and centrifugal understanding of magic in early modern Russia but never wove themselves into a uniform fabric of thought. As the Dobroe trial illustrates, Muscovite magic, as practiced, feared, and condemned in law and custom, rested on non-diabolical foundations.[9] Satan, though invoked on rare occasion, filled no essential role and bore no necessary connection with witchcraft and magic. The absence of that conceptual link led to significant consequences. In underscoring the sharp differences between Muscovite and more general European understandings of witchcraft, the goal of this chapter is not only to showcase Russia's distinctive beliefs, but also, more fundamentally, to argue that variations within witchcraft belief *mattered*, in concrete, life-and-death terms, affecting the mechanics, the targets, the processes and goals of persecution.

Theofilus and the Devil: A lively fresco from 1716 from west gallery of the church of St. Ilia in Iaroslavl showing the monk Theofilus at the very moment of selling his soul to the Devil. From Pervukhin, Tserkov' Ilii Proroka v Iaroslavle, *1915.*

Kleimo: *Detail from the Life of St. Nicholas: St. Nicholas exorcises a devil from a well. Inventory No. ERI-84 (Ermitazh Museum Collection). Beginning of the sixteenth century, Moscow School. The State Hermitage Museum, St. Petersburg Photograph © The State Hermitage Museum / photo by Vladimir Terebenin, Leonard Kheifets, Yuri Molodkovets. (See also plate 2)*

Let us return to Dobroe and Priest Davyd's complaint against his spiteful servants to see how this diabolic absence played out. Responding to the priest's plea that the matter of the roots be investigated, the tsar ordered the town governor to interrogate the husband and wife pair. When questioned, the serving man, Mishka, confessed that indeed the roots and dirt had been stuck under the ceiling in the upper chamber at the priest's house, but he placed the blame on his stepfather, Isaika Nekireev, a dragoon in the Dobroe regiment. Mishka explained that his stepfather had hidden the baneful objects in the house during Holy Week of the preceding year, "so that Priest Davyd and his whole family would wither. And from the withering disease, they sickened." Mishka's wife, Arinka, admitted that on the instruction of her mother-in-law, she had bewitched Davyd's wife and daughters by administering poisonous roots in their drinks. Following these incriminating leads, the governor sent his men out to arrest the stepfather and his wife, Agripenka, in connection with the case. When they entered the dragoon's house to make the arrest, the governor's men also found "crushed grasses tied in twelve knots and six sacks of grasses also, and a spell against gunshot wounds, written in a little notebook, and a bundle of five different grasses." The four suspects were questioned further "about the bewitchment and roots," and the transcripts of their testimony sent to the Military Chancellery in Moscow, while the provincial staff awaited instructions about what to do next. The alarming material evidence, along with the seriousness of the initial accusation, brought authorization from Moscow to proceed to torture. Clearly the authorities, both in Moscow and in Dobroe, took the matter seriously and treated it with all due rigor.

Torture won more profuse confessions. In response to questioning, Arinka explained that her husband had collected the dirt used in their spells "from the footsteps where Priest Davyd and his wife walked." She elaborated on her techniques, providing chilling details.

> In this year in September she gave the priest's wife and daughters roots mixed into their drinks on the instruction of her mother-in-law, Agripenka. And she, Arinka, stole a headdress (*kokoshnik*) and headscarf (*podubrusnik*) from the priest's wife, and her mother-in-law told her to put that headdress and headscarf under a post with a spell and to say: "As heavy as this post, so may it be heavy on the priest's wife." And Arinka carried it all out according to the instructions of her mother-in-law. And also on the instruction of her mother-in-law she tore a rag from the blouse of the priest's wife, right at the heart, and she brought the rag to her mother-in-law to use in bewitchment. And she, Arinka, pulled the rings off of the fingers of the priest's daughters and said a spell: "Till marriage, may she never weave or spin with these hands." And her mother-in-law told her to do this. Her mother-in-law also told her: "when the priest's wife leaves the house, you go up to meet her and quietly mutter a spell at her, and blow on her and she will fall over in a swoon (*otshibet obmorok*)." And she carried this all out against the priest's wife.

Questioned "about the grasses and roots and spell against gunshot wounds" that had been found in his house, the stepfather, Isaiko, initially insisted that his stepchildren were slandering him and his wife. He had not participated in bewitching the priest's family, and specifically, "about the root that was taken from him," he testified:

> He kept that root to protect himself from gunshots and other diseases. And about the salt tied up with *kuporos* (copper sulfate, vitriol) in the kerchief, [he said] he uses [it] with a stone to wash himself and his children. And he doesn't know any other spells (*stat'i*) or poisons. And what is wrapped in the leaf of *korluk*, he also doesn't know. And the spell that they took from him belonged to his wife's first husband, Kiriushka, and she brought it with her.

Isaiko's denial of criminal intent came in response to simple questioning, without torture. To move things along, and in accord with the tsar's command, the governor ordered that torture be applied, and a far more satisfactory confession followed in due course.

> The same day Isaika was tortured, given ten blows, and with the first shaking and with ten blows he said: he gave roots to his stepson Mishka and daughter-in-law, Mishka's wife, and told them to bewitch Priest Davyd and his wife and children so that they would wither and die. And he told his stepson to take dirt from the footprints where they had walked and to bring that dirt to him so that he could say a spell on it, and then he stuck it in the chamber under the ceiling so that Priest Davyd and his wife would wither, and from that disease, would die. And he told his stepson to put roots in the stove in the main chamber to work bewitchment as well. And his stepson Mishka put a root in the cradle with Davyd's grandson, the baby Ivan, so that he would die, but whether the baby died from that or not, he doesn't know. And he gave roots to his daughter-in-law, Mishka's wife Arinka, and told her to put them in the drinks of Priest Davyd and his wife and children to bewitch them, and in all of this he, Isaika, is guilty before the sovereign. He didn't bewitch anybody else.

Governor Karaulov dutifully dispatched to Moscow the complete report of the confessions that Isaika and the others had made, along with careful itemization of the precise forms of torture applied in each instance. The case record ends with his notation that "at present those criminals and enchanters (*vory i charodei*) are in jail in Dobroe," awaiting the tsar's orders.[10]

This standard-issue Muscovite case rests on an unambiguous and recognizable charge of *maleficium*, harm inflicted through supernatural means, known as *porcha* or "spoiling" in Russian. The witchcraft involved, here termed *volshebstvo* and *charodeistvo*, was imagined to function through a combination of verbal incantation, effective action (blowing, weighing down, scraping footprints), and material additives (dirt, roots). The infusion of magical ingredients into food and drink blurs the line, in modern eyes, between potion and poison, and in fact the participants themselves use both terms. Thus far, the evidence corresponds nicely with European understandings of maleficium. But when it comes to the second piece of the European picture, the satanic presence, the case of Priest Davyd vs. Mishka et al. presents us with a gaping void. Neither the accuser in his vituperative enumeration of the many crimes committed by his hired help, nor the defendants, even when enduring the weight of the strappado or repeated blows of the knout, came up with the slightest hint of a demonological narrative. Nor did the interrogators pose leading questions to encourage such confessions. The goal of the investigation was clear: the witnesses were questioned about the grasses and roots and the "spell against gunshot wounds," not about any devilish force that would endow those natural ingredients with magical power or transform a few words inked onto a scrap of paper into an effective charm. Where European courts of law drove witnesses relentlessly into formulating an adequate story to account theologically and practically for the power of their meager spells and incantations, Muscovites expressed not the least curiosity about the mechanism that transformed words or roots into power or how a vengeful servant might connect, on a cosmic scale, with the satanic and the divine.

This aloofness should come as no surprise, as Russia for the most part stood aside from the cultural and religious developments of the Renaissance and Reformation eras, separated from Western cultural currents by religion, language, and orthography, and limited in its access by the low levels of literacy and absence of printing technologies. Further, Orthodoxy in its Russian variant adopted an apophatic approach to theology, that is, the church taught that God was fundamentally unknowable to mankind, and hence there was little payoff in attempting to unravel the great mysteries of the divine. While Catholic and Protestant Europe produced a vast theological, didactic, prescriptive, analytical, and juridical literature on witchcraft and demonology, attempting to figure out its workings, resolve inconsistencies, and generally square the circle, Muscovites rarely bothered to pose the question of how magic worked. Western theologians agonized over the role of free will in succumbing to the temptations of the Devil, and wondered why God allowed the fallen angel such free rein. Troubled by the problem of how an incubus could impregnate a woman when, as denizens of the spirit world, incubi by definition had no material substance, European scholars pondered the mechanics of insemination through borrowed semen or through borrowed forms. Rejecting earlier medieval assertions that magic was mere superstition and therefore ineffective, late medieval and early modern thinkers insistently attributed witchcraft's efficacy to the Devil.

Muscovites, by contrast, kept silent on these puzzling points, and remained, as far as can be determined, untroubled by the potential logical inconsistencies inherent in magical manipulations of a divinely ordered world. They registered no efforts at codifying or organizing their thoughts on witchcraft, and left only a handful of official or semi-official texts in which witchcraft was addressed and (hazily) defined. As B. A. Uspenskii writes in a recent article, "In Rus', there did not exist the scholastic theology that would allow the explicit linkage of any deviation from Orthodox faith with demonology and heresy; in part, here there was no theology of witchcraft."[11]

Without the kind of intellectual or theological codification of its Western counterparts, Russian magic functioned in an untidy, equivocal gray zone, far distant from European satanic litmus tests that relegated even putatively benign magic into the realm of the heretical, impure, and deadly.[12] Cases involving demons, magic described as demonic, or relations with the Devil himself can be found, but they form a negligible minority of cases. Fifteen cases out of the total 227 seventeenth-century cases fall into these categories, and a handful of laws and ecclesiastical dictums employ the language of devilry. As Linda Ivanits observes, "In these instances it is, no doubt, best to consider the devil one of a number of possible unclean forces, and not a grandiose image around which a highly elaborate demonology coalesces. Such a demonology is absent from Russian folk belief."[13]

Neither Muscovite authors nor Muscovite officials viewed witchcraft as a fundamentally polarized struggle of good and evil. In her study of the theme of the satanic pact in Russian culture, Zhuravel' acknowledges that court records convey a sense that "maleficium (*porcha*), witchcraft (*volshebstvo*), incantations, or other magical activities" were viewed "outside of any opposition of the godly and diabolic."[14] Will Ryan notes that the absence of an article in Russian makes it difficult to distinguish *a* devil from *the* Devil, a grammatical murkiness that parallels the intermediary zones of the Russian supernatural world, inhabited by a wide array of spirits, forces, and beings.[15] This ambiguity allowed for pragmatism and shades of gray in the prosecution of routine witchcraft cases. Kantorovich correctly observes that because magic was not viewed as fundamentally at odds with religion:

> The guilt of the accused derived not from the sinful origin of witchcraft but [rather] was assessed according to economic principles—the degree and quantity of loss inflicted. . . . Judges reached their decisions in witchcraft cases as in any other cases. Fantastic ideas about the necessity of extirpating witchcraft in the name of some general demonological understanding were alien to them.[16]

The significant absences included not just the Devil or the demonic, but also the entire framework of cosmic struggle that so powerfully influenced European witch-hunters.

MAGICAL CRIMINALITY: MUSCOVITE LAW AND CONCEPTIONS OF WITCHCRAFT

In stark contrast to the mountains of paper dedicated to the question in Europe, Russia produced very little to represent an official or elite view of witchcraft. In terms of prescriptive sources, Muscovy left a few ecclesiastical considerations, a series of fairly terse tsarist decrees, a smattering of passing references, pointed questions in penitential handbooks, and several paragraphs in the *Domostroi* (a widely copied sixteenth-century handbook of domestic conduct). Those produced in the sixteenth century betray a somewhat more theological orientation than the later ones, and include some nods toward diabolical conceptions of witchcraft. One church disquisition, the *Stoglav*, the proceedings of the eponymous Stoglav (Hundred Chapters) Church Council called by Ivan the Terrible in 1551, contains some of the most expansive observations on the subject of magic and witchcraft. The text presents a series of one hundred problems raised by the council's participants, all the leading lights in the Russian church, who formulated their points and submitted them to the tsar for his responses. Following each set of questions are the appropriate solutions recommended by the hierarchs. Witchcraft, magic, and other "demonic" activities crop up in scattered places throughout the text. For instance, the council expounded on the particularly insidious role of bookish magic in corrupting the world:

> Most noble tsar, command in the reigning city of Moscow and in all the cities of the Russian tsardom, regarding such sorcerers, enchanters, and magicians (*volkhvy, charodei, kudesniki*) and those who look at [forbidden books of prognostication and astrology] *Rafli* and *The Gates of Aristotle* and read the stars and planets and corrupt the world using such devilish (*diavol'skie*) means and sever it from God and work any other such Hellenic demonism and all such charms (*prelesti*) that are displeasing to God and condemned by the Holy fathers, that such heresies shall from this day forth and in the future be repudiated in full.[17]

After sections fulminating against mixed bathing, predatory gangs of itinerant minstrels, drunken revelry, gambling, and the corruption of the people by false prophets, the council turns back to matters of sorcery and to "evil heretics" who keep forbidden books of prognosticatory magic and "who seduce people away from God and in those seductions cut many believing people off from God to perish." The council recommended that such evil-doers should be "held in great disgrace by the most noble tsar and punished. According to the holy laws they will be excommunicated and cursed."[18] The tsar responded quickly to the concerns raised by the council in this regard. In 1552 he issued a decree banning general immorality, such as drunkenness, swearing, and shaving beards and mustaches. More specifically he banned consulting magicians, sorcerers, or astrologers, who were held liable to punishment "according to the Byzantine church law" and "excommunication by the prelates according to the holy canon."[19]

Following the excoriation of occult books, a long section of the *Stoglav* enumerates popular forms of "Hellenic devilry" and issues a blanket condemnation of a variety of folk customs, indiscriminately labeled pagan (lit., Hellenic), demonic (*besovskii*), and even satanic (*sotanicheskii*). All sorts of revelries qualify for these epithets of opprobrium. Minstrels, swindlers, and deceivers (*skomorokhi*, *obmanshchiki*, and *moshenniki*) encourage people to jump and dance, to play "demonic games" and sing "satanic songs" on the graves of the dead. Ostensibly religious celebrations (Christmas Eve, St. John's Eve, the Eve of Transfiguration Sunday) license young men and women to indulge in "demonic songs and dancing and godless activities and they do shameful things to boys and seduce girls and they carry on practically all the night through." The council decrees unequivocally that "such ancient, Hellenic demonism absolutely should stop once and for all, and . . . such activities should be forbidden and damned."[20] By their actions, these misguided children "incur the wrath of God." "Thus according to holy law and commandments of the holy apostles and holy fathers, Orthodox Christians should not participate in such Hellenic demonry in towns or villages, and the commandment of this most noble tsar should be carried out in all towns and villages, so that Orthodox Christians should not gather for such demonry and cursed Hellenic demonry henceforth should be utterly extirpated."[21] Chapter 93 enumerates a series of pagan practices denounced by the early church councils, and concludes forcefully that "any sorcery (*volkhvovanie*) is forbidden by God because (*se bo est'*) it is demonic service (*besovskoe sluzhenie*). For this reason the holy fathers denounced and forbade such practices now and henceforth, and cast out and curse [those who engage in them]."[22]

Ryan points to this strong statement as definitive evidence that Muscovites did in fact imagine a necessary link between magic and the Devil. One could go even further and note that the Stoglav denounces "sorcerers and magicians" as both diabolic and heretical not because they jeopardize their own souls (though presumably they do), but because, on a grander scale, "with such diabolic actions they corrupt the world and sever it from God."[23] Yet the heterogeneous assortment of behaviors that fall into the "demonic" category in this text—jumping over fires, singing bawdy songs, swarming in gangs and committing crimes, playing accordions at weddings—suggests that the word serves a far broader function than that of the Western satanic pact, a tightly reasoned, specifically focused notion of a compact with the Devil. Chapter 20 of the *Stoglav*, squeezed in among several chapters dealing with Hellenic (meaning pagan) demonry, censures "all sorts of revelers (*brazhniki*) who gamble and drink to drunkenness and fail to serve their mandatory service or carry out their work." These too are charged with committing "evil" and are chastened to live "like Christians," suggesting that their most ordinary of infractions qualify as unchristian and therefore, presumably, are "repulsive to God" or even "demonic."[24]

Cross-dressing, keeping bears, bathing at night on St. John's Eve, licentiousness, laughter, and bleating like goats (*kozloglasovaniia*) are all denounced as "Hellenic demonry (*ellinskoe besovanie*)" or, alternatively, as "Hellenic delusions (*ellinskiia prelesti*)."[25] A number of the offenses in the list were transcribed directly from Byzantine prohibitions and betray the concerns of fourth-century Greeks rather than sixteenth-century Muscovites. Nonetheless, the Stoglav Council rehashed the prohibitions of the church fathers and, with a straight face, banned practices never witnessed among their own countrymen. Here Muscovy continued a trend that Simon Franklin notes in early medieval Rus': Magical practice, at least of the written variety, was "conservative," imported along with Christianity. "They were not local inventions. . . . Not only did the Rus import their Christianity; they also imported their written modes of Christian magic."[26]

The actions deemed devilish in the Stoglav can be associated with the Devil only in the loose way that all sin can be attributed to the temptations of the Great Foe, as he was sometimes named in Russian. The *Domostroi*, the household manual popular through the seventeenth century, contains similar characterizations of magic, though presented more succinctly. Bemoaning the faulty practices evident all around, the author writes: "We invite sorcerers, soothsayers, magicians, visionaries, and herbalists to our homes. With their plants we place our hopes in earthly aids that destroy our souls and prepare us for the Devil, to suffer in the pit of Hell forever."[27] Again, this apparently unambiguous linkage of magic and Satan blurs when set in the context of the hodgepodge assortment of minor lapses that draw equally sharp opprobrium. Elsewhere, the *Domostroi* lambasts witchcraft and "praising the Devil" alongside adultery, slander, and taking the Lord's name in vain. Fast on the heels of this assortment of evils follows a longer list of offenses, including sorcery and witchcraft together with "pride, hatred, wicked grudges . . . lying, theft . . . , gluttony, and drunkenness, [and] eating early and late in the day."[28] Prescriptive sources such as these contain the closest approximation of a systematic picture of witchcraft, its efficacy and its menace, to be found in the Muscovite record, but each undercuts any single message by meandering off in other directions and clustering magic with various ill-assorted infractions.[29]

In considering the jumbled concatenation of practices that fell under the rubric of devilry, it might be plausibly argued that Russians considered that "anything not explicitly Christian is the province of the Devil."[30] This would satisfactorily explain how drunkenness, laughter, animal noises, and maleficium might all be thought to reflect the Devil's mischief at work in the world. The association between all things sinful and the Devil suggests a vague Christian theodicy, in which evil is thought to derive from human weakness and Satan's malice. It would not, however, establish that magic was thought essentially to work through the direct assistance of the Devil, or that supernatural power was granted in exchange for the practitioner's contracted soul.

The idea that magic or witchcraft were seen as inherently demonic or satanic is further compromised by texts that categorized magic rather as a kind of earthy, brute criminality. In this spirit, the Newly Established Articles of 1669 mandated thorough investigations of reports about "thieves or robbers or murderers or witches (*veduny*) or about any criminals." The law specified that witnesses should inform on anyone who harbored and gave shelter to "thieves or robbers or murderers or witches or arsonists" or other "criminals," and investigators should establish precisely what was stolen, what houses or villages were burned or destroyed, and what witchcraft was practiced by such criminals. Following up on the earlier law, in 1674 Tsar Aleksei dispatched agents around the country "to investigate matters of theft and robbery and witchcraft and enchantment (*dlia sysku tatinykh i rozboinykh i vedovskikh i charodeistvenykh del*)."[31] Tsar Aleksei's association of witches with common criminals had a long history by this time. In a 1555 judgment charter of the Trinity St. Sergius monastic council, the peasants of Presetskaia volost' were "ordered not to keep in the district minstrels (*skomorokhi*) nor sorcerers (*volkhvy*) nor female fortune-tellers (*baby vorozhei*), nor thieves (*tat'i*) nor robbers (*razboinniki*)."[32] The decree constructs a typological kinship and equivalency among these various disruptive criminal elements. In a convenient shorthand, court transcripts summed up the matter as "criminal sorcery" (*vorovskoe volshebstvo*) or "magical criminality" (*volshebnoe vorovstvo*).[33]

To be sure, elsewhere, in other, contemporaneous, secular decrees, Muscovite tsars denounced magic and its accouterments and practitioners in the more spiritual terms already familiar from the *Stoglav* and *Domostroi:* forbidden, heretical, demonic, satanic, sacrilegious, outrageous, blasphemous, evil. At times, witches and sorcerers were even labeled "enemies of God."[34] Tsar Aleksei Mikhailovich, whose 1674 decree classified witchcraft as a form of brigandage, in an earlier decree of 1649 identified consulting magicians as one of many forms of "generally impious behavior," which included such serious infractions as swinging on swings, clapping hands, dancing in fields at night, talking or singing during mass, showing up at services drunk, and consulting women fortune-tellers and healers.[35] Another round of orders sent to various towns and centers around Muscovy in 1653 developed the association at length.[36] These proclamations spelled out precisely the many forms that magical practice, labeled "repellent to God," might take, and the stern measures that should be taken to stamp it out. The multiple copies of the order and the detailed reports on the way the news was made public confirm that the issue was taken seriously. The governor of Lukh, for instance, was one of many local authorities to receive the order. He acknowledged that he had received the tsar's order, instructing him to:

> announce to all ranks of service people and in Lukh and in Lukh province at the governor's offices on more than one day and on market days to have town criers shout that . . . many ranks of ignorant (*ne znaiushchie*) people, forgetting the fear of God and not remembering the hour of their death and not thinking of eternal torment, keep forbidden and heretical and fortune-telling books and writings and spells and roots and grasses and go to male witches (*kolduny*) and to fortune-tellers (*vorozheiam*) and tell fortunes with fortune-telling books and bones, and they bewitch many people to death with those roots and grasses and heretical spells, and from their bewitchment (*porcha*) many people suffer from various illnesses and are bewitched (*porchaiut*).
>
> And by your sovereign order I was ordered in Lukh and Lukh province to announce to all ranks of people that from today forth by your sovereign order they should desist from such evil activities, repellant to God (*zlye, b[o]gomerzskie*). Whoever has such forbidden and heretical writings and grasses and roots should burn those forbidden and heretical writings and grasses and roots, and this year during the Great Fast (Lent) they should come to their spiritual fathers without any hesitations (*sumneniia*), and henceforth they should not participate in any such activities, repellent to God, and should not go to male witches or fortune-tellers and should not participate in any witchcraft (*vedovstvo*) and should not tell fortunes with bones or anything else, and should not bewitch people.

Those recalcitrant "evil people and enemies of God" who refused to give up their evil ways, "by your sovereign order such are ordered to be burned without any mercy. Their houses are to be destroyed down to the foundations so that in the future such evil people and enemies of God and their evil deeds will not be remembered by anyone anywhere." Reporting on the outcome of this proclamation, the governor noted that, fortunately, in his region, "no one reported any people engaging in such evil activities, repellent to God."[37]

These decrees and prohibitions indicate that witchcraft and magic fell into a category rather more complex than simple criminal violence. Yet they too focus on the practicalities rather than either the mechanics (diabolical empowerment) of the magic or its implications for eternal judgment. Satan as the efficient cause or explanation, in other words, is nowhere to be seen.

In lumping magic with murder and other earthly crimes, Tsar Aleksei drew on the early Byzantine tradition that Russia had inherited. In an enlightening article on the evolution of Byzantine law on magic, Marie Theres Fögen notes that in the fourth century, Greek law categorized it as a secular crime, on a par with murder if it resulted in actual harm or death, and subject to secular jurisdiction. Although Fögen notes the beginnings of a change in approach already in the fifth century, only much later, in the twelfth century, does she find that the

Greeks clearly differentiated between pagan practices and Christian lapses and associated magic with heresy and apostasy rather than with murder. This shift of understanding corresponded with a change in jurisdiction, as magic moved from secular to ecclesiastical courts. In the Byzantine case, that jurisdictional shift tempered the modes of punishment, replacing execution with repentance, penance, and reconciliation.[38] The later tenor colored Muscovite didactic and prescriptive texts, but in court, in keeping with the general spirit of the early law, witchcraft was prosecuted largely as an agent of earthly harm, not as a threat to the collective salvation of Orthodox Christians.

Court transcripts from the seventeenth century rarely allude directly to specific legislation or decrees in their reports on the conduct of witchcraft investigations. Most witchcraft trials proceeded instead in an ad hoc fashion, as volleys of specific commands from Moscow and responses from the provincial governors. Nonetheless, after mid-century, quite a few of the trial reports make generic nods to the dictates of "the statutes of the *Ulozhenie* law code and other decrees and articles."[39] Since the *Ulozhenie* contained no explicit legislation on magic or witchcraft, it was left up to the judges and their Moscow superiors to appropriate articles of the *Ulozhenie* that might be relevant or to determine which "other decrees and statutes" might best apply. Fedor Dalmatov, as we saw in the previous chapter, invoked the prohibitions on poisoning. A case from Sevsk from 1666 made the elision of witchcraft and criminal banditry explicit: in his denunciation, the plaintiff charged that the malefactor in question, Oska, "is a criminal, witch, and robber (*vor i vedun i razboinik*), involved in three felonies (*razboia*)." The military governor of Sevsk who was hearing the case was inclined to believe that such a reprobate should be punished "for witchcraft according to the statute on brigandage (*razboe*)."[40] Other cases refer to the legal statutes on sons who are disrespectful to their fathers, or the fines awarded for dishonoring someone's wife or maiden daughter or minor son, indicating the kinds of infractions judges saw as comparable, in the absence of specific laws regulating witchcraft.[41]

Some trials looked to legislation concerning more spiritual offenses in their efforts to suppress witchcraft. A case from 1677 applies the statute of the *Ulozhenie* law code on blasphemy to a case of practicing magic and renouncing God: "If someone of another faith, of any faith at all, or a Russian person, should blaspheme (*vozlozhit khulu*) the Lord God and Our Savior Jesus Christ or the Mother who gave birth to him, the Immaculate Mother of God and Immaculate Virgin Mary, or the holy cross or his saints and martyrs, and if these matters are investigated with all due diligence and it is truthfully established, then this blasphemer having been identified should be executed by burning."[42]

Only two cases refer to Byzantine as opposed to Muscovite precedent, but they confirm that the relevant Greek tradition was the late antique one, in which magic was categorized as an agent of sin or physical harm rather than as an indication of satanism. A scribal note, appended in a different hand at the end of a trial report from 1668/9, quotes from Byzantine legislation, "the book of Tsar Leon and Konstantin," presenting this passage as relevant to the case.

> In the Byzantine church law (*gradskii zakon*) in the thirty-ninth part in the forty-ninth chapter, in [article?] 2 is printed: Those who work enchantment or [work] toward the destruction of man (a man?) or who keep such [magic spells?] or sell [them], should be tortured like a murderer.[43]
>
> In the book of Tsar Leon and Konstantin, chapter 2, article 4, it is written: Destroyer-enchanters [who work] to the detriment of humanity, and who call devils (*besy*), shall be beheaded by the sword. . . . For their shameful ways, for the benefit of mankind, they shall be identified and imprisoned. Or if a free person or a slave is found guilty of having given someone [a potion] to drink: a wife her husband, or a husband his wife, or a slave her master, and if, because of that, the victim falls into illness, and having drunk the potion, he falls sick or dies, the guilty party shall be executed by sword and beheading.[44]

This excerpt conveys the full array of undifferentiated ideas about magic and its dangers that Fögen describes as characteristic of the fourth century, and that resonated so strongly in Muscovite attitudes. Enchanters summon devils, administer poison, rebel against their natural superiors, and betray those they should protect. It is a capacious category, but with notable omissions. Neither heresy nor apostasy enters the picture. As far as devils enter the picture, they are lesser demons that can be summoned and commanded, not the Great Foe himself. It is worth noting that the accused in this case admitted to charges of particularly dark magic, including renunciation of "Our Lord Jesus Christ," a charge we will confront below. Still, according to the ancient Christian law invoked by the local authorities, it was the criminal harm they inflicted on the men and women around them, not their abjuration of God, that merited the death penalty.

In official prohibitions, witchcraft was denounced together with theft, murder, assault, spiritual violation, blasphemy, social disruption, impropriety, musical performance, paganism, or unauthorized prophesy, depending on the particular concern of the moment. Penalties ranged from being asked to curtail the practices in question, to penance, excommunication, exile, release on surety, beating, beheading, or execution by burning or burial alive. Even at the highest levels, Muscovite lawmakers formulated no consistent view about the nature of magical crime or the provenance of magical powers, and they displayed no discernible inclination to think through the logical or theological consequences of an explicit conception of magic as satanic.

LINES OF INTERROGATION: OFFICIAL PREOCCUPATIONS AND LEADING QUESTIONS

Just as the religious and political elites had demonstrated no interest in formulating a systematized or theorized framework for explaining the uncanny power of magic, so too they made no effort in their courtrooms to unearth evidence of a diabolical conspiracy. Like their Western equivalents, they asked leading questions and ruthlessly pursued the answers that they wanted and expected. The questions themselves, however, differed dramatically from those posed in European courts. Instead of pursuing connections to the Devil (When did you first give yourself to the Devil? Whom did you see at the Sabbath? When did you sign the Devil's book?), Muscovite judges exerted themselves to track the human lineages and practical results of magic: Who taught you? Whom have you taught? Whom have you bewitched?[45]

The contrast in the form of questioning emerges sharply in the transcripts of European and Muscovite trials. Compare, for instance, the transcript of the trial of Suzanne Gaudry, interrogated at the French court of Rieux, in May 1652, with the record of the interrogation of Mikishka Andreev Soletin, a trapper arrested in Siberia in that same year on charges of possessing a collection of written spells. In their translation, Alan Kors and Edward Peters remark on the "oddly meticulous and syntactically disordered" court record of the Gaudry case, in which the judges' leading questions draw out precisely the satanic picture they expect and need for a satisfactory conviction. Here a few of the questions are listed alone, without the prisoner's replies. They illustrate the way that the interrogators created the answers they desired to hear:

- Questioned about her age, her place of origin, her mother and father.
- Asked why she has been taken here.
- Asked for how long she has been in the service of the devil.
- Asked how many times she has been at the nocturnal dance.
- Questioned what was on the table [at the dance].
- Asked if her [demon] lover had never given her some powder.

A second round of interrogation the following day pursued the topics of interest with an even keener edge:

- Asked what is her [demon] lover's name and what name he has given himself.
- Asked where he found her the first time and what he did to her.
- Asked how long she has been in subjugation to the devil.

When Gaudry failed to respond properly to the cues fed by her by the interrogators, they generously offered her the requisite lines, including the specific names of people she had "seen" at the satanic festivities:

- Interrogated on how long it is since she saw her lover, and if she also did not see Marie Hourie and her daughter Marie at the dance (meaning the Sabbath).

The judges pressed her to admit that she had not only accepted a powder from her demon lover but had also "used it evilly."[46] The judges moved speedily along in their questioning, jumping directly from the basics (name, place of birth) to the heart of the matter: her relations with the Devil, carnal, spiritual, and criminal; and her knowledge of other participants in the "nocturnal dance." Torture is not recorded in this case, but its application is implied: Gaudry is brought "to the chamber," where the interrogation takes place. Along with the leading questions, physical torment no doubt added intensity to Gaudry's willingness to provide the answers her interrogators desired. At the end of her trial, the condemned witch received the court's mercy, in that she was promised the kindness of strangulation before being consigned to the flames.

The trial of the Siberian trapper from precisely the same year reflects both the very different topics of interest to the judges and those notably omitted from consideration. The authorities responded to the incontrovertible evidence of Mikishka's spells just as seriously as judges in the Gaudry case, as the repeated application of torture witnesses. Again, the list of questions asked points to the particular answers sought. The governor of Ilimsk, a Siberian city in the region of Irkutsk, dutifully reported to the tsar in distant Moscow that the itinerant trapper had been discovered in possession of a collection of written spells. "On the 17th [of April] 1652, Governor Bogdan Denisovich Oladin questioned the trapper Mikishka Ondreev syn Soletin and ordered him tortured severely: 'Where did he get such letters, and from whom, by name, and who gave them to him, Mikishka?' The governor questioned him harshly, whether all those spells were his, Mikishka's." Further, "the governor had him tortured to see whom he had bewitched with those letters, but with torture he didn't confess to anything." He admitted to possessing the incriminating scraps of paper, but he insisted that they were protective and curative prayers, not spells at all. "He said he didn't bewitch anyone and he didn't seduce women." Mishka signed the original copy of the confession himself.[47] The governor ordered the texts transcribed into the report that he sent to Moscow, thereby preserving them through the centuries. The texts allow us to see that what Mikishka had collected were indeed largely popular versions of prayers, what Eve Levin calls "supplicatory prayers," invoking the protection of a fully sanctioned Orthodox pantheon: Jesus, Mary, St. Catherine, St. Nicholas the Miracle Worker. Neither Satan nor any demonic force made an appearance.[48] Neither the authorities nor the trapper demonstrated the least interest in inserting him into the proceedings.

A trial of a different ilk, where demons decidedly played a role, demonstrates the same lack of official interest in Satan even more starkly, since the explicit evocation of spirits would seem to invite demonological thinking. In1629, Maksimko Ivanov, a peasant of the Pecherskii Monastery in Nizhnii Novgorod province, faced charges of bewitching the wife of a local landowner to death. The bereaved widower, Ivan Levashov, filed a complaint in which he explained that he had consulted with Maksimko in hopes of finding a remedy for his wife's state of bewitchment. The healer had given her a drink made from a certain grass, claiming that it would cure her, but instead of recovering, she died soon afterward. Levashov petitioned the authorities to imprison Maksimko and question him "about what grass he gave her." Following the pragmatic line of investigation established in Levashov's petition, the governor and his investigative team "questioned Maksimko, who says he gave her a grass to drink called *voronets* (Baneberry), and she quickly died."[49] The governors pursued this line of questioning further: "Did he give the grass to others? Were there other deaths?"

As witnesses were brought in, allegations multiplied, and accused witches exchanged further accusations among themselves. An assortment of magical practices and several more deaths were attributed to Maksimko, and a chain of denunciations dragged in three other men as well. In their testimony, with and without torture, the men confessed to some of the most elaborate and phantasmagorical magical techniques encountered in the Muscovite archives. Maksimko denounced a fellow peasant of his same village, Fedka Grigorev syn Rebrov, whom he held responsible for bewitching his son.

> And that Fedka knows all about grasses and much sorcery (*volkhovstvo*). He looks in water and calls devils (*besy*), and they tell him what's going on a hundred versts away, and what illnesses people suffer from and who bewitches them; and he recognizes people without seeing them (*za ochi*) and knows what kind of hair and marks [they have] and [their] height. And he looks in the water in a trough and says who will die and who will live and by whom they are bewitched (*isporchen*).[50]

This succulent accusation prodded the governor and his colleagues to press the witness with questions: "For whom did his companion Fedka look in water and what did he see there [and] for whom? What sorcery (*volkhovstvo*) and what evil (*durna*) did Fedka cause people?" Maksimko obligingly offered plenty of details:

Fedka had located a peasant man's runaway son, he had diagnosed the cause of a peasant woman's childlessness, and he had been called to heal the cousin of yet another peasant. Further, Maksimko informed the court, Fedka had learned his sorcery from a master sorcerer, a Mordvin (a non-Russian, Finno-Volgaic people of the Volga region) called Vetkasko. Vetkasko specialized in inflicting debilitating bewitchment on demand. For instance, a peasant called Piatunka of the village Koraskikhi "invited Vetkasko over to bewitch his neighbor. And Vetasko sent an unclean force (*nepriiaznennaia sila*) against Piatunka's neighbor, and that unclean force hit that neighbor with rods and beat him out of his house."[51]

The manipulation of an "unclean force," one might think, should have roused interest on the part of the examiners, particularly a force with sufficient material might to drive a man out of his own house. The preternatural element intensified with Maksimko's recounting of what else Fedka Rebrov had told him, but it still failed to motivate the judges to explore the eerie, metaphysical dimensions of the case.

> That Fedka Rebrov said to him, Maksimko, that he studied sorcery with that Mordvin [Vetkasko] but he didn't learn everything. [One night] he, Fedka, went to the woods to collect the bark of lime trees and he spent the night in the woods. An unclean force overpowered him, and he threw himself in the fire and burned himself all over. Those burn wounds are still visible on Fedka now. And he went to that Mordvin to complete his study. Now for the past two years or so, he, Fedka, has been bewitching people. He bewitches people by sending the unclean force, and it throttles the people he sends [it to]. And those people also die from that [unclean force].

The authorities, both the officials on the spot and the chancellery officials speaking in the name of the tsar in Moscow, found all of this testimony alarming enough to pursue the case with all great diligence, rounding up all of the suspects and launching a widespread investigation, including prolific use of torture. The specific questions they pressed on the witnesses reveal precisely where their interests and anxieties lay, and where they did not lie. On April 30, the local governors interrogated the Mordvin Vetkasko, whom the bailiffs had located and brought in for questioning. "Did he work sorcery (*volkhvuet*)? And did he bewitch (*portit*) people? And does he know Maksimko and other peasants of the village Kortashova by name? And was he ever with Maksimko? With what foul means did he cure people?" Again, strikingly absent is any identification of Satan, or even of demons or devils, as the shadow behind the "unclean force."[52] Even the unclean force itself arouses no particular interest on the part of the interrogators. Their questions probe the practicalities of the matter: the identities of the individuals working mischief, the concrete toll and material damage inflicted, the path by which forbidden knowledge was spread, and the names of teachers, collaborators, and victims. As for the particular modes or means by which the magic was enacted, the authorities expressed far more interest in the roots and grasses than the mysterious spirits of the beyond.

The mandate from Moscow in response to the governors' preliminary investigation demonstrates that the tsar and his inner circle had no more demonological vision of the matter than did their provincial representatives. The tsar commanded the governors:

> Find out who cured whom with what and who lived and who died, . . . and find out who else these criminals (*vory*) bewitched. . . . Find out by what scheming (*umyshleniu*) Maksim killed (*umorokh*) Ivan Levashov's wife. Find out what other people Maksimko and his comrades, the Mordvin Vetkasko and peasant man Fedka Rebrov, killed or bewitched, individually by name, and how long ago, and by what witchcraft (*volshebstvo*), and by whose bidding or their own [initiative]. And [find out] whether they had other companions plotting with them in that witchcraft and who by name was with them and who taught them that criminality (*vorovstvo*) and with what intentions (*i s kakimi v dushe bylo*), and which people they bewitched. Round up those people and question them. . . .

The judges' concerns were concrete and this-worldly. They interpreted the Mordvins' infractions as "criminality," and their central concern was murder rather than heresy, apostasy, or satanism.

Perhaps it is unnecessary to add another example, but the case of Mitroshka Khromoi offers such strong evidence for the absence of a satanic framework that it clamors to be included. In Galich province in 1626, a landholder, Grigorii Gorikhvostov, complained about the evil practices of a peasant belonging to his neighbor, Prince Volodimir Kozlovskoi, with whom Gorikhvostov shared a village. Mitroshka Khromoi, the peasant in question, had served briefly as a deacon of the Church of the Archangel Michael in the village, but Gorikhvostov ordered him dismissed from his post after he began to suspect the deacon of practicing witchcraft. Gorikhvostov reported: "that man sent an unclean spirit into my little house and by his bidding [the spirit] appeared in my house in the main chamber and started to throw bricks from the stove and from the ceiling and to beat many of my people," to the point of drawing blood. Further, Gorikhvostov asserted, Mitroshka had also afflicted other peasants in the village, dispatching his unclean spirit, called a *kikimora*, to plague a peasant's horse, to bewitch the priest's wife, and to wreak confusion within the herd of cattle belonging to his own nephews. The *kikimora*, he explained, drove the cattle away, scattering them in all directions.[53]

What distinguishes Gorikhvostov's complaint from those of the hundreds of others from the seventeenth century is its focus on matters spiritual. For immediate remedy of the chaos in his house, the distressed Gorikhvostov turned for help to "the goodness of God," and "ordered that prayers be sung in that room for many days and [had it] sprinkled with holy water and censed with incense, and [ordered his men] to read from the psalter."[54] Gorikhvostov questioned his people severely "about that witch (*vedun*)." He reported, "My people and peasants told me under oath that that man Troshka is a known minstrel/clown (*glumets*) and witch (*vedun*), and with his enchantment (*charodeistvo*) he bewitches (*portit*) many people and he sends out unclean spirits." His investigation turned up some disturbing evidence about a breakdown in the tsar's system of justice, and he did not hesitate to complain of the courts' inadequacies in his petition: "Sovereign, the people of the area don't inform against him because they fear him, because in Galich many witches (*veduny*) bewitch people but there has been no investigation into this and no punishment for a long time."

Spelling out the dire consequences of allowing witches to operate unchallenged, Gorikhvostov moved directly to the spiritual costs: "Sovereign, order that man, a notorious witch, taken from Galich and order him tortured without mercy for his enchantment (*charodeistvo*) and his many other forms of witchcraft, so that the Orthodox faith will not be befouled by such God-renouncing witches and people will not be further tormented with other offenses and bewitchments."[55] In another version of his petition, Gorikhvostov went farther with his soteriological line of argument: "Order someone special, whomever you sovereign appoint, sent from Moscow, and order that notorious witch, and worse than that, taken from Galich, and order him tortured mercilessly about his many acts of witchcraft and bewitchment so that henceforth such criminality will not multiply *and Christian souls will not innocently suffer torment*."[56] Horrified at the desecration of the church of God by the activities of the tainted deacon, mustering the power of incense and prayer to cleanse his house of the demonic force, concerned about the torment of Orthodox souls in the great hereafter, Gorikhvostov is almost unique in his invocation of some of the big-picture implications of witchcraft within a Christian cosmology.

Revealingly, Gorikhvostov's grim suggestions won no reaction at all from the responsible authorities. The instructions from Moscow and the actions of the local judges in the case indicate that their preoccupations stayed on the earthly, matter-of-fact level that typified witchcraft trials. As in the previous examples, the authorities in Moscow took the accusations extremely seriously. Two special agents from Moscow were assigned to the case, with authorization to muster as many provincial gunners, musketeers, messengers, clerks for writing, and executioners (torturers) as necessary to conduct a thorough investigation. Their mandate dictated that they should spare no effort, and should interrogate and torture anyone and everyone implicated in the case. The questions they were to ask, however, and the answers they sought, conformed to the usual pattern:

> Order Mitroshka Khromoi tortured harshly and burned with fire:
>
> Did he [send an unclean spirit] against Grigorii Gorikhovstov in Moscow, and in Galich against Prokofii Loginov's peasants Gavrilka Terent'ev and Mikitka Petrov and his nephews Chastunka and Kuzemka and against the wife of Priest Luka in Grigorii's village Mikhailovskoe? And by what other means did he send the unclean spirit? For how long has he been practicing such criminality and witchcraft and enchantment, and from whom he did he learn (lit. take: *vzial*) such witchcraft and enchantment, and how long ago? And whom by name did he bewitch in Galich and in other towns? And does he have confederates, other witches and enchanters and under whose auspices do they live (*za kem zhivut*) and what are they called? And who else does he know to be witches that work witchcraft and enchantment and bewitchment and bewitch people and send unclean spirits in Galich or in Galich province or in other towns? Order Mitroshka Khromoi tortured harshly and burned with fire about that criminality and enchantment, on more than one day, to discover whether he carried out that criminality and witchcraft singlehandedly.[57]

Christian souls and corruption of the Orthodox faith have dropped entirely out of the picture. The list of questions sticks to the "who, what, where, and how" of criminal investigations. This case, the exception that dramatically proves the rule, illustrates that it was not impossible for Muscovites to link witchcraft with a sweeping Christian narrative, but that this eschatological vision failed to catch on in any significant way. Even poor Gorikhvostov, the landlord who raised the concerns in his petition, was unable to sustain such an abstract conception. Muddling the magical and the criminal, his accusation raised the spiritual costs only to settle immediately back into a more down-to-earth list of concerns. The physical forms of disorder wreaked by the spirit understandably bothered him most of all, the bricks flying through the air, cattle scattering in all directions, and the priest's wife running helter-skelter (*bezobrazno*) from one village to the next. The equally this-worldly profit-making scheme by which Mitroshka made his living similarly offended his accuser: "He supported himself by these means: he bewitches many people and sends unclean spirits into houses, and whoever gives him bribes (*otkup*), those he protects/disenchants(*otvarazhival*)."[58] Corruption and chaos, more than perdition and satanic conspiracy, fueled the charges.

As in the laws and proscriptions, so too in the trial reports, *some* conception of the unnatural or supernatural crept into the official understanding of magical practice, setting it somewhat apart from other, physical forms of criminal activity. Nonetheless, the distinction from criminal assault or theft that inflicted tangible material or physical harm remained slight and undeveloped, and questions about what those supernatural forces might have been or what allowed them to act in the world remained not only unanswered but also unasked. Muscovite authorities never formulated for themselves and hence never attempted to inculcate such a satanic view into the population at large.

PROSAIC MAGIC AND THE EVIDENCE OF TRIALS

Court records reveal instead a world of magic that is aptly described as prosaic, a world of household ingredients (salt, roots, herbs, tree bark, water, kerchiefs) and homey spells aimed at achieving the most quotidian and human of ends: health, prosperity, fertility, love; or, in dark incantations, their counterparts (illness and death, privation, barrenness, shattered or purloined love).

The contents of a magician's potion supply were extremely simple—peas porridge, a buckle, an ax-handle, a towel, grasses, leaves, roots—even when working the most baleful magic.[59] A woman named Katerinka testified in her own defense in the town of Dobroe in 1690:

> the grasses that were taken from her house and brought to the town hall grow in a branch of a river. Tied in two knots are a *lolonovyi* (laurel?) leaf. Tied up in a rag in a knot is *dushitsa* (oregano or marjoram), and in a little knot is also *dushitsa* and with that same leaf she, Katerinka, dyes [Easter] eggs, and in the little knot is a garlic clove and two wax seals. . . . And the root, that's lovage, and in the knot is alum.[60]

At a trial in Sevsk in 1652, the court record scrupulously listed the suspicious items found at the home of the accused: dill weed, mint, burdock "for borscht," field hops, and various other grasses.[61] Regarding a collection of grasses presented as evidence in a case involving far-reaching charges of attempting to bewitch the sovereign, an old monastic servant named Ivashko testified:

> The grass that was wrapped in paper is good for diarrhea. It grows near the monastery in the fields in a little spot, and on that plant are little berries. Ivashko said that that grass is heavily laden with berries, and people give the plant and the berries to young children steamed in milk for constipation. . . . The grass is sharp, and they call it "wild pepper," and they heat it in water and

> drink it for difficulty breathing. He was given it to eat by Vaska, but he knows no witchcraft. He is seventy years old.[62]

In the same case, another man was called on to explain the significance of five roots found in his possession:

> In questioning he said three of the roots are . . . used for people with heart pain. They heat them in milk and drink it, and it makes them feel better. The root grows in low-lying places in puddles, and it is called *Serdeshnoe* (lit. heart root, perhaps Motherwort)." And he doesn't know what the other two roots are called, because they were left by his brother after his death, and he knows of no witchcraft (*volshebstvo*) connected with his brother.[63]

A man in another case admitted to keeping some grasses "given to him by a beggar to cure toothache."[64] In 1630, a musketeer reported that a woman fortune-teller had healed his eye: "She said a spell over water and sprinkled millet in the water, and she washed me with that water, and she put some breast milk in my eye, and she got that breast milk from the wife of musketeer Sazon Volkov."[65]

Muscovite magic relied almost exclusively on everyday items, materials easily gathered in the course of ordinary, day-to-day life. Occasionally spells required more disturbing ingredients, such as the skin of a snake, an eye ripped from a live chicken, a sheep's liver, or soap used to wash a corpse.[66] Though certainly macabre, even such repellent items were close at hand in the ordinary course of lives lived in proximity to the backyard abattoir, the ebbs and flows of disease and death. In place of salves made from the fat of unbaptized babies, the red and green powders provided by demon lovers, the mysterious phials and philters of the European necromancers' cabinets, Muscovite witches searched for a particular kind of tall grass in the fields or watercress along riverbanks.[67]

The techniques of magic were equally down to earth. A.B. Ippolitova provides a useful typology for the principles behind the function of spells and herbs: the etymological, in which the words themselves evoked the desired result (as, Heart Root, for heart pain); visual, by which some aspect of the appearance of the ingredients elicited a parallel response (as, a red flower evokes blood); gestural, in which a language of motion produced effects (crushing bark; melting wax, crossing or not crossing oneself); and a code of Christian symbolism, through which particular figures or episodes from Christian lore effected appropriate outcomes.[68] The majority of spells operated on the basis of sympathetic or mimetic magic: like produces like. "As a log withers and burns in the fire, so may my master burn and wither," intones one curse, while a love spell dictates, "As a man loves looking at himself in the mirror, so may my husband love looking at me."[69] "As that linden bark when it is crushed has neither mind nor memory, so when that Kostentin comes to the court, he will have neither mind nor memory."[70] Evocative parallelism, embodied metaphor, fragments of prayer or invocation of saintly protectors, intermixed with the occasional deployment of demons or "unclean forces," constituted the armamentarium of Muscovite magic.

Admittedly, one important attribute of magic is its ability to transmogrify commonplace items into objects of uncanny power.[71] Such metamorphoses are familiar from fairy tales: Snow White, like many unsuspecting children across Europe, falls victim to a shiny apple, and Sleeping Beauty's fate is sealed by her encounter with a spindle, the most mundane sort of household tool.[72] In a Muscovite parallel to Sleeping Beauty's wicked witch, a woman resentful about being left out of a wedding celebration in mid-century wreaked magical vengeance using everyday instruments and targeted curses. A local priest testified that "when Fedka Filipov got married in the past year 1638/39, and when the wedding party returned from the wedding and he was going upstairs to the loft with his bride, that Daritsa lit a sliver of wood (*luchina*) and she threw that sliver under the feet of Fedka and his bride on the staircase." Other witnesses added that she also cursed the groom as he passed by with the wedding party, "You will remember me!" "And after that, Fedka became bewitched and afflicted with impotence." Cautiously, the witnesses added, "but whether the bewitchment and impotence were caused by Daritsa or not, that we don't know for sure."

The community had good reason for caution: the same woman had reduced the entire district to a state of terror by bewitching people left and right, causing illness, impotence, and death. She threatened a neighbor, Evtiushka, one of her many victims, perverting the comfortable world of home and hearth analogically through a dreadful curse: "I will make him as black as the ceiling of a hut is black, and he will bend like a sickle bends." In the aftermath of her curse, her victim suffered from a wasting disease for three years, "and having withered, died."

Dozens of people stepped forward to testify against Daritsa, who had evidently actively honed her reputation for a malicious tongue and for her effective curses. Another witness testified that "in the past year 1646 during Holy Week at a feast at Grishka Semyonov's house . . . in his presence [she] threatened Luk'ian Fedotov: 'I will eat you up, Luk'ian, just like Fedka Filipov.'" Apparently she carried through on this threat, because another neighbor reported that the next year, again during Holy Week, he heard Daritsa outside the gates to his compound boasting: "Fedka writhes [in pain] (*korchitsia*) because of me, and Luk'ian Fedotov's son writhes because of me too."[73]

A sickle, a sliver of wood, a malicious reputation, and a volley of vicious words rounded out the prosaic toolkit of this active and terrifying local witch. She worked her magic at close quarters, among her own relatives, neighbors, and close acquaintances. The unfortunate Fedka, the one cursed with impotence on his wedding night, turns out to have been her brother-in-law, and a number of the other purported victims were also connected to her by marriage. Many of the accusations, as seen in the ones quoted above, grew out of incidents taking place in social gatherings, holiday feasts, or domestic gatherings. The consequences of Daritsa's witchcraft—death, impotence, wasting, writhing—were dire, despite the simplicity and quotidian character of her magical pharmacopeia.

In Russia as elsewhere in Europe, homemade cakes, beakers of beer, or buckets of mead could bring illness or death. None of the suspects discussed here would have left their testimony on record had someone not viewed their simple collection of roots and herbs as threatening or deadly. The porridge that a servant woman fed to a child in her care would have transformed, in the eyes of her employer, from dull, daily sustenance to a harbinger of death once the child sickened and the servant admitted to muttering a spell over the mush. When the servitor Ivan Koloshinskoi petitioned the tsar against the mother, brother, niece, and stepsister of his late wife, the everyday provenance of the roots that they threatened to use to bewitch him did nothing to allay his fear of the destruction and slow, lingering death they could unleash.[74] Once magic enters the scene, an eerie aura infuses the most quotidian of objects or actions. A fortune-teller who saw the future unveiled in a platter of salt described the transmogrification of ordinary white crystals into an instrument of magic when she explained that "sometimes when she looks at salt, little men (*muzhichki*) appear to her. Some cry and others laugh. If she is asked to look [at the salt] to find out about a theft, then there appears to her in the salt a man who runs bent over (*ch[e]l[o]v[e]k sugorbisia*), and by the signs she can tell who stole. And another chases after him. And who will live or die, that she sees in salt too, and there appears to her whatever she needs to see."[75]

The lurking menace of the macabre and the uncanny is abundantly evident in cases of malevolent magic, and even in magic that could be construed as benign or neutral. A book of spells confiscated in 1676 in Vologda contained a prescription for placing "beef lard between your fingers for pain and for knowing whether someone will live or die." The same book recommended "owl bones, to drive a demon (*bes*) from a house," and, "Of a bear's head: bury it in the middle of the courtyard and livestock will be found."[76] Given the capacity of magic to transform even the everyday into the dangerous, deadly, and mysterious, one might argue that the category of "prosaic magic" is itself an oxymoron.

Nonetheless, Muscovite kitchen magic, while viewed as terrifying by its self-proclaimed victims and targets and roundly condemned as dangerous, even demonic, by the authorities, never strayed into the realm of the theological, cosmological, eschatological, or soteriological. Assaults on individual members of the community remained just that: criminal attacks, inexcusable aggression. The threat was palpable, immediate, and dreadful, but it did not endanger the divine or human order or the collective salvation of Orthodox souls.

Along with prosaic ingredients and techniques went prosaic goals. After a single reference to witches' causing famine in the early medieval chronicles, Muscovite witches were not suspected of unleashing epidemics or environmental catastrophes. Neither in court testimony nor in folklore were witches implicated in bringing storms, destroying crops, or unleashing plague. These accusations did appear later, in the nineteenth century, and in the Ukrainian lands, but only two cases that I have found from the seventeenth century refer to magical destruction of crops.[77] Nor did courtroom witches fly. Baba Iaga, with her flying mortar and pestle, cannot be documented until the early eighteenth century, and her brand of cannibalistic, airborne fairy-tale witchcraft left no imprint in documented trials.[78] Muscovite magic, whether exercised for good or ill, was directed at mundane, this-worldly goals: retrieving lost objects, realigning affections, telling fortunes, healing or causing illness on an individual scale, tipping the scales of justice, acquiring wealth, causing those in power to act kindly. Spells might help women to painless childbirth, or childless couples to conceive. They might allow people to stop drinking too much, ensure virtuous conduct in wives and daughters, or, alternatively, kill babies, interrupt sexual congress, undermine business, or guarantee licentious conduct in other men's wives and daughters. Such magical interventions, especially of the malevolent variety, were not considered minor in any sense—killing babies never qualifies as a petty infraction—but in both their methods and their goals they were firmly rooted in this world, not in the great spiritual struggle that preoccupied Western demonologists.

Again, we should emphasize that in Western courts, and even in learned treatises, witches were often seen as responding to the petty human motivations of envy, greed, anger, and lust, and their accusers charged them with causing the most material kinds of harm and damage. But thanks to the efforts of the demonologists, a larger, grander template was available, undergirding what were viewed as local rivalries and paltry desires with a mighty theological scaffolding. Quarrels, hardships, and losses could be easily recast as skirmishes in that divine war. In Russia, when a wanderer was found to have in his possession a fairly large collection of assorted spells—a spell to cure hernias, one to cure toothache and against various misfortunes; a spell to make peasants fear him and another so he could win fights; one for hunting wild animals and another to catch fish; and, of course, the inevitable spells to seduce women (several of these)—the courts made no effort to place these spells in a more exalted context.[79]

DEVILS IN THE COURTROOM

On the other hand, as the cases involving "unclean forces" discussed above demonstrate, demons, devils, and other miscellaneous spirits did make rare but spectacular entrances in courtroom testimony. Employing a broad definition, we can identify fifteen demonic cases, and a number of miscellaneous spells with diabolical content. Three trials refer to a cross worn underfoot, one man wore his cross "behind his back," another was said to "go around without a cross" (although he did "keep icons in his house and pray to them"), and another was accused of removing his cross before casting spells with it. Six include charges of "keeping black books," an accusation discussed in chapter 5.[80] A Cherkassian officer charged with witchcraft in the southern frontier region was vilified as an "enemy of God," and Gorikhvostov, as described above, condemned "God-denying witches who befoul the Orthodox faith."[81] An accomplished male witch (*koldun*) named Afonka Naumenok was accused in 1642 of calling two devils (*diavoly*): Narodilo and the suggestively named Satanail.[82] One trial record contains a confession of seeing a "diabolic apparition (*d'iavol'skoe prevedenie*)," in the form of a shaggy man. Yet another includes a love spell that implores: "Oh you, Satan with the Devil (or a devil), with little ones and great ones, fly out from the Ocean-Sea."[83] Some less pointed spells invoke amorphously identified demons, such as a love spell that calls on "thirty-three demons."[84]

The four most sensational of our cases explicitly mention "god-denying letters" purportedly written by the accused to renounce "Our Lord Christ-God." Of these, one includes the full text of a dark prayer that calls on "my father Satan." The spells recorded in this case present a puzzling mixture of divine and satanic allegiances: after an apparent baptism in the name of the "cursed devils (*diiavole prokliaty*)," the speaker invokes God's angels, archangels, cherubim and seraphim, the evangelists and all the saints, in order to keep all foulness (and devils) away from him, the "slave of God." Like most written spells, this one leaves a blank place marker for the name of the supplicant: *imiarek* (say name).[85] Far less unambiguous in its allegiance is a chillingly nihilistic spell first published by N. Ia. Novombergskii. The spell, written in the handwriting of the accused in a 1663 trial in Lukh, positions itself clearly in a binary universe of God and the Devil. "I renounce our creator Christ-God and the churches of God and the most holy liturgy and the vespers and matins and all divinity and my father and mother and clan and tribe and swear allegiance to Satan and his beloved lackeys." What followed must have been even worse, since the scribe noted that "other witchcraft (*volshebstvo*) is written in the letter that I don't dare write to you, Great Sovereign."[86] What the court reporter viewed as more incriminating and horrific than the words he had just copied down defies imagination. Following the familiar pattern, the court authorities registered no discernable anxiety over or interest in this overt satanism, and instead concentrated on ferreting out all they could find about the transmission of the spell and the chain of hands involved in committing it to paper.

The case that most closely mimics Western European patterns of full-fledged satanic pact comes from Iakutsk in far eastern Siberia. The trial, which took place in the mid-1680s, featured a certain Ivan Zheglov, who confessed in the course of his trial that "he, Ivashko, renounced our Lord God and our Savior Jesus Christ and the Most Holy Mother of God and all of the saints, and taking off his cross, he wore it under his heel for thirteen days, and, having written his renunciation with his own hand, he brought it to Satan himself. He saw him [Satan] as a fiery face on a throne, and he kissed his hands and feet. And Satan gave him three demons to serve him."[87]

A.T. Shashkov, who published the Zheglov document, observes on this basis that pacts with the devil "had a place in witchcraft practice not only in the eighteenth but already in the seventeenth century," and Zhuravel' concludes that "the very mention of such 'motifs' and spells such as God-denying letters testify to the wide distribution of notions of apostasy from God."[88] They are clearly right that renunciation of God and adherence to the Devil were not unknown in connection with suspicions of sorcery. Nonetheless, it goes too far, at least for the seventeenth century, to argue on the basis of four cases for "wide distribution of the notions," or to maintain that "trial materials of the seventeenth to eighteenth centuries show that the myth of pact with the devil had firmly entered the consciousness of broad circles of Russian society in this period."[89] The number of seventeenth-century witchcraft trials that make any slight nod toward a satanic model remains small, and those that denote a clear sense of a satanic pact as underlying magical potency, negligibly so. The satanic idea was available, but was not invoked frequently or with any consistency. In spite of the occasional dramatic tribute to Satan, other models, or lack of models, served just as well and surfaced far more commonly.

Through the entire seventeenth century, Muscovite ideas about witchcraft and magic remained unencumbered by a theoretical model or explanatory framework. Magic was understood as a bit of this and a bit of that. It grew out of a broad spiritual world but offered no coherent map. Learned demonologists did not exist, and demonology, consequently, had no purchase. Prosaic, small-scale, and tangible in its very essence, Russian witchcraft could not be conceptualized as a massing conspiracy, hell-bent on overturning earthly and divine authority and subjecting the world to the tyranny of the Antichrist. Perhaps Zguta is correct in positing that it was the very looseness in theoretical exposition and the resolute focus on the mundane that lessened the stakes in Muscovy and helped keep the number of Russian trials down to several hundreds and the executions down to several dozens, rather than the tens of thousands that held Russia's European neighbors spellbound. Top to bottom, official or unofficial, magic functioned in a prosaic register.

This imprecise, shapeless understanding of magic, its power and its etiology, contributed to trials with quite different profiles than those taking place at the same time under the rubric of satanism and demonology in Catholic and Protestant Europe. In the absence of a diabolical paradigm, Muscovites eschewed the kind of militant cultural policing that encouraged European societies to persecute heretics, witches, and schismatics on such a massive scale. Muscovites were slow to identify, much less persecute, heretical groups, waiting until the late seventeenth century to launch any significant campaign against heterodoxy, and their death tolls, or even trial counts, remained strikingly low by comparison with many of their European neighbors.[90] Furthermore, in the absence of the full satanic mythos, with its elaborated early modern vision of female depravity, corporeality, and susceptibility to demonic seduction, the gender dynamics of witchcraft anxiety and witch-hunting were free to develop along a very different track

4

Love, Sex, and Hierarchy

The Role of Gender in Witchcraft Accusations

THREE-QUARTERS OF THE PEOPLE named as witches in seventeenth-century trials were male. I have identified the sex of the accused in 223 cases, involving at least 495 individuals. (The remaining cases either contain short descriptions without any details about the accused, or collective notations about "some witches," undifferentiated by sex. These include reports that "three witches were exiled," or that witchcraft had been detected but the culprit not yet identified.) Of the 223 cases, 34 involve indictments of female witches only. Forty involve men and women purportedly working together. The remaining 149 cases, or 67 percent of trials in which the sex of the accused can be identified, refer exclusively to male witches. Among the 495 individuals accused, 367 (74 percent) were men, while 128 (26 percent) were women.[1]

Why didn't women make up the bulk of the accused in witchcraft trials? In a fundamental sense, this is the wrong question, because it accepts the European model as normative. That witchcraft should be a female crime, or, indeed, that it should be in any way associated with one particular gender, are presuppositions derived from the familiar patterns. One could productively reverse the question and ask why witches were presumptively female in the European west, or, more profoundly, why was witchcraft gendered at all. Fortunately, a great deal of work has gone into explaining the feminization of witchcraft that occurred in late medieval and early modern Europe and left its mark on the witch trials of the early modern era. Theologians dwelled on the sins to which women were purportedly inclined—envy, lust, weakness of faith—and the ability of the Devil to turn those frailties to his advantage. The porosity of the female body, an accepted fact of early modern physiology, further strengthened the association between the female sex and susceptibility to the Devil. The salience of sexual union between witches and the Devil in European witch-lore added yet another support to the feminization of witches.[2] But that particular connection was in no way natural or inevitable. Indeed, Marilyn Strathern, in *Gender of the Gift*, usefully reminds us that gender need not be always and inextricably tied to sex, and this decoupling of the two concepts might allow us to find ways to question witchcraft's particular relationship to each one separately.[3]

In her refreshingly irreverent critique of the practice of reifying "gender as a category of analysis," Jeanne Boydston plays on a passage from Barbara Jeanne Fields: "If not kept strictly in their place, [categories of analysis] get above themselves and go masquerading as persons, mingling on equal terms with human beings and sometimes crowding them out altogether." Taking this warning to heart, she explores the possibility that "the category 'gender' as understood by western feminist historians on the basis of their own local histories cannot claim universal relevance." In pre-colonial Yoruba culture, for instance, historian Oyèrónké Oyewùmí finds that generational seniority and chronological age, not gender, functioned as "the primary principle of social classification."

> This does not mean that Yoruba speakers were unaware of differences between male and female bodies, or that Yoruban culture did not embrace tropes of male and female bodies, or that pre-colonial Yoruba people lived in a golden age. . . . It means simply that perceptions and representations of sexual opposition were not presumptively a *primary* field for the articulation of that particular power.[4]

The evidence from Muscovy presents a compelling case for the relevance of Boydston's and Oyewùmí's position. Gender is always an important factor in every facet of life, but sometimes other elements play a more salient role, or gender is subsumed into other categories of understanding. To assess the Russian material in its own terms requires us to set aside presumptions about gender's automatic primacy in witchcraft beliefs and to listen to the sources themselves in order to identify the particular "categories of analysis" invoked by the people most immediately involved.

In this section, we will consider the Russian case in light of Europe's insistent connection of female desire and satanic seduction, and explore the ramifications of a framework free of this central linkage. In the following section we will turn to an examination of the broader contours of Muscovite notions of gender and their implications for understanding the particular configurations of witchcraft in Russia.

As the preponderance of males among the accused demonstrates, ideas about susceptibility to or proclivity for the crime of witchcraft played out very differently in Muscovy than in most of the rest of Europe. And yet, an alternative historical route running parallel to the European mainstream would not have been impossible. All the pieces were there and could easily have fallen into place. Russian Orthodoxy inherited the same Judeo-Christian association of sin, corruption, and women through the agency of Eve, which easily could have been mobilized in Muscovite witch trials. As in Western Christianity, the connection between Eve, who succumbed to the Devil's seductions, and witchcraft was available and could have been deployed in order to link women and witchcraft. In fact, some sources make that connection explicit. The main medieval chronicle, the *Tale of Bygone Years* or *Primary Chronicle,* explains women's affinity for witchcraft in precisely this way: "In the beginning the devil deceived woman, and she in turn deceived man."[5] This underlying premise colored the experiences of men and women in the world; penitential handbooks from slightly later periods directed the question, "Or did you work magic (*Ili charodeistvo deiala*)?" more frequently toward women than toward men.[6]

Baga Iaga, the classic Russian fairy-tale witch, makes her first documentable appearance in the early eighteenth century, the date of these famous lubok *prints. She appears in exotic, somewhat androgynous clothing, emphasizing neither her gender nor her sex. "Baba Iaga and the Bald Man," first quarter of the eighteenth century, in Ovsiannikov,* Lubok, *23.*

"Baba Iaga and the Crocodile," first quarter of the eighteenth century, in Ovsiannikov, Lubok, *22.*

Other associations of women and witchcraft were also current in Muscovite culture. For instance, women were notorious for calling on the services of witches when their children fell ill, a token of weakness of faith repeatedly decried by church hierarchs.[7] Moreover the term *baba*, which could refer neutrally to a grandmother, a married woman, or an elderly woman of low social standing, also could denote a witch, pure and simple.[8] The elision of older woman and witch could easily have led to a European-style scenario, where witchcraft and womanhood were understood as overlapping categories. By the early eighteenth century, Baba Iaga, the classic witch of Russian folktales, had become a familiar cultural figure, but whether or not she was already popular in the seventeenth century is unclear. If, as Andreas Johns writes, "it seems reasonable to assume that she is considerably older" than her first documented appearance in the eighteenth century, then the folkloric model for a female witch may have already been in circulation.[9] With or without Baba Iaga, all the elements necessary to foster an association between women and witchcraft were present in the Muscovite cultural vocabulary. In the European scenario, Christina Larner points out, stereotype and cultural expectation alone could have deadly consequences in early modern trials: a self-sustaining, circular logic more or less guaranteed that "if you are looking for a witch, you are looking for a woman."[10] In Russia, in spite of the currency of similar associations and stereotypes linking women and magic, women and sin, and women and the Devil, Muscovites accused more men than women. The disconnect between available cultural tropes and the failure to mobilize them in witchcraft accusations makes the explanation of the gender question all the more challenging.

WITCHES AND SEX: THE MAGIC OF DISRUPTION, DEBAUCHERY, AND DESIRE

In European demonological and theological discussions of the topic, women were described as so uncontrollably lustful that the Devil could win their loyalty with promises of sexual satisfaction, and thereby convert them to the ranks of witches. The sexual allure of demon lovers and the undisciplined, excessive sexuality of witches attracted the attention of authors and artists alike, producing memorable images such as those by Hans Baldung Grien in the early sixteenth century. The Muscovite literary and visual corpus produced no counterpart to this line of thought. In a few Muscovite tales, women are seduced or raped by the Devil himself or by demons, but in these instances the women are represented as victims, deceived or forced into sin. Love or sex spells are some of the few that invoke Satan or demons as actors with any regularity, but they were written in male voices and called on devils to infect the female object of desire with irresistible longing: "Oh, you, Satan with devils, with little ones and great ones, fly out from the Ocean-Sea. . . . Set fire the soul of that female slave for me."[11] Significantly, the women in question are nowhere associated with witchcraft and bear a closer resemblance to the "possessed" women and girls of European lore than to European witches.

The most infernal rape in a Muscovite literary work of the seventeenth century occurs in "The Tale of the Demoniac Solomoniia," frequently invoked in discussions of witchcraft. A young bride, Solomoniia, falls into a trap carefully laid by:

> Satan—the foe and ancient enemy of all good since the very dawn of eternity, who has never ceased to battle with mankind—the devil Satan himself thought up something for the undoing of the woman—or perhaps he was sent by an evil man. And Satan came to the house in the form of a man and knocked at the door without praying but called out in a human voice, "Solomoniia, open the door!" And she rose from her bed and opened the door, thinking that her husband was coming to her. And in that moment she sensed a fierce whirlwind in her face and her ears and her eyes, and a fiery, dark blue flame appeared.[12]

Ulrich Molitor's enormously popular and frequently reprinted study of witchcraft included important early European depictions of the witch with her demon-lover. Image of a witch embracing a devil in Ulrich Molitor, Von dem Unholden oder Hexen *(Ulm: Johan Zainer, 1490?), fol. B5v. Reproduced from Albert Schramm,* Der Bilderschmuck der Frudrucke, *23 vols. (Leipzig, 1920–43), vol. 5, fig. 419.*

In the early sixteenth century, Hans Baldung Grien created some of the most explicitly sexualized visions of witches at work; some were printed and, like the Molitor image, exerted a tenacious hold on the Western, especially German, imagination. Here is one of Baldung Grien's unpublished sketches, which presents this group of witches as unmistakably sexual beings, wild, unnatural, and uncontrolled. Women of all ages, from attractive and young to the old crone, their teacher, are equally implicated in this diabolical, orgiastic scene. "A Group of Witches (Hexensabbath *II*)*," 1514, Inv. No. 3221. By permission of Albertina, Vienna. (See also plate 3)*

The unfortunate Solomoniia suffers bitterly for her mistake, spending years at the mercy of vicious water demons, who brutalize, threaten, and defile her, trying to make her abjure her faith. In a Hollywood-worthy twist, she gives birth to multiple horrific litters of blue devil-babies, "that sucked at her breast like cruel serpents." Witchcraft is only tangentially invoked in this story. The devil comes calling at his own initiative, although the narrator does allow that "perhaps he was sent by an evil man." Other than this passing nod, the linkage of satanic seduction, female desire, and witchcraft, familiar from Western lore, is absent.[13] As with the motif of the pact with the Devil, what is interesting here is that the theme of seduction of women by the Devil was present in Muscovite literature but was never linked to witchcraft per se, never attributed to female desire, and never invoked in courtroom testimony.

Not that Russian witches and their clients were indifferent to sex: sexual conquest ranks high among the goals of surviving Muscovite spells. Unlike the Western incubus fantasies, however, Muscovite magic served to win the sexual favors of mortal human beings, with no invocation of demonic partners. Moreover, with few exceptions, court records list sexual spells in the possession of *male* suspects; women were very rarely charged with using spells for explicitly sexual purposes (although women frequently sought to induce "love" or "kindness," as discussed in chapters 5 and 6).[14] Court reporters routinely abbreviated their descriptions when listing the contents of spell books, noting in convenient shorthand that the book contained "spells for women (*stikhi za bab*)."[15] Such spells generally invoked the analogic power of natural forces in winning the heart of the object of desire. Using poetic imagery and language and invoking intense emotional pain and physical suffering, these spells call on their objects to burn with desire, to be consumed by longing, to grieve and pine and starve from distraction, to sever all other human relations and to take joy only in the company of the caster of the spell.

A "witchcraft letter" discovered in the handwriting of the suspect, was copied "word for word" into the transcript of a case from Lukh in 1663–64. In it the poetic, folkloric beauty of the language activates the desperate longing that the love object should suffer:

> I, male slave of God, So-and-so, go out to an open field and as the moon shines on me and as the stars look at the moon and cleave to it, so may the female slave of God, So-and-so, look at me and cleave to me. And as the cuckoo bird grieves for her nestlings and cries for them, so may that female slave of God grieve and cry for me. And as the stars delight in the moon, so may that female slave of God delight when she sees me. And as a mare grieves for her foal, so may female slave of God grieve for me every hour of every day. I go, male slave of God, to the Ocean-Sea, and on the Ocean-Sea lies a burning white rock. On that rock stands a dry tree, and as that tree withers away, so may that female slave of God dry and wither away for me, slave of God. On that tree sits an iron man. He beats with his iron staff on the burning white rock, and as the rock catches fire, so may that female slave of God catch fire for me, carnally and fiercely and with all her flesh and being. And when she doesn't see me, male slave of God, may she grieve and cry and may she leave her father and mother and for all eternity, Amen. For all eternity, Amen. For all eternity, Amen.[16]

For the user's convenience, magical formulas allowed the user to fill in the blank, *imiarek*, with the name of the loved one:

> So-and-so (*imiarek*) goes to the Ocean-Sea; there on an island stands a hut, and in it is a bird without wings. As miserable as the bird is without wings, so may it

be for the female slave So-and-so. As miserable as a fish without water, so may it be also for female slave So-and-so. As one millstone grinds over another, so may the heart of female slave So-and-so.[17]

The latter spell survives in extensive collection of spells recorded by a cavalry captain (*rotmistr*), Semyon Vasil'eva syn Aigustov. We know of Aigustov's misdeeds, magical and other, in connection with a lawsuit initiated against him by his wife in the town of Borovsk in 1688. In a strongly worded petition, the wife, Fedosiia, charged him with repeated, violent rape of her two young daughters. To support her denunciation, Fedosiia produced a stack of notebooks and papers that her husband had left in her keeping, presumably confident in his knowledge that she could not read. The court officials could read, however, and were astounded by what they found: page after page of "spells for women," together with careful rubrics for prognostication, and a variety of other spells.[18]

Two features of this case make it utterly unique: some of the objects of his desire, his unfortunate stepdaughters and at least two of his bondswomen, are known from the testimony collected in the case record; and Aigustov sketched

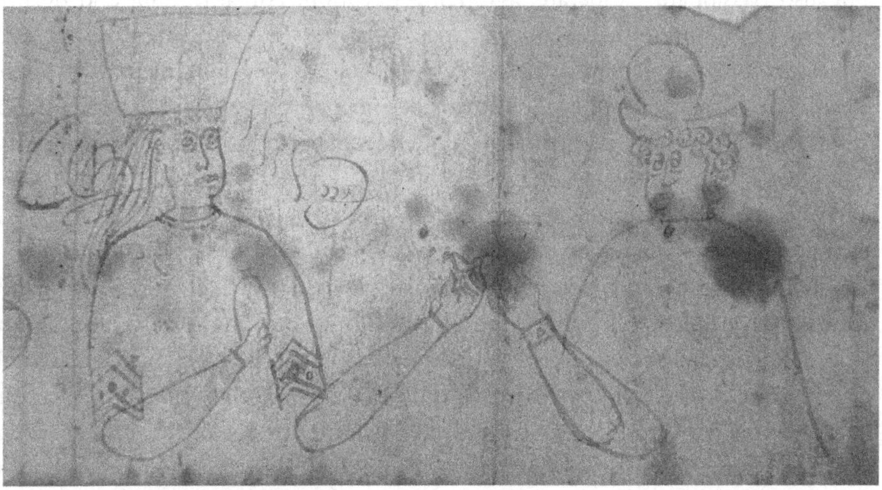

An illicit scene of witchcraft at work, from Semyon Vasil'ev syn Aigustov's magical notebook. A man (right) and a woman (left) in a scandalous state of disarray, with her hair loose and uncovered, toast each other. The scene is marked as an indecent tryst by the woman's loose hair, the untoward shared intimacy, and the drinking in mixed company. The swirling eyes on both figures may indicate the working of the drink, enchanted by spells or infused with roots or grasses. The spell book is full of powerfully evocative love/seduction spells. "Toasting Couple," image from a spell book, RGADA f. 210, Prikaznyi stol, stlb. 1133, l. 180 ob. By permission of RGADA.

into his spell book a line drawing of his magic at work. This, as far as I can tell, is the only surviving image of witchcraft in progress from the seventeenth century. In Aigustov's rendition, a young, curly haired man exchanges toasts with a large woman, who holds a small cup in one hand and a narrow bottle in the other. Her state of dissolution, presumably brought on by the man's spells and potions, is evident in her loose, uncovered hair, her unfocused eyes, and her willingness to compromise her honor by drinking in the company of a man. Despite its bland appearance to a present-day observer, inured to scenes of far more graphic sex and violence, this fully dressed couple expresses the shockingly graphic fantasy life of the man who drew it in his private, illicit notebook.[19]

In the trial, Aigustov's victims unanimously described him as an abusive husband and father and a serial rapist. They testified that he beat and injured his wife and threatened to kill her, raped his twelve- and sixteen-year-old stepdaughters and impregnated the older girl, and drove his peasants into flight in a desperate attempt to escape his assaults. This is the man who sketched the apparently quiet scene of a private tryst, and who eagerly collected spells that would bind women to him not only physically but emotionally as well. In language infused with affect, his spells promised not just sexual submission, but also passionate, desperate, agonizing devotion. An intriguing and deeply disturbing glimpse into the fantasy world of a merciless and brutal rapist, this collection of sources, particularly the widely circulating love spells with their invocation of visceral suffering, also reaches beyond the psyche of one man and suggests that love, sex, and pain, both physical and emotional, were profoundly conjoined in the Muscovite imaginary.

At the other end of the spectrum from love spells, numerous cases revolved around charges of malicious disruption of conjugal relations through magically induced impotence. This misfortune was particularly likely to be inflicted during the vulnerable liminal time of a wedding, but might be visited on an unprotected man at any time.[20] In 1647, a Mozhaisk peasant named Timofei and his son Larka were accused of afflicting at least eight different peasant bridegrooms with impotence. The distraught father of one of the afflicted men described how Timofei "bewitched my son when he was leaving the church after the wedding. Timofei came out of the gates of his compound and threw a [burning] splinter of wood under him. . . . And for that reason I suspect him."[21] Wedding guests reported that they had heard the father and son congratulating themselves after successfully destroying a fellow peasant's wedding night, saying, "That was well done by us. It's only a shame for us that some weddings came off fine."[22]

Further testimony in this case reveals a pattern that turns up in many of the instances of magically induced impotence: many of the people named as witches served also as healers of the condition, thereby encouraging suspicion that they may have caused it in the first place, in hopes of exacting some extra income for relieving it. Although some, like the vituperative Daritsa of Sevsk, were associated purely with malign magic, in the case of Timoshka and Larka, witnesses attested that the father-son team of witches repeatedly averred, "I caused it, and so will I heal it." *Stolnik* Fedor Mikhailov syn Ladyzhenskii, a landholder in Aleksin, suspected the same mechanism was at work when in 1652 he married off two of his bondsmen, "and those people were both bewitched (*pereportili*) at their weddings. Their ability to consummate their marriages was taken away (*sovokuplenie u nikh s zhenami otniali*)." Soon afterward, one of his peasants, Senka Vasilev syn, a carpenter, drunkenly boasted that he had bewitched those men at their weddings. When Fedor caught wind of these claims, he "ordered [Senka] chained by his hands and feet." Under duress, the carpenter promised to cure the men and requested only some garlic. "And that peasant, Senka the carpenter, gave his men . . . three cloves of garlic each and told them to eat them up. And those people were healed with that. And thus Senka's criminality became known; that he bewitched Fedor's people and then healed them."[23] Arshutka of Lukh "was tortured twice and with torture he confessed to everything, that he cured those townspeople of Lukh, but at weddings he released weakness (impotence) on them, and many people came from all around and he cured them."[24] Some healers maintained that they served only protective functions at weddings. One such was Ivashko Goldobin, who testified in 1692: "When there is a wedding, he, Ivashko, attends them in a protective capacity (*dlia berezhen'e*). He brings bread and salt with him, stashed separately in his sleeves, and he sits near the groom in the host's seat. Upon the arrival of the groom, he mutters magical spells (*nagovornye shepti*)."[25]

In *The Present State of Russia* (1671), the English physician Samuel Collins confirmed both the fear of bewitchment at weddings and the prophylactic resort to protective counter-magic. He observed: "Seldom a Wedding passes without some Witch-craft (if people of quality marry). . . . I saw a fellow coming out of the Bride-chamber, tearing his hair as though he had been mad, and being demanded the reason why he did so, he cry'd out: I am undone: I am bewitch'd: The remedy they use, is to address themselves to a white Witch, who for money will unveil the Charm, and untie the Codpiece-point, which was this young mans case; it seems some old Woman had tyed up his Codpiece-point."[26] Court cases inform us that Collins's impression could be generalized beyond "people of quality." Vasilii Maksimov's chiaroscuro painting from 1875 illustrates that in the nineteenth century as in the seventeenth, peasants feared the arrival of a wrathful sorcerer at a wedding. Late imperial ethnographers collected copious material on the problem of fending off the malevolence of sorcerers at weddings,

Vasilii Maksimov, The Arrival of a Sorcerer at a Peasant Wedding, *1875. Canvas, oil, 116 × 188 cm. State Tretiakov Gallery, no. 41. Belief in the vulnerability of couples to the malice of sorcerers at the liminal moment of marriage remained widespread through the nineteenth century, as depicted in this evocative painting. The drawn faces of bride and groom express their fear that the sorcerer, whom they did not invite to the celebration, will curse their marital prospects. A common practice both in the seventeenth century and in the late nineteenth was to invite a "good" sorcerer to attend the wedding as protective insurance against the magically induced impotence and infertility that might afflict a marriage. (See also plate 4)*

by holding marriages in secret, inviting known sorcerers to join the festivities, or hiring a friendly sorcerer like Senka the carpenter to weave a protective spell.

Taking money or other forms of recompense for healing impotence or any other condition could raise suspicions: "Kozlov petty gentryman Aksenka Savilov in questioning said: He was in conversation at the house of his fellow Kozlov petty gentryman (*syn boiarskii*) Timoshka Lavrov about four years earlier, and right there, while they were chatting, someone made him impotent (*i tut de evo na besede uskapili*), but who made him impotent, he doesn't know, only he petitioned Ivashka to heal him (*bil chelom emu Ivashku chotb emu posobil*) and gave him a goose and Ivashka healed him."[27] Suspicion condensed around Ivashka, who by all reports made a habit of demanding geese in payment both for medical services rendered and for protection from magically induced ailments. Aksenka's brother described Ivashka's protection racket in lively terms: "Ivashka Gubanov asked his brother Aksenka for a goose and Aksenka didn't give him a goose. And then Ivashka demanded it, saying: 'Don't forget what will happen to you.' And then he bared his teeth at him, and when his brother Aksenka gave him Ivashka a goose, he took it away and then healed Aksenka."[28]

Most accused witches initially pled innocent to the charge of causing impotence or any other infirmity or illness, claiming instead to use their special skills only to heal. Nesterko Semyonov syn, Poliak, a herdsman from the estate of *stolnik* Ivan Veliaminov in Shatsk, represented himself as a benign healer, using simple spells, prayers, and home remedies to alleviate the suffering of those around him. "He went around to Shatsk villages and hamlets to help men who can't have congress with women, and for those people he, Nesterko, said spells over wine and gave them that bewitched wine to drink. . . . And wherever someone has pain and children are sick, he deals with it; he removes the illness with spells." He categorically denied that he engaged in any "evil heresy or witchcraft (*eretichestva i vedunstva za nim zlogo net*). His skills, he claimed, were widely sought after, "and many people hire him for his medical skills (*dlia lekarstva*)." He volunteered detailed information about his curative magic. To assist men who could not have intercourse with women, he would send to the "person of the female sex" a cup of river water. It was critical to the success of the procedure that it come from the river and from no other source. Before he gave the river water to the woman, he would recite a prayer-like spell over it:

> Have mercy, Most Blessed Mother of God. Intercede for us sinners. Be merciful. Cover the sinful souls of your male slave So-and-So and your female slave So-and-So with your incorruptible mantle. In the whole world, protect them. Give them, Mother of God, love between them and [allow them] to live in congress as of old, in love, so that they now and forever will live in congress together. And when they comb their hair with that river water three times in the night, so may the woman So-and-So keep combing her husband, your slave, So-and-So, day and night and in the hours when the river flows. Eternal glory to you, and to those aforenamed people, husband and wife, eternal life."[29]

An apparently gentle man with benign intent, at least according to his self-representation, the healer was subjected to three rounds of torture, but staunchly stuck by his story. He refused to be coerced into admitting that he had caused rather than cured his clients' sexual dysfunction. The case has no surviving resolution.

Magical measures came in handy for sexual purposes, both prophylactically in offering protection against any potential magical assault on a man's virility, and curatively to restore lost manhood. Spell books confiscated from suspects in an extensive case that stretched from Vologda to Moscow in 1676 included both varieties. According to the court description, the suspects possessed "two spells for sexual function [or dysfunction: *tainye udy*, literally "secret knots," genitals] [an early Viagra prototype?], and a spell for marriage so that nothing evil should take place at the wedding." Another spell on the list involved administering a grass "to women or girls to take to protect against seduction."[30] A wandering hunter in Siberia was found carrying a large number of popular prayers and spells, including one "so that the male member would stand up (*chtoby stoiali tainye udy*)."[31] Vaska, the son of Deacon Mikiforko, testified in a case heard in Solikamsk (in the Western Urals) in 1668 that he too had copied out "a spell about sexual function." He admitted that he had tested it, but it did nothing for him. Further, Vaska acknowledged that he had given two spells to his friend Ivashko Volosheninov, a clerk at the Chancellery of Service Lands: one to seduce women, and the other so that people would be kind. "And he told [Ivashko] to say the incantation while taking an eye from a live chicken, and having ground it up, give it to women to drink."[32]

As in early modern Europe, so too in Muscovy, sex constituted a significant vein of magical practice and magical anxiety. Strikingly unlike the common picture in continental Europe, however, sexual conduct played only a small part, if any, in limning the characteristic, recognizable features of a witch. So many studies have established this linkage in the European discourse on witchcraft that lingering on the topic may be superfluous, but a quick look at almost any demonological text or trial record from the time will support the claim. In spite of recent scholarly attempts to question its impact or typicality, the infamous *Malleus Maleficarum*, much printed, translated, and cited throughout Europe, models the logical steps by which women *as women* were found to be prone to the dark arts. Posing the pressing question, "Why it is that Women are chiefly addicted to Evil Superstitions?" the author, Heinrich Kramer, called "Institoris," sets out to consider "women; and first, why this kind of perfidy is found more in so fragile a sex than in men." Insisting on the common sense inherent in his initial proposition, he points out that the preponderance of female witches "is indeed a fact that it were idle to contradict, since it is accredited by actual experience, apart from the verbal testimony of credible witnesses." An extravagant cornucopia of persuasive reasons follows, all derived from the essential nature, both corporal and spiritual, of womankind. "Some learned men propound this reason; that there are three things in nature, the Tongue, an Ecclesiastic, and a Woman, which know no moderation in goodness or vice; and when they exceed the bounds of their condition they reach the greatest heights and the lowest depths of goodness and vice." From this axiomatic premise about female nature, he ponders "the reasons that there are more superstitious women than men."

> The first is, that they are more credulous; and since the chief aim of the devil is to corrupt faith, therefore he rather attacks them. The second reason is, that women are naturally more impressionable, and more ready to receive the influence of a disembodied spirit. The third reason is that they have slippery tongues. . . .

He concludes this discussion with a bit of a non sequitur, certainly not something prefigured in the earlier discussion but stemming organically from his sense that women's inadequate bodies, faith, and character predispose them to every form of moral, spiritual, physical, and intellectual weakness: "To conclude. All witchcraft comes from carnal lust, which is in women insatiable. There are three things that are never satisfied, yea, a fourth thing which says not, It is enough; that is, the mouth of the womb."[33] Lust, then, lies at the heart of the matter, and female lust is an overweening force that propels women into the arms of Satan himself.

Even if one accepts the caveats and re-readings proposed by scholars who would have us re-evaluate the *Malleus* both for its centrality as a defining text of witch belief and for its typicality in its focus on female sexuality, it is hard to argue with the content of these passages, or with their echoes in other demonological treatises, witness testimony, and in the line of questioning so fiercely pursued in courtrooms across the continent.[34] The case report on "The Witch Walpurga Hausmännin," burned at the stake in Dillingen, Germany, in 1587, for instance, opens with a discussion of Walpurga's seduction of a serving man with "lewd speeches and gestures," and their deliberate plan to meet for "lustful intercourse." Lascivious desire led directly to Walpurga's ruin. "So when Walpurga . . . sat awaiting [her lover] in her chamber, meditating upon evil and fleshly thoughts, it was not the said bondsman who appeared unto her, but the Evil One in the latter's guise and raiment, and indulged in fornication with her. . . . After the act of fornication she saw and felt the cloven hoof of her whoremonger, and that his hand was not natural but made of wood."[35]

One would have to look long and hard to uncover any echo of these ideas in Muscovite courtrooms. Solomoniia, as seen above, was similarly deceived and sexually used by a devil in the guise of a familiar mortal man, but it was the form of her lawful husband returning from a visit to the outhouse, not the allure of an illicit lover, that led the virtuous wife to open her door. In contrast with the German narrative, it was not Solomoniia's lust that led to her downfall, but rather, as we learn toward the end, the failure of a priest to protect her properly through the rite of baptism. A few Muscovite cases contain slight suggestions that the sexual magic in question might have involved sinister linkages to the demonic. The 1668 case from Solikamsk mentioned above refers to "God-denying spells," used "for purposes of fornication with women."[36] This case seems to be the only one in which the middle step, renunciation of God if not allegiance to the Devil, is presented as useful for achieving magical sexual conquest. Not a single court case involves sexual contact with the Devil. The potent blend of sexual desire and satanic seduction that makes Western witch lore so endlessly fascinating is all but absent in Russian tales and trials alike.

Untoward sexual conduct on the part of the accused women and men attracted notice in thirteen Muscovite cases, but as a compounding offense rather than as a path to damnation or an explanation of their predilection toward witchcraft. In 1628–29, Prince Eletskoi accused his household slavewoman, Katerinka, of causing her mistress to sicken and miscarry her baby by having her lover, the household cook, add a magical root to the princess's food. Witnesses noted that Katerinka and her lover Mishka lived together in sin, and that they had plotted to run away across the border to Lithuania.[37] In Dobroe sixty years later, Archpriest Iakov of the Cathedral Church of the Transfiguration accused his serf woman, Aniutka, of casting malevolent spells on his family and killing his young son with her noxious potions and incantations. He added that after her husband had run off, deserting his wife and absconding with his master's goods, Aniutka had taken up sinfully with Levka, a carpenter in town. During her interrogation by the governor, Aniutka initially confirmed the accusation and added colorful details about her affair with the carpenter.

> Several years ago a Dobroe man, Levka the carpenter, said to her, "I've brought you what you need," and he brought something wrapped up in a pancake, and said to her, "Drink this drug (*nadob'ie*), which is for the female sex. Women who drink this won't have children." But she didn't drink it. Levka gave it to her because her husband at that time had run away, and Levka told her she should live with him in sin, and she wouldn't have to worry about having children. And this is what Levka said to her: "In case of need, I have given it to two or three young women and lived with them in sin myself, and went with them many times, and they didn't get pregnant, and they won't get pregnant in the future."[38]

In spite of her affiliation with a well-known adulterer, and involvement with magical abortifacients, Aniutka fended off all charges, successfully maintained her innocence on all counts, and eventually was set free and sent to her husband in the town of Romanov.

Untoward sexual alliances were mentioned in the life stories of several other women accused of witchcraft, but did not draw the judges' attention. The widow of a Moscow townsman petitioned the tsar from her prison cell in the Military Chancellery, begging to be exonerated of the "false and criminal scheming denunciation" of witchcraft lodged against her by an itinerant man whom she and her live-in lover had sheltered under their roof for about ten days. The witchcraft charges bore no direct connection with Matrenka's domestic arrangements, and interrogators did not pursue that line of questioning. The tsar responded favorably to Matrenka's petition and ordered the case investigated anew. Unfortunately, as in so many instances, no resolution to the case survives.[39]

In Rylsk in 1688, another Matrenka, this one the widow of a Rylsk townsman, petitioned that a market woman had insulted her publicly in the market stalls, "with all sorts of inappropriate and untrue words, and she called me a criminal and a whore (*bliad'ka*) and a potion maker (*zelenshchitsa*) and a concoctor of root magic (*korenshchitsa*), and with that she dishonored me, your slave, for unknown reasons, without basis." Hearing the evidence, the tsar's representatives determined that these slanderous words had never been uttered, thus ruling against Matrenka in the slander suit but at the same time effectively ignoring the charges of magic and fornication.[40] In 1626 a poor peasant widow in Mikhailov faced charges that she "prostitutes herself and serves as a procuress for people and plots all sorts of evil deeds (*sama de bliadet i liudem svodnichaet i s vsiakimi durnymi dely promyshliaet*)." She was arrested and tortured with fire to establish what she knew about magicians (*charodei*).[41] In these cases, assertions about violation of sexual norms happened to partner with charges of witchcraft, but the texts assert no essential conceptual pairing, and only a handful of examples of even such loosely connected innuendo appear in the court records.

Not only women got into trouble through sexual impropriety. A brief filed in 1626 from Dedilov reported that a petty gentryman confessed, with torture, to using a magical root "to go illicitly to the wife of another petty gentryman. The latter caught him in the night with his wife, beat him and robbed him, and then Ivashko hoped to use the root to get back at him."[42] In 1694 an anonymous letter was found on the steps of the governor's office in Beloozero. The anonymous author denounced Nikifor, the cellarer of the Kirillo-Belozerskii Monastery, for preparing spells to bewitch Tsar Peter Alekseevich together with his wife and son. The letter also accused him of keeping "black books" and preparing a "soap of snakes and other loathsome creatures and cats' brains and frogs' eggs" that he intended to spread on a shirt (the tsar's, presumably) in order to bewitch the wearer. Along with these charges of witchcraft the denunciation also attacked the cellarer for living in sin with a woman and fathering children with her. It suggested other "disgusting acts" committed with a deacon and a monk. Although the list of supposed offenses combined harmful magic and sexual impropriety, the charges failed to stick, and it was the author of the anonymous letter rather than its target who ultimately suffered the sting of the law. The defrocked monk convicted of composing the letters was sentenced to death, but after being taken to the site of execution, he received a stay of execution and instead was beaten in the stocks and then exiled to the Solovetskii Monastery. The poor peasant whom he had commissioned to drop the letter at the governor's office was beaten and returned in bondage to the Kirill-Belozerskii Monastery.[43]

In three cases, men were accused of using a combination of physical violence and witchcraft in their sexual assaults on women. We have already made the acquaintance of the dreadful Semyon Aigustov, the spell collector who raped his stepdaughters and serfwomen at knifepoint. He also threatened to kill his wife and marry her sixteen-year-old daughter, pregnant at the time with his child.[44] In 1670 in Smolensk, a monastic peasant named Vaska was charged with bewitching people and animals in his village. "And in the past Vaska told fortunes (*navorozha*) in that same village Pavlovo, and he swept underneath houses with a broom, and from that sweeping, two households died out (*vymerlo*)." Further, "Vaska argued with his daughter-in-law about that bewitchment and they reproached each other, and that Vaska bewitched [her] in front of lots of people, and dishonored her with sexual assault (*beschestil bludnym vorovstvom*)." He threatened peasants far and wide with various forms of magical inducement to fornication (*portit' na blud*). He was known to beat his own wife so severely that she was driven mad and wandered the streets naked, with her hair flowing loose.[45]

Despite this catalog of disturbing examples, sexual misconduct was not at all a necessary or even a central characteristic of those who fell under the cloud of suspicion for practicing harmful magic. Rather, it seems to have functioned at most as an exacerbating factor, neither essential nor even frequent in defining the profile of a witch. A final example crystallizes the matter in no uncertain terms. An ill and aged landholder in Briansk, Mikhail Ivanov syn Bezobrazov, petitioned against his own son in 1666, complaining of a farrago of offenses the young man had committed, starting with forcible seizure of the father's estate, and followed by filial disrespect, brutality, criminal assault, theft, fornication, and witchcraft. Among other crimes, the son purportedly lured one of his father's peasant women, Mashka, away from her husband, "giving her the (evil) eye and luring her to adultery (*daia glaski pro blud*)." He lived with her in sin and together they committed "crimes and witchcraft." While a fugitive, Mashka married another man, but the father refused to relinquish his title to her as his serf, despite the claim of the new husband, because, as the father pleaded, "she was granted to me by a legal document (*rospis'*), and because her previous husband is alive."[46] Sexual impropriety here forms a kind of background character indicator, but is not centrally featured as an identifying marker of a witch. Rather, the featured charge in the case is that of filial insolence.

Complaining that his son had gone so far as to state brazenly in a letter to his brother that "I don't fear our father's threats (*ia batkovykh groz ne boius'*)," the offended father invoked the law's statute concerning children's relations with their parents:

> He ceaselessly threatens me, your slave, and acts rudely with all kinds of rudeness and vexations, but in your sovereign order and in the *Sobornoe Ulozhenie* law code it stipulates that whoever steals from his father or mother, or fails to respect them, and [the parents] denounce him for his evil deeds, or fails to feed and care for them in their old age, or constrains them (*ikh suzhat*), or speaks to them rudely or files petitions against his father or mother in court, it is ordered *not* to grant them trials against their fathers or mothers under any circumstances. And such children, for their petitioning, are ordered to be beaten with a knout and given to the custody of their fathers and mothers.[47]

The law upheld Bezobrazov's position on filial disrespect. The *Novoukaznye stat'i* (though issued three years after the Bezobrazov case) formalized the principle of legal inequality between parents and children: numerous articles established that the death penalty should be immediately enforced for any son or daughter who murdered or conspired to murder a parent, while rough words, lesser violence, or failure to provide for the parents should be met with merciless beating with the knout, as the *Ulozhenie* had already affirmed. In the reverse scenario, however, that is, if a mother or father killed a son or daughter, the offending parents merely had to serve a term of one year in jail. Upon their release, they were to go to church and publicly acknowledge their guilt. "For [the killing] of a son or daughter, a father or a mother should not be executed." Similarly, offenses by servants or slaves against those they served incurred the harshest condemnation possible: "According to the Byzantine church law (*gradskii zakon*), a slave who witnesses and aids in the kidnapping of his master should be burned with fire."[48] Bezobrazov's petition echoes the principles ensconced so forcefully in the law. His paternal outrage conspicuously foregrounds the logic at work. It was the flagrant disrespect and inversion of generational hierarchies that made the irreverent son a target for such a battery of charges, including witchcraft. Magic at its most heinous posed a deadly challenge to the accepted ladder of deference and authority by subverting marriage and patriarchal control, by undermining masters' control over their serfs, parents' dominion over their children, and husbands' mastery of their wives. An examination of what those hierarchical and gendered expectations entailed should clarify what the stakes were in these and other magical assaults on the norms and order of society at large.

WHY MEN?: GENDER AND HIERARCHY IN MUSCOVITE SOCIETY

To frame an answer to this question, we need to examine the ideas about gender that shaped Muscovite and Western society in radically different ways. Comparative analysis reveals a Muscovite gender system so very different from its Western counterparts that it would be impossible to expect similar outcomes in the gendering of witchcraft accusations. This examination should make apparent why there could be no *Malleus Maleficarum* in Muscovy, why the necessary preconceptions to link women so lethally to witchcraft were simply not there.

In the early modern period, West Europeans were frantically discussing the proper roles and functions of men and women and working hard to develop and enforce new forms of Christian patriarchy.[49] Muscovites, too, certainly had their problems and preoccupations with gender roles, but there is reason to believe that in many areas other social divisions were of more concern, as the case of filial impiety discussed above intimates.

Two key factors contributed to constructing Muscovite notions of gender. First, social hierarchy within structures of service, family units, and broader communities created a powerful organizing framework that in some ways overrode gender in Muscovites' social imagination and practice. Hierarchically organized by class, age, and gender, the family, clan, or collective unit, Muscovites clearly differentiated male and female roles, but at each level, individuals were subordinated to their superiors in status and age, and then secondarily ranked by gender within category. Second, Muscovite concepts of gender derived in significant degree from Orthodox Christian teachings, which differed in essential areas from the Augustinian traditions developed in the West. Although witchcraft was configured as more a secular than religious crime in Muscovy and was tried in secular courts, Orthodoxy nonetheless shaped the underlying expectations and norms of behavior at all levels of society.

Muscovite society structured hierarchy into its every aspect. Legal stratification fixed the population into increasingly privileged layers reaching from slaves to noble boyars to the tsar himself, and composed of an infinite array of smaller collectives. Prosperous households included family members, extended kin, dependents of various kinds, servants, and slaves. Towns and villages formed their own communes, forced together by the strictures of collective taxation, service requirements, and local military musters. Within these various collectives, and within each rank or status, gender hierarchies structured another, subsidiary dimension of stratification. Rank conferred prerogatives relative to those below; gender determined the distribution of authority within rank.[50]

In practical terms, women's movement in society was more restricted than men's. Elite women were, at least in principle, confined to women's quarters (the *terem*) and forbidden to leave the domestic compound unveiled. Women were not called to serve their tsar in the military or in the many other labor capacities—as couriers, coachmen, bridge builders, guards, carters, bricklayers, metal smiths, distillers—that drew their fathers, husbands, and sons out of the home. Court testimonies record that men of all ranks often traveled to far distant regions on military assignment, in pursuit of trade, carrying out errands for their masters, or visiting relatives. Women more commonly stayed near home, and their testimony describes social interactions in church, in a neighbor's or master's home, at a wedding, at the well, or in the town square. Fewer women circulated along the roads or congregated in markets and taverns, although witchcraft testimony includes reports of some female vagrants, pilgrims, and itinerant healers.[51]

In many spheres of life men's and women's roles were defined in similar and overlapping terms. In questions of property ownership, for instance, daughters and widows as well as sons and brothers exercised claims to paternal lands. The goal of protecting properties within the clans could at times outweigh gender-based claims. As Nancy Shields Kollmann has established, honor derived from diligently fulfilling one's assigned role in the social hierarchy, whatever that role happened to be, and the tsar's courts were ready to defend both women and men from slurs to their honor.[52] Muscovy's rigid hierarchical order rested on social distinctions and the expectations they imposed, and those distinctions were made by rank and status perhaps even more than by gender. If the *Domostroi*, the household handbook of the sixteenth century, admonished men to reprimand their wives for misbehavior and beat them if absolutely necessary, it also recommended the same exemplary treatment for defiant sons and servants. Moreover, the householder's wife received similar advice for how to keep her servants, male and female, in line: "If [one of the servants] fails to heed her scoldings, she must strike him."[53] Most of the articles of the *Domostroi* discuss the universal, gender-neutral obligation to obey the clergy, the princely authorities, and all of one's elders and social betters. Isolating the treatment of women from that of all social subordinates exaggerates the chasm between the sexes. Everyone was enjoined to obedience, and everyone was vulnerable to harsh sanction in case of insubordination.[54] If in Yoruba culture age figured as the primary principle of social classification, then in Muscovy, status, rank, seniority, and gender, in more or less that order of priority, combined in a distinctive formula for calculating social standing.

WHY NOT WOMEN?: GENDER, SEXUALITY, AND THE BODY IN RUSSIAN ORTHODOXY

The mental universe of the population that turned in suspected witches was formed to a significant degree by Orthodox teachings.[55] Two central religious tenets molded Muscovite notions of gender very differently from those of their Western contemporaries. One was the status of "cognitive religion," or the value of logic and reason in Russian Orthodoxy, and the other was the Orthodox attitude toward sex and the flesh. With regard to the former, scholarship or intellectual inquiry never claimed pride of place as a route to the divine, or even to understanding. Orthodoxy, in the forms that reached Russia, was largely based on faith and ritual, on lived experience, and inner vision, and not on intellectual pursuit of the divine. Reason, that cool, refined attribute of men and men alone in the Western tradition, won no particular accolades in the Russian tradition. Rational thinking was a quality that men did not particularly seek to monopolize, or even display. Intellect was not ground for gender-based contestation or exclusion, and although by the end of the century, most young men of the landed service class and many of those of the urban estates were able to sign their names and had mastered some basic literacy, any deeper education was neither available nor particularly desirable, even for elite males. A few leading clerics achieved a sophisticated familiarity with patristics and the Eastern Christian tradition, and the seventeenth century did see an uptick in literary and theological production as the influx of clerics from the Ukrainian lands brought with them a higher degree of seminary education and greater engagement with the theological models on offer through the Jesuits and Uniates in Poland-Lithuania.[56] Through their influence, a few select young men (seven) enjoyed the opportunity to study at the Moscow Slavonic-Greco-Latin Academy, founded in 1682. Indicative of the suspicion with which some factions greeted these educational openings and the arcane books they brought in their wake, the academy's charter included a proviso that the school should not teach "any sciences banned by the church, such as natural or other kinds of magic," and should "have no instructors of those subjects. And if such teachers, magicians (*charodeia*) turn up, and they have contact with students, burn them without any mercy."[57] The minute scale of the academy, its miniscule number of students, further underscores the extent to which learned theology or rational intellectual exploration were simply off the table in Muscovy.

Paired with the downplaying of rational inquiry in Orthodox theology was a corresponding emphasis on affective response. Emotionality was not a gendered trait in the teachings of the Orthodox Church, which valued emotive qualities in males and females alike.[58] Overly effusive expression of emotion carried lamentably female valence in the judgment of many European thinkers, and could be used to dismiss the mental abilities of women in general and to disparage the manliness of men of uncontrolled affect.[59] In Muscovy, by contrast, tears of remorse, repentance, and joy characterized pious or saintly experience regardless of the sex of the weeper. A case in point, Tsar Fedor Ivanovich, son and heir of Ivan the Terrible, distinguished himself as one of the most revered Muscovite rulers by his religious devotion and his copious tears, despite acknowledged mental weakness.[60] These divergent developments have immediate implications for the development of witch lore. Where Western demonologists attributed women's susceptibility to the Devil's wiles in part to their weak, irrational minds and emotional extravagance, such invidious distinctions by sex would have made no sense in the Muscovite context.

Orthodox theology colored attitudes toward gender not only through its teachings on reason and emotion, but also through its teachings on sex, the body, and the material world. Muscovite notions of the body offer a reasonable starting point for investigating the relevant cultural terrain. Surprisingly little has been written on the topic. Aside from passing mentions in studies of Russian Orthodoxy, Eve Levin's groundbreaking book, *Sex and Society in the World of the Orthodox Slavs*, together with a number of her important articles, were the first and remain the most significant studies of attitudes toward the flesh in medieval and early modern Russia. On the basis of extensive work with sermons, confessionals, saints' lives, miracle tales, and trial records, Levin finds that the Orthodox world held the body in low regard, as a site of concupiscence and sin. Adding nuance to this finding, she shows that the church accommodated to the reality of human weakness, and aimed to contain and control rather than eliminate sins of the flesh. The most heinous sexual offenses were those that disrupted social bonds of marriage, family, and community, while private indulgences incurred less fearsome consequences.[61]

Russian Christianity simultaneously cultivated a more celebratory vision of the human body as the vessel of Christ's Incarnation. Man, created in God's image, was a pale reflection, but a reflection nonetheless of the divine perfection.[62] As the bodily incarnation of the Savior, the human form basked secondhand in the glory of the earthly Jesus. Through the miracle of the Word-Made-Flesh, the human body served as an embodiment of the Lord, and as a metaphor of the ineffable, intangible, and divine. The theme of the Transfiguration, Jesus in fully human form radiantly revealed as the Son of God, was a moderately popular one in Muscovy, as evidenced by the frequency with which it was painted in icons and the number of villages and churches named in its honor.[63] Orthodox Russians actively venerated the bodily relics, and attributed special sanctity to intact, "uncorrupted" corpses, of their saints. Within the economy of

Icon of the Transfiguration, 1685. Icons of the Transfiguration celebrate the capacity of human flesh to embody the divine. They survive in large numbers and their lesson seems quite accessible. http://snikola.ru/Ikoni/Gospodnie/Preobrazenie/3.jpg. (See also plate 5)

the miraculous, bodily contact with the physical remains were thought to yield fruit.[64] Given this appraisal of the capability of the human form to embody and channel the divine, the flesh was endowed with multiple meanings.

This claim for Orthodoxy's relative equanimity on the topic of the body has to be situated realistically. It would be foolhardy, and downright wrong, to argue that Orthodox Christianity always assessed the corporeal realm and the body itself in a positive light. Sex in particular received its due share of fiery condemnation. Confessional guides instructed priests to begin their probing of their spiritual children, whether male or female, with questions about their sexual activities. Indeed, as Nadieszda Kizenko points out, the penitential texts might

Church of the Transfiguration, Ostrov, sixteenth century. Churches dedicated to the miracle of the Transfiguration, the moment when Man is revealed as God, were and are common across Russia. Photograph from V. Kostochkin, Drevnerusskie goroda: Pamiatniki zodchestva XI–XVII vv. *(Moscow: Iskusstvo, 1972), no. 216, p. 249.*

lead one to "conclude that sexual transgression was the overwhelming concern of Orthodox priests hearing confession." V. M. Zhivov's finding that startlingly few Muscovites attended to their duty of annual confession does not lessen the Orthodox establishment's *theoretical* concern with sexual sin.[65] Nonetheless, it is worth remembering that alongside the censure and condemnation, the positive theological valence could and often did inhere in the human body, whether male or female, in Orthodox teaching and practice.

We have seen above that sexual misdeeds did not align closely with witchcraft accusations, and that women were not associated with magical sexual transgressions in accusations or confessions. Those connections failed to coalesce despite the presence in the literary annals of an ugly Christian misogyny, premised on the sexual danger that women posed. While making the occasional gesture acknowledging "the good wife," "a husband's crown and consolation," Orthodox authors left a more exuberant record of condemnation of the female sex.[66] As promised in its title, a didactic seventeenth-century dialogue, "Conversation of a Father with [His] Son about Female Evil," presents woman as the source of sin and the origin of man's downfall.[67] A much quoted passage from the mysterious Daniil the Prisoner takes an unambiguous stand on the question of women's value: "What is more evil than a lion among four-legged beasts and than a serpent . . . slithering along the ground? An evil woman is more evil than all of these. There is nothing on earth greater than a woman's evil." Daniil echoes the *Malleus* in its appropriation of Adam's fall as a brush with which to tar all women. "Through a woman, our first forefather, Adam, was driven out of paradise. . . . O sharp, evil weapon of the Devil!"[68] By innuendo, Daniil assigns responsibility for concupiscence to women, while attributing other kinds of sins to men: "A maiden ruins by her beauty; and a man by his thievery."[69] Iconographic depictions of the sins of lust and fornication frequently append pendulous breasts to otherwise androgynous or male demons, underscoring the feminization of those particular sins (although other demons wear leering faces in their genital regions).[70]

The same invidious association of women, sex, and sin surfaces in a number of non-ecclesiastical sources, suggesting that it crossed over into a more popular, or secular, milieu. "The Tale of Savva Grudtsyn," a seventeenth- or early eighteenth-century tale aimed at a secular, urban audience, purveys the same idea that women corrupt men and lead them into sexual sin.[71] Initially, the text places the blame on the Devil, rather than the woman: Incensed by the virtuous way of life he observed in the home of Bazhen, Savva's protector, "the enemy, the Devil, [who] hates all things good, . . . decided to upset his household by inducing Bazhen's wife to the vile sinfulness of fornication with the young man, to corrupt her with love of Savva." Drawing on the tropes used in Muscovite love spells, the Devil entraps the woman with an irresistible love and longing for Savva. She obligingly seduces her young boarder, a plan that proves easy for her because "woman's nature (*zhenskoe estestvo*) knows how to lead the minds of young men to fornication." But after this disparaging assessment of the essential feminine, the tale shifts the ultimate blame back to the Devil: "And thus Savva, through the perfidy of this woman, or, better to say, by the Devil's envy, stumbled and fell into the trap of fornication."[72] Lest we miss the point, or somehow misunderstand the nature of their sin, the author provides vivid descriptions of exactly what it was that they did: "They sinned endlessly, and constantly, but still they were unable to satiate their desires. And for a long time they remained in filthy sin. Even on Sundays and on the Lord's holy days, having forgotten their fear of God and the hour of their deaths, they kept fornicating, wallowing like swine in excrement."[73]

These selected passages, taken in isolation, produce a convincing impression of a Russian Orthodoxy that shared many features with the more familiar teachings of Western Christianity: susceptible to the Devil's enticement, inherently lustful, pernicious to the souls of the males of the species, women were true daughters of Eve. This summary, indeed, reflects the general consensus of the scholarly literature on the topic.

However, a consistent methodological problem haunts this scholarship, both in Russian and in Western variants. The source base, thoughtfully and deliberately selected to reveal Muscovite ideas about sexuality and gender, necessarily foregrounds issues of sexuality and gender. A collection of penitentials devoted to eking out confessions of specifically sexual transgressions, when paired with the few spicy sexual escapades in Muscovite literary works and the most highly sexualized iconography, inevitably gives an impression of a religious culture preoccupied with sexual sin and dedicated to its eradication.[74] The danger of analyzing isolated passages apart from the broader context is that such analysis removes ideas about women and notions of sexuality from the world in which they were situated. Deprived of cultural context, their significance is rendered unintelligible. In order to assess how sexual sin fit into a broader vision of sin and virtue, one needs to assemble a wider range of sources.

The intertwined themes of sex, sin, and gender in a Christian cosmology hark back, inevitably, to Adam and Eve.[75] The Fall receives plenty of consideration in Orthodoxy as it does in the Catholic tradition, but the Eastern Orthodox attributed "Adam's Fall" as much to Adam or to the wayward pair as to female weakness. "Adam's Lament," preserved in texts from the fifteenth through seventeenth centuries and presumably sung during Lent, gives voice to

Expulsion of Adam and Eve, seventeenth-century: "Novgorod school: The Creation of Adam and Eve: The Expulsion from Paradise. Fragment of painting of altar doors. Middle of the seventeenth century." Adam and Eve are depicted here as chastened sinners, but the artist draws attention to neither their gender nor their sexual infractions. From Briusova, Russkaia zhivopis' 17 veka, *Color Image, no. 114, "Novgorodskie pis'ma: Sotvorenie Adama i Evy: Izgnanie iz raia. Fragment rospisi altarnoi dveri. Serediny XVII veka." (See also plate 6)*

This image comes from a depiction of various clusters of typologically differentiated sinners in a manuscript Apocalypse, probably from the 1780s. This unhappy group is labeled charodei, *magicians or witches. They shiver, naked and exposed, as fiery serpents attack them from above. "Witches' Punishment," MS C38, f. 158v. Courtesy of Special Collections, Spencer Research Library, University of Kansas Libraries. (See also plate 7)*

Adam's regret for the loss of paradise, "created for me and for Eve," which he lost through his own unspecified sinfulness.[76] When the sin is named, it is the pair's disobedience, their refusal to follow God's explicit orders, not their sexual transgression. Eve occasionally takes the blame, as in the passage quoted above from Daniil the Prisoner, or in a widely copied passage from John Chrysostom ("If Eve had held back from the tree, we would not need this fasting"), but more generally Adam alone or the two together occupy center stage.[77] When the original couple is depicted in icons or miniatures, their often strikingly sexless bodies seem to emphasize the asexual essence of their transgression. They appear equally chastened, sharing the mortal consequences of their disobedience.[78]

GENDER, SEX, AND SIN IN MUSCOVITE LITERARY IMAGINATION

A number of "popular texts," written in the late seventeenth century, contain valuable information on the ways that gender and sexuality were lived or viewed in a Muscovite context. These tales provide an important link between prescriptive ecclesiastical sources and the evidence of lived, secular experience that we glimpse in trial records. A more secularly inclined literature was a newly evolving phenomenon in seventeenth-century Russia, and these texts grew out of a lay culture still fully integrated with religious ways of thinking. The works examined here—"The Tale of Misery-Luckless-Plight," "The Life of Iuliana of Murom," and, once again, "The Tale of Savva Grudtsyn"—dwell on matters of domestic relations and familial morality, and some explore issues of sexual conduct and misconduct at length. They do not, however, speak in a unitary voice. Unlike "Savva Grudtsyn," others do not express condemnation or even any conceptual linkage of sexuality and female sinfulness. They offer quite a different vantage point, giving us an opportunity for measuring the relative salience of various sins.

Sex does not even enter in the litany of sins and lures enumerated in the evocatively titled "Tale of Misery-Luckless-Plight (Povest' o Gore i Zlochastii)." Instead, the spotlight falls directly on the mortal sin of disobedience. The tale begins, conveniently for us, with a recap of the Creation and the Fall, which spells out a gratifyingly explicit moral message:

> *The human heart is unthinking and fractious,*
> *and Adam and Eve were tempted.*
> *They forgot God's command,*
> *tasted the fruit of the grapevine,*
> *from the great, marvelous tree,*
> *and for that great transgression,*
> *God became enraged at Adam and Eve.*[79]

Adam and Eve's sin, then, is explicitly identified as their disobedience: "They forgot God's command . . . and for that great transgression, God became enraged." Having cast the pair out of Eden, "God gave them this commandment: there should be weddings and marriages for the propagation of the race of men, and for having beloved children." The tale thus presents sexual activity within marriage as not only tolerable, but also as in harmony with God's direct command, and as resulting in "beloved children." Far from the cause of their disgrace, conjugal activity is described as Adam and Eve's obligation. But, given the "unthinking and fractious" nature of man, things continue to decline: "Humankind from the very beginning acted insubordinate, looked with disdain at the father's teaching, acted defiantly toward the mother, was duplicitous about the advice of friends." The introduction sets up the moral premise of the tale: Adam and Eve were cast out of Eden for their unruliness and for defying the Lord's command; subsequent generations were disobedient and insubordinate, defying their parents—mothers as well as fathers—and their friends. Disobedience to one's elders and superiors towers over all other sins, and sexual transgression does not merit even an innuendo in this prologue.[80]

The rest of the tale fulfills the promise and continues the moral message of the opening passage. The story starts midstream, with the unnamed youth receiving the advice and instruction of his pious parents, again, mother as well as father. Given what the prologue told us about human nature, we are not surprised to find him soon defying his parents' admonitions.

The youth was then young and foolish,
not in his full sense, and imperfect in mind;
he was ashamed to submit to his father
and bow to his mother
but wanted to live as he pleased.

His recklessness brings him into bad company. He is hounded by Misery-Luckless-Plight, who poses as a friend, and induces him to throw aside family, wealth, friendship, and a potential bride. Severing his ties with family and friends, his new companion's machinations parallel those of love spells, which require abjuring all human bonds and cleaving to the spell-caster alone. Wandering at will in the world, cut off from natural bonds and obligations, indulging his whims, the youth falls into the dreadful category of those who belong nowhere and answer to no one. Things go from bad to worse until finally, in a rather unmotivated plot twist, "the youth recalled the path to salvation and at once he went to a monastery to be shorn a monk, and Misery stopped at the holy gates."[81] "Misery-Luckless-Plight" makes its moral message extremely clear. The ultimate sin, both in the Garden of Eden and in this mortal world, is the sin of disobedience. Although along his path to perdition the young man indulges in a host of physical sins—intemperance, greed, profligacy, gluttony—it is the act of disobedience that earns him God's wrath and from which he needs to be saved at the end.

"Misery-Luckless-Plight" articulates a set of priorities in which defiance of the legitimate authority of one's elders and betters ranks as the most egregious of sins, with other, merely physical sins, cascading below in no particular order. In the "Savva Grudtsyn" tale, too, obedience and humility prove the most important of virtues, miraculously bringing salvation to the penitent sinner. The humbled protagonist gains redemption by tearfully swearing obedience to the Mother of God, promising to fulfill her injunctions unquestioningly. True to the same moral order, Iuliana Osor'ina of Murom, embodying Christian moral perfection as envisioned by her devout son and hagiographer/biographer, manifests her piety through exaggerated obedience. "She humbly obeyed [her in-laws] in all things, never disobeying them, never contradicting them, but respecting them and carrying out their wishes without fail, so that all were amazed by her."[82] Although late in life she convinced her husband to practice abstinence, her earlier life was demonstrably characterized by an actively sexual marriage, as the births of her many children attest. In the tale, her participation in conjugal life only augments her virtue, because she obeys the instructions of priest and husband in subordinating her own will and carrying out her marital obligations.

Further visual evidence from the seventeenth century underscores the virtue inherent in a pious marriage. In perhaps the most poignant woodblock print from the late seventeenth or early eighteenth century, an elderly, careworn husband and wife occupy separate squares, each attending to his or her separate but interconnected task: "The husband weaves bast shoes with skill; the wife spins flax with a will."[83] The two figures are clearly differentiated by sex, with their different headdresses and their gender-segregated tasks, and of course, the beard. They are not, however, sexually marked. Neither their somber, creased faces nor their shapeless robes betray any sexual difference.

Lubok *of virtuous man and wife, late seventeenth century. A hardworking couple divide their tasks by gender but share the burden of frugal living and hard work. The text informs us: "The Husband weaves bast sandals into the night (not quenching the fire); the wife spins thread. They wish to enrich themselves." In Sytova,* Lubok, *16.*

These seventeenth-century tales and images present a moral universe in which obedience toward authorities, whether male or female, formed the most pressing moral imperative, and where concerns about sexual activity, if present at all, occupied a second tier. Marriage and sexual reproduction within marriage figure in many secular and quasi-religious sources as constituting a positive good. While extra-marital and non-reproductive sexual activity drew predictable condemnation, clergy and parishioners alike took a pragmatic approach to helping violators toward repentance and reintegration into the community.[84] Even the Mother of God followed this line of moral reasoning and wiped clean the incriminating writing from misguided compacts with the Devil once the wayward sinners returned to the path of obedience.

Writing about early modern German and French discourses of witchcraft and magic, Gerhild Scholtz Williams argues that not all magical practice was demonized, even at the height of the witch hunts. A licit field of magical practice, characterized as "natural magic," drew on book learning and erudition, setting it in the realm of men and angels. Female magic, by contrast, was shunted off into a realm that was, by definition, one of ignorance, physicality, and evil. "The dichotomies of gender are also those of the Christian faith; they represent also the basic tenets of magic—good and evil, Adam and Eve, Eve and Mary, Christ and Satan. . . . [These Christian dichotomies] are ultimately expressions of a single, gendered dichotomy: the flesh that is woman stands opposite the spirit [and we could add, the intellect] that is man."[85] Russian Orthodox Christianity quietly parts company with the theological trends that Williams describes so cogently for Latin and Protestant Europe. Orthodoxy manifested little interest in categorizing flesh and spirit in gendered terms. Men and women alike were charged with obeying their superiors, maintaining the obedience of those designated as their subordinates, and, ultimately, with overcoming gender in order to reach sexless perfection. Orthodox-inflected gender categories and practices rendered the logic of Western associations between women and witchcraft meaningless in Muscovy, where it had no purchase on the accusers' imaginations.

IF NOT GENDER, WHAT? THE SOCIAL PROFILE OF THE ACCUSED

If accusations of witchcraft attached disproportionately to male suspects, then it would be logical, on the face of it, to conclude that witchcraft in Muscovy was predominantly a male crime, and that gender was just as relevant as in European trials but in inverse proportion. Such a conclusion would be fully logical, but only partially correct. Gender certainly contributed to the conditions under which individuals circulated, interacted, and attracted suspicion, and to the roles that they were expected to play, but it did not define the essence of witchcraft or determine the pool of the targets. People brought suspicion on themselves because they demonstrated the characteristics and behaviors associated with witchcraft, and these characteristics were not understood as constitutive of one gender or another. Rather, they were characteristics of *witches*. Men, because of their greater mobility and more open canvas for social interactions, stumbled into more potentially dangerous situations where witchcraft charges might arise.[86]

The social profile of those who fell under suspicion in Muscovite courts reveals the particular categories of people that were actually brought to trial on witchcraft charges. From an analysis of the same 223 cases in which something of the identity of the accused can be established, the following profile emerges. Thirty-three or 15 percent of the cases, a sizable subset, involved itinerants, wanderers, either indicted as the primary defendant or named as the teachers who had imparted knowledge of magic to the defendant. Itinerants may well have comprised a more substantial fraction of the accused, since the total calculated here includes only those suspects explicitly identified as such. This category included, for instance, three wandering Mordvins who conjured "unclean spirits," an "old Tatar fortune-teller woman" who "roamed around doing magic, "an itinerant horse-healer," "a wandering woman," a wandering minstrel (*skomorokh*), and a male cowherd, identified as a witch (*vedun*) who roamed from village to village.[87] These people indulged in a freedom of movement that directly challenged the regime's campaign to fix the population in rank and place and to tie the people to assigned masters, regiments, or other collective units.

As peasants were gradually transforming into serfs and urban populations became legally bound to their towns, state policies guaranteed that the population at large would aid in the policing of unauthorized movement. The Muscovite state assessed and collected taxes from communities as collective units, not from individuals or households. If individuals threw off the shackles of registration and headed off on their own initiative, their neighbors bore the brunt of their departure. The shirkers' share of the collective tax assessment transferred to the diminished numbers who remained. Residents thus had a pressing interest in curtailing the movement of their neighbors, and the townspeople's insistent demands for the return of their fugitive comrades during the seventeenth century demonstrate that they understood the coercive logic of their situation. Constant shifts of population undermined the viability and integrity of local communities and eroded or destabilized the tax base in many places, so peasants and townspeople alike appear to have welcomed, even invited, the move to lock residents in place and secure their communities. During the urban riots of 1648–49, and then consistently through the rest of the century, protesters insisted that runaways and tax evaders be forcibly returned to the towns or villages in which they were registered, to equalize the collective tax burden and distribute it more broadly.[88]

Even from the point of view of the individual, "freedom" could involve unbearable hardship if it conferred no clear alternative status or geographic tie. Freedom from slavery or bondage was an aspiration of several of the protagonists in witchcraft cases, as is discussed in the following chapters. However, perhaps even worse than slavery, at least in the seventeenth century, was the state of belonging nowhere, without any ascribed affiliation. For instance, Firska Potapov, a slave, complained in 1672 that after he had denounced his master for corruption, property fraud, currency counterfeiting, and involvement with forbidden books of fortune-telling and magic, his master had vengefully set him free. Identifying himself through his condition of bondage as "your poor and helpless orphan, Fedor Volodimirovich Buturlin's [bonds]man," Firska wrote to Tsar Aleksei Mikhailovich:

> Fedor Volodimirovich sent me out of the house, away from him, without giving me a manumission document (*ne dav otpusknoi*), and I, your orphan, with my little wife and with my little children, drift from house to house, and I am dying a hungry death. Merciful sovereign . . . order him, Fedor, [to sign a manumission document saying] that he won't search for me in the future [by invoking the terms of my earlier] enslavement agreement."

This petition gives us a fascinating insight into the logic of bondage in Muscovy. Being a slave was a terrible fate—so grim that one of the witnesses in this case averred that Firska had made up his charges against his master and others "just to make mischief (*zateiav*), falsely, criminally, in order to escape slavery."[89] But he should have been careful about what he wished: the unofficial dismissal he received landed him in a nightmarish, uncertain limbo between slavery and freedom, leaving him adrift as a man without a master and without a position in society.[90]

As part of the effort to keep track of its population, the state developed increasingly efficient censuses and record keeping, resulting in an explosion of lists.[91] Regulation of the elite rapidly proved quite effective, but surveillance of the lower orders posed a far greater challenge. As the state pushed to inhibit both geographic and social mobility, vagrancy presented a threat to the system itself. The presence of *guliashchie liudi*, "wandering people" (like Savva Grudtsyn or the Youth in Misery-Luckless-Plight), was a menace sufficient to warrant the involvement of the local governor and often was considered important enough to report to Moscow.[92] Itinerants included seasonal laborers, freed slaves, defrocked or self-proclaimed monks, priests, and nuns, and the evocatively named *vol'nye liudi*, "free people," people subject only to their own will, a term of sharpest opprobrium in a society that valued stability and hierarchy.[93]

The willingness of townspeople, artisans, and serfs to turn in vagrants on witchcraft charges suggests that ordinary people, enmeshed in a system of coercively collective responsibility, shared the official vision of movement as disruptive and potentially dangerous and a preference for stable, bonded, controlled communities. The catastrophic upheavals and economic devastation of the previous half century intensified a desperate search for stability. Hostility toward the disruption inherent in uncontrolled circulation of people surfaces from time to time in witchcraft accusations. Witnesses identified one of the men accused in an outbreak of witchcraft and possession in Lukh in the 1650s as "a landless peasant and a minstrel, who plays the zither (*gusli*) and wanders from town to town. . . . He was in Lukh only briefly and has been gone since winter. The townspeople don't know much about him because he is not a townsperson of Lukh."[94] Since reliable demographic figures are not available, it is impossible to say to what extent the 15 percent representation of vagrants corresponds with their actual presence among the accused or in the population at large, whether they were over- or under-represented. In either case, they composed a small but noticeable fraction of defendants.

A second trait slightly more weakly associated with accused witches was non-Russian ethnicity, sometimes linked, accurately or not, with paganism, or, along the western borders, with possible treason.[95] Muscovy conquered Finnic territories in the north already in the late fifteenth century, the khanates of Kazan and Astrakhan on the Volga in the mid-sixteenth century, much of Western Siberia in the late sixteenth century, and reached the Pacific by the mid-seventeenth. From the start, Muscovy was a multi-ethnic empire, encompassing many non-Russians, and the population of accused witches reflects this diversity. Among those named as witches were Lithuanians, Cherkassians (Ukrainian Cossacks), one Armenian, and a variety of non-Christians, particularly Mordvins, Chuvash, Tatars, and Cheremis. A single gypsy was mentioned as the teacher of a witchcraft suspect, but was fortunate in not being identified by name. Of the 223 cases examined here, twenty-eight (roughly 13 percent) involved identifiably non-Russian suspects, named either as the primary defendant or as a former teacher. According to witnesses, in 1630 a Tatar slave woman in the southern fortress town of Lebed' required a translator when she told fortunes and worked magical remedies for her Russian clientele. In the 1680s during the period of uncertainty about the succession, a member of the court elite brought "a *murza* prince Ibragim Dolotkozin and Tatar Kodoralei to the tsar's chamber, and they did divination there with books of prognostication and [other] writings, and predicted that Tsar Peter would sit on the throne alone." The Tatars, along with the courtier who employed them, were beaten and tortured, and "finally had their divination books and letters burned on their backs."[96]

At least some of the Finnic and Turkic sorcerers and healers appear to have been practicing pagans, and so twice vulnerable in a Russian Orthodox world.[97] The most sensational cases of spirit invocation involved suspects explicitly identified as non-Russians. Maksimko Ivanov, for instance, a self-proclaimed healer, was charged with calling demons to assist him in telling fortunes. This dramatic case, discussed in chapter 3 in connection with summoning "unclean forces," draws on a non-Russian magical tradition: Maksimko and his neighbors were Mordvins, Finnic pagans. The same trial record reports that they participated in a ritual of ancestor veneration that involved sacrificing horses. The forest rite degenerated into an all-out battle when the pagans began attacking passing Russians, and landed the whole group in court.[98] Sonja Luehrmann observes that "witchcraft suspicions may have been expressions of anxieties about living together with not fully Christianized neighbors," and formal accusations "provided a language for Orthodox Russian peasants to express a sense of threat and bring it forward to the courts."[99] This dynamic may well have been at work in instances where non-Russians fell under suspicion. Ethnic non-Russian subjects of the tsar were, in a sense, internal outsiders, and therefore would seem to have been the ideal internal enemy, ripe for accusation. Their relatively small showing among the accused, however, suggests that Muscovites were more likely to suspect their own, or at least not to foreground ethnic difference, when they sought to identify the sources of magical harm. In fact, although both itinerants and non-Russians constituted notable contingents among the accused, they remained a distinct minority relative to members of local Orthodox communities. Muscovites in general directed their suspicions at those closer to home, at their neighbors and acquaintances, at the "enemy within."[100]

Folk healers comprised yet another, more sizable subset of the accused. They appeared in fifty-three cases (24 percent).[101] This group overlapped significantly with both of the previous categories. Some healers lived settled lives and worked in their own communities, like Tereshka Malakurov, who confessed under torture to causing the illnesses that he later tried to cure. He said he had learned his craft from a healer of another ilk, a horse doctor named Oska.[102] Approximately a third of the healers targeted as witches lived itinerant lives, wandering from village to village offering their services. Non-Russians also figured prominently among the accused healers, making up about a quarter of the pool. Eleven individuals embodied all three risk factors: they were itinerant, non-Russian healers.[103]

It would be anachronistic to call these healers "professionals"; they had no formal training and they held other ranks that indicated their primary

Table 4.1 *Witchcraft trials in seventeenth-century Russia*

Cases:	227
Cases with information on the accused:	223
Number of individuals involved: minimum:	499 (495 identified, plus 4 cases without identified numbers or individuals, adding minimum of one per case)
Total number of individual suspects identified:	495
Men:	367 (74% of 495)
Women:	128 (26% of 495)
Cases involving only male suspects:	149 (67% of 223)
Cases involving only female suspects:	34 (15% of 223)
Cases involving both male and female suspects:	40 (18% of 223)
Cases involving charges against healers:	53 (24% of 223)
Cases involving charges against itinerants:	33 (15% of 223)
Cases involving charges against people of non-Russian ethnicity:	28 (13% of 223)
Satanic cases:	15 (7% of 223)

ascribed identities. Witnesses identified them as musketeers, gunners, slaves, administrators, peasants, priests, deacons, townspeople, or petty gentrymen. Some of them were simply found carrying healing spells or roots and grasses they claimed served medical purposes (*dlia lekarstva*).[104] However, most of the healer-witches among the suspects had attained reputations for their healing (and sometimes for their associated cursing) prior to their trials, suggesting that they acted and were viewed as specialists maintaining a sustained practice, not simply as providers of neighborly wisdom. A bondswoman in Iaroslavl confessed in 1664 to seeking out someone who knew about roots and grasses "or earned a living that way."[105] Ivashko Goldobin, who in 1692 in Novgorod admitted to an extensive and on-going medical practice, identified himself as a musketeer. His sideline in healing was clearly a serious one, however. After investigators discovered a vast store of supplies hidden under the floor boards of his house, Ivashko identified each of the suspicious substances and enumerated its uses:

> In the little sack is the grass called "*vasilishnik*," good for sore throat. You steam it in water. And in another little sack is ground up *deviatil'nik* grass, good against worms (*volosatki*). In the third little sack is another ground-up grass,

> of the nettle family, for *svoroba*. In the fourth little sack is another ground-up grass called "*polyn*." You steam it to cure ulcers. And tied up in a little rag is another grass to use against worms. The heap of crushed grass and seeds is for diseases of the cheek: whoever has a canker of the cheek [should use] those grasses, not ground, and also for throat ailments. The bundle of roots is against heart disease. And those same grasses and roots he, Ivashko, collected out in the fields ten or more years ago, and every year [since then], around St. John's and St. Ilia's days. . . . For twenty years he, Ivashko, has been giving those and other grasses and roots to all ranks of people whose names he doesn't remember.[106]

Ivashko's list spills over to several more pages, indicating that his was not a casual practice. Many healers appear to have specialized in a particular ailment or methodology, such as curing hernias or ulcers in children, treating impotence, predicting the outcome of illnesses, curing possession, but Ivashko's private pharmacy suggests broader reach. The evidence from the cases generally supports A. S. Lavrov's sense of healers as specialists who devoted a significant fraction of their time to and derived a significant portion of their livelihood from their medical work. Such specialists, whether healers or in the more transgressive fields of fortune-telling or cursing, risked more serious penalties than their clients, although both could run afoul of the law and incur punishment.[107] A number of scholars have posited that fewer women practiced healing, that they were blocked from the "at-risk" professions more generally, and this gendered glass ceiling inadvertently protected women from witchcraft accusations.[108] This explanation has limited traction, given that female healers make up the same fraction of accused healers, approximately one in four, as they do in the general pool of suspects, providing little reason to believe that women were discouraged from developing healing skills.

Patients or their aggrieved survivors were the people who filed charges against the healers they had consulted.[109] A puzzle inherent in this pattern of accusation is that these same healers provided essentially the only source of medical knowledge available. A few Western doctors, either trained or self-styled, worked in the employ of the tsar and the Apothecary Chancellery in Moscow, and priests and saints touted their theologically sanctioned services, but practically speaking, everyone had occasion to turn to a healer who knew some herbal cures or useful spells. In a world of universal reliance on folk healers, how could one distinguish a healer from a witch? The dividing lines emerge fairly distinctly, though necessarily indirectly, from court testimony: If no shadow of suspicion touched the healer, then he or she was able to practice freely; when clients suspected the healer of having inflicted the ailment in the first place, or when cures went terribly wrong, then accusations would follow.

Exemplifying the former, happy scenario, in Galich in 1628, two male residents charged a local widow with afflicting their wives with possession. In seeking a cure, they consulted a reputable healer, "and he said a spell over salt, and over water, and over milk, and he gave that to Ivan's wife to drink, and to pour on herself (*okachivat'sia*). And he muttered [spells] over her, and since then his wife has not been affected." The culprit was identified as someone other than the healer and the cure proved effective, so the helpful medic drew no suspicion and no charges were lodged against him.[110] By contrast, in another case of possession, this one taking place in 1660 in Sokol', the plaintiffs had strong grounds for attributing both the affliction and the cure to the same man, Karp Lomakin. Recalling an incident several years earlier, "Mikitka Kolabukhov's wife Varvara said: 'In the past year 1652 [or 1653], my husband brought Karp Lomakin to our house on horseback, and Karp cursed me and threatened, "I will make you unfit for God or man (*ne bzh'iu ni liutskuiu*)," and he loosed on me a dryness, and I dried up from that for about five weeks. I asked him to cure me of that bewitchment and I wanted to go to him in Sokol' to ask him. And he, Karp, hurrying, came and looked at me and breathed on me and told me to stand up, and with that he cured me.'" The same Karp both bewitched and healed others with whom he had fallen out: "He took off our crosses [and put them in water]. He said a spell over water, gave us to drink and he cured us of that bewitchment."[111] Sadly for him, his successful cures counted strongly against him in the court of rumor and in the court of law, because he was held responsible for the original affliction. In terms of cures gone wrong, perhaps the most spectacular was recorded in 1686 when a nun received an herbal remedy from an itinerant Cherkassian woman (one of the accused who embodied all three risk factors: itinerant, non-Russian, healer). The cure took a bad turn and the nun's arms, legs, and stomach "burst" or "tore (*rvalo*)." Witchcraft charges not surprisingly followed in short order.[112] The same dynamic emerges in 1628 when a landowner complained that a Mordvin healer "gave his wife some grass to drink to cure her of bewitchment," but instead of receiving the magical cure he had anticipated, "she died from that grass."[113] An accusation of witchcraft served as the functional equivalent of a malpractice suit.

The fact that magical healing was condemned by the church was not lost on the general public. When facing their interrogators, both accused healers and their patients emphasized that they relied on healing "without spells," or used spells "without evil content."[114] Distinguishing between what we might call "natural" and "supernatural" (and they might have called "divinely ordained" and "magical") effects, witnesses specified if someone "died his own death, with his spiritual father," or was treacherously bewitched to death or "spoiled."[115] Puzzling over the difficulty of distinguishing between the two, some witnesses admitted that "whether the bewitchment and impotence were caused by her [curses] or not, that we don't know for sure."[116] Several potential patients insisted under interrogation that they had eschewed prohibited healing methods. For instance, in 1647, Prince Mikhailo Kozlovskoi's wife, Princess Marina, was interrogated about whether she had consulted a fortune-teller when her husband had been ill years earlier.

> In questioning [she] said that before God and the tsar she wanted to hide nothing. When her husband Prince Mikhailo was sick, he tried to cure himself using doctors, but they were no help at all. And that year, about nine years ago, was two years before his death. And they heard of that old woman (*baba*) who lives in Suzdal' province from people in the area (she couldn't recall their names), and they said that she had helped them in illnesses and that the *baba* had come to them. But she told Prince Mikhailo that he should pray to God in his illness, and she couldn't help him in any way. And her husband Prince Mikhailo didn't ask that *baba* to tell his fortune over him in any way, and she, Princess Marina, warned him to be on his guard and she never asked anyone to tell his fortune, and they kept their faith in God's help. And they didn't go for any fortune-telling.[117]

Although most witnesses in court cases spoke unselfconsciously of turning to multiple sources for healing, ranging from consulting a priest to hiring a healer, to forcing a witch to retract his magic, this testimony makes it clear that the princess saw a qualitative difference among them. She understood (or expected the court to understand) the spiritual costs of consulting fortune-tellers, and of curative methods other than prayer. Although she placed little credence in the skills of the fancy foreign doctors that her husband's rank entitled him to consult, neither would she admit to relying on folk healing. Her testimony hewed close to the official line, which placed healing entirely in the hands of God. Multiple currents thus came together in encouraging ordinary subjects of the tsar to inform on the healers who served them: resentment of cures gone awry, suspicion of the itinerants and of non-Russians who often provided the services, and an underlying sense that tampering with God's will was wrong. In these ways, popular interests coincided with official attempts to punish magical healing. Official directives and local grudges ran together, gathering momentum in the campaign against witches.

The same kind of scissors effect caught a fourth group between the blades of local distrust and official condemnation. This category of people is less readily identifiable because their unifying trait is not one objectively labeled by the sources. Rather, they are unified by a shared behavior, as assessed by their accusers and judges. A close reading of the charges and the histories underlying them suggests that a common characteristic of *insubordination* or *disrespect* unified this group. In one way or another, these suspects defied or were perceived to defy the harsh strictures of a hierarchical social order. This subjective clustering accounts for a large percentage of the cases in which enough documentation survives to gain a sense of the interpersonal dynamics underlying the charges. Serving women and serfs were accused of using magic against masters or estate bailiffs in order to avenge perceived wrongs or to ameliorate their condition.[118] A nephew found himself in court facing witchcraft charges after he violated the rules of deference and generational seniority by suing his uncle for embezzling his estate. A boastful male slave became an easy target for witchcraft charges when he bragged, "If my master is ever angry at me about anything, and I say [these words], . . . then he won't do anything to me. And regarding the female sex, whomever I might want, even a *boiarynia* (high-ranking lady), I can seduce with a love spell."[119] An apprentice saddle-maker who tried to be too independent ended up suspected of witchcraft. In the midst of an outbreak of magical "spoiling (bewitchment)," a group of women sat chatting outside their homes in the town of Lukh in 1657. One offended and frightened the rest with the statement: "*I* don't fear this illness, because God will have mercy on me, but *you* will suffer this misery." Understandably, this did not endear her to her neighbors, who immediately denounced her as a witch.[120] People who chafed under the strictures of propriety and obedience to an abusively hierarchical system, a hierarchy of gender, generation, and rank, within the family, the commune, and the extended community of serfdom and collective responsibility, could be disciplined by witchcraft charges or the threat thereof.

Finally and significantly, a fifth group of people apparently came under suspicion because they actually practiced magic, or what their community defined as such. In Muscovy, without applying the term "witch" to themselves, defendants admitted without any prompting to healing, telling fortunes, finding lost objects and missing loved ones, locating buried treasure, protecting newlyweds, or restoring the possessed. Investigators discovered concealed scraps of paper bearing what were irrefutably magical spells for seducing women, causing impotence in others, or protecting from hostile spells. Witnesses produced other incriminating material evidence, including prayer-like texts and fragments of apocryphal tales meant to lend assistance in hunting, fishing, buying or selling, or winning law suits. Telltale physical artifacts—books of spells and mysterious collections of roots and grasses, knotted in complex ways and stored in small bags—were regularly discovered in the homes and on the persons of the accused. Moreover, according to witnesses' testimony, "notorious witches (*vedomye veduny*)" boasted publicly of their power and threatened those around them with their curses, thereby cementing their local reputations. Penitential guides are riddled with questions pertaining to practicing magic and consulting magicians.[121] Taken together, the evidence adduced in trials leaves little doubt that many people accused of witchcraft were, if not self-acknowledged witches, then at least dabbling in roots and spells.

Magical practice was undoubtedly far more common than the small numbers of people swept up in the trials reflects, and the arenas of practice almost certainly ranged far more broadly than the limited array—healing and cursing, predicting the future and finding lost items and missing persons, seducing lovers and winning favor—that brought suspects to court. For instance, the absence of accusations of agricultural and weather magic, so widely reported by nineteenth-century folklorists, may reflect some bias in accusation rather than an actual lacuna in practice.[122] Some areas of "women's magic" may have escaped persecution as well, which could have contributed to their low representation among the accused.[123] For the purposes of this study, my preference is to concentrate on the charges that did land people in court rather than fill in the blanks with extrapolation.

It is worth emphasizing that witchcraft in the early modern world was not a substitute category. It was not invoked simply as a mask or cover for some other deeper and more genuine offense, such as practicing midwifery, belonging to the wrong denomination, or being poor or female. As Michael MacDonald writes, "A witchcraft trial was a complex social struggle over the meaning of misfortune—of death and disease and loss."[124] Accusers, witnesses, and judges in general tried to identify witches as *witches*, that is, as people who exercised fearsome supernatural powers and bore responsibility for causing those misfortunes. This is an important caveat as we attempt to find sociological patterns in the accusations. Witches were feared primarily for their ostensible magical powers. But patterns do emerge, and they are useful in telling us what particular kinds of people seemed likely to embody the witch in a given society. Nowhere will patterns provide a single, unified answer, nor will they tell the whole story, but they can suggest a nexus of social types or issues that particular cultures and local communities came to associate with witchcraft.

Given the heavy representation of men among the accused, one might think that gender, *male* gender, would indeed be a key factor in determining who would be at risk for a charge of practicing witchcraft. But as this survey of the types of people who were at high risk for accusation demonstrates, gender was not among the primary factors. Rather, maleness was a second-order risk factor, and others were more primary. Among the accused, men and women shared the same set of primary characteristics; there happened to be more men among the targeted categories.

Men were more likely than women to roam the countryside as vagrants or healers. Of the vagrancy cases that are *unrelated* to witchcraft, almost all appear to involve male vagrants. This overwhelming gender skew in vagrancy emerges from my own unsystematic survey of cases of itinerancy listed in the formidable twenty-one-volume guide to the archive of the Ministry of Justice.[125] Although female vagabonds and fugitives certainly existed, they represented only a small fraction of the itinerant population or did not run into trouble with the law and therefore left no documentary traces. Men, whether Russian or non-Russian, vagrant wanderer, military man, or bonded laborer in service, might became embroiled with spells while on military or administrative assignment or on missions for their masters, situations their wives and sisters would not have encountered. Very frequently men accused of carrying or reciting spells acknowledged that they had copied those spells "from a Cossack while serving at the siege of Smolensk," or "I learned that evil on the Volga on the boats. I heard from about it from the barge haulers (*sudovye iaryzhnye liudi*)."[126] A case in point is that of Rodion Maslov, a resident of Belgorod, who was caught in 1679/80 with a book of spells, or more specifically, "a notebook with nine sheets, written on, and on the sheets, along the edges, dots (*tochi*) were sketched in circles." Rodion was closely questioned "about that writing, about what that writing was and who wrote it and for what reason he keeps it with him in Okhtyrka." He explained that by official orders he had been "sent from Okhtyrka to the regiment of boyar and voevoda Ivan Bogdanovich Miloslavskoi."

> And in questioning Rodion Maslov said: That notebook is a fortune-telling book (*gadatel'naia pis'ma*) written by the clerk Afonasiei Aref'ev in his, Afonka's handwriting. Afonka copied that notebook while with him on the Don. In 1676/77, Afonasei Aref'ev copied it from a text of a man from Olshanets [named] Aleshka Zakharin while [he] was with them on the Don too in service as a collector of money and sables for the sovereign's treasury. Rodion displayed three dice made of bone for gambling pieces (*protiv zernovykh kostei*) and said: that same Olshanets Aleshka made these dice and showed them how to throw them according to the writing in the notebook. Rodion threw those same dice with Afanasei Aref'ev along with the notebook and told fortunes. . . .[127]

As evident in this narrative, men circulated in a mobile world of service where they rubbed shoulders with men from other parts, exchanged drinks and threats, shared jokes and secrets, techniques, advice, dice, and manuscripts.

When non-Russian women did take up a wandering life, like the Cherkassian woman who made her patient's appendages rupture, they could be suspected of witchcraft as readily as a man in the same circumstances.

Gender provided no protection from accusation, but added no particular risk either. This contrasts sharply with the Western pattern overall. In her study of New England witch trials, Carol Karlsen shows that in most cases even when men displayed the same set of characteristic behaviors as female witches, charges of witchcraft either did not come up against them or else were not taken seriously. The charge of witchcraft was so closely tied to femaleness in New England that it was difficult to make a charge stick to a male suspect, except at times of most heightened anxiety (as in Salem). Gender alone was by far the most important defining characteristic.[128] In Russia, by contrast, the charge stuck as firmly and was taken as seriously for women as for men if they displayed the proper telltale traits. Women—defiant or vengeful, healers or itinerants—appear among the accused along with their male counterparts, and, judging by the harshness of penalties, might receive even more severe censure from the courts.[129] Gender norms shaped the situation long before the moment of accusation, in setting the fundamental conditions of men's and women's life possibilities. With men circulating widely in the world and women kept close to home, there simply were fewer women who fit the mold. Gendered activities and venues, not the physical fact or the attributed characteristics of their sex, made them suspect.

5

Undivided Spheres

Gender and Idioms of Magic

MUSCOVITE SOCIETY ORGANIZED ITSELF on principles of status, rank, and generational hierarchy, with gender inserting an additional layer of nuance within each stratum. The salience of status and seniority in calculations of hierarchy and subordination wove through every aspect of Muscovite witchcraft, coloring expectations, shaping behavior, contributing to responses, and, perhaps most important, generating particular points of friction for men and women. These social and cultural strains played out not necessarily in the most obvious arenas of difference as understood in the West, but more remotely, at one step removed.

Where studies of witches in European and Anglo-American contexts have identified distinctively male and female registers, goals, and practices of magic, Russian witches in the seventeenth century showed far less dimorphism.[1] The effort to distinguish male and female magic produces few results, but that finding in itself is an important and telling one. Confronting that impasse, we are forced to part the obscuring shroud of what we might think we "know" about the way gender works. The bifurcation of male and female spheres, familiar from European history (though constantly subject to critique in Western historiography), is hard to document in the Muscovite case, and for substantive reason. Public and private spheres were poorly differentiated, commodity exchange limited, and administrative authority vested in private hands of landholders and patriarchal heads of households. Serfdom and slavery blurred the lines between people and property and endowed landlords and householders with administrative and judicial authority, thus rendering public and private distinctions meaningless. Propelled away from generalities about male and female spheres and roles to documented specifics, the following exploration of male and female magic illuminates how magic served the needs and expressed the anguish of Muscovite men and women.

MALE AND FEMALE SPHERES

Based on the sociological differences of mobility and occupation between the sexes in Muscovite society, one might expect at least small variations in the ways that male and female witches plied their craft. As we will see, some forms of magic did attach differentially to men or women, but by and large such differences were rare and manifested themselves in subtle ways, not where one might expect them. For instance, one might anticipate that profit- and market-oriented magic would arise more frequently in cases involving men than women. Small and undeveloped as the world of commerce was in Muscovy, commercial venues—the market place or tavern—provided the setting for a good number of cases. Indeed, more men than women were accused of or confessed to receiving cash payment for magical services. In 1670 in Tula, a male healer was caught red-handed with the implements of his illicit trade (roots and grasses) and the payment that he had received for his efforts to cure an ailing woman: a piece of canvas and one ruble, ten altyn. In a case prosecuted in Lukh in 1658, a former patient reported that a male healer "took that ulcer away from me, but he also took from me two grivnas of money for that." In the same town in 1663, a priest acknowledged that he had purchased a "witchcraft letter" from a church sexton for six rubles in copper money. Witnesses attested that an itinerant male healer in Voronezh had taken payment of twelve lengths of canvas for healing two women in 1700.[2] Yet, while more evidence survives documenting men trafficking in magic in return for payment in money or goods, men did not have a monopoly on cash-for-magic transactions. In 1630, for instance, a musketeer reported that a "Tatar woman fortune-teller healed his eye and took from him an altyn of money," and then, while holding his hand, she tied something over his eyes and "told him to say a prayer to St. Nicholas."[3] Although fewer cases tie women's magic to payment, female entrepreneurs appear in proportion to their representation among the general pool of the accused, roughly one in four.

A small subset of cases revolved around accusations of utilizing magic to attract customers to the spellcaster's wares and to drive them away from those of competitors. These cases also feature male practitioners more often than female ones, again maintaining roughly the four to one ratio. In 1666, an archpriest of Akhtyrsk testified that a certain Cherkassian weaver named Vaska had confessed to him that he had worked sorcery with stolen communion hosts and "lured people to his shop heretically, so they would come see his wares and would love them, and would cool toward the goods of other weavers."[4] In 1671 in Tula, the criminal (*vor*) Ivashka Vlas'ev syn Popov, a landless peasant from Nizhnii Novgorod, was apprehended with "a bag of grasses and roots and canvas and one ruble, 10 altyn." Questioned, Popov admitted that he had taken the canvas and cash from a townswoman in Tula whom he claimed to have cured of a case of "shrieking." Tortured to confirm his testimony, Popov confessed that "he had been in many towns working such criminality and sorcery and black magic." In particular, "in Dedilov he taught the tavern keeper Mikitka Luk'ianov sorcery and [to inflict] shrieking and bewitchment and gave him various grasses so many people would squander money on drink in his tavern, and for this he got one ruble."[5] In 1636 a tavern keeper in Orlov complained that another tavern keeper in town "brought a root of unknown type from the field and said that that root would make me have lots of drunken people [in my tavern]."[6] Magical marketing was not exclusively a male prerogative, however. In a 1638 case, an old women confessed that "she also has other skills: when merchants have goods that they can't sell, she casts spells for these merchant people over honey, and tells them to rub themselves with that honey while she casts spells: 'Like ferocious bees root about and swarm, so may buyers swarm these merchants for their goods.' And because of that spell, customers swarm these merchants for their goods right away."[7]

If Western studies have identified commercial magic as a male purview, they have even more strongly correlated the sphere of fertility, childbirth, and the nursing and care of children with women's practices and anxieties.[8] This self-evidently female locus of anxiety would seem a promising place to look for gendered witchcraft of a female variant in Muscovy as well. Muscovites also considered matters of reproduction to be prone to magical interference, for good or ill. The time of childbirth and post-partum recovery was a particularly vulnerable period, during which new mothers were sequestered from men and lived in a closely supervised cocoon of protective women. Even priests were prohibited from defiling that female realm with their male presence; in case of imminent death of mother or infant, a priest could administer last rites or emergency baptism from the doorway.[9] M. V. Korogodina finds that confessional guides associated exclusively female practitioners, *babas*, with love and fertility magic.[10] Nevertheless, this area that should by all rights function as an entirely female sphere turns out in the Muscovite case to be open to practitioners of both sexes. Surprisingly, only seven trials of our collection involve spells directed toward fertility, pregnancy, or childbirth, although many more record complaints about bewitchment and killing of children, often along with other family members. Of the seven directly touching on conception, pregnancy, and birth, three attributed miscarriage or infant death to the machinations of witches. In the words of one distraught father, "the children that are born to him soon die from that bewitchment."[11] All three of these attacks on unborn or newborn babies were attributed to female witches, conforming to what one might anticipate both from Muscovite childbirth practices and from European analogues.

However, Muscovite evidence never seems to stick to expected patterns. The rest of the accusations of pregnancy-related magic fell on male practitioners. One man was found with a collection of spells including several related to matters of reproduction: one "for women's quick delivery of babies," another "for the dulling of the senses of a wife so that she will not suffer with childbirth," and a third, "a concoction to give to your wife to drink to find out if she will give birth to a son or daughter."[12] In a second case, two men copied out spells including one meant to influence the sex of a child, "so that women would give birth to babies of the male or female sex."[13] These examples both rest on the evidence of written spells, which were found exclusively in the hands of men, but evidence of male involvement in issues of pregnancy derive from oral testimony as well. Fedka Grigorev called Rebrov, a Mordvin peasant of the Arzamas district, looked in a trough of water to see "why the wife of the peasant Fadei Onisimov has no children, and he said [it was] because she gets no fruit (*ploda*) from her husband."[14] Finally, the carpenter Levka, whom we met in the previous chapter, allegedly boasted of having an effective contraceptive or abortifacient.[15] The interest of men in influencing the sex of their offspring or averting the advent of offspring altogether might fit easily into a model of patriarchal heredity, but their direct involvement in easing the pain and speeding the pace of childbirth, an arena of life from which they were strictly barred, is startling. Even in this most segregated of female activities, men were most frequently identified as the sources of relevant spells and curses.

It is possible that the source of our evidence distorts the sample: women's magic in the context of childbirth may have been so routine as to escape prosecution, whereas male meddling in this arena provoked concern. Given the small number of accusations that reached the courts, it seems likely that some forms of popular ritual perturbed no one and thus never provoked legal inquiry. Still, the fact that trials document the prosecution of men and women on pregnancy-related charges in numbers proportional to their representation in the general population of the accused suggests that anxieties about childbirth were no more skewed in one direction or another than those of any other field of magical activity.

The most likely sites of gender divergence, at least based on abstract assumptions, then, show shared rather than distinctive patterns of magical practice by men and women. If not distinguished by locus or goal, perhaps Muscovite notions of magic depended on gendered ideas about the character traits (and flaws) of the practitioner? European societies associated certain affective states with women, and, by extension, with witches. In studies of witchcraft accusations in Europe and Colonial New England, scholars have noted that anger, envy, lust, ambition, and vanity were understood as signal attributes of witches, and more generally as defining weaknesses of the female sex. Bad-tempered, foul-mouthed women were easily tarred with the witch label, although, as Carol Karlsen cautions, it is important to resist falling into the trap set by the repressive norms of the time, which defined meekness and silence as female virtues, while condemning outspokenness or strong opinions in women.[16]

As embodied by some of the splenetic characters that appeared in the previous chapter, some of the Muscovite women accused of witchcraft were described by their neighbors and acquaintances as spectacularly disagreeable. Some even seem to have made a profession of their unpleasantness, like Daritsa, described above, who terrorized her entire district with curses and threats of impotence. In her testimony, a peasant woman recalled Daritsa's menacing words at a wedding: "*Muzhik*, son of a whore (*shliukhin syn*), you will beg at my feet!" Storming from house to house, feast to feast, and town to town, Daritsa blanketed the population "with all sorts of bad words and mortal oaths."[17] By anyone's standards, this was not a meek, well-behaved woman. But in their testimony, none of her accusers framed her aggressiveness as violating any gendered norms, nor did they suggest that her behavior was particularly outrageous because it was conducted in a female voice. In fact, her husband, Nekraska Trofimov, volubly bragged about his wife's power, saying, "there is no [other] such wise-woman (*znatnitsa*) that knows what Nekraska's Daritsa knows!" More to the point, Nekraska acted equally outrageously, and the couple's conduct was reported evenhandedly by witnesses, with no particular edge in the description of one or the other. Testimony attributes precisely the same words, threats, and curses to husband and wife alike, with no additional accompanying commentary. Thus, for instance, a group of witnesses reported that: "At a feast at the home of the widow Daria Anofrieva's daughter, . . . Nekraska got in a fight with the widowed priest Danila, and Nekraska said to the priest Danila: 'I will eat you up, somehow!' " At another feast, according to witnesses, Nekraska threatened Svirido Sviridov, saying, "Your son-in-law Fedka will never sleep with his wife, and *you* won't sleep with your wife either!"[18] Irascible, undiplomatic, belligerent, and rude, husband and wife shared a common set of negative traits that triggered suspicion equally, without regard to gender.

For every woman tried for cursing a victim, four men would be investigated for shouting ominous threats ranging from the literal and specific ("There will be a fire under your grain shed!") to the chillingly open-ended ("You will see what will happen to you!").[19] Whether uttered by men or women, Muscovite curses were, as Jane Kamensky describes their New England equivalents, "the verbal equivalent of blank checks for bad news." In Shatsk in 1647, a woman jilted in love worked a spell with a curse and a hair from a corpse: "As a dead body does not stand up, so may he, Fedor, perish forever."[20] In 1628 a widowed townswoman brought suspicion on herself when she visited a fellow townswoman and threatened: "You will not live long in my house, [not?] until spring!" In 1660 a dragoon from Sokol' cryptically menaced his comrades with the words: "A man won't have time to blink an eye before I will count every hair on his head!"[21] Kamensky notes that "the full force of a curse ripened over time. . . . This 'remembered quality of curses followed their linguistic form: they were acts of "overpowering speech" delivered in the future tense.' "[22]

In early modern European and North American understandings, an unbridled tongue was viewed as a particularly female proclivity. Cursing and scolding were behaviors that erased the fine line between witches and all of womankind.[23] In Muscovy, anger and ill-temper were apparently equally (and generously) distributed throughout the population and, in practical terms, were equally condemned regardless of the sex of the offender.

In a quest for gendered uses of magic, assumptions imported from European models prove sterile guides to the Muscovite situation. Officials and witnesses seem to have found the gendered traits that were most pronounced in early modern European thought irrelevant to the practice or persecution of witchcraft.

GENDER AND MAGIC AS SYMBOLIC COMMUNICATION

In a world with few available options for self-expression, magic and witchcraft offered Muscovites modes of thinking about the world and expressing themselves in it. Viewing witchcraft as a symbolic form of communication brings into focus the two detectable areas of significant disjuncture between men's and women's use of that magical idiom. In her analysis of "the discourses of magic and witchcraft in early modern France and Germany," Gerhild Scholtz Williams argues that women suffered the brunt of the European witch burnings not only because of the late medieval and early modern intellectual currents that turned witchcraft into a female crime, but also because women were shut out of participation in the debate. Denied the kind of education offered to men, women lacked access to the fundamental tools required for entry into the conversation, much less control over or ability to shape and define discourse.

> Determining who was in—orthodox faith, licit in the practice of magic—and who was out—heterodox, illicit—depended increasingly on the individual's ability to shape and to participate in the language of a chosen and therefore privileged group. The fact that women, especially the old and the poor, represented a large and constant group at the margins, . . . meant that more than anybody else they were susceptible to being pushed beyond society's protective orthodox boundaries.[24]

Control over discourse played an equally decisive role in the struggle against witchcraft in Muscovy, but the tools and terms of the debate were necessarily altogether different, and the boundaries of the acceptable were set in altogether different ways. With no high-culture tradition of spiritualized scientific or natural magic on offer as an antipode to impure, diabolical magic (also not a readily available concept), the resonances of literacy and of orality, of learned and popular, of male and female, were different, and control of "the discourse" a much trickier, more elusive task.

Active practitioners of magic, clients, victims, and even officials, witnesses, and bystanders employed the idiom of witchcraft to augment and expand other modes of communication and expression. Participants from all positions on the spectrum of experience engaged in a common discursive field and utilized a shared conceptual vocabulary and toolkit. Within this unified field, Muscovite men and women generally spoke the same language of word and deed but on occasion expressed themselves in different registers. The sections that follow, on textual magic, largely but not entirely associated with men, and "shrieking," or possession, largely but not entirely associated with women, consider the various languages of magic, the range of expression, and the efficacy, power, and impact of those communicative modes in Muscovy. Strikingly, even in these areas of magical expression where gender divisions emerge most strongly, the men and women involved voiced their experience of witchcraft—and the court scribes transmitted their testimony—in overlapping idioms.

THE POWER OF THE PEN: MAGIC AND THE DANGERS OF UNSANCTIONED LITERACY

In July 1699 the Most Reverend Nikita, Archbishop of Kolomna, lodged a complaint with the governor against a renegade monk for possession of a root and a little booklet (*malaia knishka*). The archbishop was moved to bring the action after a retired stableman named Senka Kazimer denounced the monk, accusing him of witchcraft (*volshebstvennoe delo*).[25] The defendant, who identified himself as Afonasei of the Resurrection Monastery, a simple monk, openly confessed his crimes, but insisted that Senka, the Judas who turned him in, had colluded with him and, in fact, had been the instigator and the brains behind their joint enterprise. According to Afonasei, earlier that year the two men had gone to Moscow and stayed with Senka's father-in-law, who gave Senka the problematic booklet. Senka recognized that the book was mysterious (*zagadochnaia*), but neither of them knew for sure what kind of magic it contained. When the pair left Moscow and headed to the nearby town of Kolomna, the clever Senka cooked up a scheme for turning the book into a sure-fire moneymaker. Baldly stated, "Senka told the monk to pretend that he knew how to tell fortunes (*vorozhit'*), and they would be able to collect money." Once in Kolomna, they put their plan into action. "The monk and the informer Senka went among the monks and among all ranks of Kolomna residents to their houses with that book, and, not having any idea what they were doing, looked purposely as if they were reading that book, and told fortunes. Pouring water into vessels, they would look in that water and pretend to tell fortunes, and pretend to drive out unclean spirits."[26]

Witnesses from Kolomna confirmed that the charlatans had circulated through the town and local monasteries and convents. The informer, Senka, placed full responsibility on his erstwhile partner, testifying that people of all ranks invited the monk into their homes and "he, the monk, reading, pours water into a vessel and looks into the water and tells fortunes by that little book, and predicts about buried treasure . . . and [pretends to] drive unclean spirits out of houses. Following this fortune-telling and prediction . . . he, the monk, dug up the land of that monastery, in the presence of the monks, but whether they found treasure in that monastery or not, he, Senka, doesn't know."[27]

The testimony and the booklet itself caused consternation, first in the archbishop's residence and then in the governor's office. The problem was that the book was written in some language other than Russian, and no one knew what it said. The governor reported that "in Kolomna that book was shown to those people who know the languages of other lands so that someone could read it," but no one in Kolomna could figure it out. Flummoxed, the provincial officials packed up the book and the monk, "locked in chains," and sent them under guard directly to Boyar Tikhon Nikitich Streshnev in the Military Chancellery in Moscow, because "there is no one in Kolomna who can read the letters of the above mentioned book."[28]

The sham fortune-telling derived its entire inspiration and plausibility from the power and mystery of the written word. The monk admitted with disarming frankness that he and his double-crossing accomplice carried out a deliberate and premeditated fraud, but both the initial idea and the success of the scam built on the inaccessibility of the text. The recondite writing established their credentials, endowing their pseudo-fortune-telling with an edge of mystery and danger that drew clients to them and filled their wallets.

An aura of mystery surrounds and elevates incantatory speech wherever magic is practiced. In Russia as elsewhere, practitioners impressed their clients with muttered, inaudible, and incomprehensible susurration and atmospheric obfuscation. Witnesses testified that they listened as the accused muttered spells over troughs of water or root-infused teas, "but what those spells were, I do not know." The murkiness of magicians' articulation is reflected in the terms for their craft: *sheptat'/sheptun* (to whisper, whisperer) referred to the act of spell making or prophesying.

If speech was deliberately obscured for dramatic effect, in a predominantly illiterate society, writing by its essence added an element of the arcane to any situation. A long tradition of esoteric writing, from the gibberish-covered magical bowls of ancient Babylon to the papyri and amulets of ancient Egypt, from medieval grimoires to Prospero's books, endows writing itself with mystical power. In most of these cases, the text presents itself with occult trappings, visually exhibiting its divorce from all things mundane through ornate, archaic, or indecipherable calligraphy, cryptic letters, runes or symbols, or unfamiliar language.[29] In Muscovy, in light of the pervasive illiteracy, writing did not have to be particularly arcane, archaic, or elegantly calligraphic to appear mysteriously powerful. To the illiterate majority—by Gary Marker's estimate rudimentary literacy reached 3 to 5 percent by the late seventeenth century—the way that scribbles on paper could communicate thoughts across time and space must have held some essential mystery, regardless of appearance.[30] The efficacy of those indecipherable marks in transforming lives and changing outcomes was evident

The Life of Antonii Siiskii, 1648, l. 172, Old Russian School. Courtesy of the State Historical Museum (Gosudarstvennyi Istoricheskii Muzei), Moscow. GIM, 23905, Shchukinskoe sobranie, No. 750, 1648; ff. 171 v–172. Ecclesiastical and some formal secular documents were copied out in calligraphic lettering and adorned with ornate rubrication and illumination. Early printed bibles and tsarist decrees mimicked the calligraphy and ornamentation of their hand-copied forbearers. (See also plate 8)

to anyone who had any dealings with the state authorities, landlords, or masters. As for presentation, although the church developed calligraphic traditions in liturgical manuscripts and even carried over the elaborately interwoven letters and ornate rubrics in the early printed editions of biblical texts, secular documentation was copied out in the business-like rapid script of the chancelleries, with no frills and no decoration. Underscoring the point that magic in Muscovy was essentially unconnected with and not about religion, the writing habits observable in surviving spells and spell books fall almost unwaveringly into this secular manuscript tradition (although some manuscripts of high magic, such as chiromancy, use the trappings of ecclesiastical calligraphy and rubrication).[31]

In a world where the written word was understood to be primarily the prerogative of men of power and their delegates, unauthorized writing could, and did, raise questions. Given the untoward uses to which men like Afonasei and Senka might turn it, some of these questions were apparently well justified. Where Williams posits that in the West literacy and education protected men who dabbled in the occult sciences from the stigma of black magic, in Muscovy to some extent the opposite obtained. Literacy and even the possession of

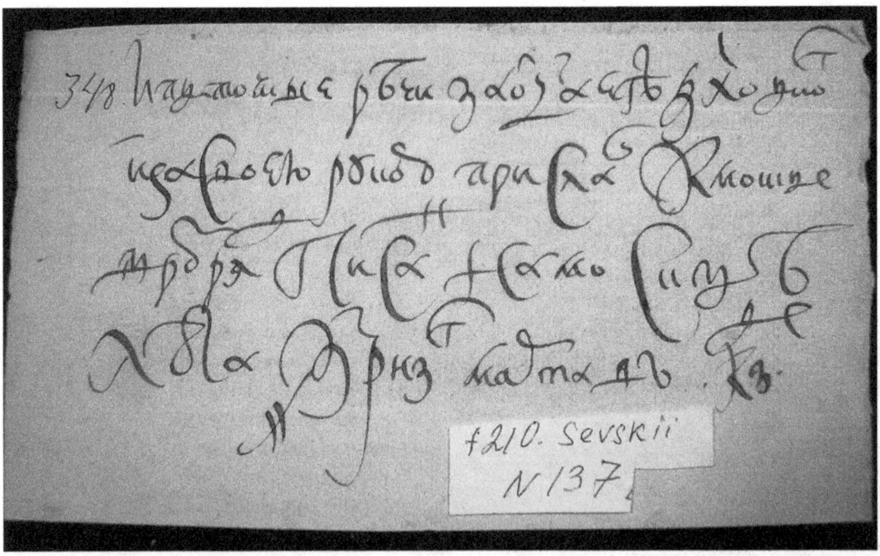

*A page from a chancellery document, in good Muscovite bureaucratic fashion, reports on a report sent to the Military Chancellery: "And testimony taken under torture (*pytochnye rechi*) signed by his spiritual father and by his [own] hand I sent to Moscow to the Razriad. Written in Moscow in the year ZRNZ [7157 = 1649], March 27." The unadorned presentation and no-frills chancellery hand are typical of both administrative documents and written spells. RGADA, f. 210, Sevskii stol, stlb. 137, l. 348.*

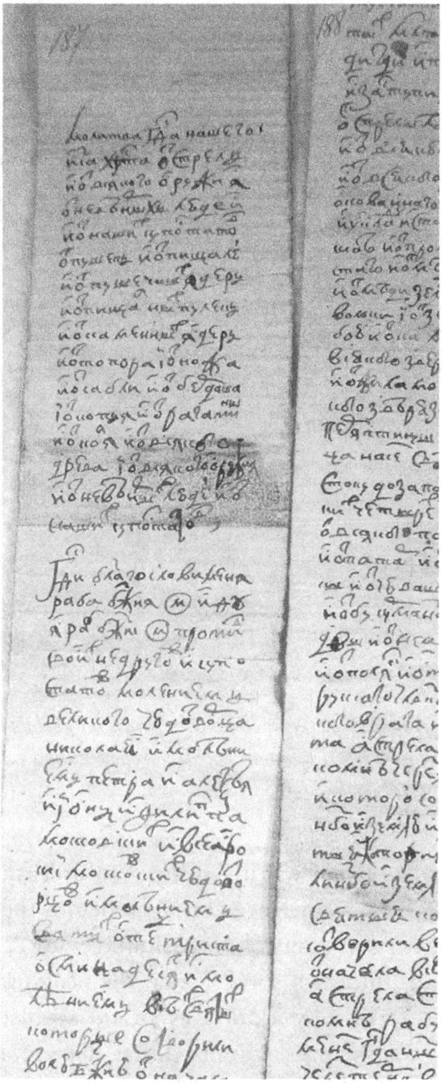

Page from a spell book, confiscated and presented as evidence in the trial of cavalry captain (rotmistr) *Semyon Vasil'ev syn Aigustov for witchcraft and rape. RGADA, f. 210, Prikaznyi stol, stlb. 1133, ll. 187–88. Spell books were written out in the workmanlike handwriting* (skoropis') *that characterized administrative memos and decrees. The page on the left opens with a supplicatory prayer or spell that calls on "our Lord Jesus Christ" for protection against gunshot or arrow wounds or against "any kind of weapon," against all untrustworthy people, and against "our enemies."*

scraps of writing put men at risk for witchcraft accusations. Trials very often originated with the sighting of a piece of paper in the hands of a person who had no obvious official need or license to be handling such explosive material. If that paper was found to have writing on it, the implications could be grave. Perfilii Fedorov Rakhmaninov, former governor of Galich, fended off a charge of witchcraft lodged against him when he was found possessing a bit of anise wrapped in paper with the name of the herb written on it. Although the suspect explained that he used the sweet smelling anise to counteract the foul odor of

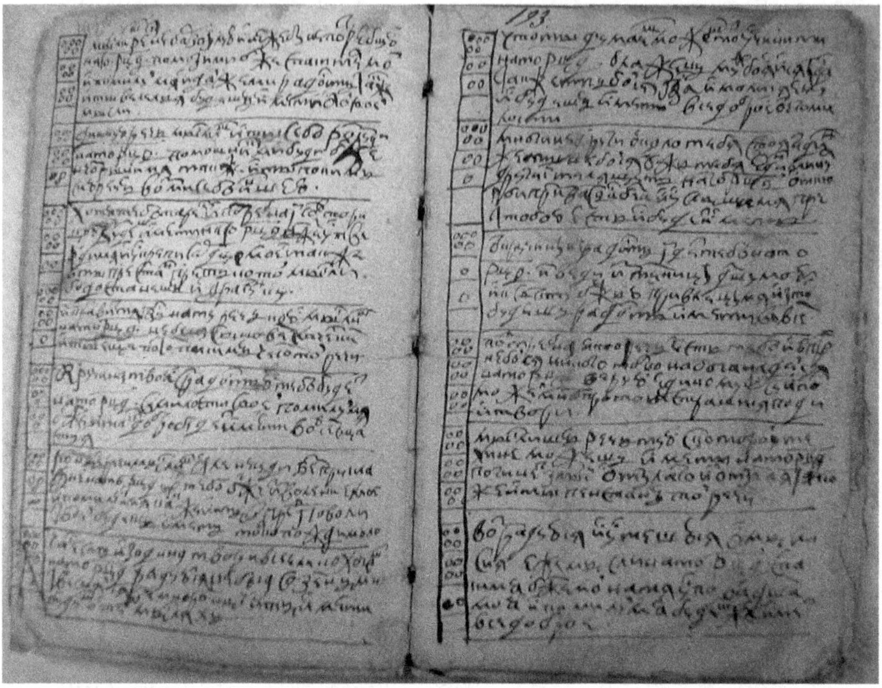

From the spell book of Semyon Vasil'ev syn Aigustov. These pages show combinations of dots resulting from throwing dice. Each combination predicts a particular, rather open-ended and vague outcome. RGADA, f. 210, Prikaznyi stol, stlb. 1133, ll. 192v–93.

ulcerating sores in his mouth, this harmless bit of writing sufficed to unleash a full investigation.[32] In 1676 a peasant from Galich was brought before the governor in Kostroma under severe suspicion because he was found with "a root and with some kind of writing of an unknown sort." Fetka, the peasant, testified that the writing had been given to him by a priest as an aid against fever. Brought to a confrontation with Fetka, the priest admitted that "he wrote it out with his own hand and gave it to Fetka against fever." He claimed that "the writing was copied out of the Bible." The governor uncharitably interpreted the priest's declaration as proof of his guilt: "And by that token it is evident that this priest works witchcraft (*volshebstvuet*) because in the Bible, Sovereign, such articles are not written anywhere. [So] I, your slave, ordered an investigation and had that priest write something to compare with that writing, and that writing I sent to you, Great Sovereign, in Moscow together with this report."[33]

Possession of writing also triggered an investigation in Toropets, when a local servitor grabbed a paper out of the hands of a man in a tavern, only to discover that the paper contained two spells, one against gunshot wounds, the other against fever. The investigation pulled in two other men, a minstrel and a musketeer. The minstrel claimed he learned the spells from his brother, but had been drunk when he dictated them to the man in the bar, because "he is a drinking person." The musketeer said he learned the spells from his father, now missing in territories handed over to the "Germans." After imprisonment and two torture sessions, the men were released, with promises to refrain from keeping such spells in the future.[34]

Muscovite authorities were deeply concerned with retaining a monopoly on all forms of power and control and with eliminating disorderly spontaneity. The pen posed a clear and present danger when wielded by the wrong people. As Elena N. Eleonskaia noted in her 1917 study of early modern witchcraft, "any scrap of paper, and even more so, a letter or a notebook, were grounds for an accusation of sorcery."[35] Writing out of season, without obvious reason or authorization, provoked unease among the general population as well. Muscovite subjects proved ready and willing to denounce those among them given to carrying bits of paper on their persons or known to put pen to paper by their own volition.

Illustrative of the anxiety incurred by undisciplined literacy, an anonymous and decidedly suspicious set of papers found in Beloozero in 1694 precipitated an investigation at the highest level, focused entirely on the act of writing.[36] Heading up the stairs of the governor's office to report to work early one morning, a guard came across a kerchief tied with a thread. Untying it, he discovered an official-looking document sealed with an official seal, and several papers covered with writing. Terrified by his discovery, he rushed directly to the governor's home, presumably waking him up, so he could hand over the incriminating papers. The governor too was appalled by the horror that had landed in his lap: a forged document sealed over his own name, thereby implicating him in a seditious act of abusing the sovereigns' names (an act formally defined as treason in the 1649 law code). Claiming that he had not dared read the other papers, he sent them directly to the co-tsars, Ivan and Peter Alekseevich, and to the boyars in the Chancellery of the Great Palace (*Prikaz Bol'shogo dvortsa*) in Moscow. There, the papers were read and catalogued. One perplexing and disturbing document in the bunch was a sliver of paper bearing a cryptic list of alphanumeric characters.[37] The original fragment is preserved in the case file.

These clusters of letters in strips likely represent the tosses of "bones" or dice by which fortune-tellers predicted people's futures. A guide to reading "bones" or "beans," confiscated from a slave in Tobolsk in 1630, lists predictions under permutations of the letters А, В, Г, Д, representing the numbers one through four. Each toss of three dice is associated with an outcome: "В Г Г: The heart trembles and rejoices, and illness and health only seem to be the force of another hand. . . . Distance your enemies and a peaceful time [will follow]."[38] Another manual (see figure above) illustrates the pages of the terrible

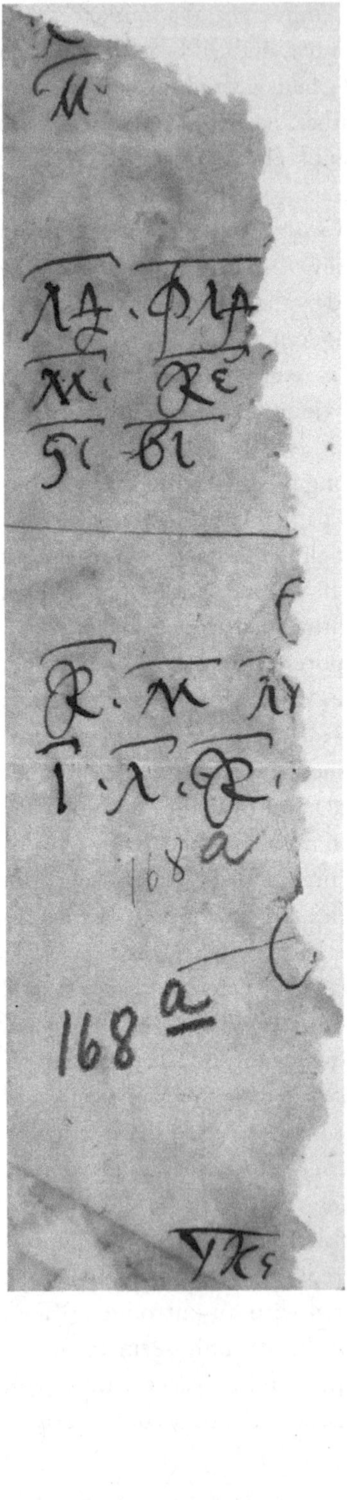

A mysterious sliver of an "anonymous letter" or scrap of writing with coded letters, presumably part of a fortune-telling rubric to be used when throwing dice (bones or beans), was discovered in 1694 in Beloozero. The discovery of this slip of paper, taken as a clear token of "criminality and magic and evil intentions," precipitated an all-out investigation in order to hunt down whoever had written it. Officials were instructed to search for people of any rank, lay or clerical, high or low, or even female. RGADA, f. 210, Belgorodskii stol, stlb. 1032, l. 168a.

Aigustov's spell book with similar patterns for fortune-telling, but his provides interpretations of combinations of dots, representing the sides of dice, in place of alphabetic clusters.

So serious was the discovery of this slip of paper that the chancellery officials determined that the anonymous letters (*podmetnye pis'ma*) signaled "criminality and magic and evil intentions (*vorovstvo i charodeistvo i zlye umysly*)." Orders arrived from Moscow instructing the governor:

> to search where people live, whether in [monastic] cells or in houses, to see if there are any kinds of criminal writings or roots or other poisonous substances, and whoever is found to have such things, those things should be taken and described and they themselves and their cellmates and servants should be questioned about that, and if some discrepancy arises among them, they should be confronted with each other and they should be questioned harshly according to the *Sobornoe Ulozhenie* and other decrees and statutes.

The governor was ordered to compare the handwriting with that of likely suspects and show the original to many people, in hopes of identifying its author. The Moscow authorities stipulated that not only monks and townsmen should be questioned:

> Then investigate whether . . . there are people of any rank or prisoners sent from Moscow who might engage in such criminal plots, or among upstanding people or servants or servitors in the settlements outside of the monastery or people of any rank whatsoever, men or women, widows and girls who might themselves know how to read and write, because anonymous letters can sometimes turn out to be from women.[39]

Although the orders stressed that women could be literate and could pen such dangerous works, the reminder illustrates how exceptional such an eventuality would have been.[40] It also underscores the anxiety spawned by the amorphous threat of underground literacy. The danger could lurk anywhere.

The instructions of how to proceed further in the case of the mysterious letters underscores how seriously the authorities took a case of unauthorized writing, a matter that they labeled *velikie dela*: "weighty matters."

> Whoever is identified in this way, whether of the male or female sex, and is identified in an honest investigation, their homes should be searched to find evidence of secret activities (*tainyi obychai*) and searched for any written materials and for any anonymous letters like the ones described above, and

> their handwriting should be checked against that of the anonymous letters. For additional evidence, make them write something in front of you and if by the evidence of their writing they turn out to have written the anonymous letter, question them about the matter and whether they themselves wrote those letters and whether they know about these weighty matters and whether they saw or heard from someone or they composed those letters and wrote them simply frivolously, for no reason, or why, and was it through their own evil intentions or on the instructions of someone else, and with whom they sent those letters to Beloozero or did they bring them themselves?[41]

Once the suspects were identified, the orders specified that they were to be questioned, tortured, and locked up in chains. Under no circumstances should they be permitted those dangerous controlled substances: paper and ink (*bumagi i chernil im davat' ne velet*).[42] The special investigator brought along an executioner from Moscow to carry out the multiple rounds of torture and, ultimately, the execution of those convicted in this flagrant abuse of literacy.[43]

Writing itself carried ambivalent potential. Miskha Svashevskoi's case offers a good example. A man whose life was shaped in all dimensions by official paperwork and interactions with the bureaus of state, he used his unusual gift of literacy to maneuver his way from bondage to freedom, but then that same literacy ultimately took him from freedom to the pyre. For Mishka, literacy entailed both empowerment and risk. He served as a serf- or slave-bailiff on the estate of *stolnik* Fedor Tikhonovich Zykov in Vologda province in the 1670s. There, inspired by one of his fellow bailiff-clerks, he forged a deed of manumission over his master's falsified signature. With this sleight-of-hand, Mishka freed himself from bondage and, through the magic of the pen, transformed himself into someone entirely different. For good reason the law code of 1669 included the stipulation that clerks should be closely supervised to make sure that they gave out no exemplars of documents to anyone at all.[44] Once liberated, thanks to his ability to read and write, Svashevskoi moved quickly into the circle of chancellery clerks in Moscow, where he may have picked up piecework as a copyist. He styled himself a "*d'iak*," or high-ranking chancellery administrator, on a document he copied for the Novgorodian Chancellery. This self-aggrandizement won specific mention in the enumeration of his crimes. His illicit literacy took on occult shades when his hidden past came to light, and a search turned up a host of spell books hidden in a hole in the floor of his former master's storeroom.[45]

Closely questioned about the sources of his various spells, Mishka named a large number of people who had provided him with texts or with material to copy. He had been inspired to forge his way to freedom in the first place by a fellow bondsman on Fedor's estate, Vaska Alekseev. He named "a resident of Vologda" as the source of a dangerous collection of spells involving summoning demons. Under torture, Mishka identified the Vologda man as a prominent merchant by the name of Gavrilo Feteev, and also implicated Gavrilo's illiterate brother. The denunciations continued to snowball. Another little book of spells "was written by Fedor Zykov's man . . . and Mishka took that notebook from [another of Fedor's men], Pron'ka Buslaev, in the storeroom while Pron'ka wasn't there."[46] Others on the estate had pestered Mishka to provide them with spells. Once in Moscow, Mishka came in contact with more spell collectors. According to his testimony, the Moscow chancelleries were rife with spell enthusiasts. Mishka claimed he had commissioned a palace clerk (*dvortsovoi pod'iachei*), Karpushka Tarakanov, to copy down spells as he read them aloud from a book, perhaps the one borrowed from his colleague, Iakushko Shguki, also implicated in the case. Once these men were named, they too endured harsh interrogation and torture. Karpushka explained that he had found a collection of healing spells lying around in the offices of the Chancellery of the Great Treasury. The clerk Iakushko was questioned and tortured, and implicated his friend Karpushka along with his friend's father. Pressed further, "Iakushko said he also took a different book of spells from his cousin, clerk of the Chancellery of Service Lands, Oska Timofeev, but he did nothing with it and gave it to no one to copy."[47]

This mushrooming list of individuals involved shows broad circulation of these spells. Mishka said he had copied an even more radioactive spell, a "renunciation of Christ-God," from Ivashko Volosheninov, clerk of the Chancellery of Service Lands, from originals in Ivashko's hand. He confessed to copying a twelve-page notebook of spells also from Ivashko's stash, "but he didn't see whose handwriting it was, because Ivashko told him what to write from that notebook, all the while holding it in his hands."[48] Ivashko extended the chain of suspects when interrogated under torture about the origins of his God-denying spells. As the questioning continued, Mishka and Ivashko named yet more sources in the ever-expanding web of exchange of spells, including another Vologda resident, a highly placed state secretary, and his son. The biggest fish named in this extraordinary network of spell collectors and spell copiers was Artamon Sergeevich Matveev, favorite of the late Tsar Aleksei Mikhailovich, recently fallen from grace after the death of his royal patron. Although the evidence adduced here comes from a single court case and a single trove of spells, it implicates at least sixteen men, plus the unknown person who dropped some spells that Ivashka found near the Prechistenkii Gates and the mysterious clerk who left his magical notebook on the floor of the Great Treasury.

The power of the written word is evident in every aspect of this case. Recall that it began with Svashevskoi's forged letter of emancipation. The landlord, Zykov, initially announced to the boyars in Moscow simply that his slaves (*kabalnye*) had run away from him. Only later did he learn about the falsified manumission documents. "That same day," a fellow *stolnik* by the name of Andrei Kolychev asked Zykov, "what kind of man had he let go who could write?" A literate slave was too precious to let slip away, but the danger went beyond simple loss. A literate fugitive was an unpredictable menace when loosed on the world. Kolychev knew the inside story, because one of the fugitives, Vaska Alekseev, had taken refuge with Kolychev's brother-in-law, Prince Semyon Zvenigorodskoi. The runaway had presented Zvenigorodskii with an official-looking manumission document that was, to all appearances, legitimate and signed in Fedor's hand.[49]

Fedor Zykov eventually got his hands on one of the forged releases and turned it in to the authorities.

> The letter he said belonged to his man Vaska Tatarinov. And here is what is written in the release document:
>
> Memo of *stolnik* Fedor Tikhov syn Zykov: I, Fedor, manumitted my bondsman Vaska Sergeev syn Tatarinov at his will, to live wherever he wants to live, and I and my wife and my children and descendants (*vodicham*?) have no further claims on him. In the year 1676, October 20th.[50]

The memo looked genuine and functioned effectively in the world to transform a slave into a free man, a textual shape shifting that threatened the stability of society and identity.

The written word was imagined to have a potent materiality. When the content of confiscated material was particularly blistering, local officials protested that they had not read the papers or even looked at them, or they explained that they did not dare to copy the "unseemly words" into their reports. For instance, when a hunter was brought in with a collection of spells on his person, the governor of Ilimsk reported primly to the tsar: "I ordered cathedral priest Obrasim and customs official Ivan Kriukov to read that writing, and I myself, your slave, did not read that letter."[51] In the case of the anonymous documents dropped on the town hall stairs in Beloozero, the timorous governor reported that he ordered the document read aloud, "but I didn't dare stamp and examine the letters, and so in the presence of those people I ordered them listed and sealed and sent to you in Moscow on that same day."[52] The act of reading could unlock the power of a spell. Mishka Svashevskoi explained to a friend that he had a copy of a particularly blasphemous spell but refrained from reading it. One had to be careful about such things: "if he should start to read it without knowing what it was, he wouldn't be able to rid himself of demons (*besy*)."[53] Even without looking, however, or without the ability to read, the bearer of a spell might benefit from its talismanic force. Many of those found carrying spells on tattered scraps of paper declared themselves unable to read. In 1693 an unfortunate fellow, Kozlov resident Ivashko Adamov, was tortured with hot pincers and "the wheel (*koleso*)" to force him to tell the truth about a "criminal written spell for weapons (*vorovskoe zagovornoe pis'mo o ruzhiia*)." The most the torturers could elicit from him was that he "got the writing during the unsettled time in 1682 in Tambov province at the Trinity Monastery," and from there he took it home and wore it on his person while at home. "And he didn't read it to anyone, nor did he let anyone copy it. He kept it at his home only, and he himself, Ivashko, cannot read."[54] The paper and ink alone, the words on the page, sufficed to work their amuletic effect, protecting him from gunshot wounds.

In a cruel mirroring of the offenses committed, the joint sovereigns Ivan and Peter Alekseevich sentenced the illiterate Ivashko to a punishment that fit the crime: the spell discovered in his possession was to be "burned on his back," after which he was to be held in the stocks, beaten mercilessly with a knout, and exiled for the rest of his life.[55] The same gruesome punishment was inflicted on one of the men implicated along with Mishka Svashevskoi for copying and keeping books of spells: "He should be beaten with the knout and all those spells should be burned on his back, and he should be exiled with his wife and children to Siberia and registered as an agricultural peasant."[56] Searing human flesh with texts set aflame, this pattern of punishment reflects a potent sense of the physical power inherent in writing.

The focus on the act of writing surfaces again in one of the cases that opened this book. In April 1647, Iurii Shestakov, a clerk of the Zemskii prikaz, informed against Garasimko Kostiantinov, a servant of the New Savior Monastery in Kozlov, on the grounds that he, Iurii, had witnessed that servant holding some kind of "unseemly" writing (*neistovye pis'ma*). Iurii tore the paper out of the servitor's hands, sealed it, and turned it in to the authorities. The boyars and other men of duma rank who heard the case found this blatant act of spontaneous reading and writing (understood as "criminality") of unidentifiable documents (presumptively assumed to be "heretical notebooks") as alarming as did the clerk Iurii. The boyars questioned Garasimko closely, not so much about the content of the letters as about the origins and nature and explanation of his literacy. The day after receiving Iurii's denunciation, they interrogated Garasimko:

about whether those heretical notebooks (*ereticheskie tetratki*) were his and whether he wrote them and who taught him such criminality (*vorovstvo*) and from whom he copied them.

And the servitor Garasimko in questioning said that he learned to write from the same master as the clerk Iurii Shestakov, but afterward, during his wanderings, he forgot how to write, and he learned to write again from Iurii Shestakov and Iurii gave him many letters in his own hand to copy. And for the sake of learning, he copied those letters, but whether he copied those notebooks or not, he doesn't remember.[57]

Now that Iurii himself had been reciprocally incriminated, he too was called on to testify. He admitted that he and Garasimko had indeed learned to write from the same master, and in fact they had been close friends and lived together for many years. Nonetheless, he protested rather unconvincingly, Garasimko hadn't returned from his wanderings to study with him, and moreover Garasimko couldn't possibly have learned to write from him, because Garasimko was years older than he, Iurii. As a defense against Garasimko's innuendos, Iurii protested that he had served the sovereign faithfully by informing against his criminal friend.

On the first day of the trial, the notebooks themselves were produced in evidence. The record laconically remarks that "in those same notebooks according to the investigation was written over and over again in many places: *slave of God, Garasim*."[58] The harmless, even pious content did nothing to allay the court's fears. In fact, they ignored the content entirely and focused monomaniacally on the handwriting and the act of writing. Presiding Boyar Ivan Morozov insisted that Garasimko should write out those same words in the presence of the court, so that his writing could be compared with the incriminating document. "And the notebooks were shown to Garasimko. And having looked at the notebooks, Garasimko said: 'It is possible that writing is his writing, but honestly, he can't identify it because he wrote a lot during the course of his studies.'"[59]

Garasimko's testimony and defense also focused on the act of writing. Tortured to confess, he admitted to having copied the notebooks but structured his defense by harping on his simplicity and lack of forethought. In "torture testimony," he explained that when he was a boy, in Voronezh province,

walking along the road, I found some writing—two notebooks with spells against gunshot wounds. And being stupid from birth, not knowing how to write, I started to copy out one of the notebooks and it was my first attempt at writing. . . . I found those writings and copied one of the notebooks from

> stupidity, not knowingly, from simplicity. And now I, unfortunate one, lie under guard. I am oozing pus from the wounds resulting from torture. Wretched and in great deprivation, I am perishing and dying of hunger.[60]

For his dreadful crime of wanting to learn to write and copying out a few innocuous words, he was tortured hideously, but in the end, he was released on surety.[61]

Texts belonged in the sanctioned venues and in the hands of authorized clerics and officials, not in the pockets of wandering hunters, stablemen, or lowly monastic servants. When writing escaped the corridors of power and floated free among the population, villains might steal the power of official or sacred words for their own lawless ends. Ordinary Muscovites appear to have shared their rulers' suspicion of rampant, unchecked literacy, which in its unfathomable way, threatened the stable hierarchies that held Muscovite society together. Even when deployed by trained clerks like Vaska Alekseev and Mishka Svashevskoi, whose jobs involved their writing skills, writing outside the safe confines of those official functions—for pleasure, in pursuit of private goals, or just for the sake of writing—incurred suspicion and carried a degree of risk.

"BLACK BOOKS" AND THE MENACE OF THE WRITTEN WORD

Several of the cases discussed so far hint at yet another level of danger posed by unsanctioned writing. Some of the suspects were charged with keeping "God-denying letters" and "heretical books," described in the same language used in the official decrees that condemned such works. Tsar Aleksei Mikhailovich's 1653 decree, sent to all corners of the tsardom with orders to have it read aloud by town criers in marketplaces on crowded market days, chided "ignorant people, who, having forgotten the fear of God and not remembering the hour of their death and not bearing in mind the consequent eternal torment, keep *forbidden heretical and fortune-telling books and letters and spells*, and roots, and grasses. . . ."[62] Forbidden heretical and fortune-telling books, also known as "black books" (*chernye knigi*), appear with some regularity in the official texts condemning magical practice from the beginning of the sixteenth century on. The *Domostroi* condemned "black book magic" (*chernoknizhestvo, chernoknizhie*), along with the use of spells, "sorcery and witchcraft as propounded in *Rafli* and almanacs [and other astrological and prognostic texts], censured books, . . . and any other Devil-inspired art."[63] Penitential guides instructed priests to inquire of those taking confession: "Did you keep forbidden books or keep them at home?"[64] "Black books" make an appearance again in Grigorii Kotoshikhin's enumeration of the various forms of punishment assigned to particular crimes in Muscovy in the 1660s. Kotoshikhin asserts that *chernoknizhestvo*, along with sacrilege, stealing from a church, sodomy, and, interestingly, unauthorized exegesis on religious texts, earned execution by burning alive.[65]

Though frequently condemned in ecclesiastical texts and law codes, black books enter the transcripts of actual trials rather rarely. Of the 227 seventeenth-century trials for magic and witchcraft that I have examined, a grand total of 6 involve charges of keeping black books.[66] One of the most serious charges of keeping black books comes from the case of Mishka Svashevskoi and the circle of runaway bondsmen and chancellery clerks discussed above. This trial clarifies what seventeenth-century Muscovites had in mind when they threw about charges of keeping "black books." When Fedor Zykov discovered that the fugitive Svashevskoi had forged a manumission document, he "questioned people in his household about that emancipation document, using force to make them speak." The slave Vaska Tatarinov informed his master that in addition to writing his way to freedom, "Mishka Svashevskoi has *black books*, and Mishka copied them from books that belonged to Boyar Artamon Sergeevich Matveev." After hearing this dire report, "Fedor did not question his people more but ordered all of them clapped in irons and informed the boyars about it."[67] This was a wise move on his part, since Matveev was a big fish, and his involvement took the case to a higher level still.

When Zykov's case reached the boyars, Matveev was already facing high-level charges of practicing magic and keeping black books himself. This was a tense and precarious time in the capital. Tsar Aleksei Mikhailovich had died in January, and a shake-up at court accompanied the succession to the throne of his son, Fedor. One of those to fall from power was Matveev, a favored adviser of the late tsar but out of grace under the new regime. Moscow was rife with dangerous and sometimes deadly rumors, and the Danish ambassador to Russia, Friedrich von Gabel, reported one of the stories that apparently were making the rounds at the time. The ambassador repeated the accounts of eyewitnesses who claimed that they had watched as Matveev and his foreign collaborators (including, variously, a baptized Jew, a German doctor, and a Russian diplomat of Romanian origins) "locked themselves in a room and read a black book (*chernaia knizhka*)." They "made the devil swear to do their will but the devil excused himself and asked that first they should ask a small dwarf who had hidden behind the stove to leave, since he could do nothing while there were people present who had not surrendered to him." When they discovered that the dwarf Zakharka was indeed hiding behind the stove, Matveev kicked him, breaking his ribs, and threw him out of the room. Afterward, "the devil had to dance to their pipe and was said to do tricks, taken from heaven, meaning that he could darken the sun and the moon."[68] Matveev and his supporters insisted that the books in question were merely "anatomical diagrams, medical advice, Arabic numerals and algebraic exercises," in other words, precisely the kind of foreign, imported texts that would set off alarms.[69]

Once Svashevskoi's slave manumission case was tied to the high profile Matveev trial, Zykov's men were carted off to Moscow and interrogated. Although they provided tidbits of information incriminating Matveev, for the most part their testimony stuck to the circulation of magical texts within their own world of serf-bailiffs, runaway slaves, and low-level clerks. Questioned before the assembled boyars in the Golden Hall in the Moscow Kremlin, Miskha Svashevskoi said: "Vaska [Alekseev] has a notebook hidden in the floor of the porch of Fedor's house, written in his own hand. *And in it is written a renunciation of Christ God.*" Vaska reversed the charges, saying:

> Mishka has *black books*, and he, Vaska, knows that he does because three weeks or so ago Mishka showed him a notebook with his own hands at Fedor's house on the porch, and that notebook was written in Mishka's hand.

Vaska noted that Mishka had boasted to him of his black books "while drunk," but the books were frighteningly real. "Mishka was drunk, but those written pages lie in Mishka's storeroom, in the ground. . . . And Vaska saw a renunciation of Christ-God written out in that notebook."[70]

The boyar court dispatched a high-ranking state secretary to investigate, and his findings bore out Vaska's testimony. In Mishka Svashevskoi's storeroom, a box with letters was taken out of the ground. "And in the box was a notebook with twelve pages, and of those, five were written on. . . . On the first page . . . and onto the next page was written a spell for withstanding torture. On that same page in two lines and on the following four pages was written a renunciation of faith and of the Lord God himself, and a spell for calling demons (*besy*) and for seducing the female sex. . . ."[71] This final spell, and not the seemingly graver renunciation of God, was the one that Mishka had not dared read aloud, lest he be beset by demons.

This evidence finally provides a glimpse into what, specifically, characterized "black books." Mishka's circle did not participate in a world of imported Greek esoterica, but rather, in their eyes, his books qualified as "black" because they contained incontrovertibly maleficent texts involving renunciation of God and the summoning of demons. The use of this powerful label was a risky business. Actual charges of "black books" remained rare and were often retracted under pressure, suggesting a degree of fear and awe that lingered around these particular forms of writing, banned in law because of their association with specifically heretical, treasonous leanings and foreign, "Hellenic" learning. However, the explosiveness of an accusation of keeping black books also reflected the broader, widely shared suspicion of unshackled literacy evident in Muscovite society. The horror of *chernoknizhestvo* displayed in intensified form a far more generalized fear of literacy run amok, of illicit copying and circulation of texts, and of the capacity of writing to serve the disruptive ends of subversive individuals instead of the authorized goals of sanctioned hierarchy.

Simon Franklin argues that early Rus' pursued a path to literacy somewhat different from that of most of medieval Europe, where learning was funneled fairly consistently through the interlocking channels of church and state, religion and administration. In Rus', by contrast, Franklin finds, alongside the rise of an ecclesiastical form of writing, a spread of casual literacy, symptomatic of a diffuse, informal, pragmatic acquisition of reading and writing skills.[72] The same dispersion and informality continued to characterize education in the Muscovite era, as evident from the curriculum vitae of Garasimko, described above, who learned to write from a local man, forgot all he had learned as he grew to adulthood, and picked it up again on his own by copying any bit of writing that came into his hands, receiving casual instruction from a friend.[73] Muscovy developed few formal schools or institutions of learning. Boys learned to read and write from anyone they could find: from their fathers, local priests, clerks, or estate bailiffs. This anarchic acquisition of literacy made it uncontrollable, and one never knew quite who could read or write or what they might be reading or writing.

The dangers of such writing, as we have seen, could be tangible, effectuating the mysterious metamorphosis of slave to free man, of lowly estate bailiff to well-placed chancellery clerk. When writing was involved, suspicions intensified and simple misdemeanors might be interpreted as heinous crimes. In the same extensive investigation that implicated Artamon Matveev, for instance, a clerk of the governor's office in Vologda had to answer witchcraft charges pertaining to his own extensive library. The court carefully catalogued the "printed and manuscript books confiscated from Senka Vasileev in his house on December 12, 1676." The collection consisted entirely of editions of Psalms, Gospels, and lives of saints.[74] A suspicious list indeed! But the very fact that the man owned books raised suspicions and constituted important evidence in the case.

A patently different appreciation of literacy was at work than that obtaining in early modern Europe, where literacy might confer protection and elite status.[75] In Muscovy writing words on paper without explicit orders from one's sovereign, administrative superior, or master could easily lead to trouble. Not all writing incurred suspicion, of course, and the seventeenth century witnessed a countervailing tide of newly developing literary genres, such as the tales discussed in the previous chapter. The first "autobiography," by the schismatic archpriest Avvakum (who, perhaps not incidentally, was executed by fire in 1682), and hybrid biographical hagiographies appeared in the seventeenth century. Private letter writing increased, sermon writing developed, and within the chancelleries, in the same circles of *prikaz* clerks in which Svashevskoi and the others indulged their fascination with black books, other men engaged in creative writing of poetry and historical fiction, producing faux treaties, letters, and diplomatic texts.[76] In spite of this small and fully licit literary flowering in the same period, a powerful current of suspicion of freelance literacy flowed through society and put men, more likely to command at least a small degree of literacy, at greater risk than women for attracting witchcraft charges.

BEWITCHED WIVES: SHRIEKERS AND DISCOURSES OF AUTHORITY

Women however did occupy their own corner of the world of witchcraft, and in it they raised their voices loudly, if not clearly. One of the channels for women's voices was the bewitched state of possession, which afflicted them disproportionately and offered an unusual opening for registering their experiences in official documentation.

In December 1648, Tsar Aleksei Mikhailovich sent a memo around to all the towns of his realm, warning his town governors to be on the lookout for misbehavior that had lately been disturbing the peace in Moscow: "Disorder of all sorts is taking place. Many people sing devilish songs with repulsive words, on Saturday evenings and Sundays. And . . . on the feast of the birth of Christ and on the feast of the Transfiguration, they gather to play games in devilish collectives and priests and monks and all ranks of Orthodox Christians go around Moscow drunk. . . ." Among other behaviors meriting censure, many people went about "shrieking (*klikali*)," in a state of distraction or affliction caused by witches (*kolduny*).[77]

The tsar may have overreacted; cases of this particular affliction, normally translated as "possession," were not terribly common, or at least they rarely reached the courts. Among the court cases analyzed here, only 18 mention possession, and of those 18, the 3 largest outbreaks all occurred in a single province, Lukh, within the space of several years.[78] Possession left more of a mark outside of the legal system, in saints' lives and other religious texts, but on the whole, the incidence seems to have been quite low in the seventeenth century, or at least remained unrecorded in written sources. Nonetheless, the shriekers displayed bizarre and terrifying symptoms much like those manifested in cases of spirit possession in other cultures, so even a single case would have been deeply disturbing to observers.

In keeping with their general tendency to leave life's experiences untheorized and loosely categorized, Muscovites left few records of their thoughts on possession. Even the vocabulary of possession is vague. Although petitioners responded to the reference in the tsar's decree and shared his alarm at outbreaks of this particular form of supernatural affliction, there was no stable term to describe it. Witches were understood to "spoil (*portit'*)" people, and afflicted individuals suffered from "spoiling (*porcha*)," but those generic terms could also signal a wide variety of other curses and afflictions, from illness and death to lovesickness or infertility. Moreover the identical word could refer to the natural spoilage of crops or the deterioration of gunpowder because of leaky storage facilities. The possessed were reported to "shriek (*klikat'*)," usually in inhuman voices. They hiccupped and barked (*ikali i laiali*), made noises like birds, and unleashed strings of shocking invective. Witnesses of their paroxysms reported symptoms that included extreme vertigo, temporary blindness, debilitating melancholia, and, on occasion, loss of consciousness. In extreme cases, the affliction might be lethal. Several documents refer to the afflicted as "*oderzhimye*," literally, possessed or held, and as "possessed by various afflictions" or "possessed by various unclean spirits."[79] Devilish presence (*d'iavolsoe nakhozhdenie*), a term employed in apotropaic spells, also signifies possession. Several but not all of the suits, as well as many of the tales recounted in hagiographic texts, attribute the sufferers' maladies to unclean forces sent by witches.[80] The language of "spoiling" captures the loose and indeterminate Muscovite sense of the etiology of the affliction, which could be attributed to witches' curses, the invasion of the body by spirits, or causes unknown. The one quality of possession that remained uncontested until Peter the Great introduced a new skepticism toward the subject in the early eighteenth century was that those afflicted by possession were the unwilling victims of the supernatural, not witches themselves or perpetrators of fraud.[81]

NOT PLEASING TO GOD OR MAN: THE SHRIEKERS OF LUKH

In 1653, following up on his earlier blanket prohibition on impiety, Tsar Aleksei Mikhailovich sent a memo to the governor in Lukh, with orders to send criers around to public gathering spots in the towns and villages of Lukh province to remind people to set aside their sinful habits and to live godly lives. To everyone's relief, the governor was able to report back with a clean slate: "I, your slave, carried out your sovereign order, and after that, Sovereign, no one reported any people engaging in such evil activities, repellant to God."[82] Just three years later, the picture looked far darker. Between 1656 and 1659, Lukh was wracked with a terrifying series of witchcraft cases, implicating two-dozen practicing witches and at times sweeping the entire town into their orbit.[83] At the heart of these episodes was an outbreak of possession, by far the biggest documented in the century.

On St. Nicholas's Day in the spring of 1656, a certain widow named Tatiana was overcome by a strange fit while attending a church service. In a delirious state, she began crying out that two other women of Lukh and a townsman, Igoshka Salautin, had bewitched her with ensorcelled bread.[84] The contagion spread, and fits of bewitchment engulfed other townswomen. In response to the complaint lodged by the husbands and fathers of the afflicted women, orders reached the Lukh governor, Grigorii Kaisarov, instructing him to investigate the "disease of witchcraft" or "magical disease" (*volshebnaia bolezn'*) that was afflicting people in Lukh. The orders specified that he should "call together people suffering from the magical disease" and observe for himself whether "in their bewitchment they start to shriek and hiccup in various bestial and animal and birdlike voices." The tsar admonished Kaisarov to order the harsh torture and execution of "many people of the male sex" found guilty, and to order "those of the female sex buried in the earth so that in the future other such people will not bewitch anyone."[85]

In their testimony before the governor and then before a special investigator sent from Moscow, the afflicted women uniformly stated that they could not remember what they said or did while in the clutches of bewitchment. They remembered only standing in church when they began to feel faint and queasy. Their hearts began to pound as if about to explode, and chills, aches, and fevers wracked their bodies. When they reached their homes, they described losing their sense of orientation, and being gripped by "great terror." The world went dark around them, and the walls began to close in on them, and to spin and shake (*sharkat'*) around them. They described fits of delirium, interrupted by periods of unbearable pain that came in recurrent waves, continuing for weeks or months.

Male witnesses, the husbands, fathers, and fathers-in-law of the afflicted women, provided more complete catalogues of symptoms. They lamented that their wives and daughters growled like bears, honked like geese, and barked like dogs. They cried out in the voices of wild beasts, birds, bears, hares, and cattle. They hiccupped "in voices." They grimaced, fell to the floor, and cried out accusations. In their madness, they bit themselves and other people, and said things "not pleasing either to God or to man."

Over the course of the next two years, a total of thirty-five Lukh townspeople (thirty-three women and two men) displayed symptoms of possession, while another ten (all male) suffered from other forms of bewitchment, manifested as disease or impotence. In connection with the case, fifteen husbands and fathers of victims and about seventy-five additional male witnesses from Lukh and at least ten of their wives were questioned. At the beginning of the eighteenth century, official censuses listed three hundred adult townsmen in Lukh.[86] Assuming that an equal number of women inhabited the town, those bewitched men and women (forty-five) together with those questioned (one hundred) represented roughly one-quarter (24 percent) of the adult population of the town.

The two women initially implicated, the widow Lukeritsa Zakharovna and a married woman named Orinitsa Iarofeevna, were expeditiously tortured and imprisoned, but the investigation turned its attention to five men and their families. Lukh townsman Igoshka Salautin, one of the first three charged in the case, and his brother Ianka Salautin, a "fine young fellow (*detina*)," were accused of bewitching the wife of Luka Frolov, another Lukh resident. In her delirium, Luka's wife cried out the words "master" and "*porutchik*," or guarantor. Her disjointed words led Luka to identify the Salautin brothers as the culprits, "because I had a loan contract with him [Ianka], and his brother Igoshka] was guarantor."[87] The broadest range of accusations revolved around the town healer, Tereshka Malakurov. Witnesses alleged that he kept charms, herbs, and talismans in his house and that many people went to him to be healed. Fedka Popov and the priest Matvei reported that they had paid Tereshka for medical consultations when their wives had become possessed.

Attention then shifted from townspeople to outsiders, such as Arkhipko (also called Arshutka) Fadeev, a monastic peasant from the countryside, and Ianka Erokhin, a wandering minstrel (*skomorokh*). The minstrel was targeted for accusation after an altercation with Manka, daughter of a leading citizen and wife of a local fisherman. The incident began when Manka's husband invited the minstrel to her father's home during Lent and ordered her to fetch some wine for his guest. Her father reported that his daughter retorted, "You know my father doesn't like minstrels, and I won't bring you any wine!" After that, her kerchief disappeared and simultaneously, her fits began. Her father (interestingly, not her husband) lodged the complaint on her behalf, arguing that the coincidence of events made it obvious that the minstrel was at fault.[88]

The final person accused in this first wave was an unlikely candidate, Fedka Vasil'ev Kozmin, the son of a prominent townsman. His father, a shoemaker, served the town administration responsibly in official capacities and had never been known to cause trouble. Fedka was accused by a woman who cried his name while possessed but also when fully in control of her faculties. She noted that he wore a cross in the heel of his shoe, an unambiguously satanic fashion statement.

All of the accused were imprisoned and questioned with torture, except for Fedka Vasil'ev, who prudently vanished as soon as the situation grew dangerous and was not located for over a year. All denied the sorcery charges at first questioning, admitting at most to healing epilepsy and curing hernias in small children "using words." They denied any knowledge of witchcraft, but several of them admitted that they provided protective counter-magic at weddings, warding off malign forces. A few of them confessed that they also knew how to cure impotence.

Several rounds of torture, including beating, burning, and water torture, elicited from all the men but Igoshka Salautin complete confessions in conformance with the inquisitors' leading questions. Battered by his second ordeal in the torture chamber, Tereshka Malakurov confessed that he was in the habit of chanting incantations to be carried off by the wind or by a stray dog. He attested that he scattered salt around the streets and crossroads, "and whoever comes along will be taken ill, and will be overcome by misery and by trembling and will cry out with various voices, and others will hiccup and gnaw at themselves and bite other people."[89]

Under extreme duress, the suspects not only elaborated on their own putative witchcraft but also incriminated each other and named still more witches. Tereshka was tortured to such an extreme that he incriminated his wife, Olenka. He confessed that he had taught her everything he knew and that she had transported spells out from the prison for him and had even worked her own curses independently. Olenka was imprisoned and tortured until she corroborated her husband's testimony in full. On July 27, 1658, in accordance with the tsar's order, Tereshka Malakurov, Ianka Salautin, Arkhipko Fadeev, and Ianka Erokhin were executed. Olenka, Tereshka's wife, and probably the two original female suspects as well, were buried in the earth up to their necks and left to die. Igoshka Salautin refused to confess his guilt even after repeated torture and the execution of his brother, and so he remained alive. Fedka Vasil'ev had yet to be found.

The executions did not put an end to the matter. Igoshka Salautin, adamantly refusing to admit guilt, was tortured again. His mother, the widow Nastasitsa, was arrested, along with his young brother Mitka. Each was tortured three times, but refused to confess. A final surge of accusations ensued one year after the executions. This time charges revolved around the belated bewitchment of a little girl, Nastasitsa, Tomilo Ezhov's daughter, who was bewitched as she passed by the prison. According to the record of her testimony, "on June 23, 1659 . . . she says she came with loaves of bread to the prison window and a young fellow with red hair approached her. And she left that window and went to another, and that same fellow came up to her, and from that window smoke and wind hit her, and she was overwhelmed by misery, and when she reached home she began to ache and to cry out and she turned out to be just like the other bewitched women."[90]

The incident sparked a renewed epidemic of possession. Many of those who had recovered from their previous episodes with the help of prayer and time found themselves once more seized by fits and hysteria. The names of several townswomen floated as possible sources of the contagion, but more consistently, accusatory fingers pointed again to the widow Nastasitsa Salautina and her two surviving sons, to Fedka Vasil'ev, who at last had been found and imprisoned, and to an assortment of other suspicious characters.[91]

The new town governor, Nazar Olekseev, reported to Moscow that the guilty parties had distributed "roots and grasses of various kinds and salt, tied in knots . . . around Lukh, around the streets and at the gates, and from those grasses and roots and knots, Sovereign, much bewitchment breaks out, and in their shrieking those bewitched wives shriek and in the future they will continue to shriek," unless the tsar took immediate steps to staunch the flood.[92] The problem, however, persisted. In March 1660 a new governor, Mikifor Obruttskoi, forwarded a petition from two townsmen of Lukh, complaining that two women had been bewitched again. The women would grimace and shriek, and the other Lukh wives who had previously been bewitched now placed the blame on "those same witches, Fetka Vasil'ev and Igoshka and Mitka [Salautin], and their mother, the widow Nastasitsa Salautina," who were still able to work their terrible magic from their prison cells. The petitioners explained the witches' motivation: "They bewitched Ivashko's wife because he, Ivashko, took the communal petition [complaining about the earlier bewitchment epidemic] to Moscow, and Senka Bukhalov's wife they bewitched because while serving as a guard at the prison, he locked those witches up in prison, and so they released their witchcraft (*volshebstvo*) against his household in order to kill his entire household."[93] Here the documentary record dries up, so the fate of this second group is unknown, but given the tsar's willingness to execute so readily in the previous round of investigations, the prospects for those under still interrogation must have been bleak.

THE POSSESSED

In the eyes of officials and townspeople alike, the presumptive profile of the possessed was married or widowed and female, to which they also added children. In their petitions, the Lukh townspeople consistently reported, using the typically self-deprecating Russian diminutives, that their "little wives and children (*zhenishki i detishki nashi*)" were suffering from bewitchment. "The townsmen whose wives are possessed bring them to the elders in the municipal tax (*zemskii*) office and report orally that their wives are bewitched and they list the names of those against whom they cry out in their bewitchment."[94] When the affliction broke out with renewed vigor in 1658, Governor Olekseev reported to Moscow: "Again in 1658 there began in Lukh in the town among many townspeople's wives all kinds of shrieking and painful bewitchment (*klikotnaia i lomotnaia porcha*)." The default presumption about the possessed was female, but a few token men were included in their numbers.

The inconsistency of language and demographics is embodied in a list of the possessed that Governor Olekseev composed and attached to his report to the tsar in June 1658. Olekseev was deeply troubled by the rash of witchcraft plaguing his region, and, in addition to enumerating eight cases of magic using roots and grasses that he was currently investigating, he described the dreadful condition of "townspeople's wives and children suffering with possession from unclean spirits. During godly liturgy and during prayers [they] dream of various evil and cry out in bewitchment from their side [of the church] against provincial people, and they say, such-and-such a person bewitches them." Locating the disruptions on "their side" of a sex-segregated ecclesiastical space, the governor underscored the extent to which the condition affected only women and young children. Urging the sovereign to order a full investigation "about the bewitched wives and widows of Lukh townspeople," Olekseev sent along a (partial) "list of the Lukh townspeople's bewitched wives who were bewitched in the past year 7164 and in 7165 and in this 7166." The list of "wives and children" ran as follows:

7164 (1655/56): townsman Fedor Stepanov syn Popov's daughter-in-law the widow Tatianitsa and the beggar girl (*ubogaia devitsa*) Oksinitsa.
7165 (1656/57): townspeople Ivan Ievlev and his wife Marinitsa, and Iakov Trofimov's wife Annitsa.
7166 (1657/58): the wife of Fedor Martynov, Matrenitsa, and his daughter-in-law Ofronititsa; the wife of Luka Frolov, Ulititsa; the wife of Mikifor Ivanov, Ofrimitsa; the wife of Ivan Ivanov, Ogrofenitsa.[95]

This list represented only a small subset of those afflicted in Lukh during the seven years during which the problem sporadically erupted, but it is nonetheless telling about the presumptions about and experience of possession. The bewitched "wives" listed here included one widow, one girl, one married couple, five wives, and one "daughter-in-law," perhaps a widow, since she is listed without reference to her husband. In simpler terms, of the ten people listed, there were two widows, six wives, one girl, and one adult man. Elsewhere in the same document, Governor Olekseev noted with concern that the grasses and roots that the witches had purportedly strewn around the city "will bewitch townspeople of the male and female sex and children."[96] From the entire collection of documents from Lukh between 1653 and 1660, we can identify forty sufferers. Of those, three were male (7.5 percent).

Equally colorful, though smaller scale, episodes of possession came to the attention of the courts from other regions of the Russian land and through the course of the entire century. The earliest mention of "hiccups" in the judicial records occurred in1606 in Perm, in the Urals. In that year, two separate complaints of false accusation of causing "hiccups" reached the governor's court. A church deacon accused a local peasant man of afflicting his wife with hiccups, and a tradesman (*torgovyi chelovek*, perhaps involved in the regional salt trade?) charged a townsman with unleashing the same afflictions on another townsman, so one woman and one man were allegedly "possessed." The accused in each of these cases protested the slanderous charges, and through their protests, sent to Tsar Vasilii Shuiskii in Moscow, we know of the cases.[97] Twelve years later, in 1628, in the region of Novgorod, two court stablemen (*zadvornye koniukhi*) complained to the tsar and the governor of the bewitchment of their wives, describing the symptoms in vivid terms. Petr Khmetevskii testified that while he was away from home serving his sovereign, a neighbor woman came by his house and threatened his wife, saying that she did not have long to live. "And having said those words, Ovdotitsa went away from the house. And on May 11 his wife Mar'ia became bewitched. She wails like a cuckoo and shrieks like a rabbit, and he, Petr, brought a Chukhlomets townsman Pervushka Ul'ianov to heal his wife from bewitchment." The second stableman, Ivan Churkin, added that "he let his wife go to visit Petr Khmetevskii's wife while she was bewitched, when first she cried out on May 11, in the year 1628, and many women held her, Petr's wife. And three days later, after Petr's wife [was possessed], his, Ivan's, wife was seized by bewitchment. She cried out for a whole day, day and night, and the next whole day she was without consciousness of her surroundings."[98] Later in the century, in Tula in 1671, an itinerant healer was accused of bewitching a local landholder's wife with roots and grasses. Under torture he confessed to teaching five other men various kinds of bewitchment, including causing hiccupping and shrieking, attracting women, and improving business in a tavern. Without getting into specifics of number or gender, "he confessed that he bewitched many of the tsar's people and so was guilty before the tsar of [using] grasses and roots and various sorcery, and many people were afflicted, hiccupped, cried, and [suffered] various afflictions."[99] At the end of the century, in 1692, Ivashko, a peasant in Tot'ma, on the Volga, pleaded guilty (with torture) to bewitching a peasant woman by saying spells over salt and water, setting loose on her "an aching misery (*toska, lomota*)," and causing her to "shriek in bewitchment in wild animal voices."[100]

In this general pool of possession cases the question of gender becomes harder to determine, because unlike the Lukh records, not all of the court reports provide complete information on the possessed. Of the cases from outside of Lukh, only nine enumerate and identify the victims; the rest mention unspecified numbers of afflicted people. In 1670, the governor of Shuia worried about a large influx of pious pilgrims who flocked to the newly discovered miracle-working icon in his town, bringing with them their loved ones, hoping for a cure. "These out-of-towners bring with them people possessed (*oderzhimy*) by various afflictions, afflicted by various unclean spirits, and in the town of Shuia during godly services these afflicted people dream up all kinds of mischief (*mechtaiutsia vsiakimi koznodeistvu*)." The governor's report does not identify the "afflicted provincials from other towns" or provide a breakdown by sex, although he did identify the one local townswoman who shared in the affliction.[101] In 1677, a man new in the area (*prishlyi chelovek*) and his wife were accused of heresy and the bewitchment of "many people of the male and female sex in Kurmysh, and from their bewitchment people shriek."[102] The possession cases that do list numbers and genders allow us to add twelve women and possibly as many as four men to the Lukh tally, giving us a grand total of fifty-six individuals, forty-nine (87 percent) of them women and up to seven (about 13 percent) men. Muscovites were perfectly comfortable describing possession as an affliction affecting both men and women, and in their miracle tales they preferentially listed men as the recipients of saintly healing. When it came down to naming names and identifying actual individuals in court, however, possession turned out to be overwhelmingly a female condition.

Of the four non-Lukh men possibly meriting the classification of possessed, three clearly fit the bill, since the documents label them as such with some degree of precision. The earliest one, the 1606 case of hiccups from Perm, mentioned above, unambiguously pairs the term "spoiling" and hiccups, thereby clearly signaling possession. In a case in Sokol' in 1660, two cousins, both dragoons, accused Karp Lomakin, a member of their regiment, of "spoiling" both them and their wives, but the nature of that "spoiling" is a little unclear. After an altercation with Karp, one of the cousins reported, "bewitchment seized me in the belly and I began to cast about in my soul (*z dushi metat'*). And from that bewitchment I lay without memory like the dead for a whole day, but the next day I came back to myself." His cousin experienced similar woes: "Bewitchment seized me and took hold of me. And at night it swept my entire soul."[103] These descriptions sound very like possession, but neither the men themselves nor the court scribes attached the customary nouns or verbs (*oderzhimye*, *besnovatye*, shrieking, hiccupping) that definitively signaled that state.

The murkiness of the terminology offers some insight into the problem of gender and possession. Traveling to a distant town at his master's orders to take care of estate business, a bondsman named Ivashka Leontev camped in a meadow along the road. Ivashka returned severely shaken, with a frightful tale that he felt needed to be aired in court. He explained that as he lay in the meadow that night, a cry came to him from the woods, and in that cry he heard sinful, indecent, improper words (*bludnye, skarednye, neprigozhie rechi*), and "he heard that night in the woods a bird cry, speaking improper words with a human voice, and from those words, he was seized with terror."[104] His terror is understandable enough, and even the court clerk seems to have shared it; he crossed out the description of the improper words and the human voice, perhaps finding it all a little too strange. What is telling here is that no one involved in this case characterized it as possession. The key words for recognizing the symptoms, particularly shrieking or hiccupping, are not invoked, and the animal voices are interpreted as exogenous rather than internal to the afflicted. Ivashka was eager to talk about his brush with the uncanny and to use the court as a forum for his tale-telling, but he did not invoke the mantle of possession, and neither did those around him. While possession could, in principle, pertain to men or women, in the theater of the courts, it was viewed as an essentially female language.[105]

This strong finding requires some commentary, as the record of secular courts differs significantly from the impression derived from religious sources. Surveying icons and saints' lives from medieval Rus', Worobec finds saints performing exorcisms and expelling demons from possessed *men*. She observes that Russian ideas about possession shifted slowly over time: "Depictions of demon possession changed subtly over the centuries as the focus shifted in the fifteenth century from saints' experiences to those of laymen and laywomen, and then in the late eighteenth century to those of predominantly women."[106] The pattern observed in seventeenth-century court cases confirms Worobec's suggestion that this was a period of transition and the normative image of a victim of possession was in flux. When possession was considered in the abstract or encountered at a saint's shrine, it might be still considered a characteristic of men and women alike (afflicting "townspeople of the male and female sex"); but when viewed in the specific context of court hearings, it shifted resolutely to the realm of women.

In icons, saints' lives, and miracle tales, men continued to attract unwanted infiltration by demons and to benefit from the curative powers of saints. Among the miracles of St. Sergei of Radonezh, for instance, his seventeenth-century publicist included the healing of a number of men afflicted by demons. One of them, a youth, struggled so ferociously with his attacking demon that his body turned black from wounds. In his fits, the boy whistled like a bird and his cries inspired terror in those who heard him.[107] At of the Icon of the Mother of God and the shrine of Saints Gurii and Varsonofii in Kazan, women received miraculous cures for various physical ailments, but it was a young man, Aleksei, whom the icon freed from demon possession. Aleksei received a vision, in which he was told that "God had allowed him to become possessed because he had left his home [in Mozhaisk] without his father's permission." After fulfilling a promise to the saints to devote a year to their service, and after "proving [his] obedience, he was healed." Matthew Romaniello emphasizes that in their miraculous cure, their explanation of the initial fall from grace, and the conditions they imposed, the saints enforced "strict commitment to piety and obedience to all authority."[108] Their lessons upheld the very pattern identified throughout this book: magic and the miraculous were invoked where the smooth fabric of hierarchy was most frayed. For Aleksei as for his literary contemporaries Savva Grudtsyn and the Youth from "Misery-Luckless-Plight," filial disobedience provoked a fearsome supernatural response. Ekaterina Mel'nikova describes a number of incidents from lives of saints, almost all featuring men as the afflicted in need of miraculous aid. Saint Sergii of Radonezh, for instance, expelled a demon from a possessed man, as depicted in the scene below. From the Life of Savva Storozhevskii, Mel'nikova recounts the story of *sytnik* Simeon, "tormented by a demon," and of a man named Kozma who "had an unclean spirit" and arrived at the saint's shrine in such a violent state that it took two men to control him. A youth arrived with "a very fierce demon," and another man arrived "tormented by a demon, bedeviled." Alongside this parade of possessed men, St. Savva also extended his aid to a bedeviled woman who, while possessed, lunged at people like an animal and rolled about on the ground.[109]

To some extent, the predominance of men among the possessed in icons, saints' lives, and miracle tales may have resulted from the endurance of Christian tropes in the literary and cultural production of the church. According to Mark 5:1–20, Jesus, the original Christian exorcist, worked his miraculous cure on a male sufferer, "a man with an unclean spirit, who had his dwelling in the tombs. Nobody could bind him any more, not even with chains." "Always, night and day, in the tombs and in the mountains, he was crying out, and cutting himself with stones." Jesus ordered the unclean spirit to leave his host, and asked the spirit his name. The spirit replied, memorably: "My name is Legion, for we are many." The outcome of the story is equally unforgettable. The spirit, not wanting to be banished from the country, spotted "on the mountainside a great herd of pigs feeding. All the demons begged him, saying, 'Send us into the pigs, that we may enter into them.' At once Jesus gave them permission. The unclean spirits came out and entered into the pigs. The herd of about two thousand rushed down the steep bank into the sea, and they were drowned in the sea." The tale of the miracle of exorcism spread rapidly: "Those who fed them fled, and told it in the city and in the country," and the biblical version became the blueprint and template for Christian exorcisms in the centuries that followed.

Detail, kleimo—*Scene from the Life of Saint Sergii of Radonezh, "The Healing of the Demon-Possessed," first third of the sixteenth century. From the collection of the Central Andrei Rublev Museum of Ancient Russian Culture and Art, Moscow. In Muscovite imagery, the possessed were usually not represented as writhing on the ground, but rather their deranged state was indicated by semi-nakedness. Sometimes their concerned relatives restrain them with chains while the saint works his miraculous cure. The recipients of the saints' miraculous exorcisms are nearly always male. (See also plate 9)*

St. Nicholas the Miracle Worker heals a demon-possessed man. In this late sixteenth-century representation, the demon is seen departing through the mouth of the afflicted. The possessed man is again shown as semi-naked and barefoot. "Istselenie besnovatogo (Healing of the demon-possessed)," from an icon of St. Nikola Gostunskii with scenes from his life. Murom Icons: Medieval Russian Painting in Russian Art Museums. Murom Museum of History and Art *(Moscow: Severnyi palomnik, 2004), fig. 16.9, p. 126. (See also plate 10)*

Muscovites appear to have turned the biblical archetype into a self-fulfilling prophesy, making life imitate art. In quest of healing, men may have felt more entitled to approach the saints directly, to journey to the shrines where their relics resided, to leave their lives of toil, and to seek remission from friends in high places. For women, more restricted both in their movements and in their ability to set aside their domestic responsibilities, the obstacles to seeking a cure at a monastery or the tomb of a saint loomed large. The quasi-saint Iuliana Osorina, the pious woman who waited all her life to devote herself entirely to her religion, offers a perfect example of this phenomenon. Serving her in-laws, bearing children for her husband, she bore her familial burdens until finally, late in life, she was emancipated from those ties.[110] Isolde Thyrêt's comparison of men's and women's interactions with the sacred suggests that women had only very restricted access to the premises of monasteries and in particular to the inner sanctum where the saints' relics were housed, whereas male supplicants were generally welcome. Thus not only was it difficult for a woman to wrench herself away from her obligations at home and to travel across distances to find a cure, but once she arrived, she also might be barred from physical contact with the relics of the saint she sought.[111] For all of these reasons, it seems plausible that men actually did flock in greater numbers to the saints for their miraculous healing, while women of necessity stayed closer to home. Of course, it was fully possible to benefit from a saint's intervention through virtual contact: through a vision or a dream, rather than through physical proximity. Thyrêt finds that these kinds of visionary connections were more frequently attributed to women. Still, the preponderance of women among the possessed in the court records supports the idea that men more frequently sought remedies from saints, or that hagiographers were more likely to boast of their miraculous cures, while women turned elsewhere. Their husbands and fathers, while keeping the afflicted women under their own roofs, appealed for help to healers, local priests, and the courts. On the question of absolute numbers—either to determine how commonly possession events occurred or what the overall gender distribution—the sources give us little basis for judgment.

How to interpret the troubling phenomenon poses equally challenging questions. The vast literature on spirit possession across the globe and through history offers a number of promising models, among which is the idea of possession as an elevated mode of communication. Many of the most interesting studies underscore the ways in which the altered state of spirit possession liberates the sufferer from the normal strictures that govern expression and behavior in their societies. Not coincidently, cross-culturally, those who most commonly experience fits of possession are those most beset with constraints, the lowest of the social heap. For them, the restrictive trammels of convention exert the most stifling effect under normal circumstances, and the lifting of those weights offers the most relative freedom. In European and Anglo-American manifestations, possessed young women spoke without inhibition, in the deep, rough, irreverent masculine voices of their inhabiting demons. They articulated powerful currents of anger, rebellion, and disrespect, and engaged in criticism and conversation otherwise altogether prohibited to them.[112]

From Puritan England and New England to the convents of France, Italy, and Spain, and all across Europe, young women, the primary though not exclusive demographic of possession, used the privileges and exclusions of their magically altered state to work through the pressing moral, social, and religious conditions in which they lived, to question, to mock, to revile the encumbering strictures of their lives.[113] Possession magically loosed their tongues and bodies and gave them a vivid, dynamic, and expressive new lexicon for thought and communication. Their messages, emanating from a zone of satanically protected free speech, were conflicted, but on the whole intelligible. They chafed at the rules of a society geared toward silencing, diminishing, overworking, and controlling them. Sadly, though, the actual experience of possession was far from liberating. If possession often licensed defiant speech, equally frequently it gagged its victims, leaving them catatonic, silenced and mute, with immovably curled tongues or eerily distended throats. Moreover, the price of forthright speech was high, and the authorities exacted their due by mortifying the possessed, body and soul, in the most brutal ways imaginable. In combating the forces of Satan, learned exorcists joined forces with their demonic foes in tormenting the women's twisted bodies and excoriating their conflicted souls.

Testimony from the possessed women in the Lukh investigation comports with the anthropologist I.M. Lewis's observation that among the African groups he studied, the most "depressed and deprived" categories of people were subject to possession.[114] One of the possessed was a crippled beggar girl. Several of the widows emphasized their particularly straitened conditions. Two women were described in the court report as beggars reliant on charity: "a poor person who feeds herself in Christ's name."[115] Another woman, too sick to make the trip to the governor's office, testified before the officials sent to interview her at her home: "I am a poor, simple person and don't go out anywhere with people and don't go around to feasts."[116] Most of the women described their initial attacks occurring during church services and continuing at home. Their ongoing struggle over the subsequent weeks and months may have lightened for them whatever was most oppressive to them in the long Orthodox services and the endless drudgery of domestic subordination. However, the sheer pathos and desperate straits of the women, whether in their ordinary lives or in the transported state of possession, resist romanticizing. These outbursts are hard to see as triumphal arias; rather they scream with the penetrating tones of desperation. The explanation of possession as a mode of liberatory self-expression for the oppressed and the silenced fits well with the evidence from Muscovy and parts of the globe, but it risks overlooking or minimizing the excruciating manifestations and the agonized content of that self-expression. Possession gave voice to desperation and anguish, but did not transcend or erase it.[117]

A second critique of this analytical position rests on the individual agency that it imputes to the afflicted. The idea that possession served as a release for the oppressed presumes a highly individualized sense of self, a subjectivity striving for self-expression. Historians struggle to establish the parameters of subjectivity even in the most recent past; to discern such interiority by the dim light of Muscovite sources would be impossible; even if the historical actors did indeed maintain a sharply delineated sense of self.[118] Considering possession as a more inclusive communicative arena offers what seems to me a more fruitful interpretive approach. The violent, enigmatic spectacle of possession offered a mode and opportunity for expression not just to the suffering women but also to a broader cast, including their husbands and communities. As Michael MacDonald establishes in his study of the Mary Glover case, which fascinated all of London in 1603, possession is by its essence not an individual but rather a collective experience. Fundamentally theatrical, possession is staged in a dialogic give-and-take between the afflicted and her audience; it is performed according to a demanding script, with specific gestures and references taught and learned through exchange between the various actors in the drama. "The theater of possession and exorcism was theater in the world, and it was consequently acted out by and before people whose social roles and prestige differed widely. The extent to which a possession was judged to be persuasive or unpersuasive was determined partly by a shifting matrix of power relations."[119]

In each of the Muscovite possession cases, it was the husbands, fathers, and fathers-in-law who brought the matter to the attention of the authorities, and thus they were the first publicly to categorize the women's affliction and endow it with meaning. Priests, town officials, and courts authenticated those interpretations as the case moved through layers of officialdom. Court clerks recorded the drama and copied the parties' accounts into the official record. Possession therefore offered a language and extended mode of discussion and debate not only to the shriekers but also to a broader community. If the afflicted women found voice in their torments to express deep discontent, then the men responsible for the safekeeping of hearth and home also were licensed to use the idiom of possession to articulate the anxieties and distresses of being responsible for households veering out of control. Accountable in the public eye for the orderly conduct of their wives, children, dependents, and bondsmen, male heads of household participated actively in the somatic discourse of possession.

In discussions of women's roles in witch trials, scholars have debated the extent to which the sources, written by men, recording the transactions in male-dominated institutions of church and court, can be said to preserve women's voices at all. The question "can the subaltern speak" has surfaced in these discussions, leading some commentators to suggest that male mediation so utterly appropriated women's voices that we cannot hope to unearth a female viewpoint. While some scholars point to the testimony of female witnesses, women's confessions, or the reports of midwives or other women serving as medical experts as documentary evidence of women's contributions and concerns, others caution that all of these instances of female speech were subject to the ventriloquizing distortions of male scribes. Even the few accounts penned by women, such as the autobiography of the Mother Superior of the Loudun convent who recorded her own impressions of her possession experience, were mentored and directed by male spiritual guides, edited by male executors, and published by male publishers.[120] The impetus in this chapter has been to cut through the competing gender binaries presumed in these historiographic debates, and to reframe the question in a way that encompasses all involved parties by approaching possession as a site of discourse and a language of expression. Men and women, the possessed, their advocates, and their audiences, engaged in a mutually comprehensible conversation, a structured, theatrical exchange of words, gestures, and ideas, rather than in a battle where the sexes fought for monopoly rights on the contemporary and historical record. In keeping with Muscovite conventions, the one figure whose voice is not heard in the Russian conversation is the Devil. In their hiccups, barks, and honks, and in their imprecations and curses, not one of the possessed or their chroniclers acknowledged hearing the voice of Lucifer, Beelzebub, Leviathan, Astaroth, or any of Satan's minions familiar from Western trials.

With these two languages of the uncanny, spell writing and possession, Muscovite men and women inscribed their lives with meaning and negotiated lines and limits of power. Each associated predominantly with one particular gender, neither idiom was confined to one or the other in the Muscovite imagination. Although more men were known to write, and although our sample reveals only a single case in which a woman used writing to record a prayer or to work a spell, the authorities were explicitly open to and on guard for such a possibility.[121] Although women comprised the overwhelming majority of those reported as possessed in seventeenth-century courts of law, the general notion of possession was open to all comers, and the danger to men was acknowledged. Even the most sharply polarized modes of magical communication and efficacy were deemed available to men and women alike. No conceptual barriers, no notional innate distinctions between men and women, prevented the participation of all in the fearful, covert, ongoing magical conversation. That conversation, and men's and women's roles in it, was shaped and constrained, in turn, and to some degree determined, by the oppressive distinctions of gender, rank, and hierarchy.

6

"To Treat Me Kindly"

Negotiating Excess in Muscovite Hierarchical Relations

IN 1664 IN THE COURT OF THE PROVINCIAL GOVERNOR in Iaroslavl, a prominent local landholder, the *stolnik* prince Mikhailo Fedorov syn Shaidiakov, lodged a complaint against his household slave woman Fenka. He explained that "by the will of God," both he and his wife had fallen ill earlier that year. When he questioned his domestic servants, they fingered Fenka, charging that she had bewitched Prince Mikhailo and his wife by adding enchanted roots and grasses to their food. In response to the prince's petition, the governor ordered Fenka brought to court and questioned. The court report records her testimony, in which she admitted to adulterating their food with magical substances, but she also explained the extenuating circumstances behind her actions. As it happened, she had stolen some crosses and rings from her mistress, Prince Mikhailo's wife, Princess Katerina, and the prince and princess discovered the missing items in her possession.

> They took those crosses and rings from her, and Princess Katerina had her punished. From that time, she, Fenka, started to think and to search for people who could give her grasses and roots to make Princess Katerina be kind to her as she was before. She went to the hamlet of Skripino to the peasant woman Daritsa, Fedor's daughter, Nesterko Isaev's wife, and asked her about grasses and roots, whether she had some or knew someone who earned her living that way. Daritsa said that there are indeed such grasses and roots to make Princess Katerinka be kind to her as she was before. Daritsa said that her brother, Nadyr Murzin Kutumov's peasant, Troshka Fedorov, has them.

On the two women's request, Troshka brought the requisite roots to his sister's house and instructed Fenka in their use. "Troshka showed her three roots.

He scraped one little root into a jug while she watched, and he gave it to her and told her to give it to Princess Katerina in her food. Two little roots he told her to keep herself and to hang in the entrance gate." Following Troshka's directions precisely, she administered the potion in two doses. She added one to the princess's fish soup, the second to her drink (*kvas*). Instead of the desired result, the princess fell ill and lay in bed for about two weeks. Fenka staunchly insisted, however, that "she never asked Troshka or anyone else for deadly roots, and she never had any intention of bewitching the princess to death. And she didn't give the root to Prince Mikhailo or to anyone else."[1] The record breaks off without a resolution. Fenka and Daritsa were being held for questioning. Troshka had eluded capture but the search for him was on. A note scrawled on the back of the final page commands: "The Great Sovereign ordered . . . that they should question the woman and the peasant and anyone else to whom the investigation leads about the roots and grasses and about bewitchment, and conduct a thorough investigation. And if torture should be called for, if it turns out these charges are real, send a report. 1664 August 3."[2]

EXPECTATIONS OF KINDNESS AND MERCY

Fenka's tense relations with her master and mistress reflect a presumption, common to witchcraft cases in which such personal interactions can be traced, that in an ideal scenario, masters and mistresses should treat their servants "with kindness." Fenka asserted that such a blessed state obtained "in the past," but shattered under the strain of the discovered theft. The prescribed harmony, or, less glowingly, the watchful truce or suspension of violence, between unequals had been ruptured, and magic purported to offer a route to reestablishing the prior terms of engagement. From Fenka's point of view, the princess was unfairly holding a grudge, punishing her without pity, and withholding the clemency required by her superior status. From the perspective of the prince and princess, an uncomfortable sense of their own obduracy may well have encouraged them to interpret their illnesses as magical retribution. The traces of a "moral economy" guide the dynamics of their interaction.[3] Witchcraft functioned as a powerful mediating and mitigating force, asserting and enforcing, from below as well as from above, the consensual norms that made Muscovite hierarchical inequality workable.

Hierarchy was the natural condition of life in Muscovy, and everyone from the lowest serf or slave to the tsar himself answered to a higher master. Woven tightly within the warp and weft of hierarchy, living and breathing the pressured air of hierarchy, every Muscovite of every station depended on the goodwill of his or her superiors. Hierarchies metastasized from top to bottom, and the challenges of mitigating their harsh exactions drew everyone into a self-replicating web. Survival meant winning the favor of a patron, the blessing of a powerful court figure, the clemency of a judge, or the leniency of a master. Within Muscovite society, patronage, mercy, and kindness were not mere niceties or personality traits; instead they were the necessary softening agents that made the otherwise harshly stratified and cruelly exploitive system tolerable and lent it stability and staying power. Throughout society, didactic texts preached the virtues of mercy and kindness toward the less fortunate. Admittedly, the bar for what constituted kindness was set horrifyingly low: kindness consisted of refraining from rape, murder, starvation, burning, dismemberment, or excessive beating, although a reasonable amount of beating was deemed perfectly acceptable. Still, this universally shared understanding of limits on the conduct of power gave the poor and the powerless some small access to redress and could mitigate their conditions of servitude.

Practically speaking, those in power frequently breached the terms of this moral contract, and the vast inequities of power left the violated with little recourse against them. Aggrieved underlings could run away, they could exact their own violent reprisals (a dangerous course of action), they could petition the authorities, begging for mercy, or they could deploy magic. Pushed to desperate measures, the needy and the oppressed found hope of remediation and means of alleviating their affliction in the magical artillery at their disposal.[4]

Methodologically, such an assertion raises a host of questions. In asserting that the downtrodden employed spells and potions against their superiors, we risk accepting uncritically the accusations lodged against purported witches by their masters, commanding officers, or husbands. If we take a more cautious stance and recall that we have to rely in large measure on testimony of the accusers and confessions coerced and shaped and recorded by the courts, we shift into a different evidentiary realm, where testimony reflects the fears of the accusers and the court officials as much as it records the actual actions of the accused. The premise of this chapter builds on that of the previous one in viewing all concerned parties as participants in a single, integrated interpretive field of thought and contention. Witchcraft testimony reveals a striking overlap between the anxieties expressed by accusers and the desires articulated by the accused, suggesting that magic was widely understood as a field of struggle in which the moral limits of hierarchical abuse were negotiated, projected, and enforced. The beauty of magical retribution, and of the moral economy model, is that both derive their force from the fact that transgressors and victims shared a sense of where the boundaries lay, even if the particulars and justifications looked very different from different perspectives. When aware, consciously or subliminally, of their own excesses, masters made themselves vulnerable to

Plate 1. Burning *v srube*. Executions by burning were relatively rare in witchcraft cases, but when they did occur, the condemned were burned alive inside a small wooden structure rather than at the stake. Here is depicted the execution of the Judaizers, condemned as heretics at the Council of 1504. Seated in judgment, from right to left, are Metropolitan Simon, Grand Prince Ivan III Vasilevich, and his son, Vasilii Ivanovich. Miniature from the great illustrated chronicle compilation overseen by Metropolitan Makarii during the reign of Ivan IV, the *Illustrated Chronicle Compilation Listevoi letopisnyi svod*, 1570s (RNB. f. 4. 232. l. 644). *Litsevoi letopisnyi svod XVI veka: Russkaia letopisnaia istoriia*. Bk. 18, 1503–1527 (Moscow: Akteon, 2010), 43.

Plate 2. *Kleimo*: Detail from the Life of St. Nicholas: St. Nicholas exorcises a devil from a well. Inventory No. ERI-84 (Ermitazh Museum Collection). Beginning of the sixteenth century, Moscow School. The State Hermitage Museum, St. Petersburg Photograph © The State Hermitage Museum / photo by Vladimir Terebenin, Leonard Kheifets, Yuri Molodkovets.

Plate 3. In the early sixteenth century, Hans Baldung Grien created some of the most explicitly sexualized visions of witches at work; some were printed and, like the Molitor image, exerted a tenacious hold on the Western, especially German, imagination. Here is one of Baldung Grien's unpublished sketches, which presents this group of witches as unmistakably sexual beings, wild, unnatural, and uncontrolled. Women of all ages, from attractive and young to the old crone, their teacher, are equally implicated in this diabolical, orgiastic scene. "A Group of Witches (*Hexensabbath* II)," 1514, Inv. No. 3221. By permission of Albertina, Vienna.

Plate 4. Vasilii Maksimov, *The Arrival of a Sorcerer at a Peasant Wedding*, 1875. Canvas, oil, 116 x 188 cm. State Tretiakov Gallery, no. 41. Belief in the vulnerability of couples to the malice of sorcerers at the liminal moment of marriage remained widespread through the nineteenth century, as depicted in this evocative painting. The drawn faces of bride and groom express their fear that the sorcerer, whom they did not invite to the celebration, will curse their marital prospects. A common practice both in the seventeenth century and in the late nineteenth was to invite a "good" sorcerer to attend the wedding as protective insurance against the magically induced impotence and infertility that might afflict a marriage.

Plate 5. Icon of the Transfiguration, 1685. Icons of the Transfiguration celebrate the capacity of human flesh to embody the divine. They survive in large numbers and their lesson seems quite accessible. http://snikola.ru.Ikoni/Gospodnie/Preobrazenie/3.jpg.

Plate 6. Expulsion of Adam and Eve, seventeenth-century: "Novgorod school: The Creation of Adam and Eve: The Expulsion from Paradise. Fragment of painting of altar doors. Middle of the seventeenth century." Adam and Eve are depicted here as chastened sinners, but the artist draws attention to neither their gender nor their sexual infractions. From Briusova, *Russkaia zhivopis´ 17 veka,* Color Image, no. 114, "Novgorodskie pisma: Sotvorenie Adama i Evy: Izgnanie iz raia. Fragment rospisi altarnoi dveri. Serediny XVII veka."

Plate 7. This image comes from a depiction of various clusters of typologically differentiated sinners in a manuscript Apocalypse, probably from the 1780s. This unhappy group is labeled *charodei*, magicians or witches. They shiver, naked and exposed, as fiery serpents attack them from above. "Witches' Punishment," MS C38, f. 158v. Courtesy of Special Collections, Spencer Research Library, University of Kansas Libraries.

Plate 8. The Life of Antonii Siiskii, 1648, l. 172, Old Russian School. Courtesy of the State Historical Museum (Gosudarstvennyi Istoricheskii Muzei), Moscow. GIM, 23905, Shchukinskoe sobranie, No. 750, 1648; ff. 171 v–172. Ecclesiastical and some formal secular documents were copied out in calligraphic lettering and adorned with ornate rubrication and illumination. Early printed bibles and tsarist decrees mimicked the calligraphy and ornamentation of their hand-copied forbearers.

Plate 9. Detail, *kleimo*—Scene from the Life of Saint Sergii of Radonezh, "The Healing of the Demon-Possessed," first third of the sixteenth century. From the collection of the Central Andrei Rublev Museum of Ancient Russian Culture and Art, Moscow. In Muscovite imagery, the possessed were usually not represented as writhing on the ground, but rather their deranged state was indicated by semi-nakedness. Sometimes their concerned relatives restrain them with chains while the saint works his miraculous cure. The recipients of the saints' miraculous exorcisms are nearly always male.

Plate 10. St. Nicholas the Miracle Worker heals a demon-possessed man. In this late sixteenth-century representation, the demon is seen departing through the mouth of the afflicted. The possessed man is again shown as semi-naked and barefoot. "Istselenie besnovatogo (Healing of the demon-possessed)," from an icon of St. Nikola Gostunskii with scenes from his life. *Murom Icons: Medieval Russian Painting in Russian Art Museums. Murom Museum of History and Art* (Moscow: Severnyi palomnik, 2004), fig. 16.9, p. 126.

Plate 11. Torture as depicted in scenes from recent Muscovite history in the *Litsevoi letopisnyi svod*: hands hacked off, whipping while hanging from the strappado, here shown, on the right, as a quite delicate process with a fine thread apparently tied around the culprit's chest, suspending him from the rack. Miniature from the great illustrated chronicle compilation overseen by Metropolitan Makarii during the reign of Ivan IV, the *Listevoi letopisnyi svod*, 1570s (RNB, f. 4. 232. l. 644). *Litsevoi letopisnyi svod XVI veka: Russkaia letopisnaia istoriia*. Book 20, *1541–1551 gg.* (Moscow: AKTEON, 2011), 98.

Plate 12. Knouting: The Russian knout is a form of whip attached to a wooden handle. The whip end itself is usually made of leather, but hardened into a sharp, cutting blade. Here a group of landholders from Novgorod are knouted by order of Grand Prince Ivan III. *Litsevoi letopisnyi svod XVI veka: Russkaia letopisnaia istoriia*. Book 20, *1541–1551 gg.* (Moscow: AKTEON, 2011), 100.

Plate 13. Icon of St. George with scenes from his life. Tempera on panel, gilding and silvering, 76.5 x 59 cm. Russia, first half of the sixteenth century, Inventory No. ERI-235, The State Hermitage Museum, St. Petersburg. Photograph © The State Hermitage Museum / photo by Vladimir Terebenin, Leonard Kheifets, Yurii Molodkovets.

Plate 14. Detail, Scenes from the Life of St. George. Above: Suspension from the rack or strappado. Tormentors rip the saint with metal claws. Below: Torture with burning hot metal shoes, which they adjust with metal pincers like those used by Muscovite torturers. Icon painters and chronicle illustrators depict the torture endured by martyr-saints and by criminals and heretics in similar ways. The icons and miniatures both display in slightly abstracted forms the devices of torment that were actually used by Muscovite courts. The State Hermitage Museum, St. Petersburg. Photograph © The State Hermitage Museum / photo by Vladimir Terebenin, Leonard Kheifets, Yurii Molodkovets.

Plate 15. Detail of Icon of The Miracle of St. George and the Dragon, with scenes from life. Here St. George is beaten with a whip to the point of drawing blood. Late seventeenth century. Inventory No. ERI-463. The State Hermitage Museum, St. Petersburg. Photograph © The State Hermitage Museum / photo by Vladimir Terebenin, Leonard Kheifets, Yurii Molodkovets.

Plate 16. Cross-kissed oath. From *Litsevoi letopisnyi svod XVI veka: Russkaia letopisnaia istoriia*. Book 20, *1541–1551 gg.* (Moscow: AKTEON, 2011), 192.

magical retaliation. Whether or not their dependents/victims actually used witchcraft against them, violators of the social norms saw righteous vengeance menacing them with every blade of grass that found its way into their houses or every unidentifiable substance they spotted in their soup. Magic functioned at the margins of the acceptable, patrolling the boundaries, threatening retaliation, and animating moral norms.

Merciful treatment of the defenseless was widely touted as a requirement demanded of those in power. It is evident that those lower down the social scale were well aware of that expectation and played on it strategically in their interactions with the tsar, with highly placed officials, or with their masters. Supplicants constantly invoked the terms of the general moral contract, playing up the pathos of their own abject state. In a typical example, the sisters and daughters of a monastic servitor imprisoned on charges of possessing spell books implored in a 1646/47 petition to Tsar Aleksei Mikhailovich:

> Your poor and helpless and bitter orphans, servitors of the Savior Monastery, the little daughters of Garaska Bogdanov and his sisters, two little girls, Dunka and Afenka, Bogdan's daughters, petition you! Sovereign, that brother of ours lies under guard miserable, covered in pus-filled sores, and is perishing in terrible deprivation. . . . And we poor and bitter ones wander around homeless between houses without refuge and we are dying of hunger, and our father and mother are [dead?], and other than him we have no clan or tribe and no friends. And we have no safe haven. And now, sovereign, we poor and bitter little girls are coming of age, and without friends we will perish. Merciful sovereign tsar. . . . Favor us, poor and perishing bitter orphans, for the sake of the Savior and the most Blessed Mother of God and for your sovereign's own many years of health and for our poor, dying, bitter tears. Order our unfortunate brother released from great privation and from incarceration, and returned to us, poor ones. Free him on surety bond that we poor bitter orphans . . . will not be reduced to tears, and will not entirely perish.[5]

Moving words, even if formulaic in mode and voice. Occasionally, even often, such pleas hit the mark. Garasko's sisters and daughters won his release from prison with strong securities for his future good behavior.[6]

Subjects of the tsar, however humble, had strong reason to anticipate that he, or any of their many superiors in the Muscovite hierarchy, would respond with mercy to their pleas. Mercy was not an optional caprice, but a fundamental obligation imposed on and expected of all Orthodox Christians, the powerful most of all. Orthodox political theology demanded that those in power display mercy and charity toward the weak and defenseless, and these obligations were stated and reiterated in every medium and venue, from the didactic fresco cycles decorating the tsar's throne room in the Kremlin to the petitions of protesters seeking to remind their rulers of their duties as Christian monarchs.[7] Eve Levin finds in popular religious texts, "the most serious failing, earning the most extensive condemnation, is the lack of mercy."[8] As expressed by a group of gentry petitioners during the bloody riots of 1648, "God chose your Sovereign father of blessed memory and you, Great Sovereign, . . . and entrusted to you, Sovereign, the tsarist sword for the punishment of evildoers and the reward of the virtuous." The petitioners complained that the tsar had been failing to act on behalf of the downtrodden, and had been allowing corrupt officials and "powerful people" to run roughshod over the defenseless. "Remember that you, Sovereign, were called to the tsardom by God himself, not by your own wish." They reminded the tsar of his coronation oath, sworn on the cross, to protect the poor and weak, and added that the people were grumbling about his failure to deliver on his promises: "We hear among all the people moaning and wailing because of the injustices of the powerful people . . . and everyone is weeping to the sovereign saying that the sovereign does not stand up for us poor people, for the lowborn and the defenseless, handing over his realm to thievery."[9] In principle, divine, ecclesiastical, and popular expectations bound the tsar to temper his stern rule with a generous admixture of mercy. Likewise, his subjects all the way down the social ladder enjoyed whatever degree of status and privilege they held with the expectation that they would soften their authority with compassion. Fathers bore responsibility for feeding, clothing, and negotiating appropriate marriages for their children; masters shouldered the same responsibilities for their serfs and slaves.

The obligation was spelled out in no uncertain terms in didactic media that saturated the culture, but, given realities of Muscovite life, not every tsar fulfilled his God-ordained mission, and petty tyrants at all levels of society remained unmoved by their subordinates' woes. Masters and officers demanded excessive labor from their serfs or soldiers, local authorities accepted bribes and ruled in favor of the highest bidder, and men and women of all ranks brutalized those below them in the pecking order.

Magic provided a way to confront the relentless intrusions and exactions of omnipresent hierarchy and to navigate between the expectations of mercy and justice and the realities of cruelty and brutality. An examination of the uses and suspicions, confessions and accusations, surrounding magic and witchcraft not only illuminates the ways that ordinary people understood tsarist power, but also sheds light on the otherwise opaque recesses of conjugal families and slave- and serf-holding households. Trial testimony casts a stark, revealing light on the kinds of abuses and violations of moral reciprocity that led Muscovite men and women to test and to fear the efficacy of the supernatural. Evidence from witchcraft trials reveals that magic was viewed as an extension of the politics of petition and supplication by other means. We will begin with a look at the most public, official venues in which magic was invoked, and then turn to the sphere of the family, household, and serf-holding estate.

WINNING THE LOVE OF THE POWERFUL: SPELLS FOR PATRONAGE AND FAVORABLE OUTCOMES

Muscovites of all social levels found themselves interacting with agents of tsarist power on a regular and often unwanted basis. To this extent, advocates of hard-line, statist interpretations of Muscovite history are quite right: the tsarist state and its apparatus, which Richard Hellie labeled a "hypertrophic bureaucratic government," extended into the smallest pores of society.[10] Admittedly, the extant source base gives a skewed sample—those unfortunates that we see in court by definition were those who ended up in court—but the variety of people and charges heard in those courts suggests that one never knew when one might end up answering accusations before a tsarist official. Striking in these cases is the courts' ability to track down individuals wherever they were in the vast Russian lands and drag them in for questioning. Given the high likelihood of entanglement with the law, arming oneself prophylactically for such encounters was simply good practice.

For all sorts of men, particularly highly placed men or men on the move—soldiers, wanderers, *vol'nye liudi* (people at liberty/free people), hunters, merchants, and healers—spells offered a way to try to level the playing field. Provident Muscovite men carried them along whenever they wandered from home and kept one or two secreted somewhere easily accessible. Spells were found in men's pouches, tucked in their belts, tied on their crosses, and hidden under their hats. One man admitted he had lost a spell that had fallen out of his sock.[11] Among the spells listed as evidence in witchcraft trials are a legion of incantations to ease interactions with authorities: "a spell book for when you go to trial"; "a spell to protect from torture (or to withstand torture)"; "a spell so that people would love you"; "a spell so that people would love and fear one, and in it also is written a cross in a circle, and in that circle and around it is written 'Saints of God.' Pass a fern frond through silver, and nothing bad can happen to you. About the eagle: take out its right eye and carry it under your left breast to turn away the tsar's or a prince's anger. 2 spells so that princes and boyars should love you. 3 spells so that people should love you and say nothing against you"; "a letter, and in it was written a spell to change the hearts of angry people"; "a spell so people would love you and fear you."[12] "As the powerful cannot live without bread and salt, so may they be unable to live without so-and-so."[13] Over one hundred such "spells to power" survive from the seventeenth and eighteenth centuries.[14] In her taxonomy of spells, E. B. Smilianskaia finds that "spells to power" comprised 20 percent of all those recorded in the 240 trials she examined from the eighteenth century, second only to healing spells (30 percent) and ahead of both love magic (16 percent) and curses (15 percent). Smilianskaia and A. L. Toporkov point out that this genre of spells tends to have more emotional than substantive content. Rather than aiming to achieve any specific outcome (wealth, vindication, or emancipation, for instance), they invest in an affective currency, with the goal of engendering fear, love, or kindness in their powerful targets.[15]

Given the hierarchical nature of Muscovite society, we might expect that highly ranking individuals would have the judges or other officials in the palms of their hands, and only relatively humble folk, runaway bondsmen or low-level chancellery clerks, would feel the need to resort to magical means to receive fair treatment in the courts. As it turns out, this was not the case. The mighty and powerful felt just as vulnerable in their interactions with the tsar and his inner circle as did everyone else, or perhaps more so. For example, a case prosecuted in Moscow but originating in Tula pitted two well-born men, both named Prince Ivan Volkonskoi, against each other, each claiming that the other was the guilty party in copying out a spell for tipping the scales of justice. The text of the spell, reproduced in the court transcript, ran as follows:

> By the mercy of God, lover of mankind, look at me, slave of God, Prince Ivan Volkonskoi, with angelic and paternal and maternal heart, [so] that Kostentin Teterevin . . . will not be able to bring suit against me. And as you go out of the courtyard, pick up the first linden bark that drops from a tree and crush it in your hands. Then, when you come to the court, throw that bark under him, and as when that bark is crushed, it has neither mind nor memory, so when that Kostentin comes to the court, he will have neither mind nor memory.[16]

The court investigated the complicated genealogy of the spell as it changed hands prior to being marshaled against its specific target. A convoluted story emerged, which demonstrates the wide interest in this kind of protective spell across the social spectrum. One Prince Volkonskoi had used the spell, written out for him by a chancellery clerk named Voinko Iakunin, "to influence a suit in the Great Treasury Court (Bol'shoi prikhod)." "And in this year 7158 (1649/50) in connection with that written spell, Voinko Iakunin was questioned and tortured, and with torture Voinko admitted the spell is written in his handwriting. He wrote it in his youth, following the dictation of Don Cossack Fedor Aleksandrov." The line of incrimination spreads out in both directions from the chancellery circles, to include highly placed princes and a lowly frontier Cossack. Anyone might end up facing a stern judicial panel on real or trumped up charges at any time. The arms of the state were long, and its eyes penetrating.[17]

Spells intended to affect the outcome of a trial were common enough that already in the previous century the Stoglav Church Council of 1551 devoted one of its hundred chapters to condemning the practice. In this earlier period, the topic of anxiety was less the subversion of a trial than the supernaturally rigging the outcome of a judicial duel, fought to determine guilt or innocence through "God's justice.[18] The council's uneasiness about magic influencing trial outcomes was reinforced by common practice. Books of spells confiscated from witchcraft suspects recommended several magical techniques that litigants could use to ensure judicial victory. The secret to success, according to one spell book, was to place a black snake's tongue wrapped in green and black cloth in one's left boot prior to the duel. "And when necessary, also put three garlic cloves in that same boot, and under your right armpit tie a hand towel and take [it] with you when you go to court or to the field of the [judicial] duel."[19]

By the seventeenth century, judicial duels had long been eliminated, and the resolution of trials rested in the entirely mortal hands of the judges. Judicial spells adapted to the times, shifting to magical erasure of the memory of the opposing side, as in the Volkonskoi case, or to win the heart of the judge, silence the opposition, or protect against self-incrimination under torture in others. Levontei Fedorov, a cathedral deacon from the fortress town of Sevsk, was tried in 1647 for possession of a fortune-telling book (*vorozhebnaia kniga*), by which he "told many people's fortunes (*vorozhil mnogim liudem*) and worked sorcery (*volkhvuet*)." A witness in the case, the gunner Mikhailo Makarov, testified that he had asked the deacon whether he had other similar books. The deacon reportedly replied, "I have a lot memorized. I have some so that if I'm in court, my opponent will be found guilty and I will be exonerated."[20] Two years later, a prisoner in a Moscow jail informed on his cellmate, the prisoner Fedka Popov. The informer reported that Fedka "had a letter [with writing] on both sides, and Fedka took that letter out from inside his shirt . . . and showed it to another prisoner, Ivaska Rospopa, because he Fedka can't read or write." Ivashka read the letter out loud, permitting their fellow prisoners to overhear its seditious content in full: "Ivashka Rospopa read that letter and it said, 'Whoever carries this letter on his person, in trial the guilty will be found innocent and the innocent guilty.'" The spell promised effects even in the judgment of the hereafter: "Whoever dies with this letter on his person will escape eternal torment." Horrified by the parlous content, his two cellmates grabbed the incriminating paper and tore it to shreds, so that nothing at all remained for the authorities to examine.[21]

Among the most dramatic cases in which the rich and powerful turned to magic to win favor from their superiors was the scandalous case of Andrei Ivanovich Bezobrazov, an important *stolnik* of the realm. Bezobrazov's problems began in 1689. He received a posting to the Terek River, where he was to serve as military governor. An honorable but dangerous posting, this placement did not appeal to him in the slightest. He tried to avoid the order by lying low in his provincial estate, but the sovereigns' order pursued him, requiring him to proceed to Moscow for orders and deployment. Reluctantly, he complied and returned to Moscow, but "feigning illness, he wrote a deceitful petition to the great sovereigns, claiming that he was old and wounded and lay sick in bed, and was unable go on this service assignment because of his illnesses." When the wily sovereigns dispatched a doctor to check out the story, Bezobrazov took a more confrontational stand. After further histrionics and malingering, he installed himself in a boat in the middle of the river, avoiding repeated orders to head to the Terek without delay. During his month-long stint on the river, Bezobrazov conducted a two-fold assault on the tsars and their inner circle, with the intent of making them "long for his company." He adopted a political strategy startlingly saturated with affect. The first line of attack was an almost daily stream of petitions to the tsars and letters to the boyars and other influential people, and letters to his wife and friends, urging them to plead his case. In one of his "deceitful" petitions to the co-tsars Ivan and Peter Alekseevich, Bezobrazov wrote, begging for their pity:

> As I was traveling to service, on the road I was taken ill and from that illness became weak (*driakhl*) and deaf, and lost my memory, and my head spun and I see poorly, because I'm an old, incapacitated little man (*chelovechenko*), my arms and legs are all broken, and I have lots of other illnesses, and in Kolomna, they lay me out, your slave, and gave me communion and anointed me with holy oil. Have mercy, Sovereigns, on me, as God will! Sovereigns, do not order me sent to the Terek. I could not survive in such distant service because of my advanced age and my terrible sickness and memory loss. I have served you, great sovereigns, for forty-eight years, and from birth I am sixty years old. Order me and my illnesses examined, and then it will be clear to you, Great Sovereigns.[22]

He flooded other potential patrons and intercessors with pitiful appeals as well:

> My lord, [who has been so] kind to me, Prince Petr Ivanovich! Greetings in Christ, the eternal, merciful lord, and may you enjoy all joy, and [the same]

> to all those who are in your kindness. And protect your health and wish you all good, my lord. Remember, my kind lord, the kindness of your grandfather, Prince Semyon Vasil'evich, and the kindness of your father, Prince Ivan Semyonovich, and your kindness to my father and to me. I beg your merciful intercession: let me, lord, remember your kindness for all eternity and to pray to God for your eternal health and for your entire righteous house. Intercede for me, lord, with your kindness, so that by your intercession I will not be sent to Terek, because of my advanced years and my terrible illnesses and wounds.[23]

Bezobrazov's petition unambiguously reminds his patron of his obligations to those dependent on his benefaction. To his wife he sent increasingly desperate instructions about how to frame her supplications on his behalf, and how to obtain cash to grease potentially helpful hands. "If only someone would favor me!"[24] This was the mantra for survival in Muscovy's hierarchical world, for a highly placed man like Bezobrazov as for a humble household slave or wandering vagrant.

Meanwhile, being a practical man, Bezobrazov strove to extend the techniques of supplication and clientage into the supernatural realm. With the help of an assortment of fortune-tellers, enchanters, and even his wife, he launched a magical campaign to change the sovereigns' hearts. According to testimony in the case:

> On the boat, the sorcerer Dorofeika talked with Andrei Bezobrazov and wanted to do this: to set loose on the wind a destructive spell against great sovereign tsar Peter Alekseevich and [his mother] the great sovereign tsaritsa Natalia Kirillovna and [his uncles] the Naryshkin boyars and their wives, so that they would pine for him, Andrei Bezobrazov (*po nem toskovali*).

Later, once the jig was up and Dorofeika, Bezobrazov and a bevy of assorted magicians had been arrested, Dorofeika was tortured. With two elevations on the strappado accompanied by one blow of the knout, he testified that "Andrei Bezobrazov told him to go to Moscow and there to arrange things so the great sovereigns would be kind to him. And he told him that he would do it and would let loose on the winds such spells as he had said, and from which would come good." He then recited the verse that he had loosed over Tsar Peter and his mother as they were going from the Savinskoi Monastery to Moscow. The spell starts out with a fully acceptable Christian invocation but rapidly descends into chilling metaphor:

> Lord Jesus Christ, Son of God, have mercy on us. I lie down, crossing myself, I go out, praying; from the house by the doors, from the courtyard through

the gates, by way of the road to an open field: In the open field stands an oak. Under the oak is a golden chair. On the golden chair sits a maiden Marem'iana, spinning golden thread; and where the slave does not see Tsar Peter, his tracks will be hidden, his heart will contract.

I, slave Dorofei, come. I prostrate myself. I submit. I release a key in the Ocean-Sea, so that with that key they won't sail the ocean sea for all eternity. Amen.[25]

Bezobrazov took assistance wherever he could find it. His wife also advised him on how to proceed in order to turn the sovereigns' hearts toward him.

Andrei Bezobrazov's wife told him to write on little pieces of unbleached linen the name of Tsar Peter Alekseevich and Tsaritsa Natalia Kirillovna and the Naryshkin boyars and their wives, and royal carver (*kravchii*) Prince Boris Alekseevich and State Secretary Avtamon Ivanovich, and she wrapped wax candles in those pieces of linen with writing on them, and she sent her people around to churches with those candles wrapped in linen and told them to light them and place them before the icons.[26]

Neither the unremitting petitions nor the various spells and candles accomplished the desired end. Rather than pining for his company, the sovereigns ordered the execution of "the criminal and apostate" Andrei Bezobrazov, along with seven of his magical consultants. His wife was sentenced to lifelong confinement in a convent. Lesser punishments, combinations of knouting and exile, were meted out to four others.[27] In spite of the inefficacy of the spells, the case illustrates the desperation that pushed even highly placed people to strive to win the kindness, love, and favor of their superiors.

A second set of cases reaching to the tsar and tsaritsa themselves involved women who worked in the tsaritsa's workshop as "gold-embroiderers," presumably embroidering the elaborate golden altar cloths that women of the royal family bestowed on favored churches or shrines.[28] When one of the craftswomen, Dar'ia Lamanova, was observed sprinkling powder in the tsaritsa's footsteps, she confessed under torture that she had sprinkled ashes in the tsaritsa's footsteps on the advice of an old fortune-teller named Nast'ka, in order to make the tsar and tsaritsa love her and treat her kindly. When Nast'ka, at her initial interrogation, denied any involvement with the case, Dar'ia called on her to confess:

Remember, she said to her, how Mistress Avdot'ia Iaryshkina told me about you, and I came to you on her advice and, having ripped off the collar of my

> black blouse, I brought it to you, and with that same collar I brought you salt and soap. And you asked me if Avdot'ia was my real name, and I told you that it was, and you burned the collar of my blouse at the stove, and you said spells over the salt and soap, and when you were done with the spells, you told me to sprinkle that in the sovereign's footprints, where the tsar and tsaritsa and their children and people close to them walked; and you said that then I would have no harsh treatment from the tsar and tsaritsa and the people close to them would love me.[29]

When torture loosened her tongue, Nast'ka dropped her denials. She confessed to having worked magic, but reiterated Avdot'ia's assertion that the goals were benign. She had instructed her clients to sprinkle the enchanted ashes in the tsaritsa's footprints, "but not for any evil intent, but rather so that when the tsar and tsaritsa stepped over that ash, *whoever had cases pending before the tsar, they would succeed in their suits, and then they would receive the tsar's kindness and the people close to him would be good to them.*" Once again, magic was imagined as a tool employed to mitigate harshness, precipitate kindness, and bring successful resolution of suits. Naturally, once detected by the tsarist authorities, it achieved none of its promised results. In this case the mistresses of the tsaritsa's workshop got off relatively easily. Dismissed from their posts, they were barred from holding rank at court ever again. The lowly townswomen who had guided their magical experiments, mostly blind, all elderly, were exiled together with their husbands to various Siberian towns.[30]

"TO TAKE AWAY HIS ANGER AND CRITICISM": MAGIC AND MARITAL ABUSE

Even more common and more necessary than spells to ease interactions with powerful officials were spells to mitigate harsh domestic situations. In the case in the tsaritsa's workshop, the bewitchment of the tsaritsa understandably attracted most official interest and has continued to preoccupy historians, but the bulk of the confessions extracted during interrogation pointed closer to home. Dar'ia Lamanova admitted her guilt in summoning the old fortune-teller (*vorozheia*) from across the Moscow River. She explained that the old woman "works love spells (*privorazhivaet*), and she can take away the anger (lit. heart) and jealousy of men toward women." "She says spells over salt and soap, and then [women] can give the salt to men in their food and drink, and wash themselves with the soap." Getting to the crux of the matter, Dar'ia elaborated on the fact that all of these women had cause to use the witch's services to quell their husbands' rage. About the friend who referred her to the fortune-teller, Dar'ia said "Avdot'ia used [the enchanted salt] on her own husband too, and she made his anger and criticism (lit. heart and mind: *serdtse i um*!) go away; whatever she, Avdot'ia, does, he just keeps silent and says nothing to her. And that same old woman gave something enchanted to Anna Tiapkina (another needleworker from the tsaritsa's workshop), so that her husband, Aleksei Korobanov, would be kind to her, Anna's, children."[31] Tracked down and questioned, the unfortunate fortune-teller, the aged, sightless Nastas'itsa Ivanovna, initially denied everything, but when "tortured severely and burned with fire," she confirmed all the accusations and provided the words of perhaps the most eloquent spell in the annals of Russian marital magic:

> As people looks at themselves in the mirror, so may the husband look at his wife and never get enough looking.
>
> As quickly as soap so quickly washes away, that quickly may the husband fall in love with his wife.
>
> As a blouse is to the body, so may the husband be light.[32]

The poetic images evoke simultaneously the fervent hopes and grim realities of these women's lives. Where they wished for idealized relationships, adoring gazes, and light caresses, the marriages they knew were the antithesis of this vision, a domestic world filled with vicious rages and a rain of heavy blows.

The testimony of the tsaritsa's craftswomen underscores the extent to which the same tensions of hierarchy that plagued what we might label "public" interactions infected the most private and intimate of relations, those within the family. In describing their efforts to win love and kindness from their husbands, the women used precisely the same language that men and women alike used in regard to tsar and tsaritsa. Within their own homes, Muscovites were just as vulnerable to indignities and assaults from those empowered to command and abuse as they were in the broader world. They turned to the same blind *babas* for incantations and ashes to soften their husbands' hearts and stay their hands. Wherever they were, the same desperation impelled the wives to do what they could to protect a modicum of physical safety and social dignity. This isomorphism of the home, the court, and the workshop highlights the impossibility of making public/private distinctions in a world where politics and power were negotiated through intimate relations of kinship, marriage, and patronage, and advancement was achieved through the cultivation of emotive bonds of love, longing, and kindness.

Wives of all social standing, from gentrywomen and the tsaritsa's craftswomen to peasants and slaves, sought protection from their husbands' brutality. Some women turned to the courts, where they not infrequently won their suits by calling on the tsar's mercy for their sad plight.[33] In cases of extreme abuse, where women were crippled or maimed, starved, locked in chains, or driven mad by their husbands' rough treatment, the courts might uphold their claims, free them from their obligations to live with their husbands, return them to their father's home, or place their husbands under strong surety guarantees for future good behavior. In the absence of such legal intervention, women turned to their networks of friends and acquaintances for help. The court embroiderer Lamanova described how she had tracked down the helpful witch in the era before Internet searching: "she summoned her friend Stepanida Arapka from across the Moscow River to go to the old woman fortune-teller (*vorozheia*). . . . She got to know her [the fortune-teller] through her friend, also a craftswoman in the palace, Avdot'ia Iaryshkina."[34] Networks of women sharing the same plight offered hope of halting the daily brutalities that so many of them endured.

In a slightly earlier case that also transpired in the tsaritsa's Kremlin embroidery workshops, another needleworker pleaded innocent to trying to bewitch the sovereigns. Under threat of torture, she confessed that she had indeed resorted to magic, but with her husband rather than the tsaritsa in mind. "A *zhonka* (low-class woman) called Tan'ka came to the tsaritsa's . . . workshops. She complained to this *zhonka* that her husband treats her badly; and [the woman] gave her that root, the one she dropped [in the path of the tsar and tsaritsa]. [The *zhonka*] told her to put that root on a glass mirror and to look at herself in that mirror and her husband would treat her well."[35] With depressing regularity, women accused of using roots and spells explained that they reached for magical protection only to make the conjugal beatings stop. The underlying truths remain inaccessible, but the trope of marital abuse served at the very least as a completely commonplace, plausible, and often successful, line of defense.[36]

Abusive husbands and in-laws make frequent appearances in witchcraft cases, usually initially in the role of accuser. Only gradually does the counter-charge of abuse emerge as the wife explains her situation and motivation. In 1623, for instance, in Voronezh province, a peasant man named Lunka, the serf of a Cossack ataman, denounced his wife, Fetinitsa, for bewitching his brother with a root and causing his death. As tangible proof, Lunka brought the root to the town hall. Questioned by the provincial governor, Fetinitsa testified that her mother gave her the root, which she had been given in turn by another peasant woman of their village. According to Fetinitsa, her mother instructed her to make a tea with the root and give it to her brother-in-law to drink, with the assurance that he would not die from that root. After drinking the potion, her mother promised, "He will be good to you."[37]

Fetinitsa's simple statement, recurring in so many trials, lays out before us a world in which a woman's urgent need to make her husband or in-laws "be kind to her" met with instant recognition. Spousal and more generally domestic abuse was unexceptional enough that no one bothered to inquire why each of these women claimed to need help in pacifying their husbands, or why, for instance, Fetinitsa might harbor a desire to make her brother-in-law "be good to her." The fact that women might seek magical remedies for their desperate situations made perfect sense, and even won the backing of the courts, which recognized that certain limits had to be observed.

Famously, the *Domostroi* recommends exactly how, where, and why a husband should and indeed must beat his wife. The guidelines display remarkable sensitivity when they note the importance of tact in wife-beating. The beating should be administered in private, to avoid humiliating the woman in front of the servants, and it should be framed in a properly didactic way to make the point. Moreover, the text urges caution: do not use wooden or iron rods, avoid beating on the face, ears, or abdomen, so as not to inflict blindness, deafness, paralysis, toothache, or miscarriage.[38] This passage, the most notorious in the *Domostroi,* suggests that wife-beating was indeed not only accepted but also appreciated (by men) as a necessary tool of household governance, just as knouting, maiming, branding, and execution were all understood as necessary and salutary accouterments of tsarist rule. At the same time, there were, as Nancy Shields Kollmann argues, (some) limits on patriarchal abuse.[39] A good thrashing might benefit the soul, but maiming, crippling, or killing crossed the line. The checks on violence built into this ideal vision of family life were meager and most often ineffectual, but nonetheless, they were explicitly set in place.

The line between spells to rectify their domestic situations by making their husbands "be kind" and spells intended to wreak vengeance, to sicken, or kill, was a fine one. Very frequently, the accused wives pleaded the former version as their defense while the husbands charged them with more sinister intents and practices. For example, a young gentrywoman was accused in 1678 by her husband and in-laws of trying to bewitch them by putting pieces of coal and clay, hemp fibers, a dead mouse, and some grains of wheat in their beds. She admitted that she had "bewitched her father-in-law because he acts unkindly toward her," but only with the hope that the spells would make him and the others "love her" and "treat her kindly." She used some of her husband's "manly essence" to inspire him "to passion." When tortured, she retracted her confession. She claimed that her husband and his parents had forced her into making a false confession to magical acts she had never committed. In fact, she now testified, she had put nothing at all in their beds and worked no magic against them; she insisted that she had incriminated herself falsely, to win their approval.

> I slandered myself without grounds, because I was seized by terror. When I lived at my in-laws' house, they started to question me, and I said to them that I don't know anything. Because of that, they didn't love me. But when I concoct stories against myself in some way, they love me, and so I slandered myself in all sorts of ways without any grounds. Then my father-in-law would start to question me about some kind of heresy (*eretchestvo*) and I would start saying all sorts of stuff about myself in their house.[40]

Whether this testimony refers to physical as well as emotional abuse is unclear, but the connection between the young woman's "terror" and her resort to magic, whether imagined or not, displayed an evident logic to all those involved, the oppressed daughter-in-law, the suspicious parents-in-law, and the court dignitaries.

DEADLY INTIMACIES: WITCHCRAFT AND DOMESTIC SERVITUDE

The constricted, bounded, protected perimeters of the domestic was seen as potentially housing the most deadly serpents, those unseen and unsuspected, those closest to home. In her study of Ukrainian witchcraft trials, Kateryna Dysa evocatively describes this potentially explosive relationship as "dangerous proximity."[41] Abuses in these more intimate relationships were constant and, for the dependents, unavoidable. In this context, along with wives, household slaves, and particularly female domestics, were those most at risk for witchcraft accusations. In the cramped space of the household, slaves and serfs confronted their masters and mistresses every day, and when those relationships went awry, dependent bondsmen and women had few resources for redressing their wrongs. Male and female household servants were accused of trying to ward off their master's anger by making use of defensive spells, like one attributed to a household slave in 1648 by his master, a Belev serviceman named Vasilii Pavlov. Pavlov testified that, "My man Ivashka Ryzhei threatened in the presence of my man Gavrilko Filipev, saying, 'If my master is ever mad at me for any reason, then I will say [this spell], going to the threshold or wherever, and he will be able to do nothing to me.' "[42]

A sense of just how routine the practice of beating household servants was can be gleaned from a pair of letters sent back to his estate by our friend Bezobrazov as he stewed on his boat in the middle of the Oka River, waiting for magical or human interventions to take effect. Learning from his wife that his major domo (*dvorovoi khodatai*), Grigorii Shcherbachov, had behaved insolently toward her, Bezobrazov wrote to her:

Vasil'evna! For the lord's sake be patient, although he angers you. He has all the documents for the estates! If I live, I will [deal with] Grishka; I will send Tsygan to take over affairs from Grishka and take care of things. And if in the future he disobeys you or becomes rude, beat him with a knout or batogi.

To Shcherbachov himself, the enraged Bezobrazov thundered:

> Grigorii Shcherbachov! Where do you get off being rude to my wife and angering her all the time? You forgot, dog, beggar (*stradnik*), how you cut my man with a knife, and I saved you from death, you beggar. This is how you repay my kindness?! You should be ready to die on my word or my wife's. And if you dishonor my wife in the future or act rude to her, I will find out and order you beaten with a knout, leaving only the barest bit of life in you![43]

Questions might arise about how representative Bezobrazov might have been in the treatment of his menials, given that he was a particularly appalling character. Not only his ultimate conviction and beheading but also a whole series of run-ins with the law throughout his career show that he was a villain through and through, even by the rough standards of the day. His treatment of his serfs and slaves was so egregious that whatever license was allowed to masters failed to justify it.[44] Others of his contemporaries were also singled out for punitive action when they crossed the line from violence to excessive violence. In his study of slavery, Richard Hellie discusses several such cases, where slaves successfully sued their masters for what he terms "gross sadism," which "seems to have been condemned both by the Muscovite authorities and by public opinion."[45]

We have ample ground to suppose that a high degree of violence constituted the norm, the commonplace background against which Bezobrazov's actions were viewed as extreme. The *Domostroi,* again, takes great care in spelling out the proper occasions on which beatings not only may but should be administered to servants, as well as the precise manner and degree of their administration. Servants should be kept in line with harsh and immediate discipline. Both the male and female heads of households were responsible for applying the rod to servants as necessary. The prim *Domostroi* thus affirms the intemperate Bezobrazov's advice to his wife regarding the impertinent servant. Regarding the wife of the head of the household, the book admonishes: "If [one of the servants] fails to heed her scoldings, she must strike him."[46] As we have seen in his letter, Bezobrazov agreed wholeheartedly.

A heavy baseline of violence against domestic slaves and servants reverberates through the court records. In 1672, a slave-bailiff named Firska Potapov accused his master, Fedor Volodimirovich Buturlin, of corruption, property fraud, currency counterfeiting, and involvement with forbidden books of fortune-telling and magic. This is a rare case where charges of magic pointed up rather than down the social ladder. The Monastic Chancellery and then the Military Chancellery heard the charges but found the slave guilty of slander. They returned him to his master, who gave him an angry welcome. According to the renewed protest that Firska smuggled out with the help of his cousin, "Fedor Buturlin, avenging himself against Firska for the fact that he had informed truthfully about the corruption case, held him in his house in chains and in irons for more than a year. . . . And in addition Fedor beats him at his house and tortures him." After several more rounds of petitioning and denunciation, the boyars decided to send Firska back to his master once again, but they expressed some concern that Fedor should fulfill his minimal obligations as master. Firska would be returned to his master as previously, but this time protected by "a signed document stipulating that Fedor was not to maim or kill him."[47]

In a case in Velikie Luki in 1628, a peasant woman named Katerinka faced witchcraft charges because her mistress, Prince Fedor Eletskoi's pregnant wife, had mysteriously sickened and miscarried. Her master ordered her beaten and conducted a search of her meager possessions. The investigation turned up some curious items: a locked box containing something wrapped in a kerchief and three paper packets, wrapped and tied, containing crushed grasses, "but what those grasses are is unknown." In her pre-torture testimony, Katerinka explained that "in the big paper was water-pepper (*perets vodenoi*) and in the smallest paper packet was a powder called *strekil'*, or in Russian, *vish* (a spongy plant that grows on riverbanks). And in the third paper packet was plain old grass (*trava tak*)."[48] Tied up in the kerchief she had some soap made of crushed ginger. Katerinka said that she had used these items as soaps and salves for her eyes and face: "And I kept that *strekil'* not for magic and I didn't put it in anyone's food, and I kept it to rub on my face for cleanliness."[49] These innocent explanations did not satisfy her interrogators, who subjected her to several rounds of torture, which, according to the tsar's command, was to be administered "*na krepko* (forcefully)."

Katerinka's story provides a revealing example of how witchcraft charges were used to address transgressions of the expected moral compact between community members. Not only did Katerinka suffer the torment of constant beatings in her masters' house, but in addition to this normal violence she also endured more particular kinds of abuse. She confessed during torture:

> I sprinkled the salt that Baba Okulinka gave me in the princess's food, and I took that salt from the old woman because, you see, I am a widow. Many people have tried to arrange marriages for me, but the prince and princess refuse to give

> me out in marriage. And that woman, Okulinka, told me, "When you give the princess that salt in her food, they will let you marry." And I took about a pinch of that salt from Baba Okulinka, and for that salt I gave her a headdress (*povoets*) worth about a *grivna*. All of that salt went into the princess's food, and I don't have any of it left. And I gave the princess that salt . . . because she had a grudge against me. But I never intended to bewitch the princess. And unfortunately, the illness started, and she miscarried her baby, but not from bewitchment.[50]

Katerinka's account includes all of the familiar elements of turning to magic to stay the master's hand, to turn malice into benevolence, to induce "kindness." In addition, Katerinka voiced a particular, legitimate gripe against her masters. When landlords assumed title to young, unmarried peasants, they assumed an obligation to arrange marriages for them. A standard memorandum transferring ownership of a peasant girl to a new landlord asserts, "and it is up to [the new master] and his wife and their children, to give her out in marriage while keeping her within their household, or wherever outside the house they wish to give her."[51] The church exerted pressure on landlords to arrange timely marriages for their peasants in order to prevent them from falling into sin outside of marriage, and the *Domostroi* similarly stressed the need to provide for suitable Christian marriages for serfs and dependents.[52] Masters who refused to allow their peasants to marry failed to fulfill their obligations and were guilty of undermining the values and behavior of the community at large.

Legitimate or not, Katerinka's justification of her use of magic did not protect her from further violence, this time inflicted by the court rather than by her master. To get at the bottom of the story, the tsar's representatives ordered her and all the others implicated in her story tortured mercilessly, four times, with blows, hot pincers, and fire. The resolution to this investigation unfortunately does not survive, so we have no way to know how the authorities weighed the different moral valences of the case. The documentation begins mid-stream, so the case has no beginning, and it breaks off sixty-five manuscript pages later, with no decision yet made. As it ends, after four rounds of torture, Katerinka, her lover Mikitka, the cook, and two other men were being held under close guard. Their jailer, Vaska Ondreev, was ordered to keep them alive and to prevent them from escaping the hands of justice either by running away or slitting their own throats. Baba Okulinka, the supposed purveyor of salt and spells, did manage to escape whatever punishment the courts might have prescribed; she died a few days before the end of the trial during her third round of torture.[53]

The more intimate the relationship, the more likely such charges were to arise. While all bonded and dependent laborers were vulnerable to the violence of a master or bailiff, household slaves were especially liable to face explosive situations. Among household slaves, cases involving women seem to be more numerous, or at least more developed in the court records. This is a significant finding on several scores. First, given the great preponderance of men among the general pool of witchcraft suspects, the higher prevalence of women in the subset of household slaves accused of witchcraft points to a unique dynamic fueling the exchange of suspicions in this particular context. Second, though less directly linked to the theme of witchcraft, this dynamic sheds light on the relationships and interactions of slaves and masters within the seigneurial household, something that is otherwise very difficult to see in Muscovite sources.

The psycho-sexual dynamics of the master-female slave or mistress-female slave interaction remain largely inaccessible to historical analysis, although it is clear in many of these cases that rape, desire, or exchange of sexual favors heightened the intensity of emotion bound up in those relationships. More readily traceable are the kinds of roles that female slaves played in the seigneurial household that forced them into relationships of profound, and apparently uncomfortable, intimacy with their masters' families. Slave women prepared the family's food, cared for the children, tended to pregnant, laboring, and nursing mothers, and kept clothing and other domestic items in order. In their magical practices, or in their masters' anxieties, those household objects and intimate exchanges became sites of vulnerability. Accused witches acknowledged slipping snake skins into the evening cabbage soup and blowing on it with a spell before serving it to the unsuspecting family, or reciting a curse over a bowl of peas and thereby killing the master's son.[54] The line between potion and poison is always porous, and in Muscovy apprehension about those who made and served food reflected that ambiguity. Since so much of Muscovite magic depended on tangible contact with the elements of enchantment, preferably ingestion, the frequency of accusations involving food and drink is understandable. Infusions made with roots and grasses or other, less palatable ingredients (soil from graves, semen, breast milk, human hair, sheep's liver) delivered a potent punch.[55]

Articles of clothing similarly allowed tangible, intimate contact with the body of the wearer, offering more immediate access than many a master was comfortable with. A stolen kerchief or blouse, casually picked up in the course of moving through the house, could result in bewitchment or even possession. Masters and mistresses viewed their household help through a murky cloud of suspicion, since they never knew when access to every corner of their unguarded domestic life might provide an opportunity to destroy them. Literally every move a domestic servant made might pose a danger.[56] Masters' accusations convey a pervasive set of anxieties about the unintentional empowerment and unlimited access, the unwanted but unavoidable intimacy, and the inevitable vulnerabilities incurred when food, childcare, and childbirth were entrusted to involuntary household slaves. Several of the cases that pitted masters against household slave women revolved around pregnancy and miscarriage, as in the case of Princess Eletskaia and Katerinka, or around the poisoning/potioning deaths of young children.

Perhaps the most appalling case of seigneurial abuse and magical retribution comes from Elets in 1695–96. Elets landholder Semyon Frolov denounced his bondswoman, Mashka, Stepan's daughter, for "criminality and heresy (*vorovstvo i eretichestvo*)" and for attempting to bewitch and kill him with poisonous grasses and crumbled pig stomach. In her recorded testimony, Mashka confessed to every lurid detail of Semyon's denunciation. She agreed that she had attempted to poison and bewitch him. She admitted that she had consulted a host of knowledgeable friends and specialists to figure out how to work her magic, and that she had obtained special herbs from none other than the local priest and had followed his instructions to sprinkle them in Semyon's food to free herself from his abuse. Thanks to the herbs, the priest purportedly assured her, Semyon would no longer "have (*vladet'*)" her, the verb here connoting sexual possession.[57] Mashka added that her own son, Afonka, served as the go-between, bringing the herbs and instructions to her from the priest. Even as she followed her master's storyline in this lavish confession, she employed the familiar trope of magic as a tool to blunt the edge of domestic cruelty. Mashka's testimony offers a wrenching narrative and merits presentation in full.

> And the above-mentioned woman said in questioning that in the past she was married to a resident of the town of Talets, Ivan Maksimov syn Danilov, and her husband served as a soldier in the sovereign's regimental service. In the past, her husband lived with her, Mashka, in Elets with the Trinity Priest Iakov of their own free will (*dobrovol'no*) for about five years, because their own house had burned up without a trace, and they became impoverished.
>
> And in the past year 7203 (1694) at the Feast of the Intercession of the Most Pure Mother of God [October 14], a townsman of Elets, Vasilei Repin, brought her husband to another Elets man, to Semyon Frolov. Having made her husband drink himself into drunkenness, Semyon Frolov got him to write some kind of agreement for himself, and from that time, in accordance with that agreement, her husband and she lived in Semyon's house on his estate in Elets province in the village of Ponikovets since the Intercession of the Mother of God.

One wonders if Mashka repeatedly invoked the "intercession" of the protective Mother of God with any trace of irony, or simply as a date marker.

> At that time Semyon lived on his estate too. And at the beginning of November, in the evening, Semyon gave her wine and forced her to drink it against her

> will. And at night, after she had fallen asleep, he came to her in her sleep and hit her on the cheek, and took her by force to bed and slept with her in one bed for the whole night and lawlessly fornicated with her.

Coincidentally or not, a mere month after Mashka and her husband had joined Semyon's household, Semyon's wife died.

> After her death, he took her, Mashka, to his bed and he fornicated with her frequently and slept with her in one bed. And he didn't let her see her husband or sleep with him.

At that point, the violence that had been directed only at Mashka took a more inclusive turn.

> [Semyon] said of her husband, "That is a soulless creature (*bezdushkaia tvar'*)." And he told her, "If you go to your husband, I will beat you and kill you." She told her husband about that and because of Semyon's threats, her husband wouldn't come anywhere near her. And if it happened that they crossed paths, Semyon would beat her husband with mortal blows. But her husband didn't inform on him and she feared his threats and deadly blows if she denounced his sinful forced fornication.

As it turned out, Mashka was not the first victim of Semyon's roving eye.

> His household slave woman Domnitsa, Kiprian Gerasimov's wife, knows how he took her to himself for sinful fornication because he would send her, Domnitsa, to bring Mashka to his bed. Domnitsa told her that Semyon forced sinful fornication on her too and corrupted her when she was still a young girl.

When Mashka's husband died in the second week of the fast of St. Nikola of that same year (March 1695),

> Semyon, having come from the town to his estate, started fornicating with her during the Great Fast (Lent) as before, forcibly. And from Semyon's lawless fornication she, a widow, found herself pregnant in the sixth week of Lent. And now she is pregnant with that child.

With the dreadful circumstances of her life on the Frolov estate out in the open, Mashka's testimony took an abrupt turn. She backtracked on her confession and denied committing any magical attack on her oppressor:

> She didn't bewitch Semyon Frolov with any kind of heresy, and Semyon's household slave woman Afroska, Iakov's daughter, didn't give her any dried pig's stomach to mortally bewitch Semyon Frolov to death, and she knows of no heresy that she is guilty of. She didn't ask the woman Afroska to crumble any poisonous grass in Semyon's porridge in order to bewitch him.

In front of the court, she retracted every bit of her previous story, about the priest providing the herbs, about her son bringing them to her and conveying the priest's instructions about crumbling it in the master's food so that he could no longer "have her." She explained why she had gone along with the fabricated confession earlier, and why she was now denying it so emphatically. She had initially maintained her innocence in spite of the hideous torture she had undergone.

> She confessed all of that only *after* torture, because they were going to torture her son Afonka and shake him on the rack, and her son cried out then and so she made all that up about herself. . . . She pitied her son Afonka because he was little, only eleven years old, and couldn't stand the fear of torture.[58]

The boy was only eleven as he faced the rack, the knout, and burning hot pincers.

Aside from revealing the shocking depths of domestic abuse on the seigneurial estate (and in the torture chamber), the testimony of Mashka and her defenders reveals that underlings formulated for themselves a clear sense of what constituted run-of-the mill exploitation and domination of the quotidian landscape, and what qualified as inexcusable excess. What it also shows, surprisingly enough, is that the courts might come to the defense of these misused serfs and slaves, if they could establish that their oppressor had crossed that elusive line. Frustratingly few cases survive in complete enough form to track resolution, but those that do reveal clear patterns. Arguments from pathos *worked.* Demotion in rank sufficed as punishment for the tsaritsa's gold-embroiderers, who were hoping to gain the tsaritsa's favor but also to win their husbands' love and stop the beatings. Their penalty for tampering with the tsaritsa's footprints could have been far worse. The young gentrywoman accused by her husband and in-laws of attempting to bewitch them by putting mice in their beds was cleared of all charges, and it was her accusers who were forced to find guarantors to sign a surety document constraining them from mistreating her in the future.[59] In another case in which a master accused his slave woman of bewitchment, she managed to turn the tables on him by establishing his extraordinary brutality against her. The master was stripped of his officer's rank and held in jail, while his erstwhile slave woman, though still languishing in prison when the records end, had received the tsar's "favor" and could hope for release on surety bond once her case was finally reviewed.[60] The view from below of what constituted a moral order was sustained by the authorities above. Magic and the courts performed parallel work, inviting tense, perilous negotiations about the appropriate or tolerable boundaries of exploitation, and groping toward resolutions that might soften the edges and rein in the most egregious violations.

Given the ubiquity and intensity of officially prescribed torture, explicitly described as "severe," or "merciless" (*na krepko, besshchadno*), we must bear in mind that these basic protections were as basic and bare-bones as can be. Lest we slip into a vision of cozy, pre-modern harmony, another passage from the case of Katerinka and her lover, the cook Mikitka, can efficiently quash that golden glow. During his third round of torture, "Mikitka repeated the same thing. Then they burned him with fire. And with fire Mikitka still didn't confess to anything. They kept him on the fire until he couldn't speak at all and his screaming didn't stop. They took him from the fire as if dead."[61] In the next chapter we will consider the rationale that lay behind the court's application of torture. For the moment, however, it is worth noting that despite the courts' willingness to subject suspects to the inhuman and dehumanizing ordeal of torture, an encompassing moral economy allowed those most abused by the ferocity of hierarchical power some small shred of protection and recompense.

PROJECTED GUILT AND FEARFUL ACCUSATIONS: THE MASTERS' STORIES

Not only the witches and their judges internalized and acted on a shared sense of justice and the obligations imposed by the "paternalistic tradition"; even the brutal masters and abusive husbands implicitly acknowledged through their behavior that they had transgressed the limits of the acceptable. It is probably fair to say that most twenty-first-century readers of Mashka's, Fetinitsa's, or Katerinka's life stories find themselves sympathizing with the victims of seigneurial abuse, and shedding few tears for the masters. Yet the masters' side of the story also needs unpacking, perhaps even more than those of their dependents. Their conduct through the course of the investigations and trials speak volumes about their awareness of their own vulnerability to the (well motivated) vengeance of dependents who served and surrounded them.

Their unspoken recognition of their own trespasses took two forms. First, in lodging witchcraft accusations against their domestic servants, the masters singled out those individuals who had borne the brunt of their violence and abuse. Second, when their brutality came to light, a number of these abusive masters left their homes and holdings and fled, thereby acknowledging their misconduct. When Prince Mikhailo Shaidiakov and his wife sickened, their thoughts turned to the women of their immediate households whom they had wronged. When Semyon Frolov felt queasy after drinking a contaminated concoction, when the peasant Lunka's brother died of a mysterious illness, they remembered uncomfortably the people most likely to harbor grudges against them and the most justified in doing so. When Prince Fedor Eletskoi forced Katerinka and her companions to confess to their efforts to bewitch him, his princess, and the baby they were expecting, he may have indirectly acknowledged his own unease with his harsh treatment of her and his refusal to allow her to marry. Her resentment fell right at his door, and at some level he must have felt he deserved it. Although it is impossible to say to what extent the perpetrators consciously or even unconsciously recognized that they were doing wrong, or at what point that sense began to dawn on them, their readiness in singling out and charging their victims suggests some kind of projection of their own guilt. Since we know these tales of witchcraft only through the complaints of the masters and the coerced confessions of the accused, it seems reasonable to view the alleged acts of witchcraft not so much as "weapons of the weak" as projections of the strong. In other words, given the dynamics of court interrogation, we cannot assess the authenticity of confessions or the reality behind the accusations with any confidence. We can, however, assert with certainty that the masters feared their subordinates' resentment enough to lodge formal charges.

Explaining the masters' actions as a product of guilt and fear, of course, rests on a number of untestable assumptions about the inner workings of the mind and conscience and will inevitably raise some objections. The psychological mechanism of projection brings us back full circle, not back to E. P. Thompson's "moral economy," but to another theoretical thread developed in the early 1970s scholarship on early modern England. In their pioneering studies of English witchcraft, Keith Thomas and Alan Macfarlane explore the murky intersections between the psychology of guilt and the enforcement of social morality. Converging on the importance of "charity refused" as a catalyst for witchcraft accusations, they examine the ways in which changing moral systems were worked out on the ground in a currency of magical belief, practice, and fear. Poverty pushed elderly women not into indigence but into reliance on their neighbors, into occasional begging and frequent requests for favors and loans of bread, milk, or other small subsistence items. Such importunate begging came at a time—the late sixteenth and early seventeenth century—when the dismantling of the Catholic Church in England toppled charity from its status as regnant virtue, and when Poor Laws instituted formal requirements and institutions for poor relief, hence further diminishing incentive for private charitable giving. According to their model, the clash of new norms of reduced charity with the vestiges of older expectations and internalized guilt about failure to aid the poor led to a complicated psychodynamics of guilt projection onto the poor beggar women.[62]

In seventeenth-century Muscovy, a parallel mechanism seems to have been at work. Here too, social change was brewing, but change of quite a different sort. With the expansion and entrenchment of serfdom, landlords came to stand in a new and not yet fully articulated relationship to their serfs. More proximately, uncomfortable awareness, however subliminal, of their own transgressions may have provoked uneasy masters to project their iniquity onto others. Where Thomas and Macfarlane see conscience as the key factor in precipitating witchcraft charges in Protestant England, fear seems just as palpably at work in the projections and suspicions of Muscovite accusers. They were at some level conscious of their own infractions, fearful of their victims' retribution, and sharply aware of their own vulnerability to those they had mistreated. Scripted though their accusations were, their fears may even have corresponded with reality: the abused serfs and wives had ample cause to mutter the occasional curse or to slip an herb or potion in one of the meals they were forced to prepare. Whether or not the serf women placed roots in their masters' rafters or crumbled pigs' bellies into their porridge, though, they had the power to make their masters cower in fear and to turn to the authority of the state for protection. In fact, we have stronger basis for assertions about the accusers' motives than those of the accused, since the former were the ones who were moved and motivated to air their stories in court. They were the ones who felt something so amiss that they had to take action.

Fear seems to be the operative term in explaining why husbands and masters were so quick to detect hexes in the actions of their dependents. Fear left its traces most clearly in an extraordinary episode that took place in Vologda in 1671. A large group of serfs and domestic slaves, seven men and four women, was arrested for the murder by bewitchment of their master, Vasilii Zubov. All of the suspects were imprisoned and tortured with fire concerning their "bewitchment of Vasilii Zubov with grasses and roots and spells." Although the interrogators seem to not to have probed to establish motive for the peasants' dastardly deed, the case record mentions in passing that one of the peasant men had been held by his master in chains and had been tortured by him or on his orders before escaping from irons and vanishing without a trace.[63] There may well have been a history of ill-treatment during the master's lifetime. Since the case allegedly involved murder as well as witchcraft, the courts pursued the case energetically, following each lead as far as it would go, and applying torture to all. Ultimately, most of the peasants cleared themselves by withstanding interrogation under torture. By order of the sovereign, four of the suspects were ordered released and officially registered to the late Vasilii Zubov's closest surviving relative, his nephew, Boris Afanas'evich Zubov, or, if not to him, then to one of the other survivors, a brother and several cousins and nephews, all listed by name.

This is where the case becomes particularly interesting. The relatives refused to accept the gift of peasants they being were offered. This was an era of fierce competition for labor, and landholders generally jumped at the chance to augment their workforce, but Boris repeatedly insisted that "he did not have any need for them and in the future he wanted nothing to do with them." The next in line, various Zubov cousins, shared Boris's reluctance to take on these dangerous servants. Luka Zubov added that Vasilii had granted all of his people freedom upon his death anyway, a claim that none of the peasants made themselves.[64] While one might initially wonder why a landlord would spurn such a generous bequest, when one remembers that these particular peasants had a record of surreptitiously killing off their landlord with roots, spells, and grasses, it makes sense that fear might trump material interest. "Since no relatives of Vasilii Zubov will claim them," most of the suspects were granted release documents and set free "at will."[65]

Psychohistory requires reading in the dark, creating interpretations out of our own common sense and imposing it, in the absence of evidence to the contrary, on the unresponsive people of the past. In this case, however, as in the English case, enough evidence mounts up to substantiate the projection hypothesis. Court records report in one investigation after another that as soon as the serfs or slaves revealed their versions of the story and disclosed their masters' predations, the masters vanished from the scene. The despicable Semyon Frolov, despite his seeming utter lack of heart or conscience, must have understood the danger when Mashka, his much-abused slave, aired her side of the story. Although he and other abusers probably did not give the least consideration to the rights and wrongs of the situation until the scales of justice began to tip against them, they were quick to recognize their tenuous moral standing once it was shoved in their faces, and they ignominiously fled. Once confronted in court, these men were forced to acknowledge to themselves what they had done. Semyon, for instance, dropped his efforts to pursue witchcraft charges after Mashka exposed his vile conduct toward her and others. He failed to respond to repeated summonses to court where the case he had been so eager to prosecute was being heard. The court summary reports that "Semyon Frolov never came to answer Mashka's charges, despite numerous summonses, and did not come for a confrontation or truthful investigation into his sinful fornication or to answer for his disobedience." One local official plaintively reported:

> I sent them many memos, and in response to my letters the provincial governor wrote to the Spiritual Chancellery and said that Semyon was acting defiant, so the priestly elders rounded up lots of people and priests and sent them to get him, but he still acted defiant, and ran away and hid. . . . Overall, Semyon acts defiant, and for his defiance he is cut off from entry into the church of God, but he still is defiant toward me, your pilgrim.[66]

Compounding his guilt before the law, several witnesses testified that he had "boasted outright" to them about his sexual conquests.[67] Seeing flight as the better part of valor, recognizing his guilt in the eyes of both community values and law, he absconded.

Mashka, by contrast, came out of the skirmish far better off than before. Official papers provided by the governor of her natal town established that she was not and had never been Semyon's slave. She was a free woman, the wife (now widow) and daughter-in-law of gunners in the sovereign's army, small landowners in their own right. While held under guard in connection with the suit, she had borne a child, a girl, from Semyon. Nonetheless, she and her son and presumably the new baby, along with all the other suspects in the case, were freed and exonerated, reinstated in their legitimate status, and held only to surety bonds for their good conduct.[68]

Semyon Frolov was far from the only man of relative standing and power to find his witchcraft accusations running offtrack and himself at the wrong end of the stick, his actions deemed outrageous and his accusations dismissed as frivolous and false. This pattern repeats itself in several other cases where masters seemed to sense that they had crossed the line, projected their insecurity onto their victims, and then vanished rather than face justice.[69] Muscovite courts took failure to appear at court as admission of guilt. For instance, in a reciprocal slander suit where a couple sued a local official for rape, infanticide, and corruption, as well as "heresy" and "keeping black books," and he sued them back, the trial record reports that instead of appearing for the court-ordered confrontation with the accused, the husband "fled and the time is up and thus the matter is concluded." His wife, too, "seeing her guilt, did not come to the confrontation, and the time limit was up three times over, and in the writ that set the time limit, it was written that if either party failed to show up at the confrontation within the given amount of time, then that party would be held guilty without confrontation."[70] The presumption of guilt attached to no-shows in court strongly suggests that the defiance and flight by abusive masters represented an admission of guilt, or at least of a guilty conscience.

The fact that certain stories won favorable outcomes in court serves as a reminder that testimony was always at some level strategic and shaped by cultural scripts, and some narrative strategies worked better for particular kinds of people than others. Descriptions of flagrant violence and abuse, like the claim that their magic was directed toward healing rather than cursing, proved an effective defensive trope, employed by men and women alike. Other exculpatory factors figured more prominently in the defenses of men or women, respectively. Men more commonly appealed for mercy on the grounds that their dalliances with spells or roots and grasses were not deliberate acts. They described their actions as "unthinking," committed thoughtlessly out of stupidity, or while inebriated, or when they were very young.[71] Women, on the other hand, were the prime users of the defense strategy discussed in this chapter, the claim that they had worked magic with no ill intent, but rather to stay the hands of their masters or husbands. Ample evidence demonstrates that men too found magic useful for winning the favor of the powerful, as many of the catalogues of confiscated spells list spells to "make the prince and princess love you," "to make the sovereign be kind to you," or "to soften the tsar's anger." Yet very few of the many men accused of witchcraft defended themselves by saying that they had used magic to soften the edge of abuse. Although pathos provided grounds for appeal for men as well as women, and men continually made bids for mercy on the basis of poverty, misery, illness, youth, old age, or general piteousness, they eschewed the argument that they turned to incantations to dissuade their superiors from brutalizing them. This quirk in male testimony explains why most of the stories discussed in this chapter (and the next) feature female protagonists; not because men did not participate in the same world of subordination and moral expectations, but because they did not air those stories in court. Winning the master's kindness was not part of the male defensive script, even though, as we know, they collected spells to win the love and kindness of superiors with great gusto. In this particular situation, we are fortunate in having evidence, the surviving spells, to prove that the absence of this line of defense was an artifact rather than a reflection of male magical practice. It inspires a healthy humility in our reading of the surviving sources. Here we can see that courtrooms evoked specific stories from particular kinds of witnesses, stories edited in strategic ways for judicial audiences.

The documents provide no firm guidelines for sorting out which side was telling the truth. It is fully possible that both sides were telling the truth as they perceived it, or that neither was. The formulaic quality of supplicatory language in petitions, the current of insistent misery and abjection that runs through all interactions with authorities and superiors, the standard-issue mold of the charges raised by masters and the counter-charges lodged by accused witches, all suggest that accusers and accused alike were conforming to cultural scripts in formulating their strategies.[72] However, the scriptedness of their accounts in no way undermines the argument that norms of moral hierarchy were widely acknowledged and offered both explicit and tacit guidelines to the proper exercise of power and the limits to exploitation in an unequal society. Life very often conforms to expectation, and cultural scripts guide not only confessions but also behavior. Victimhood was up for grabs. Each of the accusers mobilized the powerful rhetoric of victimhood in lodging charges against his domestic servants, and each of the defendants in these cases, from widely varying times and regions, understood which formulas of suffering to follow in her quest for exoneration. Muscovite masters and the chancellery officials who sat in judgment answered to the same framing moral precepts that guided serf and slave defenses.

In her study of eighteenth-century witchcraft, Smilianskaia argues that "the goal of a spell 'toward authorities (*ko vlasti*)' . . . is the inversion of the roles of the ruler and the ruled, and, in the final instance, the authorities' loss of their essence, of their powerful force, of the ability to act and react."[73] By inspiring "muteness, trembling, terror or else kindness, ardor (*prosvetlenie*), or joy in those holding power in the presence of So-and-So, the worker of the spell," such spells aimed to transpose "those feelings that should have been felt by the subject himself in a collision with a court of law, with civil or ecclesiastical authorities, by the subject before the emperor or the serf before the master," from the subordinate to the powerful.[74] The impulse behind such emotional transposition derives from the same intense, dangerous intimacy that led masters to project their fears on their servants.

In her work on honor litigation, Nancy Shields Kollmann finds that the tsarist courts carried through on their promises in many ways, upholding the claims to dignity and worth that injured subjects brought to trial.[75] One might expect, however, that supposed witches, particularly those who confessed to various kinds of magical practices, might step outside the protective circle in which the moral contract applied. After all, in Western contexts, witches defined the limit-setting aberration, the heretical, the satanic, the unclean and impure. With the witch in Catholic and Protestant Europe, all bets were off, and mercy could not apply. In Muscovy, the contrast was quite stark. Witches, together with other seemingly disreputable categories of people, appear in the long list of compensation fees for insults to the honor of various ranks of people enumerated in the Law Code (*Sudebnik*) of 1589 and its successor, the Law Code of 1606–1607 (*Svodnyi Sudebnik*), issued during the Time of Troubles. The existence of witches "was acknowledged by the administration, and they were under the protection of the law."[76] This is an extraordinary finding. Though condemned in law and prosecuted in the tsar's courts, "witches" enjoyed a small but significant degree of respect in Muscovite law and practice. Witches, like all others, dwelled within the embrace of the hierarchy of dependency and the hierarchy of protection.[77]

7

Trials, Justice, and the Logic of Torture

IN 1663 OR 1664 IN THE TOWN OF LUKH, a deacon and a monastic peasant were brought in for questioning before Governor Aleksei Kablukov in connection with a spell for seducing women. To guarantee that he obtained complete, truthful confessions and following the letter of the law, Governor Kablukov ordered the men tortured. After their ordeal, the peasant was released but the deacon languished in jail. The deacon tried to go over the head of the governor by petitioning the tsar for mercy. In his appeal, he admitted that he had indeed copied out the incriminating spell at the peasant's request, but he knew of "no other guilt before you, Great Sovereign." He described what he had gone through during his interrogation about so slight a misdemeanor: "That governor tortured us three times with various tortures: he burned us with fire and with hot pincers and broke our ribs, and he tore me, your orphan, to pieces with weights. And from those tortures I, your orphan, lie in prison like one dead, and I am dying of hunger."[1]

In most witchcraft trials, testimony "led to torture" and suspects and witnesses were hoisted on the strappado, stretched with weights, burned with hot pincers, beaten with knouts, and, more rarely, subjected to water torture. Some cases refer to a torture chamber (*zastenok*) in which the ordeals took place, but they may have been applied in public at other times, as depicted in the illustrations included in Adam Olearius's account of his visit to the court of Tsar Mikhail Fedorovich in the 1630s. Olearius recorded with palpable shock the kinds of torture routinely employed in Muscovite trials.

> They use various horrible methods of torture to force out the truth. One of them involves tying the hands behind the back, drawing them up high, and hanging a heavy beam on the feet. The executioner jumps on the beam, thus

Depiction of water torture, from Erich Palmquist, a Swedish military engineer who spent time in Muscovy in the seventeenth century. From Erich Palmquist, Någre widh sidste Kongl: Ambassaden till Tzaren Muskou giorde observationer öfwer Rysslandh, des wagar, pass meds fastningar och brantzer *(Stockholm: Generalstabens Litografiska Anstalt, [1898]; facsimile of 1674 edition, n.p.). Bell 1898oPa, from the collection of the James Ford Bell Library, University of Minnesota.*

A scene of public punishment and execution, as depicted by Adam Olearius, diplomat in the service of the Duke of Holstein, who spent time at the Muscovite court in the 1630s. His account was published originally in 1647, with illustrations added in an updated 1656 edition. The work was then frequently reissued. Here the illustration is taken from Auszführliche Beschreibung der kundbaren Reyse nach Muscow und Persien, *2 vols. (Schlesswig, 1665), 1:274. f Typ 620.63.645 illus., p. 274, Houghton Library, Harvard University.*

> severely stretching the limbs of the offender from one another. Besides, beneath the victim they set a fire, the heat of which torments the feet, and the smoke the face. Sometimes they shear a bald place on top of the head and allow cold water to fall on it a drop at a time. This is said to be an unbearable torture. Depending on the nature of the case, some may, in addition, be beaten with the knout, after which a red-hot iron is applied to their wounds.[2]

Olearius's horror seems slightly disingenuous, since torture was still widely employed throughout much of Europe at the time, but his report fit well with the general expectations about Russian brutality and tyranny that Western travelers brought with them.

Investigations for witchcraft prove particularly relevant to a consideration of the meanings of torture, because torture was routinely applied in such cases, and applied with an intensity paralleled only in trials for treason, heresy, and

Torture as depicted in scenes from recent Muscovite history in the Litsevoi letopisnyi svod: *hands hacked off, whipping while hanging from the strappado, here shown, on the right, as a quite delicate process with a fine thread apparently tied around the culprit's chest, suspending him from the rack. Miniature from the great illustrated chronicle compilation overseen by Metropolitan Makarii during the reign of Ivan IV, the* Listevoi letopisnyi svod, *1570s (RNB, f. 4. 232. l. 644).* Litsevoi letopisnyi svod XVI veka: Russkaia letopisnaia istoriia. *Book 20, 1541–1551 gg. (Moscow: AKTEON, 2011), 98. (See also plate 11)*

rebellion. In investigations of any lesser offenses, voluntary testimony and material evidence sufficed, but for murder and other major felonies such as witchcraft, Muscovite law favored coerced testimony.[3]

Even after suspects had already confessed, torture was prescribed to guarantee the veracity of the confession or to double-check whether or not more hidden truths, particularly names of co-conspirators, lurked within. Most reports of torture merely note that the suspects were "tortured with various tortures," without supplying details.[4] In other cases, the official reports coolly spell out the particulars with precise accuracy. In 1644 Vaska, a Cherkassian of Akhtyrka, was accused of using stolen communion hosts in his practice of sorcery. "So Vaska was brought to torture and in torture was given twenty

Knouting: The Russian knout is a form of whip attached to a wooden handle. The whip end itself is usually made of leather, but hardened into a sharp, cutting blade. Here a group of landholders from Novgorod are knouted by order of Grand Prince Ivan III. Litsevoi letopisnyi svod XVI veka: Russkaia letopisnaia istoriia. *Book 20, 1541–1551 gg. (Moscow: AKTEON, 2011), 100. (See also plate 12)*

blows and burned with fire."[5] Suspected of writing magical spells, the monastic servitor Garasimko Kostiantinov "was tortured harshly. He was raised on the strappado twice, and while raised, he was given forty-two blows. His head was shaved and water was poured on his head and he was burned severely with fire."[6]

Torture was a routine part of witchcraft investigations. As spelled out by the Moscow authorities in instructing the local governor about how to conduct a witchcraft trial in Beloozero in 1694, "If the investigation leads to someone warranting torture, then torture them harshly, individually, about criminality and sorcery and evil intent in truth, and if that questioning implicates someone in criminality and sorcery and evil intentions, then take those people and chain them in irons under strong guard and surveillance so that they don't escape."[7] Anyone named by a suspect could swell the ranks of the tortured. Even the original plaintiff was at risk. If the accused denied the charges or reversed them, the interrogators might give the accusers a turn on the rack. "If under torture they do not say anything against themselves, torture those people who brought them in for arraignment to verify their accusations. If those people who brought them in for arraignment confess under torture that they [planted the evidence against those they had accused], inflict punishment on them for such a felony. Beat them with the knout on the rack so that they and others like them will learn henceforth not to do that."[8] Thus the plaintiff, along with the accused, was vulnerable to torture in the courts' efforts to ferret out the truth. One wonders what intensity of feeling must have lain behind accusations, when filing a suit could lead the complainant to the torture chamber. Brutal, sustained, repeated torture lay at the heart of the judicial process for the handful of crimes deemed exceptionally heinous, among which witchcraft stood high on the list.

The specter of torture has haunted this entire study. Almost every curious tidbit or heartrending story preserved in the archives of witchcraft trials bears the traces of a human figure in pain. Almost every narrative carries the distorting imprint of leading questions that wrenched the requisite answers from convicts who were broken by the simple but effective technologies of interrogation. This chapter addresses the problems ineluctably rising out of the annals of torture. In a dark age of our own in which torture has returned, a revenant reanimated from the dust heap of history, these questions force themselves on us with urgent intensity. Why did Muscovite courts use torture? How did they understand its efficacy and its role as mediating factor between the body and truth? How did they distinguish between legitimate and illegitimate violence? Why did they identify witchcraft as a crime meriting administration of particularly spectacular regimes of torment?

TORTURE THEM HARSHLY, IN TRUTH

In *The Rack and the Knout (Dyba i knut)*, E. B. Anisimov explains the perverse logic behind the application of torture in early modern Russian courts:

> If it was decided to torture the prisoner, then even an honest confession (or that confession which the proceedings required) would not save him from torture, since torture, by the understanding of the day, served as the highest measure of human honesty. Even if the accused repented, confessed, even so he was usually tortured, as was written in the documents, "for the real truth."[9]

Anisimov's telling use of quotation marks indicates his skepticism regarding the truthfulness of the confessions elicited by such violent means. The kind of "truth" produced in the torture chamber was a constructed one, truthful in its correspondence with cultural expectation and official mandate, but far less reliably so relative to any independent, Platonic ideal. Yet truth as a social form, created through negotiation and consensus, may stand in for "the real truth" within the framing norms, or limiting blinders, of a society. Despite the distancing quotation marks, Anisimov acknowledges in places that his judges *thought* they were doing their utmost to discover the truth. He credits the Russian courts with employing torture to uncover their idea of truth, even as he condemns the cruelty and illogic of the practice and remarks on the social malleability of truth itself.

At the most obvious level, investigative torture (that is, torture administered with the purpose of eliciting information rather than as punishment for a crime) is mandated in an effort to discover the truth. This is the justification trotted out by defenders of the practice across time, from early modern witch-hunters to former U.S. Attorney General Alberto Gonzales.[10] In *The Body in Pain*, the book that in many ways initiated and continues to frame discussion of this topic, Elaine Scarry dismiss the torturers' claim that their resort to "enhanced interrogation techniques" serves the lofty goal of discovering the truth. She argues that torture is not about eliciting truth, but rather about commandeering the voice of the victim and eliminating his or her personhood. "It is for this reason that while the content of the prisoner's answer is only sometimes important to the regime, the form of the answer, the fact of his answering, is always crucial." In her reading, torture is not about securing the truth or even about eliciting information; rather it is about power and voice. "The question and answer also objectify the fact that while the prisoner has almost no voice—his confession is a halfway point in the disintegration of language, an audible objectification of the proximity of silence—the torturer and the regime have doubled their voice since the prisoner is now speaking with their words. The interrogation is, therefore, crucial to a regime." The torturer's goal is not knowledge; rather it is the obliteration of everything for which the prisoner might live.[11]

Scarry's perspective overturns any rational, evidence-oriented understanding of torture, and her insights apply well in Muscovy. It is impossible in these cases to minimize the elements of sheer sadism and gratuitous demonstration of power. Yet torture, like any other human phenomenon, must assume culturally specific inflections. To understand the particular ways in which the practice of inflicting pain on others was rationalized and justified by a regime that ostentatiously legitimized its rule by claims to righteousness, it is important to look to the ways that the society itself spoke about and employed torture. As is so often the case, Muscovites left us little to work with. They compiled no philosophical treatises on the subject and wrote up no ruminations on its jurisprudential meaning, but they did leave behind indirect evidence about official ideas about torture, its utility, and its limits. The fragments of evidence that survive are especially valuable because they derive not from any deliberate cover-up, self-justification, or propagandistic campaign, but rather from unapologetic, unremarkable internal correspondence concerning routine practice. Without in any way condoning the horrors of torture, a nightmarish manifestation of human cruelty whether in the seventeenth or twenty-first century, the discussion that follows delves into the courts' own records to establish the ideas that underlay Muscovite use of investigative torture.

In seventeenth-century Russia, the quest for truth features explicitly in the law and in orders to presiding judge-administrators. Investigations were to be carried out "truthfully," "honestly," "without bias."[12] The 1649 *Ulozhenie* law code devoted many of its nearly one thousand articles to insisting on the importance of collecting truthful evidence. "If the people being interrogated testify in the investigation not according to the truth: they shall be in great disgrace with the sovereign and shall be punished for that. Instruct the investigators sternly about this, and write to them in their working orders with great emphasis that they must conduct the investigation justly, under the sovereign's oath, not favoring a friend and not wreaking vengeance on an enemy. They must see to it and take utmost care that the people being interrogated do not collude in family groups [and] lie in the investigation."[13] Laws, decrees, and instructions to governor-judges reiterated that the goal of judicial inquiry was to discover the truth, and that torture offered the most reliable means to that worthy end. Brutal though this procedure was, its ruthless logic was at least nominally deployed in a quest for truth, not merely as an exercise in cruelty.

In Muscovite courts, torture could vindicate as well as convict. If individuals could preserve their claim to innocence in the face of torture, the tables would turn. Certitude in the reliability of torture in extracting the truth from unwilling flesh required that if suspects could withstand torture and not confess to the crimes with which they were charged, they would have to be deemed innocent. As the *Ulozhenie* explained, "If they proceed to give that same testimony [i.e., maintain their innocence] under torture as in the interrogation, release them without sanction. . . . Only if they proceed to give that same testimony under torture as in the interrogation, release those people accordingly."[14] This principle governed witch trials throughout the century, both before and after the promulgation of the *Ulozhenie.* For instance, in 1647 in Voronezh, both the accused and the accuser were subjected to harrowing torture, but the testimony remained contradictory and the governor could not assign guilt or innocence. The court report concludes with the statement: "This matter was not resolved in the governor's chambers with torture. And other than [what they had already said], the clerk didn't say anything else against the servitor, and the servitor with torture said nothing else against the clerk." Given the stalemate, both men were released with surety bonds.[15]

The exculpatory potential of maintaining innocence was well understood by even the most humble of the tsar's subjects. In 1671 a peasant woman from Vologda was tortured to see what she knew about her husband's plots to bewitch and kill their master, but the woman, Fedoska, explained that her husband had run off and abandoned her and so she knew nothing of his activities. "I know nothing about that, and in questioning and with torture I said nothing to incriminate myself, and now I sit in prison in the Military Chancellery." Fedoska understood that she had passed the test by withstanding the ordeal in the torture chamber. Because she had admitted to nothing, she begged, "Order me freed so I don't die a poor and hungry death." Her appeal worked to good effect. The chancellery ordered her and several others released "because they had cleared themselves."[16] Torture was presumed so efficacious that it could exonerate as well as condemn. Faith in its reliability in establishing guilt or innocence was so high that among the many iniquities attributed to Boris Godunov in the propagandistic tales dedicated to sullying his memory was the fact that he "ordered [people] executed without torture."[17] Remarkably, his refusal to grant people their right to torture, and thereby to vindicate themselves, weighed heavily against him.

Judges and officials acted with a confident sense that bodily anguish would call forth truthful confessions, but they also recognized that a prisoner in agony might falsely confess to whatever crimes he was told to admit. This concern hovered over some trial records, supporting the contention that it was the quest for truth, not (purely) the urge to inflict pain, that motivated the judges. A 1644 case in Rylsk, in the southwest, for instance, turned complicated when the validity of a confession came into doubt because it was elicited through torture. Grishka Titov, a petty gentryman of Novgorod Severskii, was arrested for possession of "many criminal letters (*vorovskoe pis'mo*) and spells for all kinds of evil and spells for catching animals and against gunshot wounds (*prigovory vo vsiakom durne, i zagovory zverinye i pishchalnye*)." Grishka admitted he kept "heretical, incantatory writings (*zagovornoe ereticheskoe pis'mo*)" in a trunk that he left with a friend, the hegumen's son, Deacon Ivan, in Moscow in the Monastery of the Conception. "The trunk was sealed with Grishka's seal. And the trunk lay in a cellar under the stall with shirts, and Deacon Ivan knew about that writing of Grishka's." Subjected to torture, Grishka confessed that not only did he collect spells, but he also had committed arson "at the bidding of his father-in-law, Hegumen Iona." Later, however, Grishka retracted his confession in a petition to Tsar Mikhail Fedorovich. He explained that the governor "ordered him tortured with harsh tortures, and, not being able to endure the torture, he spoke out against himself, claiming that he set fire to [the area around] the millpond by the bidding of Hegumen Ioana. But he did not set the fire, and at that he time wasn't even in Rylsk." Held in jail for forty-five weeks, broken by torture, and "dying of hunger," Grishka begged for the tsar's mercy. The tsar granted his request, ordering Grishka released on surety while his accuser was further interrogated.[18]

The law encouraged and officials sought a "happy" medium that would keep their suspects alive and talking. Officials strove to keep torture within bounds, to make it serve the purpose but not exceed what was survivable. Muscovite courts did not apply torture in a random or thoughtless way. Rather, tsarist legislation specified when torture could or could not be applied, and in what forms. In principal, no more than three rounds of torture were permitted for any given prisoner, and the most elaborate techniques were to be applied only in cases of particularly monstrous crimes, such as witchcraft.[19] Violations of these norms or application of torture without the tsar's approval brought down heavy sanctions on wayward officials.[20] As with the conventions concerning "proper" forms of beating for wives or slaves, the moral bar was set dismally low, with death as just about the only outcome that clearly exceeded the allowable. When the torturer's customers expired on the rack or died from their wounds, burns, or trauma shortly thereafter, reports had to be written up and sent to the central chancelleries to defend the local authorities from negative repercussions.[21] Of course, there is a significant degree of irony in the officials' stance, since torture is by definition premised on abuse, and further, as Edward Peters writes of the more elaborately structured jurisprudence of torture in European courts, "Precise, limited and highly regulated in law and legal theory, torture became quickly roughened in the hard world of applied law among the hardened personnel of the court system."[22]

Ordinary Muscovites recognized that torture was meant to be applied according to proper procedure, by authorized individuals acting in their official capacity in formally designated torture chambers. The central authorities were responsive enough in enforcing the minimal safeguards of the law that supplicants were emboldened to protest against perceived procedural violations. When retired musketeer Volodka Kuznetsov petitioned in Oboian' (not far from Belgorod) to have his wife released from prison, he argued her case on several levels. First, he claimed, the charges against his wife were false and slanderous, lodged by a neighbor and his wife out of spite. "In the past, my neighbor . . . Vasilii Chirkin has inflicted offenses and oppression on me, and in 1667/68 he instructed his wife Agafeia to slander my wife, claiming that my wife Ovdotitsa came to her in her house and taught her witchcraft (*charodeistvo*), [taught her] to cut out the heart of a baby goat and to bewitch him, Vasilii." Second, he continued, not only were the charges untrue, but his wife had also been subjected to torture without due process. "My wife was tortured without your sovereign order and without investigation, and was taken to the torture chamber three times, and was mortally wounded with the knout, and her arms were displaced from her shoulders and she can't use them, and until this day she lies on her death bed. And the administrative clerk Iakov Timofeev syn Cheplygin holds her in prison until this day, for unknown reason, and your order hasn't been carried out regarding her, and she is dying of hunger in jail for no reason." Finally, Volodka expressed indignation that after all his wife had endured, his enemy's wife, "having slandered my wife, has not been questioned in the torture chamber." Not questioning the efficacy and appropriateness of torture, the aggrieved husband begged that his wife be released from prison, "so that she, sitting in jail without cause owing to calumny, will not utterly perish." In her place, the slanderer should take a turn on the rack.[23]

In a parallel move in 1671, the Kostroma resident Osip Leont'ev syn Laptev, spending his second year in jail after his brother Ivan had denounced him for keeping satanic spells, petitioned the tsar, protesting that the town governors had subjected him to torture, "out of friendship to my brother Ivan." Not only were they blatantly violating their obligation to administer justice fairly, but they also "tortured me severely (*na krepko*) about Ivan's untruthful, slanderous, baseless calumny and lying petition." "During two hours of torture they raised him thirty times and poured water" on him, and all this, they inflicted on their own initiative, "without your sovereign order and without [having conducted] a general search."[24] To avoid precisely such charges of torturing without authorization or not following prescribed procedure, most governors included in their initial reports deferential passages like one sent from the governor in Orel to Moscow in 1636, describing the crime in question and explaining that he had placed the suspects under guard "until your sovereign order arrives. Without your sovereign order, I don't dare torture them."[25]

Even when fortified with official orders, local judges encountered moments of troubling uncertainty in the course of carrying out their duties. A case heard in the town of Chern' in 1647 compelled the governor to doubt the propriety of continuing with torture when he was confronted with the fragile corporal humanity of one of his subjects. It is a sobering account.

On November 16, 1647, a Cherkassian inmate in the town jail informed against one of his fellow prisoners, a low-level servitor named Volodimir Sevriukov, claiming that Sevriukov had been concealing two suspicious roots in the pocket of his trousers. This denunciation reached the chancellery in Moscow, and in response an order was dispatched to the governor in Chern', telling him to interrogate Sevriukov about the root. "Find out why he kept the root on him, and investigate harshly. If it leads to torture, then question [those to whom it leads] hard under torture, so that they will speak the truth." The logic of this order played itself out, drawing an expanding list of suspects into the torture chamber. After initially denying all knowledge of the roots, Sevriukov eventually admitted that a certain "Ivashko's mother, Ragata's widow, known as Rogataia Baba," had given him the roots to heal his young son from illness. This admission came while Sevriukov was hanging from his wrists with his arms wrenched and tied behind him, on the strappado. Even with the encouragement of torture, he insisted that although he had administered the roots to his son, he had no idea how they had found their way into his pocket. Hauled into court and dangled on the rack beside her accuser, Rogataia Baba admitted that she had supplied one root, the less incriminating, "naked" (smooth) one, to Sevriukov's wife, Annitsa. She had instructed the mother to wash her sick child with an infusion made from the root, and for further protection to tie the root to the cross he wore on his neck. The old woman denied any knowledge of the "hairy" root. Incriminated by this new link in the chain, Annitsa joined Rogataia Baba on the rack, where she disclosed that she had secretly slipped the healing root into her husband's pocket in hopes of protecting him from illness and harm. Her protective magic had gone horribly awry. Both women broke down with further torture and admitted that they had indeed dealt with both roots, the more ominous hairy one as well as the apparently harmless smooth one.

Up to this point, the court record unfolds in the chillingly standard, impersonal tone of so many of the reports of judicial torture. Each suspect is drawn into the net and subjected to one round after another of torture. The report describes the torture itself tersely: "Volodka's wife and Rogataia Baba were raised in torture." This particular case, however, ends on a jarring note. In its concluding words, the flat, administrative narrative of the case record gives way to the following horrifying observation in the voice of the presiding governor: "That Rogataia Baba is old and blind, and she fainted during torture." He then adds: "I gave her those roots to feel with her hands. She felt the roots with her hands and brought them to her nose to sniff."

Tempting though it is to read some trace of humanity and moral qualms into this description, the actual context in the document suggests that the governor's dilemma may have remained a purely administrative one. Fearing the tsar's wrath and unsure how to proceed, given the fragile state of his prime suspect and witness, the governor explained, "I your slave do not dare torture Rogataia Baba further about those roots, lest she die during torture." "I ordered Rogataia Baba and Volodka's wife placed under guard . . . until your order arrives about whether I should torture that Rogataia Baba more about the roots. And I will do whatever you order." Unmoved by the prisoner's age or ill health, the tsar replied promptly that the governor should free Sevriukov and his wife, mere consumers of roots, "but keep Rogataia Baba and see if she has any previous witchcraft record."[26] The record breaks off with the old woman still in jail, although no further torture had yet been recommended. The image of Rogataia Baba feebly sniffing and running her fingertips over the surface of the suspicious roots confronts us with the human toll taken by this legal practice exercised in the pursuit of a nominal truth.

The courts' quest for truth was bedeviled by problems that torture could not resolve, and sometimes even exacerbated. Experience demonstrated that torture was not a fail-safe way to force people to tell the truth. Some determined suspects managed to maintain their claims to innocence throughout multiple rounds of torture. Yet others carefully tailored their confessions to protect their friends and relatives, particularly when forced to name their teachers and co-conspirators. Marfitsa, a young woman married to a townsman in Murom, was accused of bewitching her husband, her father-in-law, and several serving women of the household. In response to the complaint, "*Stolnik* Roman Voeikov interrogated Khariton Borisov's daughter-in-law, Marfitsa, about that witchcraft and bewitchment and tortured her to find the truth. And with torture she confessed to witchcraft and bewitchment (*volshebnoi porchi*). [She confessed] that she put a stake (*rozhen*) in her father-in-law's bed to cause illness of the heart, and she gave girls and women biscuits with shoots of *uzhev*. . . . She bewitched her father-in-law because he acts unkindly toward her. [She bewitched] the woman Ulitka out of jealousy." When the governor demanded to know "who taught her witchcraft," Marfitsa confessed that she had acted "by the instruction of her sister Anna, and a Mordvin of Shatsk province named Ievka . . . , but whose son he is, that she doesn't remember." Offering up details about her initiation, Marfitsa continued to describe the role of her sister and of other vaguely identified Mordvins, and set the action in a remote village in distant Shatsk province. "Her sister Anna gave her enchanted garlic *(nagovornoi chesnok)* for her in-laws. [The garlic] was bewitched at Anna's sister's house in Shatsk province in the village of Berezovo by the Mordvin Kichatko." When the governor's agents successfully tracked down all the people implicated in her testimony and confronted her with them in the torture chamber, Marfitsa retracted every piece of her confession. "*Stolnik* Roman Voiekov, in order to get at the whole truth, tortured her a third time harshly and burned her with hot pincers, and with torture she began to retract her testimony, saying that she never bewitched her father-in-law or mother-in-law or her husband and their people, their girls and women, and never gave them any kind of grasses, and her sister Anna never said anything to her about enchanted garlic and neither did the Mordvin. With those statements she had slandered the people implicated in her previous testimony." Voiekov "questioned Marfitsa to find out why she had implicated those people" in the first place. "And Marfitsa said that . . . she had accused the other [Mordvins] so that she wouldn't be tortured." She had evidently done her best to keep their identities nebulous to protect them from the long arm and eerily sharp eyes of the law (by "forgetting" their patronymics), but it is in connection with her sister that her testimony is most heartbreaking. She explained to the judge that "she had spoken of her sister Anna in connection with this witchcraft and bewitchment because she had heard that her sister had died." To end the searing torment, Marfitsa had selectively named a person close enough to her to be plausible, but safely beyond the reach of the law, securely resting in the grave. Tragically, the tsar's officers succeeded in finding Anna alive. Their reunion in the torture chamber must have been a moment of agonizingly mixed emotions: joy at discovering the other lived, horror at what their reunion now entailed.[27]

Even as they underwent a second, third, or occasionally a technically illegal fourth round of torture, many witnesses managed to protect the living by naming teachers long dead, with generic first names (Ivashko), informal nicknames, and forgotten patronymics, long lost in the mists of time and space.[28] For instance, a clerk of the Lukh treasury admitted that he wrote down a satanic spell "for women," but limited the spread of blame by saying that "he copied it from a Lukh townsperson who has since died, because it has now been fifty years and more."[29] Adopting the same approach, in 1629 Maksimko Ivanov, a monastic peasant of Arzamas, admitted with torture to administering lethal grasses to a neighbor's wife. Required to name his teachers, Maksimko stated, "A man passing through showed him that grass, but he doesn't remember his name."[30] In 1647 in Shatsk, the governor interrogated a peasant man named Tereshka Ivlev. The governor "ordered him tortured hard and burned mercilessly with fire." He denied almost all the charges brought against him, and he successfully shielded others from sharing his fate. He testified: "I don't know about my daughter-in-law Avdotitsa, where she ran and with whom, because she didn't live with me but lived in the village of Sotnitsyno belonging to Boyar Prince Nikita Ivanovich Odoevskii. And I learned that evil [witchcraft] on the Volga on the boats, I heard about it from barge haulers (*sudovye iaryzhnye liudi*), but whose boat on the Volga and in what year and under whom in particular I was serving, that I don't remember, because it was long ago when I was young."[31] With this impressively vague testimony, Ivlev managed to steer clear of incriminating anyone except perhaps his other daughter-in-law, who was already up to her ears in trouble and undergoing torture by his side.

Exchanges between the chancellery and local officials express a pragmatic concern with the misuse of torture to coerce witnesses or to produce false confessions. Not infrequently subjects of torture later retracted confessions made under duress, explaining that they had manufactured false stories to stop the unbearable pain and avert further torment. The same Marfitsa, accused of bewitching her husband and in-laws, when "she was suspended again on the rack and was brought to the fire, and hung [over it], . . . said, 'I confessed to those things because I couldn't endure the torture, and with those false confessions I slandered myself.' "[32] Investigating a witchcraft case in 1629, the governor of Arzamas tortured the peasant Maksimko in accordance with the sovereign's order and exposed several of the many drawbacks of using torture as a means to the truth. Maksimko, "unable to endure the torture," named five other peasants as his accomplices in working magic. Of the five, two ran away, "fearing torture," but the rest resisted the pressure to confess: "The Mordvin Vetkasko was tortured to death, but said nothing to incriminate himself or the others during torture. And Andriushka was tortured too and also said nothing to incriminate either himself or the monastic peasants."[33] These men showed remarkable fortitude, holding firm in the face of unimaginable pain. Western jurists were aware of and troubled by the possibility that certain criminals might resist the persuasions of torture. Some built a pragmatic critique of the practice on the premise that the worst offenders would prove either the most obdurate or the most likely to lie cravenly to end the torment, thereby circumventing the pursuit of truth that supposedly justified investigative brutality. Western demonologists worried that the Devil might protect his acolytes from feeling the pain at all, and European courts searched the bodies of suspects for amulets or charms that might serve that cause. In this same spirit, though divorced from diabolical agency, Muscovite subjects armed themselves with protective "spells against torture."[34]

Muscovite authorities appreciated the risk that, with or without magical talismans to help them, malefactors might keep silent or lie deliberately even while enduring the agony of the torture chamber. During one of his many rounds of torture, the same Garasimko who suffered strappado, blows, water, and fire, turned the tables against his accuser, Iushka Shestakov, by denouncing him as a sorcerer. Iushka protested that "in your sovereign decrees and in the *Ulozhenie* law code it says that . . . if during torture criminals accuse [their own accusers] out of resentment, then . . . it is ordered *not* to believe their denunciations."[35] In accordance with his own law, the tsar dismissed the charges against Iushka as spurious because they had been taken from Gerasimko during torture. This legal position, if played out logically, should have cast the entire premise of "investigative torture" into doubt.

If Muscovites understood the possibility that people could and did lie while suffering excruciating pain, and even built in legal protections against such circumstances, then why did the courts continue to rely on torture as a means of eliciting the truth? This contradiction, like all of those roiling around the torture controversy, retains its urgency. In today's post-911 world, despite a general aversion to cruel bodily practices, a widely shared belief in the authenticity of pain-induced confessions continues to license the application of torture under extraordinary circumstances.[36] The questions remain eerily the same, but those parallels may mask the gulfs of understanding from which very different societies reach similar conclusions.

TRUTH AND TORMENT: UNDERLYING LOGICS OF TORTURE

To the extent that one can accept at face value the notion that courts viewed investigative torture as a means for establishing truth, one must next interrogate the underlying logic that posited an association between physical pain and truthful confession. Why should a body in pain necessarily be presumed to speak more truthfully than a body at ease?

An equation between pain and truth is by no means universal. On the contrary, today only a person of "sound mind and body" can reliably certify a will or other legal documents. This stipulation derives from a presumption that clear thinking and *freedom from pain* best certifies reliability. In Song China, according to Christian de Pee, jurists maintained that only *unforced* testimony would illuminate the truth. "This culture . . . held a positivist view of the legal enterprise: human intelligence, if properly trained, would always be able to see through false accusations and false confessions, discern the hidden messages of body language, and establish the truth of a case." Torture in this view could only distort the picture and shatter the fragile expressions and other physical indicators that a jurist was trained to read.[37] Throughout Europe by the late eighteenth century, "once pain was reconceptualized and represented as a meaningless and mechanical physiological response devoid of social meaning, torture lost its integrity and its perceived ability to draw the truth from the body."[38] More subjective conceptions of truth, as a slippery and negotiated terrain of varying perspectives, a product of consensus among sober minds, or a scientific notion of testable and self-correcting knowledge, would offer yet other equations, where neither pain nor the body would feature into the articulation or identification of truth.[39]

Each of these various approaches to defining and discovering truth drew on particular cultural premises that for one reason or another did not require or admit pain as an investigative device. By the same token, cultures that valued torture as a means to establish truth drew on their own respective modes of understanding the nature of the body. In early modern Europe, for instance, an Augustinian pessimism about the corrupted state of the human will cast a pall of doubt over consciously formulated confessions. For that reason, spontaneous cries wrenched from the flesh of the tortured might hold more weight in the eyes of the court than did consciously mediated speeches, freely made.

Whatever its intellectual, theological, or visceral grounding, faith in the unique ability of physical violence to wrench truth from the unwilling flesh provides the conceptual lynchpin in any claim for the efficacy of torture. Lisa Silverman, in a study of judicial torture in early modern France, writes that in early modern courts of law, "human suffering [was] seen as a means to knowledge." Pain, in this sense, serves as a way of knowing, a bodily epistemology. But why should pain bring truth to the surface? The work of torture differs from other means of discovering truth in that it purports to bridge a divide between the palpable, knowable realm of the flesh and the elusive zone of the unseen, unrecoverable past. "The publicly and legally acknowledged purpose of judicial torture was precisely to render truth visible and audible through the infliction of pain."[40] Torture serves as what the anthropologist Webb Keane describes in a different context as "the practical expression of an ontological dilemma." Keane notes that communication between the realm of the physical, knowable, and concrete and the metaphysical, disembodied, and spiritual necessarily poses a conceptual and practical problem. "One way to put the dilemma is this: to the extent that living humans seek out relations with an invisible and silent world, then they will tend to encounter difficulties centering on their own materiality as well as that of the world they experience and the media for action that are available to them." To transcend the limits of their own materiality, people must develop "material practices [that] make the invisible world a presupposable ground for experience," and find ways to "produce the immaterial using the material means available to them." Torture, like reading entrails, constitutes a way of achieving what Keane labels "*transduction across semiotic modalities*."[41] It may be productive to consider torture in these same terms as a technique for bridging the seemingly impassable gulf between the incommensurable "semiotic modalities" of abstract truth and corporeal flesh. The corporeality of the body served as a repository for truth, which could be extracted, *transduced*, through the experience of pain.

While the productive concept of "transduction" provides a general picture of why torture was considered a useful and effective tool for the implementation of justice, the particular relationship between truth, pain, and the body in the Muscovite metaphysical imaginary is difficult to pinpoint. In Muscovy, as elsewhere, the vulnerability of the human body to pain was understood to offer a bridge to span the gulf between physical and immaterial registers, but, true to form, Muscovite legal experts did not do us the favor of leaving explicit explanations of their ideas. The sources they did produce, laconic legal documents, indicate implicitly that Muscovy hewed its own course, diverging from the various European and Chinese, modern and pre-modern, paradigms characterized above. Since Augustine had little purchase in Orthodox theology, the contamination of the human will was not a subject of concern. Truth appears to have been conceived as an almost corporal reality, an entity that could be physically drawn out through manipulation of the human body. In this scenario, pain functioned as the medium of communication between the corporeal flesh and the embodied reality of truth.

Orthodox teachings provided a foundation for viewing the body itself as a mediator, a transducer, between the sacred and the profane. The incorruptible bodies of saints served precisely this function, as physical embodiments of the sacred and as vehicles transmitting the miraculous to the corporal world of the living.[42] Martyred saints earned their sacred stripes through ordeals of torture, displaying the body's potential for sacrifice and for steadfast adherence to truth. The bodies of criminals performed the reverse function, occluding the truth within obdurate bodies.[43] With a basis in the underlying ambivalent theology of the body as both an agent of sin and the chosen and glorified vessel of Christ's incarnation, Muscovites could rest easy with a double-barreled certainty of the efficacy and righteousness of torture. The body was a cesspool of sin, an obstacle to the discovery of truth and deserving of punishment as brutal as the torments of hell; it was also the chosen form of the incarnate Christ, capable of containing, and therefore of revealing, truth.

The disinclination of Muscovite jurists to put their thoughts down on paper again disadvantages us in the attempt to link these kinds of religious discourses with judicial ones. No law code, decree, or court transcript alludes to sacralizing violence, martyrology, or the miracle of the Incarnation. Quite the contrary; Muscovite legal records are distinguished by their dry, secular, bureaucratic tone and language. Recent work on quotidian and administrative practices, however, find that Orthodox teachings informed the ways that Muscovites of all ranks understood the world around them and shaped the ways they lived and viewed their lives, even in the most banal and unspiritual endeavors.[44] In formulating their understanding of torture and its relationship to human corporeality on the one hand and to essential, intangible truth on the other, Muscovites could easily draw on a ready cultural vocabulary that made all the necessary connections for them.

Icons made those connections manifest in visible form. Among the most popular saints depicted on Muscovite icons was the holy martyr St. George (of dragon fame), whose sufferings at the hands of the Romans received attentive treatment in the "scenes from the life" that framed his image in icons. These detailed miniatures carefully depicted the implements of torture, and, somewhat shockingly, placed in the Roman tormentors' hands precisely the same tools—strappado, weights, hot pincers, fire, and the lash—that executioners used on a regular basis in the tsar's courts. Some shared principle of truth's immanence in the flesh must have helped resolve the dissonance between the vilification of one set of tormentors as godless tyrants and the righteous affirmation of the efforts of another set as loyal and honest officials.

Aside from ideas about interactions between the sacred and profane, another arena premised on communication between the ineffable and physical realms, one particularly pertinent to this discussion, was the lively sphere of Muscovite popular and magical culture. The magical spells that the courts were so determined to discover through torture reveal the same pattern of embodiment and personification of abstract concepts that seems to have characterized judicial notions of truth. In the same way that truth hid in the physical bodies of the accused, fusion and confusion of the literal with the metaphorical also allowed emotional states to assume bodily form. Muscovite spells, particularly love spells, endowed emotional conditions with physical form and addressed them directly, as active participants in the drama of enchantment. Love spells frequently enumerate isolated body parts, each of which should suffer the torments of longing and desire. The somatization of emotion is on display in a spell from the spell book of Semyon Aigustov (discussed in chapter 4), in which each separate part of the body is afflicted with unbearable yearning. Each afflicted limb and organ becomes a receptacle for the unholy desire infused by the spell.

As that fire burns. . . .
So may that female slave burn for me.
White body,
Ardent heart,
Black liver,
Impetuous head with brains,
With clear eyes,
With black brows,
With sugary lips.
As suffocated,
As bitter
As a fish without water,
Just so may the female slave So-and-So be miserable, bitter, for me.[45]

One particular emotion, *toska* (misery, longing, woe), plays an active role in these spells, either as a tangible, transportable object or as a personified agent, or both. Another section of Aigustov's long love spell sends Woe to infect his female prey:

Oh, you, Satan with [your] devils,
With little ones and great ones,
Fly out from the Ocean-Sea,
Take my fiery Woe,
Go around the white world,
Do not set fire to stump, or log, or moist tree,
Not earth, [nor] grass,
But set fire the soul of that slave for me.
On the Sea-Ocean,
On the island of Buian,
There stands a bathhouse,
And in that bathhouse lies a board,
And on that board lies Woe.
I, the slave So-and-So, came,
"What's with you, Woe,
That you grieve and are sad?
Don't grieve, Woe,
Don't be sad, Woe,
Come, Woe,
Come to female slave So-and-So, Woe;
So she will grieve and be sad."[46]

Icon of St. George with scenes from his life. Tempera on panel, gilding and silvering, 76.5 x 59 cm. Russia, first half of the sixteenth century, Inventory No. ERI-235, The State Hermitage Museum, St. Petersburg. Photograph © The State Hermitage Museum / photo by Vladimir Terebenin, Leonard Kheifets, Yurii Molodkovets. (See also plate 13)

Detail, Scenes from the Life of St. George. Above: Suspension from the rack or strappado. Tormentors rip the saint with metal claws. Below: Torture with burning hot metal shoes, which they adjust with metal pincers like those used by Muscovite torturers. Icon painters and chronicle illustrators depict the torture endured by martyr-saints and by criminals and heretics in similar ways. The icons and miniatures both display in slightly abstracted forms the devices of torment that were actually used by Muscovite courts. The State Hermitage Museum, St. Petersburg. Photograph © The State Hermitage Museum / photo by Vladimir Terebenin, Leonard Kheifets, Yurii Molodkovets. (See also plate 14)

Woe's agency, as a delimited, active force, is also apparent in descriptions of possession. Muscovites conceived of *toska* as something that could be sent to people, and witnesses remark that "*toska* overtook her," attributing physical, corporeal power to a metaphor, which in turn produces physical consequences.[47] In tales from the same era, personified Misery roams the earth as the eponymous sufferer of "*Gor'e-Zlochastie (Misery-Luckless-Plight)*," and blue demons incarnate misery as they besiege, brutalize, rape, and impregnate the unfortunate "Demoniac Solomoniia."[48]

Detail of Icon of The Miracle of St. George and the Dragon, with scenes from life. Here St. George is beaten with a whip to the point of drawing blood. Late seventeenth century. Inventory No. ERI-463. The State Hermitage Museum, St. Petersburg. Photograph © The State Hermitage Museum / photo by Vladimir Terebenin, Leonard Kheifets, Yurii Molodkovets. (See also plate 15)

Metaphor assumed physical instantiation not only in fanciful magical lore, but also in a brutally tactile way in Muscovite legal sentencing. Punishment "fit the crime," though in far less lighthearted ways than those imagined by Gilbert and Sullivan. Courts condemned convicts to have their hands cut off for writing illicit documents. People caught in possession of magical spells might be sentenced to having those same spells set aflame and burned on the flesh of their backs.[49] Bandits, rebels, and thieves had the letters of their crime branded onto their faces for all to see.[50] The more routine lashes of the knout left equally legible traces, scarring and marking the criminal for life. "These operations," Keane observes of spirit writing, "typically result in either materializing something immaterial or dematerializing something material."[51] Elaborate dramas of punishment likewise allowed for a literal enactment and physical instantiation of the essence of crime, a ritualized embodiment of concepts of violation and retribution.

To some degree, this marked tendency toward blurring of the metaphorical and the literal obviated the need for complex methods of "transduction across semiotic modalities." By reducing the gulf between incommensurable essences, by conceiving of the immaterial in solid, substantial forms, Muscovites sidestepped the dilemma. Through the conceptual transmutation of an immaterial, intangible abstraction, truth, into an embodied, extractable entity, Muscovite logic could successfully reduce the factors to a common denominator, a shared modality, through which the flesh could be coerced into transmitting the truth. Like Woe, Truth could assume form and substance within the corporeal frames of the people who embodied it.

MORALITY AND MAGIC: PUNISHING UNAUTHORIZED TORTURE

In spite of the absence of explicit meditations on the ethics of torture, Muscovites recognized the ambiguities, practical, legal, and perhaps ethical, of torture, and struggled, just a bit, to erect an administrative structure that would rein in its potential excesses. Supplications from the victims of wrongful torture show that they had a quite refined understanding of those rights and wrongs, or at least an understanding of what kinds of grievances might win the sympathy of the courts. Torture had its appropriate, even righteous, time, place, and circumstances, but, when wrongly applied, it constituted egregious abuse. Location offered one relatively clear standard by which to assess whether torture was legitimate or not. Torture outside of the authorized context of the courtroom was viewed as an abomination, a transgression worthy of legal punishment and moral censure. Nor could just anyone torture another human being at will. In principle, only delegated officials acting under formal orders from the tsar had the right to apply torture.

Under no circumstances could private individuals rightfully torture another person by their own volition. This prohibition applied even if the person subjected to private torture was a violent criminal caught red-handed in the act. Not only was the practice frowned on, but the presumed thief was also entitled to receive recompense for the injury inflicted to his honor and his body. The *Ulozhenie* stated: "If someone, after apprehending a thief, and without bringing him to the [Felony or the Moscow Administrative] Chancery, proceeds to torture him in his own home: the thief shall exact from him his dishonor compensation and maiming fee." Instead of undertaking interrogation on his own, the injured party was to bring the thief to court and initiate formal proceedings against him: "Concerning that for which he tortured him: he shall sue that thief for the theft at a trial. Order that the thief shall not be tortured outside of the chancery."[52] The courts proved particularly vigilant in enforcing this rule if torture was applied in an effort to silence or distort evidence, in other words, to obscure the truth. When Firska Potapov, whom we have encountered before, protested that his master was holding him in his house in chains and in irons for more than a year and subjecting him to beatings and torture in order to prevent him from reporting a case of corruption and lèse majesté (*gosudarevo slovo*), the courts responded with some sympathy (although not with great alacrity), to try to uncover the truth.[53]

The shared understanding that torture belonged only in authorized places and could be exercised only with an official mandate emerges clearly in a number of witchcraft cases where suspects were released after arguing that their accusers had forced their confessions. In the section that follows we return to several of the cases of domestic abuse discussed in the previous chapters, but with a different set of questions in mind. Here we explore the problem of coerced confessions and unauthorized domestic torture. One of the most dramatic of such cases originated in the jurisdiction of Dobroe in 1690. In that year, Archpriest Iakov of the Cathedral Church of the Transfiguration dragged his "longtime serf woman (*starinnoi i kreposnoi*)," Aniutka, into the governor's office, charging that she had conspired with her fugitive husband to rob and burn their master's household, and, even worse, to bewitch him, his wife, and his young son to death. She had put snake skins in their soup and had conspired with other women to mutter incantations over their food and drink. Armed with material evidence, the archpriest provided for the governor's inspection a paper packet containing the snake skins. He informed the court that, having discovered her machinations,

> I, your pilgrim, commanded that she be put in chains, but her husband came with his gang at night by moonlight and got her out of the chains and took her away from her imprisonment to [the town of] Romanov. And he absconded to Romanov with various articles of clothing worth ten rubles and all kinds of goods worth seven rubles.

On the basis of this compelling narrative, the governor ordered Aniutka questioned. Initially she exceeded expectations by confessing not only to the particulars of her master's denunciation but also to seeking advice from an extended and elaborate chain of evil magical practitioners who guided her through a long sequence of malignant incantations, deadly potions, and murderous spells. Not only did she slip snake skins into her master's soup, but she also bewitched an axe handle so that it would chop off the hand that wielded it, she burned a towel with an incantation to make her master and mistress wither, and she cast the mistress's buckle into the stove to cause her to burn in torment. As for the archpriest's little son, Aniutka admitted to placing bewitched peas before him while murmuring, "As a spirit wanders the earth, so may this food cause him, Mikhailo, to wander the earth." According to her confession, after eating the peas, the little boy "lay down to sleep and after that he fell ill and lay sick for about two weeks and then died from that food. And he, Mikhail, was about five years old."

The prosecution's case looked fail-safe, until Aniutka backtracked abruptly and retracted everything. To sort out this newly complex situation, the governor ordered her brought to the rack, "to terrify her (*s pristrastiem*), but she was not tortured."[54] While in the torture chamber, confronted with the implements of torture, she explained her recantation and the circumstances under which she had been forced to make her original incriminating statements. She asserted that "she had confessed out of fear of the archpriest's torment." Offering up the ugly details, she described how "the archpriest beat her for a long time with a whip and a cudgel (*polenom*) and imprisoned her in chains and kept her underground and terrified her." He threatened her, saying, "I will take you to the town and if you don't accuse Aniutka Denisov and Katerinka Podoprishikha and Orinka Parshikov and Avdot'ia the widow of the priest and Levka Novikov of giving you snake skins and teaching you to bewitch people, then I will order you burned in two." Critical to note here is the pattern discernible in the behavior of the abusive master and the court's response to Aniutka's story. Like the other abusers we have encountered in the previous chapter, her master sensed that he had dug himself a hole from which he could not escape. In the aftermath of Aniutka's damning testimony, he did not return to court to contest her version or the verdict. Through his failure to appear, he lost his case, and his serfwoman, his workman, his stolen goods (if such there were), and, presumably, his local reputation.[55] The court report concludes with the statement: "In accordance with everything written above, the archpriest's working woman Aniutka [and the other people implicated in the archpriest's story] *were ordered released*." Aniutka was freed both from prison and from the abusive domination of her master, and was sent to join her husband, the fugitive former workman. Still assigned to the supervision of a man, this time her husband, Aniutka was nonetheless affirmed in her rights as a human being to live without the extremes of physical violence and coerced lies that had brought her to the court's attention.

Torture played a triple role in Aniutka's exculpation, sequentially implicating, condemning, and vindicating her. On the first level, because she had been wrongfully tortured by her master, she occupied the moral high ground as she stood before the authorities. For usurping the court's exclusive right to torture a suspect, the archpriest had stepped onto dangerous terrain, encroaching on the tsar's sovereign jurisdiction. Second, because her initial confession had been wrung from her through his unauthorized torment, her retraction of the story could be seen as serving the quest for truth, while his coercion constituted tampering with the evidence. Third and finally, her retraction and new testimony gained the luster of truth by withstanding the encounter in the torture chamber with the fearsome prospect of the strappado. Torture in the proper venue was deemed a legitimizing certificate of authenticity; misplaced, it was a wrongful device to manipulate and distort the truth.

Another case where a master's violence in extracting a confession backfired is that of Oksiutka, a free woman, who was wrongfully enslaved by Ilia Okhlebaev, a provincial servitor of Sevsk. Okhlebaev took Oksiutka into his household, ostensibly to help her out, and then enslaved her children and forced her to marry one of his men. When he and his wife sickened and each of the couple's babies died young, he charged Oksiutka with consulting a local witch, Baba Daritsa, and with causing their illnesses and deaths through spells and potions. From her prison cell, however, Oksiutka managed to turn the tables. She exposed the vicious way her self-appointed master had first lured her to his household under false pretenses, with intent to enslave her, and then had wrung a confession of witchcraft out of her through force:

> Wanting to take away my freedom (*menia nevolit'*), that Ilia beat me and tormented me ceaselessly, and he told me, poor one, to accuse Daritsa Nikiforova, a musketeer's wife of Sevsk town, of dealing in roots, and I poor one, unable to bear the torment from him, accused that musketeer's wife on his instruction. . . .

The two women were sent from Sevsk to Moscow for further questioning. There both withstood torture and maintained their innocence. In 1651, in her fifth year of imprisonment in Moscow, Oksiutka appealed directly to the tsar in a petition, begging that he release her from the dungeon, "so that I, poor bitter orphan, do not die a pointless death of cold and hunger while sitting in prison." Okhlebaev had done his best to fend off her countersuit with a claim that the women were lodging false charges against him "with criminal intent," duplicitously alleging that he had tortured Oksiutka into her confession, but his excuses did him no good. Although the two women still were locked in prison when the records of the case trail off, the tsar's sympathies in the matter were quite clear. He had ordered a new investigation in response to their appeal, and, "as a result of the investigation, Ilia was retired from his captaincy, and sat in jail."[56]

A case from 1700 brings us from brutal interactions between masters and servants to the equally raw relations within Muscovite patriarchal families. Fedor Dalmatov, a provincial servitor from Zemliansk in Voronezh province, charged that his daughter-in-law Marfa had brought "a great evil" to his household. He reported that the perfidious woman had given "his wife, her mother-in-law, the skin of some disgusting creatures in her drink, and from that she is suffering and dying. And she also gave grasses to his daughter Maria so that she withered. And now his wife and daughter are suffering from that and will ultimately die." When questioned by the authorities, Marfa admitted to the charges and dragged her own mother, Ovdot'ia, and her sister-in-law Nastas'ia into the ugly business as well. But when she was questioned again in the presence of her kinswomen, Marfa retracted the confession and the denunciations and insisted that she had been forced into these statements because she was "unable to endure the blows" inflicted on her by her father-in-law.

> In questioning, Marfa testified that in this 1700 year [in the week before Lent], on the Saturday, her father-in-law, Fedor Dalmatov, brought a stranger to his house and he placed her before this man. That man called himself a wise man (*znatok*), and he told her, "I know that you bewitched your mother-in-law and Fedor's children with poisoned potion. You gave your mother-in-law the skins of loathsome creatures and the children grass, and your mother gave you those skins of loathsome creatures and the grass. And that man, who called himself a wise man, told Fedor to beat her, Marfitsa, with a whip, so that she would confess to what he had said, that supposedly she had bewitched her mother-in-law and Fedor's children. And her father-in-law with his son, her husband, took whips and beat her with deadly blows, and having beaten her, chained her. Once she was chained, the wise man took the key to those irons for himself. And they kept her chained for a week, and terrified her. And as her husband and her father-in-law were taking her to the Spiritual Chancellery in Zemliansk for questioning, they frightened her further and told her, "If you don't start talking and admit to all of this, and accuse your mother, we will beat you with whips and torture you with all sorts of tortures." And she, Marfitsa, fearing and not able to bear their blows and torment, confessed and accused her mother as they had instructed her, according to their words and warnings (*ustrast'ki*?). But she confessed to that bewitchment all falsely.

No resolution survives for the case, but the fragmentary record suggests that Marfa's position was gaining credence in the courtroom, and the bullying pair of father-in-law and husband were on the road toward losing their trumped-up case. Dozens of local residents testified to the good and upright character of the women, and Marfa's mother and sister-in-law registered forceful counter-petitions in which they presented strong cases for their innocence. They took responsibility for using herbs and grasses to make healing teas, and, with a flair for courtroom drama, they imbibed their own potions before the eyes of the judges, thereby providing convincing evidence that the concoctions were harmless.

Gradually, blame in the case shifted to the rogue "wise man," identified as Iakushka, who turned out to be a known troublemaker, a harborer of grudges and resentments, with a record of shaking down local residents with threats of bewitchment. The neighbors testified in large numbers that he promised healing but worked no cures, and that he forced all and sundry to pay him exorbitant sums of money to avoid his curses. Witnesses reported that Iakushka had boasted: "I told Fedor to chain his daughter-in-law because her brother insulted me and wanted to beat me up. If only her brother, Priest Timofei, had begged me on his knees, I wouldn't have said anything about his sister's witchcraft, and I wouldn't have told Fedor to chain her up." One witness reported that Iakushka said, "if only Priest Timofei had given me money, five rubles or less, I wouldn't have said anything about his sister and bewitchment to Fedor Dalmatov."[57]

With the evidence mounting, the case ends with the usual frustrating lack of resolution, but given the proclivity of Muscovite courts to follow the logic of evidence, it looks as if the scales of justice must have tipped in the right direction. Marfa and her mother and sister most likely were released, although whether Marfa was returned to her father-in-law's household remains unknown. Most likely she was, although perhaps with some legal protections. Her situation may have paralleled that of the other Marfitsa, discussed above, who claimed that she too was forced to confess to practicing witchcraft against her husband and in-laws. In that case, the woman was released back to the care of her husband and his parents, but they were firmly bound by a signed surety to refrain from abusing her in the future.[58]

Not all cases resulted in as satisfying resolutions as these cases suggest. Earlier in the century, another husband, a peasant named Lunka in the Voronezh region, beat his wife Fetinitsa into accusing her mother and another woman of bewitching his brother Grishka to death with a root. In court, the governor and assistant governor of Voronezh reported: "Lunka spoke against his wife Fetinitsa before us, your slaves, [saying] that his wife had bewitched his brother Grishka, and she bewitched him with a root, which he brought to us. And that Fetinitsa was questioned and tortured following her husband's testimony."[59]

When first questioned, Fetinitsa backed up her husband's story with her own testimony, although softening the account slightly. She admitted that she did administer a root to her brother-in-law, not to harm him but to make him "be kind." She blamed her mother with providing her with the root, obtained in turn from "another woman of the village of Usmon, Grishka Polstovalov's wife Akulinka." When the mother denied all charges under the duress of torture and insisted that her daughter's testimony was false, the authorities had Fetinitsa "tortured again in the presence of her mother and in front of Grishka's wife Akulinka." Even while facing the women she was incriminating, Fetinitsa stuck by her husband's story, but when she was handed over to a regimental Cossack for safekeeping while she recovered from her ordeal, she changed her tune. She protested that she had been forced to confess to all the spell casting and that she had unjustly slandered her mother and Akulinka "at the instruction of her husband Lunka, because she was not able to tolerate his beatings."

As a result, the brute Lunka was arrested and subjected to interrogation under torture himself. The court took the women's charges seriously, but the judges' concern did little to improve Fetinitsa's lot. Her challenge to domestic hierarchy perturbed them as much as or more than the domestic violence and weighed against her. "*Because she had spoken against her husband*, the governors ordered Fetinitsa tortured for a third time." On the other hand, her steadfast denial under renewed torture would have counted in her favor: "And with torture that Fetinitsa said the same thing, that she had slandered her mother and Akulinka at the instruction of her husband, not being able to bear his beatings." "My husband brought that root to me and told me to slander my mother, and at the instruction of my husband, I slandered my mother. And I did not get that root from my mother."

The records end in July 1623 with an order from the tsar instructing the governor of Voronezh to have Lunka questioned and tortured. The order concludes with the proviso that "if with torture he doesn't confess, then you should order his wife tortured hard about that root: where did she get it, and who instructed her to bewitch Grishka, and why. And whomever she implicates, you should find those people and question them, and investigate harshly. And if the interrogation should justify torture, then you should torture those people about the root, . . . and you should send us a report of what they say." In this case, the court's diligence produces only an ever-expanding spiral of torture. The alleged provider of the root, "Grishka Polstovalov's wife Akulinka was brought to torture. And after torture she lay for a week and then died."[60] Akulinka's death was collateral damage. Everyone touched by the strands of incrimination met the fierce heat of the burning pincers and the agony of the rack.

Similarly Katerinka, a household serf in Elets who also made an appearance in the previous chapter, maintained during investigation in 1628–29 that her confession, like those of the other women and men discussed here, was coerced by her master, Prince Fedor Eletskoi. She explained that after the prince's wife fell ill, he "ordered me beaten and . . . started to question me about the princess's bewitchment. And he said to me, 'if you incriminate yourself, nothing will happen to you. And so, on the basis of what he said to me, I slandered myself and said that I gave the princess enchanted salt in her food and that the Baba Okulina gave that salt to me.' "[61] Her master therefore had doubly wronged her and had ample cause to fear that she might have resorted to magical retribution: not only had he prevented her from marrying, but he had also beaten her to force her confession. On the basis of these reciprocal accusations, Katerinka and a number of other serfs and slaves, male and female, were repeatedly subjected to torture with hot pincers and fire in the official court setting in order to sort out the conflicting evidence. What happened to Katerinka and the others incriminated in the case is unknown, but the pattern is clear. Officially authorized torture functions to test charges of illicit torture, which, in turn, was employed to elicit coerced, and therefore suspect, confession.

Male as well as female dependents found themselves forced by their superiors to confess to crimes of witchcraft, and then tortured to authenticate their claims. In 1672 in Kostroma province, a peasant woman of the estate of the infamous Andrei Bezobrazov was hauled into court along with a male healer after the woman confessed she supplied a fellow peasant with some grasses to remedy possession. Under questioning the woman, Avdiushka, retracted her earlier confession, with a now-familiar exculpation:

> She slandered herself with those confessions without basis, because she was unable to tolerate the torture of Andrei Bezobrazov's bailiff (*prikashchik*) Sereshka Terent'ev. The bailiff Sereshka tortured her three times in his house in the landlord's compound. He beat her with bastinados and wanted to burn her with fire. . . .
>
> And in Kostroma at the governor's office, she said, she incriminated herself falsely, at the instruction of the bailiff and the elder and peasants, claiming that she had sent grasses to the peasant woman Alenka with her son Sidorka. But, she said, she never took any grass from Sereshka and she didn't send her son Sidor to the woman Alenka, and didn't tell her to sprinkle it in food.

Sereshka Borov, the peasant healer implicated as her supplier of magical ingredients, echoed her story of forced false confession.

> In questioning Sereshka said that he didn't give any grasses to the woman Avdiushka. And he heals babies and livestock using only incense (*rosnyi ladan*) that he ties onto his patients and puts in water to drink. But in the case record, his previous testimony is recorded as saying during questioning that he healed babies and some people by saying incantations over water and salt, and he gives this water to his patients to drink, but now he says that he confessed to those things being unable to stand the torture, and that he had falsely accused himself. Actually he says he healed babies and livestock only by using incense, and without any incantations.

To clarify matters, by command of the tsar, the governor of Kostroma had the witnesses tortured:

> In examination Sereshka was tortured hard and burned with fire. . . . And Avdiushka was tortured hard and burned with fire, and with torture and fire she still did not confess, and she maintained that she had said all those things incriminating herself and Sereshka Borov slanderously, by the instruction of the bailiff Sereshka Terent'ev.

The bailiff, questioned in turn, maintained that he had interrogated the two suspects after their fellow peasants denounced them, but he insisted that he only "questioned them orally but did not torture or torment them." The case breaks off, sending the suspects under guard in Kostroma "to the prison of disgrace (*v opal'nuiu tiurmu*)," pending the outcome of a general investigation.[62] Nonetheless, the bailiff's fervent denial demonstrates his awareness that abusing the peasants in his charge and coloring the contents of their confessions would appear, in the eyes of the court, as misconduct and might well tip the case against him.

In each of these cases, officially mandated torture served, in the eyes of the authorities, to peel away the layers of falsehood manufactured through illegal, private, unauthorized torture. The binary assessment of torture, producing falsehood when used by an individual's whim but reliable when applied by the courts with the tsar's imprimatur, illuminates the morality of torture, of witchcraft, and of Muscovy more generally. Punitive actions taken against domestic torturers express the same moral sanctions as those levied against brutal husbands and masters in the previous chapter. More specifically, however, in the context of the courtroom, the moral commitment to truth made private torture not only a violation of Christian mercy and an irresponsible exercise of power but also a serious criminal infraction involving deliberate distorting, suborning, or silencing of witnesses. "Truth," the holy grail of judicial investigation, was unproblematically understood as that which authorized interrogation and lawful use of torture would elicit, through wise and merciless questioning by the tsar's appointed officials.

TORTURE AND TERROR

The evidence adduced in this chapter suggests that Muscovite law and the upstanding officials in its service, misguided though they may have been, considered torture a necessary and even righteous tool to be deployed in the pursuit of truth. And yet, this cannot be the whole story. Constrained and confined by the documents that happen to survive in state archives, any study of torture in historical context must recognize its own limits. Dispassionate court records present only the horrifying but always self-justifying official picture. Very rarely can we crack the smooth surface. No inside view of the torture chamber has surfaced in Muscovite archives, beyond the appeals of the tortured, but an astonishing, devastating firsthand account from a witch trial in seventeenth-century Bavaria survives: the interrogation of Johannes Junius, burgomaster at Bamberg. Junius was accused of witchcraft and brutally tortured in 1628. Writing with hands broken and mangled in finger screws, he described the cynicism of his judges in a letter he attempted to smuggle out of prison to his daughter:

> I had to tell what people I had seen [at the witch-sabbath]. I said that I had not recognized them. "You old rascal, I must set the executioner at you. Say—was not the Chancellor there?" So I said yes. "Who besides?" I had not recognized anybody. So he said: "Take one street after another; begin at the market, go out on one street and back on the next."[63]

While he was still resisting the judges' pressure, the executioner, with chilling honesty, urged him to confess anything, whatever the investigators wanted, or else the torture would never end. "Sir, I beg you, for God's sake confess something, whether it be true or not. Invent something, for you cannot endure the torture which you'll be put to; . . . one torture will follow after another until even you say you are a witch." Eventually, inevitably, Junius complied, "forced to say through fear of the torture which was threatened beyond what I had already endured." "They are all sheer lies and made-up things, so help me God. . . . For they never leave off with the torture till one confesses something; be he never so good, he must be a witch."[64]

The official genesis of the court records from seventeenth-century Muscovy prohibits such revelations. The documents that survive also obscure the self-conscious sadism that the all-too-numerous modern accounts by torture victims describe. In a painful account of his time in French colonial prisons in during the Algerian War, the journalist Henri Alleg records that "bursts of laughter" greeted his efforts at maintaining his dignity or retaining his proud silence in the face of the most brutal tortures. His tormentors jeered:

> "Everybody talks. You'll have to tell us everything—and not only a little bit of the truth, but everything!" During all this time I was being taunted by the "blue berets" standing around me.
>
> "Why don't your friends come and rescue you?"
>
> "Well, well, what's he doing stretched out like that? Relaxing?"[65]

Unbelievably, his mocking interrogators in Algeria in 1958 glorified their similarities with the Nazi torturers who had been defeated in France just over a decade earlier.

> “This is the Gestapo here! You know the Gestapo?” Then, with irony: “So you wrote articles about torture, did you, you bastard! Very well! Now it’s the tenth Paratroop Division who are doing it to you.” I heard the whole band of torturers laughing behind me.[66]

Similar revelations are appearing with shocking regularity from multiple venues, including, most recently, Abu Ghraib, and providing insights that one would prefer not to see.[67] Once the veil is removed, it is harder to accept that a lofty quest for truth was the motivation, however misguided. Something else motivates the torturer, making “the abject night terrible.”[68]

Jean-Paul Sartre, in his blistering introduction to Alleg’s account, deems the idea that torture is used to elicit the truth risible.

> What emerges from the events [Alleg] describes, is that [the torturers] want to convince themselves and their victims of their invincible power: sometimes they present themselves as supermen who have other men at their mercy, and sometimes as men, strong and severe, who have been entrusted with the most obscene, ferocious, and cowardly of animals, the human animal. . . . The main thing is to make the prisoner feel that he does not belong to the same species: therefore they are undressed, they are beaten, they are mocked; soldiers come and go, proffering insults and threats with a nonchalance which they want to make as terrible as possible.[69]

Their murderous taunts support Scarry’s notion that their goal was to shatter the life, the core, the very being of their target. Their continued torment of their prisoner long after any information he knew would have lost its effective utility further underscores the gulf between their claim, that they were seeking critical truths, and the reality, that they were subjecting a human being to torture for the sake of torture. Torturers, in Sartre’s words, are sadists, fallen angels, war lords with terrible caprices.

Muscovite authorities made no apologies when they mandated that torture should be applied “without mercy,” though mercy formed the centerpiece of their political theology. It is hard to escape ultimately agreeing with Scarry and with Sartre: “Torture is senseless violence, born in fear.” It has its own relentless, self-perpetuating, diving logic.

> The purpose of it is to force from *one* tongue, amid its screams and its vomiting up of blood, the secret of *everything*. Senseless violence: whether the victim talks or whether he dies under his agony, the secret that he cannot tell is always somewhere else and out of reach. It is the executioner who becomes Sisyphus. If he puts the question at all, he will have to continue for ever.[70]

Torture manufactures the answers that it seeks, but always demands still more, still more hidden information. In European witch trials, torture educed elaborate confessions of impossible crimes: flying on brooms, goats, or even men to distant Sabbaths; compacting with the Devil and fornicating with demons; sending out spirits to possess others, sacrificing babies and consuming their flesh or reducing their fat into salves and unguents. Such outlandish confessions demonstrate unambiguously that torture and truth do not walk in tandem. Some confessing witches may have come to believe their own stories, to internalize the assumptions about sin, Satan, and the destructive power of envy or anger as tangible forces in the material world. But that belief, that truth, was manufactured through careful ideological work, and was forged and polished in the fires of the torture chamber. Russian witches confessed to far more plausible crimes: making teas from roots, casting salt at crossroads, putting dirt from dead men's graves in their enemies' soup. If occasionally they confessed to summoning unclean spirits or watching little laughing men frolic about on a platter of salt, such phantasms still hew far closer to a credible picture of actual practice than the naked night-flying, demonic sex, shape-shifting, and cannibalism of their European counterparts. Nonetheless, the case records document the proliferation of confessions under torture and bear witness to the fact that coerced confessions were, even in the eyes of the authorities, far from reliable windows on truth.

This is the fallacy of torture. Its defenders claim that although it is not pretty, it works, and extreme times call for extreme measures. But if early modern people could be tortured into admitting to any story line that might stop the pain, so too will modern men and women. In light of torture's ability to create rather than reveal the truth, the resurgence of torture as an extension of the tools of interrogation, its return from the dark pages of history to which the rational thinkers of the Enlightenment consigned it, is chilling. Again, Sartre provides mordant commentary on the rehabilitation of torture as a technique of governance so quickly after the horrors of the Third Reich. What served as a heartfelt wakeup cry to France in 1958 sadly serves the same purpose in the United States and throughout the world in 2013: "The decline has been gradual, imperceptible. But now when we raise our heads and look into the mirror we see an unfamiliar and hideous reflection: ourselves."[71]

8

Witchcraft, Heresy, Treason, Rebellion

Defining Muscovy's Most Heinous Crimes

TORTURE PLAYED ITS PART IN serious criminal cases, but only the most heinous of offenses warranted the superfluity of blows or the exorbitant application of fire, water, and hot pincers that constituted the norm in prosecuting witchcraft. Most crimes were adjudicated on the basis of testimony, material evidence, and character witnesses, without recourse to torture at all. Even for those serious crimes that did lead to torture, the torture itself was for the most part administered with a restricted range of techniques: most commonly blows with the knout and/or suspension on the rack. In her study of the entire legal system and survey of hundreds of trials, Kollmann identifies only three types of crime that unleashed the full arsenal of the torture chamber, with suspects undergoing multiple sessions and a battery of different horrific techniques: knouting with unendurable numbers of blows (up to one hundred recorded for one session), strappado with weights, hot pincers, burning with fire, water torture. The three crimes that drew the most elaborate torture were treason, heresy, and witchcraft.[1]

It is pressing, as this book draws to a close, to consider why witchcraft joined heresy and treason in unholy triple alliance as the most terrible of all crimes, meriting the most brutal of all investigations. If the interpretations presented in this book are correct, it should not have ranked so high, or rather, so low. After all, as argued in earlier chapters, what distinguished Muscovite witchcraft beliefs from those widely held in Europe at the time was the absence of an overarching satanic narrative that could endow the acts of witches with destructive cosmic significance. Muscovite witches, we have seen, were not imagined as massing in vast conspiracy to overturn monarchical and divine authority, nor were they generally conceived as sworn agents of the Devil. They were not seen as members of heretical, anti-Christian cults. Nor were they were seen as sexually voracious corrupters of men. Why, then, did their prosaic practices and kitchen magic trouble Muscovite authorities and subjects so profoundly that they merited the fullest violence of the law and the most extreme forms of torture? This finding would seem to undermine every assertion of the previous chapters. What about witchcraft constituted it as a crime of such enormity that its investigation required pulling out all the stops?

In the scholarly literature, an easy elision with the historical experience of the Catholic and Protestant West makes the association of witchcraft with treason and heresy seem natural and unsurprising. In Western demonologies, heresy and its intrinsic treason against God were understood as integral and defining characteristics of witchcraft. This argument builds on strong evidence in European material, but has generally been appropriated rather than explored in the Russian context. Muscovite law and belief did not follow the Europeans in placing healers and fortune-tellers and purveyors of curses and love spells in the same imaginary space as heretics and rebels who defied divine and earthly order as part of a great subversive movement. Instead, the extreme reaction to the crime of magic, following the general line of argument pursued throughout this book, derived from an understanding that witchcraft constituted an egregious assault on the fragile, individual, personal bonds that kept the moral order of hierarchy, dependency, and bondage in check.

HERESY AND WITCHCRAFT?

From a European perspective, the intellectual clustering of witchcraft, heresy, and rebellion makes perfect sense, indeed, seems an obvious and intuitive one. The importance of the shift in understanding the essence of witchcraft's threat in late medieval Europe has become entrenched in scholarly explanations for the rise of prosecution. According to Pope Hadrian, writing in 1523, witches were guilty of "heretical pravity": "Many people of both sexes, . . . forgetful of their own souls' salvation and straying far from the Catholic Faith, made a certain sect, utterly denying the Faith which they received in Holy Baptism, spurning beneath their feet the Holy Cross and treating it with vilest contumely, above all abusing the Divine Sacrament of the Altar, taking the Devil to be their Lord and Master, promising him worship and obedience, and with accursed incantations, charms, sortilege, and other foul magic rites ever doing grave harm and hurt to men, animals and the fruit of the earth . . . , to the deadly peril of their own souls, giving offense to the Divine Majesty of God."[2] This papal mélange says it all. The reclassification of witchcraft from a form of maleficium, the inflicting of harm, to a form of heresy, the abjuring of God and swearing of allegiance to the Devil, opened the door to the concerted early modern effort to hunt and burn witches. John Calvin, representing a very different voice of

Western Christianity, defined witchcraft as "an overthrowing of God's service and a perversion of the order of nature." The heretical turning away from God, "attributing God's office to satan," constituted rebellion, and, even without evidence of harm, sufficed to define witchcraft as an abomination, deserving the ultimate punishment. According to Calvin, one voice among many to weigh in on the subject, "although other vices were to be pardoned, yet this one ought to be punished and utterly rooted out."[3] The same draconian logic applied on the secular side of the equation. For the sake of divine and terrestrial order, witchcraft, a deadly combination of heresy and treason, had to be ruthlessly extirpated.

In Muscovy, as we have seen, no such grand narrative encompassed notions of witchcraft, and although the terms "heretic" and "heretical" do crop up, there was no systematic linkage of the concepts. Relatively few litigants adopted the term "heretic" when denouncing alleged witches, and when they did, most used it loosely as a synonym for witch.[4] In this context, it rarely if ever alludes to a systematic, organized set of unorthodox beliefs or practices, much less a collective heterodox movement. Although there were plenty of accusations of heresy as a stand-alone crime or in combination with other forms of rebellion or criminality, in only twenty-two of our cases was the word "heresy" recorded as part of the accusation.[5] One case from the end of the century records charges against the "criminal and heretic" Liubim Anikiev syn and his son Ivashko. According to a petition filed by one of their purported victims, the father confessed with torture "to this heresy: he bewitched (*isportil*) my wife." In the eyes of this plaintiff, bewitchment, the bread and butter of witchcraft, qualified as an act of heresy.[6] In 1677 a number of residents of Kurmysh petitioned against a vagrant, Senka Ivanov, and his wife for heresy and bewitchment. "In questioning and with torture they said that they bewitched with heretical words and poisons many people of the male and female sex."[7] Even though the accusations introduce the term "heresy," the elements of the charges look in no way different from the run-of-the-mill, prosaic magic that formed the core of seventeenth-century complaints: spells, and poisons, roots, and "spoiling." The troops fighting against the rebel Stenka Razin captured a criminal and heretic nun (*vor i eretik staritsa*) who had led troops and bewitched people with the usual stock of roots and spells, so they too saw the dual descriptors of heretic and witch as a plausible pairing, here throwing in rebellion to boot.[8] Conceptual distinctions between the terms were left unexamined, and few of their compatriots shared this association.

In one trial the label of heresy refers to acts of recognizable sacrilege described in the accusations. In this trial, a Cherkassian weaver was charged with stealing communion bread from the local church and using it to lure people "to come to [them] and look at [their] wares, and so they would love his wares and so that they wouldn't patronize his fellow weavers in Akhtysk." Standing by the implements of torture, the weaver admitted that "he took church communion bread out of the ciborium and from the church. . . . And having taken that communion bread, he soaked it in water and sprinkled that water on his wares so that people would come to him and would love his work, but he didn't cool people toward his fellow weavers, and he didn't bewitch anyone with it. And having fortified his work, he ate the communion bread."[9] The court scribe applied the word "heretical" in describing the weaver's "sorcery" (employing the term associated with non-Russian magic, "*volkhovanie*"), but in prosecuting the case, the authorities pursued the criminal manipulation of commerce and let the matter of heresy drop. A small cluster of cases associated accusations of heresy with keeping "black books," an association made with some consistency in the decrees and prohibitions issued from on high. But more commonly, the adjective "heretical" simply intensified the noun "witchcraft," without implying any particular religious deviance, and the two terms functioned interchangeably. The label indicated awareness that the church frowned on magic, but did not invoke any substantive notion of magic as part of an organized, doctrinal, or fundamental divergence from Christian teaching or Orthodoxy community.[10]

A POLITICAL CRIME?

In searching for a common denominator unifying Muscovy's triad of most grievous infractions—treason, heresy, and witchcraft—a number of scholars have suggested placing them all under the rubric of "political crimes." Politics proves more illuminating than the red herring of heresy for identifying the core anxieties at the heart of witchcraft prosecutions, but the rubric of politics, too, is useful only within limits. Since the beginnings of scholarly interest in the topic, Russian witch trials have been cast as a variant of political trial. N. Ia. Novombergskii framed this particular understanding when he chose to publish a selection of witchcraft trials as an appendix to his two-volume collection of "sovereign's word and deed" trials, that is, trials involving accusations of treasonous speech or acts.[11] Will Ryan attributes both the "political colouring" and the preponderance of male suspects to the fact that the courts hearing witchcraft accusations were predominantly military courts, which skewed the pool of suspects toward men, and in particular, men who drew the ire of people of power, people in a position to prosecute. He argues that the country was under-governed and the chanceries understaffed, so only cases involving "male persons in the employ of the state or the Church" were likely to receive formal trial.[12]

Many of the trials do fit nicely within this political-military framework, but it can be misleading. Muscovite courts listened attentively to the complaints of men and women of all ranks, from boyars and archbishops to serfs and slaves. Investigations responded to initiative from below, and no subject of the tsar was too lowly to expect, or even to receive, what George Weickhardt calls "due process and equal justice" from the tsar's officials.[13] The cases presented throughout this book document trials instigated by petitions submitted by townspeople, peasants, bailiffs, priests, monastic servitors, deacons, and slaves, women and men, as well as boyars, abbots, and tsars, people from all over the tsardom, not only those residing in major cosmopolitan centers. Not just the highborn, the influential, or the powerful and not only the witches and fortune-tellers in their employ found themselves entangled in witchcraft trials before the courts.

If we define as "political" only those cases involving magic directed at individual members of the ruling elite, connected with acts of rebellion, or explicitly labeled as treasonous or seditious in the court report, roughly forty-five (20 percent) of our cases meet the criteria. Drawn from records of trials, this number excludes rumors of sorcery that swirled around various rulers and high court figures of the time but never reached the stage of legal prosecution. At the other end, the figure also necessarily omits the presumably even more common village rumors that never hardened into formal charges. Some cases easily meet the standards of the political, but how can one categorize the case of an elderly fortune-teller named Daritsa, brought before a panel of distinguished judges in the Chancellery of the Great Palace in 1647, where it was discovered that she had foretold the brief rise to the throne and rapid fall of Boris Godunov fifty years earlier.[14] This sounds like reckless meddling in a dangerous realm of court politics and would certainly suffice to land her in hot water on those (political) grounds. Yet this particularly piquant bit of political prognostication came to light only as the investigation unfolded half a century later. The charge that landed her in court was that she had used her preternatural vision to help a peasant named Simonka identify the thief who had absconded with his "stuff." It was not the threat she posed to the tsarist succession but rather her practice of everyday village magic that earned her the attention of the court.[15] In identifying the thief, she was perhaps seen as usurping the authority of the courts or as capturing spiritual energy on which the church claimed a monopoly. On this we can only speculate; but her infraction seems far removed from any useful definition of politics.

Other cases have indisputably political features. In the time of Ivan the Terrible, the untimely deaths of two of the tsar's wives were attributed to magic, that of his first wife, Anastasiia Romanovna, and later, Marfa Sobakina, who lingered in life only two weeks after the royal marriage. In 1616, Tsar Mikhail Fedorovich's intended bride, Maria Ivanovna Khlopova, sickened prior to her wedding, inclining the tsar's mother and other advisers to deem her unsuitable because of her purported inability to bear children. The tsar reluctantly accepted the change of plans but, convinced that jealous members of the Saltykov family had deliberately bewitched his betrothed, he exiled the presumed culprits, who had "whispered" among themselves.[16] Touching on politics in a lower register, several witchcraft cases involved efforts to bewitch governors, four involved clerks from various central and local chancelleries, a few concerned suspicious border-crossings, ten involved "sovereign's word and deed," and several were precipitated by the discovery of anonymous letters that were deemed "treasonous." A few allude to events of the "unsettled times" of various rebellions but show little direct engagement with the background of revolt. An unusual case featured Andrei Matveev, son of Artamon Matveev (of "black book" fame, discussed in chapter 6), as both plaintiff and judge.[17]

A. S. Lavrov correctly notes that after decades of relative calm under tsars Mikhail and Aleksei, the political aspects of witchcraft trials intensified in the late seventeenth century. While plots against royal brides dotted the first three-quarters of the century, after Aleksei's death in 1676 and reaching a crescendo during the chaotic transition before Peter consolidated his rule, cases involving anyone acquainted with the tsar or his inner circle came to approximate treason more closely.[18] The late seventeenth century does depart from the earlier decades of the century, with spikes both in overall numbers of trials and in those bearing directly on the life and health of the sovereign and his family. Peter the Great and his immediate family attracted a disproportionate share of magical attacks, or at least such accusations seem to have been most actively policed and recorded during the tumultuous first decades of his reign. At least six trials investigated efforts to bewitch Peter and various family members: his brother and co-tsar Ivan. his mother Natalia Kirillovna, and his children.[19]

In 1694 an anonymous letter thrown onto the steps of the governor's office in Beloozero alerted the governor to a ripening plot. Within the Kirillov Monastery, treason was afoot. According to the letter and subsequent confessions under torture, the cellarer of the monastery and the brethren were conniving to make a "soap of snakes and other loathsome creatures and cats' brains and frog eggs," a compound of the sort that "a wife might [use to] bewitch her husband." The plotters meant to imbue a shirt stolen from the sovereign, Peter Alekseevich, with the potion, with intent to kill. Investigated as a case of treason, the anonymous letter was quickly traced back to a monk by the name of Ioanikii. Ioanikii, the authorities concluded, had schemed maliciously in his cell to frame the innocent cellarer and other monks with these false charges. Ignominiously defrocked and returned to his secular status and pre-tonsure name Ioanikii, now known again as Larka Lopukhin, was condemned to death "for his criminality in that he composed criminal letters and in those letters wrote many unseemly words touching upon the sovereigns' health and blamed those criminal letters on the cellarer of the Kirillov Monastery and the brethren." Led grimly to the execution site, the convict received the news that the sovereigns, "in memory of their mother the great sovereign and pious tsaritsa and great princess Natalia Kirillovna, rescinded the order for execution. And they ordered that the defrocked monk for his criminality be punished: he should be beaten with a knout and sent in exile to Solovetskii Monastery and held with great surveillance with all diligence, and do not to let anyone see him, and do not to allow him pen or ink."[20] This is a revealing case in that it illustrates how all parties effortlessly imagined witchcraft as a tool, even *the* tool, of political treason.

Similar machinations were ascribed to the suspects in the notorious Shaklovityi scandal of 1689. A leading administrator and state secretary entrusted with leadership in the most important chancelleries in Moscow, Fedor Shaklovityi proved himself a devoted servant of the regent Sophia, half sister of Peter the Great. Implicated in fomenting a mutiny in favor of the Sophia in 1689, Shaklovityi was tried and convicted of attempting to assassinate Peter and members of his immediate family. He was speedily executed in that same year.[21] An incriminating bit of evidence arrived posthumously in the form of another anonymous letter, written with the standard fill-in-the-blank slot for a name, familiar from generic magical spells. The letter began as follows:

> To Tsar Peter Alekseevich! Your true slave *IMIA REK* (fill in the blank) informs you about the wizard (*volshebnik*) Iudka Vasil'eev syn Boltin, that he, Iudka, took counsel with Fedka Shaklovityi against you, sovereign, and against your mother, Tsaritsa Natalia Kirillovna and against tsarevna Natalia Alekseevna, to feed you, sovereigns, with a poisoned potion and roots (*okormit' otravnym zelem'i korenem*) in Moscow and on campaigns on many different days in Preobrazhenskoe Monastery and in the Maiden Convent. And a variety of poisoned potions were prepared in food and in drink, but on that day, you weren't there in the Maiden Convent. God protected you, sovereigns, from such an evil act. And on the road many times Iudka scattered grasses and roots where your sovereign travels would take you on campaign, and God protected you from those grasses and roots. Your great sovereign's carriage never went to that place. But he, Iudka, worked that kind of evil for a long time against you, sovereigns. If you had passed through those roots and grasses, sovereign, at that very moment you would have fallen ill. And those roots and grasses were there on many days.[22]

The long letter continued, recounting the history of Iudka's training in witchcraft, which he learned from another peasant, now dead, and of his close relationship with Shaklovityi. Iudka often came to Shaklovityi's house at night, the letter claimed, and sat there for hours, talking and exchanging vows of friendship, brotherhood, and filial love.

> And when they cut off Fedka's head, [Iudka] left Moscow and went the village and said these words, and he still says them now: "For the sake of my father I will die, and if God prolongs my health, from mourning my father Fedor Leont'evich's death, I will get even with my father's enemies, and I will complete the enterprise. Have mercy on me."
>
> Sovereign Tsar Peter Alekseevich! For your eternal health and that of your mother and sister, it is time to carry out an order against this criminal. The sorcerer Iudka Boltin and his brother and those criminals, and that which Iudka said with tears is known to you Sovereign.[23]

Politics and witchcraft could complement each other, and thoughts of treason readily moved to fears of witchcraft. Even libelous or anonymous denunciations made a bid for plausibility by drawing the two themes together.

Given the broader span of trials, however, it is hard to maintain the position that witchcraft trials were essentially political. The surviving corpus of cases tells a quite different story, providing a useful corrective on three counts. First, the vast majority of cases that found their way to trial involved alleged targets and accused perpetrators who could claim no connection to the political elite. Witchcraft trials, as we have seen throughout this study, pitted peasants against one another, estate bailiffs against serfs, masters against slaves, husbands against wives, tavern keepers, Cossacks, Mordvins, Chuvash, musketeers, priests, deacons, weavers, healers, and wanderers against one another. If roughly 20 percent of the cases touched on political actors, the remaining 80 percent did not, at least not in any straightforward way. When, after a night of carousing together, a dragoon in Sokol' accused one of his fellow dragoons of magically causing him to "be taken with nausea and to vomit for a long time," the justice system moved into high gear, penalizing a night of heavy drinking with torture and imprisonment.[24] The petition submitted in July 1659 by the Lukh town elder and taxpayers of "the whole town" about the bewitchment epidemic that was engulfing their wives provoked similarly vigorous investigation: "The tsar sent special investigator (*syshchik*) Ivan Savinov syn Ramanchiukov to torture [the accused]."[25] In August 1622, when "Ivan Voronin's peasant" complained to the Cossack ataman in the village of Usmon' that his wife had bewitched his brother to death, the ataman duly passed the denunciation on to the governor and vice-governor in the provincial capital, Voronezh, and they in turn forwarded the case to Moscow and to Tsar Mikhail Fedorovich. No one in this case in any way qualified as a political figure, nor can they even be called persons in the employ of the state. Nevertheless, the inquiry moved forward with the full attention and involvement of the central authorities, accumulating forty-eight manuscript pages of documentation over the course of nearly a year of to-ing and fro-ing before the case record runs out.[26]

Understaffed or not, the Muscovite chancelleries took an active interest in all cases of witchcraft brought to their attention, and many cases such as this, between peasants of a single landlord, were prosecuted in state courts rather than falling to the arbitrary jurisdiction of estate or village courts. Peasants suspected of witchcraft in remote villages such as Usmon' or Mordvins in the village of Brekhovo in Shatsk province found themselves in contact with authority all too frequently, as the state proved its efficacy in tracking down "anyone to whom the investigation leads and tortur[ing] them harshly to find out the whole truth." Our knowledge of such cases rests on the surviving archival records, which in turn were compiled thanks to the state agents' efficient outreach in rounding up suspects, however obscure, and reporting "to us the great sovereign about whatever they say and whomever they implicate in their interrogation and eye-to-eye confrontation and torture."[27] The arms of the state were longer than one might expect, and its legendary under-governance proved chimerical to those undistinguished suspects swept up by their friends' and neighbors' denunciations.[28]

Noting the broad sociological spectrum represented in witchcraft trials, Eve Levin asks, "why should the government act on denunciations from insignificant persons against equally insignificant 'witches'?"[29] It is an important question, both because it underscores the extent to which witch trials investigated the concerns of the humble as well as the mighty, and because it encourages a serious consideration of the specific threat of witchcraft. The tsar's justice strove to shore up and maintain the uneasy inequalities that formed the basis of Muscovy's tense and fragile social compact. Defending the strictures of hierarchy from abuse from above and from subversion from below, whether in the context of the Kremlin or a peasant hut, witchcraft trials performed a profoundly political function.

This finding leads us to the second corrective to the idea that the majority of witchcraft cases were political. It seems the meaning of the term "political" itself requires closer scrutiny in a Muscovite context. At some level, every witchcraft charge and every trial carried weighty political implications. It is difficult to figure out who in the Muscovite tsardom might *not* have been, in some way or other, a person in the employ of the state or the church. All male Muscovites of whatever station were bound to serve the church or state. The better-placed men served the tsar as diplomats, secretaries, generals, or military officers. Those of middling status served as cavalry or infantrymen, Cossacks, gunners or musketeers, merchants or apothecaries. Lower-level servitors fulfilled their obligations as scribes, clerks, bricklayers, postal messengers, coachmen, tavern keepers, beekeepers, smiths, miners, craftsmen, grooms, or kennel masters. Those at the bottom of the social scale, peasants, serfs, and slaves, served the tsar by laboring in the fields and houses of his gentry landholders. Religious hierarchies followed equivalent gradations in the service of the Lord, and women occupied the service rung of their fathers or husbands. The tsar's non-Russian subjects slotted into whatever service suited the sovereign's purposes and filled his coffers. Who then was not in the employ of the state or the church? The "wanderers" and "free people" who made up a noticeable fraction of accused witches in some sense gained their notoriety as rare exceptions to this rule of universal service. The potent danger they posed lay in their ability to evade the restrictions of what Roland Mousnier calls a "liturgical," or "service society," and to make their own way, free of obligation and of bonds of affiliation.[30] Their anomalous status and their vulnerability to witchcraft accusations underscores their deviance from a different norm, according to which all subjects served the tsar and therefore all interactions carried some degree of political charge.

Third, Muscovy's economy was not based on market capitalism or on institutional structures but on personal relations of patronage and dependency. Goods and power circulated along axes of human (and divine) relationships, and were negotiated in a vocabulary of intimacy and beneficence (or, when they went awry, of cruelty and hostility). If we return to the anonymous letter implicating the sorcerer Iudka for his relationship with Fedor Shaklovityi, we encounter the startling affective language in which their relationship was presented:

> And when Iudka came and sat with Fedka, there was no one in the house other than one other man, and they, Fedka and Iudka, spoke among themselves of love. They stood up and prayed together and kissed a holy icon, and kissed each other, and Iudka called Fedka "father," and Fedka called Iudka "son," and [they swore] that neither friend would tell on his brother or would say anything of what they had discussed. And if one of them should be implicated by some denunciation of their business, he would not confess to anything even until death.[31]

The anonymous author of this screed played on the actual workings and structures of politics, turning the relationships of patronage and clientage into corrupt, perhaps indecent, conspiracy.

Although this depiction shines a sickly light on the men's loving connections and fictive kinship relations, in routine and idealized settings as well, political relations were expressed in a vocabulary of love and hierarchically ordered familial bonds. "The political" was expressed through supplication and prayer from below, patronage and munificence from above. Political allegiances were cemented through marriages, and status was achieved by birth, calculated in kinship terms. Honor was a critical currency in which standing was affirmed.[32] In such a world, defining cases as "political" or not does little to advance our understanding, since the personal was political in a very direct sense and the political was also the theological. One category blurred into another such that divisions evanesce.[33]

The looseness of the definition of "political sorcery" turns out to be analytically productive, encouraging a careful reassessment of what actually constituted the political sphere and, by extension, what posed a political threat. A society's collective nightmares prove revealing of the particular issues confronting it at a given time. In Muscovy, those nightmares involved the overturning of the moral order as it was constituted in relations between people at each rung of the social hierarchy, from top to bottom. Magic was frequently deployed, suspected, and feared, precisely at those moments when superiors overstepped the bounds of those highly personalized relationships. Witchcraft, therefore, *was* political, and *did* constitute a threat to the social order, but in the personal, relational way that Muscovite politics were structured.

WITCHCRAFT AND REBELLION

The seventeenth century, rife with rebellion throughout Europe, brought unrest to Muscovy as well. Suspicions of evil magic regularly surfaced during the great uprisings, and they took lethal form in the action of rebels as well as in the retribution meted out by the regime. From below and from above, conspicuous manifestations of "time out of joint" provoked anxious speculation about dark magic afoot. Rioters attributed their oppression to corruption, greed, and witchcraft, while the tsarist authorities were equally free in charging their opponents and challengers with sorcery. Sometimes, top and bottom joined ranks against a perceived violator, as the examples of Artamon Matveev and Fedor Shaklovityi, denounced from below and condemned from above, demonstrate. Rumors of witchcraft adhered to Boris Godunov, the first tsar to rule without the benefit of grand princely lineage. The "Tale of the Reign of Tsar Feodor Ioannovich," an anti-Godunov jeremiad, attacked the fallen ruler for, among other sins and crimes, consulting with sorcerers, male and female witches, and fortune-tellers (*volkhvy, volshebniki, volshebnitsy, gadateli, vorozhei*).[34] These subversive whispers were already circulating in 1604 and early 1605, when his reign was pressured by a rising tide of rebellion spearheaded by a pretender to the throne, known as the First False Dmitrii. The Pretender, who successfully installed himself on the throne of the tsars, succumbed to the plots of his erstwhile supporters at court and to the knives of the mobilized rank-and-file in Moscow. They, in turn, were inflamed by whispered intimations associating him with Polish Catholicism and with sorcery. A chronicle composed shortly after the events, the Chronograph of 1617, maintained that Dmitrii worked "magic with devils." Foreign eyewitnesses reported that his successor, Prince Vasilii Shuiskii, had Dmitrii's mutilated corpse publicly displayed surrounded by the masks and instruments of minstrels to publicize his affinity for dark magic.[35]

Intimations of witchcraft accompanied both elite plots and mass rebellion throughout the century. During the wave of urban revolts that engulfed the tsardom in 1648, Boris Morozov, brother-in-law and chief adviser to the young Tsar Aleksei Mikhailovich, personified corruption and greed in the eyes of the common people. Although no taint of witchcraft seems to have attached to Morozov himself, an anonymous Swedish account reports that his major domo (*upravitel'*), a man by the name of Mosei, was reputed to be "a great wizard," who had forecasted hard times for his master and other boyars: "Great misfortune threatened them." The Swede maintained that Morozov haughtily dismissed the prediction, but shortly thereafter, Mosei lay dead from the blows of the mob, Morozov schemed his return from exile, and many boyars and princes had been torn to pieces by the crowd.[36]

More deadly rumors circulated during the unsettled years at the end of the century, when the succession was murky and Peter the Great's half sister Sophia angled for the throne. The taint of witchcraft attached to several of the most hated dignitaries and commanders in the rebellions of 1682 and 1689. The 1682 uprising began after a regiment of musketeers, incensed by the excesses of their commander, Colonel Semyon Griboedov, submitted a petition against him to the tsar, Fedor Alekseevich. Griboedov and other officers, they complained, had violated the precepts, now familiar to us, of restraint in hierarchical exploitation. They forced the soldiers to break stones at his estate outside of Moscow during Lent, made them work on Sundays, and treated them "like criminals exiled to hard labor or like people tortured for treason or crime."[37] Responding to the moral imperative that governed Muscovite society, the tsar and his boyars found the generals guilty of failing to live up to their obligations as superior officers and had them beaten mercilessly with bastinados, with their shirts removed. Nonetheless, the punishment did not fully appease the musketeers and soldiers, and in May 1682, after the death of Tsar Fedor, violence erupted.

One of the early victims was Artamon Matveev, whose fondness for foreigners and their impenetrable books heightened the murderous rage of the crowd. The revolt was now directed in part against corrupt boyars, favorites, and state officials, and in part against the elevation of Peter Alekseevich (later Peter the Great) to the throne ahead of his half brother, Ivan. Floating rumors, key throughout the rebellion, maintained that the Naryshkin family, partisans of the young Peter, had killed the unfortunate Ivan, scion of the Miloslavskii line. The Mazurinskii Chronicle records that "musketeers of all regiments and soldiers" rampaged through the Kremlin, seizing targeted individuals and subjecting them to mutilation and dismemberment. Undaunted by constraints of deference, the enraged musketeers marched to the Kremlin late at night, directly to the royal chambers. They "rudely demanded [that] Ivan Kirillovich Naryshkin, Natalia's brother [and uncle to the young tsar, Peter]" and the foreign doctor, Daniil be handed over to them. Tsaritsa Natalia and Peter tearfully begged that they be spared, but the musketeers remained unmoved. They dragged Ivan Kirillovich and the doctor away and subjected them to torture in the Kostentinovskii Tower. After torturing them, they brought Ivan Kirillovich to *Lobnoe mesto* on Red Square "and cut him up with pikes and axes and carried out all manner of mutilation: they cut off his head and arms and legs." They placed these gory mementos on long pikes and paraded them through the city, mocking them.

Along with the body parts, they paraded through the streets a pike topped with a strange-looking fish waving like a banner. The fish was long and thin, with long fins, and they had found it at the home of the state secretary Ilarion Ivanov. The unfortunate Ivanov had drawn the attention of the mob the day before, when they had captured him with his son in the Kremlin and cut them both to pieces.[38] The long-finned fish, elsewhere named a "cuttlefish," reeked of sorcery to the enraged mob, adding to their resentment of the powerful Ivanovs. The Chronicle of 1619–91 elaborates vividly on the infamous fish: In the storehouse of state secretary Ilarion Ivanov, some of the musketeers found "some ocean-going fish with many fins that hung from them like mustaches, long and thin, like hair. Taking the fish, they brought four fish, some with seven fins, some with eight, to the dead bodies in the square. They called them flying snakes. And they set up a pike in the middle of the *Krasnaia* Bridge, with two fish dangling from it. Another two they hung on a pike near the body of state secretary Larion [Ivanov], and there they wrote a notice saying that with these snakes the traitors had wanted to destroy the tsar's clan and the musketeers. [They planned to] mix them into the wine and bring them in wine casks to the musketeer regiments. And when they would drink the wine, they would die." The musketeers' fabricated account follows the general outline of other anonymous and libelous fictions we have seen. Their notice imputes malicious motives and magical methods to the Ivanovs in their imagined pursuit of imaginary crimes. With the clarity of hindsight the author of the chronicle added that the fish were actually perfectly harmless.[39]

In each of the chronicle reports, Ilarion Ivanov's fate appears in immediate proximity to descriptions of the attacks on a foreign doctor in the tsar's employ, a character alternately named Daniil the Doctor or the tsar's doctor, Stefan the Jew. Although the women of the royal family, both Naryshkin and Miloslavskii, begged the mutineers to spare the doctor (whoever he was), the rebels "tortured doctor Daniil by beating him with three knouts and then they led him from the place of torture to *Lobnoe mesto* in Red Square, where they cut him up and mutilated him as they had Ivan Naryshkin. They cut off his head, arms, legs, and raised his torso repeatedly on pikes."[40] Enjoying intimate access to the tsar's person, practicing a kind of healing distinct from and alien to the Orthodox approach of supplication and prayer, the foreign court doctor had long occupied a precarious position in Muscovy. A century earlier, during the perilous years of Ivan IV's rule, Eleazar Bromelius, a Westphalian, "sometimes a cozening imposter, doctor of physic in England, a rare mathematician, magician," was suspected of poisoning and sorcery and fell from grace in 1579. He, like Doctor Daniil/Stefan, met his death by torture, but in his case, the sentence was officially prescribed rather than meted out by an angry crowd.[41]

Suspicions of magic spread in tandem with outrage at corruption, violence, and excess perpetrated by the powerful. They emerged at precisely the same kinds of points of fracture that generated quotidian, private magical clashes. The predictable recrudescence of those suspicions at times of political upheaval speaks to the way that Muscovites of all levels explained political and social disharmony as evidence of witchcraft. Outraged musketeers saw magic at work behind the abuse they endured at the hands of their officers. Ruling elites detected traces of witchcraft in the rise and fall of royal favorites, generals, and brides. People at all levels of society turned their thoughts to witchcraft when they perceived moral trespass. The oppressed joined those in power in imagining witchcraft where they saw corruption, extortion, and treachery. This unanimity of belief demonstrates that something broader and more diffuse was at stake than protecting a church or state monopoly on spiritual or worldly power. To the people at the bottom of the ladder, those most abused by the strong and powerful, as well as to those on the top, threatened by the magic of defiant underlings, witchcraft signaled profound violation. In diagnosing witchcraft as the canker gnawing away at social harmony, both the rebels in the streets and the rulers in the Kremlin found explanations for the failures of a moral hierarchy secured by mutual obligation and personal piety. Magic, or suspicion of magic, was not a one-way street, but rather a branching intersection, along which accusations, suspicions, and deployment of witchcraft flowed in all directions.

MUSCOVITE NIGHTMARES: SORCERY AND PERVERTED JUSTICE

At the very core of the Muscovite moral order sat the figure of the tsar, divinely entrusted with the weighty task of guiding and preserving a pious, Orthodox realm. The sovereign's courts served as the locus in which stern and merciful justice was administered and disseminated to subjects of all ranks throughout the land. The sanctity and incorruptibility of the courtroom, as an extension and embodiment of the tsar's rule, thus assumed enormous importance. In the Muscovite social imagination, the pursuit of justice was an urgent matter and required vigilant defense against magical perversion. Here, if anywhere, Muscovites interpolated witchcraft into a nightmarish vision nearing the level of horror of Western satanic apocalypticism. This dark imaginary, as I will argue, still did not pose the threat of a diabolical conspiracy to challenge Christian order, but it did draw the threat of witchcraft into a broad and terrifying fantasy. The imagined target of witches' assault was the universal justice that maintained the fragile order in check, the court system that upheld the morality of Muscovite hierarchy.

The idea that Muscovites viewed their courts as models of rectitude flies in the face of many centuries of sedimented wisdom. The more common assumption maintains, on the contrary, that these courts were bogs of corruption, inherently structured to favor the highest bidder or the best connected. Many modern scholars take up this position, arguing that the courts were so crooked that magic offered the sole, rather pathetic, hope for the poor and weak when they entered the maws of "justice." M. V. Kogorodina notes that in the sixteenth and seventeenth centuries confessional books addressed both to ordinary parishioners and to powerful magnates included the question: "Did you judge corruptly or on the basis of bribes?"[42] Penitential guides paralleled the law codes in their preoccupation with corruption of the courts and dishonest litigation.

Scholars draw on a range of strong evidence to support this dispiriting view of the Muscovite legal system. Widely circulating popular tales, dubbed "democratic satire" by the Soviet literary scholar V. P. Adrianova-Perets, lampooned the courts as sites of bribery and foolishness.[43] A sense of the profound dishonesty of the courts and inherent bias against the weak fills petitions from the time, and the resulting outrage contributed to the series of urban riots that engulfed Moscow and other towns in 1648. In a petition submitted during the Moscow riots, a group of gentry landholders from Vladimir complained:

> Chancellery officials are inclined to bribery and to craftiness. No one is allowed out of the chancelleries anywhere without paying a fee, and no one anywhere is given the sovereign's service payment without their taking a cut. Everything is being sold for high prices, and in the towns, because of these chancellery people, the taxpaying community has perished and is currently perishing.[44]

As Brian Davies has shown, bribery was so deeply engrained in the Muscovite system that local communities complained when an anomalously upright governor refused to accept their "gifts," thereby leaving them with no means of influencing his verdicts. Gift giving served as another palliative strategy for dealing with the inequities of Muscovite hierarchies of power. By winning the "friendship" of a governor-judge, by initiating him into the currents of local society, communities could ensure judgments in keeping with their sense of propriety and their local knowledge. The practice of giving and receiving gifts could work in harmony with rather than in contravention of legal injunctions that judges should rule "neither favoring friend nor penalizing enemy," and that they should seek the truth by any means necessary. This personalized form of justice allowed for rulings based on the kind of "truth" gained through intimacy and human connections, "truth" defined by the kinship and patronage clusters that, in turn, structured society.[45] Justice, like truth, was constructed according to reigning norms and defined according to Muscovite understandings.

A number of scholars take seriously the courts' claims of dedicated pursuit of truth. Horace W. Dewey, Ann M. Kleimola, and most recently, Nancy Kollmann, point to officials' surprisingly serious engagement with their duties, as spelled out by law and decree, and highlight their careful weighing of evidence as presented in the course of investigations. George Weickardt underscores the curious commitment to "due process and equal justice" in Muscovite trials, despite the fundamental inequities woven into the very fabric of the law. Within the defining constraints of inegalitarian social structures, Weickhardt finds, Muscovites had a strongly developed sense of entitlement to the fair application of the law as decreed for people of their rank. It should be noted that none of these authors overstates the case; they fully acknowledge the many flagrant violations and exceptions that darken this bright vision.[46]

Witch trials by and large show the courts working hard to follow the law, obey orders from Moscow, and glean (or construct) the truth, according to their conception of it. The bulky stacks of back-and-forth correspondence, reports, and orders collected in the files of witchcraft trials reveal a tendency on the part of the courts to take each successive petition seriously, thereby privileging, at least temporarily, the most recent accusation in an ongoing, sequential set of complaints and counter-arguments. The appeals processes allowed people of any rank to protest when the minimal rights allotted to them were trampled or ignored, and protest they did.[47]

The stakes of keeping the courts honest, by the standards of the day, were extremely high. If Muscovite rule was predicated on the tsar's or grand prince's special link to God, then his justice system too necessarily relied heavily on deciphering and carrying out God's judgment.[48] Viewed as extensions of the sovereign's own, personal authority, the courts shared in his sacral aura. In the not-too-distant past, suits had been resolved by ordeal, in which God's verdict manifested itself physically. As late as the mid-sixteenth century, God's will was served through the judicial duel, where litigants or their champions battled for vindication on the field of justice. By the seventeenth century, these rites of direct divine intervention had fallen out of favor, but the imprint of the sacred on the realm of the courts persisted. The "cross-kissed oath" retained its saliency as a way of allowing direct transmission to earthly courts of God's truth (*pravda bozhiia*) or God's judgment (*sud bozhii*). Cross kissing was routinely used in the seventeenth century to solemnize an oath and to ensure the truth of statements made by witnesses.[49]

If justice went awry under the sovereign's jurisdiction, as suggested by the grumbling about corruption in the 1648 petitions, the land would "perish."[50] Davies coins the useful term "theodicy of bureaucratic malfeasance" to underscore the extent to which bureaucratic corruption might portend subversion of the divine order.[51] If the tsar's own administrators and courts of justice were manifestly corrupt, then something had gone seriously amiss, something that could not simply be imputed to the occasional venal individual but rather to some evil afoot far more profound and far more insidious. The logic of this political theodicy pointed to supernatural causes.

Texts exploring this nexus of anxiety were particularly rich in the mid-sixteenth century, when a number of authors decried the pernicious effects of magic at work deep in the heart of the growing judicial-administrative apparatus, and most worryingly, at the tsar's court and throughout the judicial administration. Although this study has concentrated on the seventeenth century, these texts are so rich that they demand attention here, despite the chronological backtracking involved. Their traces remain distinctly visible in both law and magical practice in the seventeenth century.

When Ivan IV raised the question of sorcery at the *Stoglav* Church Council in 1551, the church fathers voiced their increasing concern with the issue by requesting that the secular authorities join their campaign to stamp out magic. In addition to having the metropolitan excommunicate fortune-tellers, astrologers, and other magicians, the tsar should order their execution.[52] In response, the tsar issued an order banning general immorality, such as drunkenness, swearing,

Cross-kissed oath. From Litsevoi letopisnyi svod XVI veka: Russkaia letopisnaia istoriia. *Book 20,* 1541–1551 gg. *(Moscow: AKTEON, 2011), 192. (See also plate 16)*

shaving beards and mustaches, and kissing the cross (taking oaths) falsely. The decree also specifically prohibited patronizing magicians to pervert the course of justice:

> nor should they . . . go to wizards or to sorcerers or to astrologers to have them cast spells, and magicians should not attend judicial duels. And those disorderly people, who, having forgotten the fear of God and the tsar's order, start to swear falsely in God's name or kiss the cross falsely and besmirch each others' fathers or mothers, . . . or bring magicians to judicial duels, and if they are discovered in this through inquiry and if the denunciation comes from trustworthy witnesses, then those people shall be held in great disgrace by the tsar and grand prince according to the Byzantine Church Law (*gradskii zakon*), and they are to be excommunicated by the prelates according to holy canons.[53]

Particularly interesting in this decree is the special ban on magical interference in judicial duels. The church leaders at the *Stoglav* council had raised this issue the previous year, alerting the tsar that:

> In our Orthodox Christendom some people litigate dishonestly: after lodging a false accusation, they kiss the cross or holy icons, they fight judicial duels and they shed blood. And at the same time wizards and sorcerers are giving them aid, based upon their diabolic learning. . . .[54]

The hazards consequent on allowing this kind of dirty work were enormous. The *Stoglav* fathers set them out clearly. In the most immediate, earthly sense, magical perversion of justice led to discord and murder: "Trusting in this witchcraft, the false accuser and the slanderer are not reconciled: they fight judicial duels, and, having accused [someone] falsely, they kill [him]." In the grander scheme, the costs were even more dire: "By these diabolic acts they are seducing the world, and they wrest [it] away from God."[55] This is as close as Muscovite texts come to voicing a fear of witchcraft as a soteriological threat to the divine order. No Muscovite thinker, however, fully developed those sweeping implications, and the danger posed by witchcraft remained confined to the concrete world of judges and their courtrooms.

The reign of Ivan IV (1533–84) represents a highpoint in textual concern with sorcery in the courts and as a hidden danger lurking on all sides. Letters and historical narratives associated with Ivan's reign depict him as prone to an almost obsessive suspicion of magical conspiracy. In 1547, early in his reign, a tumult erupted in Moscow as the city blazed in a huge fire caused, according to carefully planted rumor, by witchcraft. *The Chronicle of the Beginning of the*

Reign of Ivan Vasil'evich reports that scheming boyars spread "hostile calumny" among the people, alleging that "through means of sorcery a human heart had been taken out and soaked in water and sprinkled with that water, and because of that all of Moscow had burned." The common people then elaborated on the core idea seeded by the boyars and wove in their own understanding of sorcery as signaling abuse of power. Five days after the fire, the grand prince ordered an investigation and had his boyars question the urban taxpayers about the fire. The assembled crowd testified that "Princess Anna Glinskaia [the young ruler's maternal grandmother] with her sons and people performed sorcery: She took out a human heart and put it in water and with that water, riding around Moscow, sprinkled [it], and because of that, Moscow burned down." Voicing the same association of misuse of power and sorcery that we have already noted in the urban uprisings of the following century, "the tax-payers said this because at that time the Glinskiis were close to the sovereign and in favor, and their people [caused] the taxpayers violence and robbery."[56] The princess and her kin made likely suspects because of their illegitimate exploitation of power and position.

Ivan's own suspicions ran along similar lines to those expressed by the rebellious Muscovites. The untimely deaths of several of his wives underscored for him and his inner circle the real and pressing danger posed by witchcraft. The church council that met in 1572 to rule on the canonicity of remarriage for the serially widowed tsar affirmed that his first wife had died through the magic of evil people (*zlykh liudei charodeistvom*) and poison, and the second and third were also craftily poisoned.[57] Although questions about authenticity haunt several of the texts associated with Ivan, feverish interest in sorcery runs so consistently through so many sources from his reign, in letters, polemics, confessional guides, ecclesiastical rulings, and chronicles, that it seems legitimate to associate him personally and his time with intensified fear of witchcraft.

Maria Korogodina sees in this preoccupation the influence of scholars and churchmen from the south and western Slavic lands who arrived in Muscovy in the first half of the sixteenth century, bringing with them a strong interest in magic.[58] Ivan Peresvetov, one such immigrant from the Lithuanian Grand Duchy, epitomizes this trend. In a cautionary allegory written for the edification of Ivan IV in 1549, Peresvetov's fictional cast of evil advisers employed magic deliberately to lead a pious Greek emperor astray: "Sorcerers and heretics take the tsar's (emperor's) happiness away and his tsarist wisdom, and set his tsarist heart aflame toward them with heresy and by means of sorcery, and [they] weaken his army. . . . Such people deserve to be burned with fire, and other cruel deaths should be given to them so that evil won't spread."[59] This scenario evidently appealed to Peresvetov's imagination. He dwelled on it at length, spinning out the sad details of what happens to a kingdom blighted by sorcerers at the helm. He set his parable in Constantinople, just prior to its fall to the Turks. Faced with the necessity of explaining why Orthodox kingdoms suffer defeats by infidels, a variant of the age-old question of why a good God allows evil in the world, Peresvetov invoked supernatural sabotage as one cause of the Turks' conquest of Byzantium: "They [the sorcerer-magnates] enfeebled the emperor's armies with their spells, and by deceitful, heretical means, and with sorcery. And with that they handed over the Greek empire and the Christian faith and the beauty of the church to Turkish foreigners, to be abused."[60]

Peresvetov's parable allowed him to elaborate on the implications of the magical infiltration of a system of justice. In the final days of the Greek empire:

> The tsar's magnates . . . plotted by their craftiness and by the Devil's temptation to dig up the dead thievishly from newly buried coffins and to cover up the empty graves. [Then they] pricked that dead person all over with a spear or cut off [parts of it] with a sword. They smeared [the body] with blood, and they threw it in the home of a rich person. [Then] they set up a slanderer as plaintiff, one who knew little of God, and having judged him in an unfair court, they robbed his home and his wealth from his home. In this unclean manner they enriched themselves according to the Devil's enticement, but there was no tsarist punishment of them, by which they angered God in everything and forgot the teachings of God and the holy fathers.[61]

The intricate stratagems attributed to the sorcerers in Peresvetov's allegory could easily have been attributed to human rather than supernatural agency: ordinary mortals could act out the ugly scenario—planting bloody corpses in the homes of innocent rich people, framing them in court and extorting money from them—just as easily as those adept in the black arts. He attributed the macabre deeds to sorcerers because he operated in an ideological universe in which God's justice *should* have come through directly, physically. If justice ran off course, forceful and plausible explanation was required, and the interference of sorcerers provided that explanation. More than ordinary venality was afoot.

Though written a full century before the witchcraft trials, this cluster of texts from the reign of Ivan the Terrible exposes an intense, focused fear of witchcraft in the Muscovite courtroom that endured through the seventeenth century.

According to Muscovite political theology, the well-being of the society required divining and carrying out God's judgment. Any derailing of God's justice needed forceful and plausible explanation, which the activity of witches provided. An eagle feather under an armpit or a spell that promised, "if I am in court, my opponent will be found guilty, and I will be exonerated," threatened not only to distort one particular verdict, but also to corrupt the sanctified field of the tsar's justice.[62] The discovery of tangible evidence in the possession of the accused—written spells and hidden talismans offering protection from torture and guaranteeing favorable verdicts—confirmed the sense that the sovereign's sacral duty to administer in truth was being actively and magically undermined. In the face of manifest evidence of supernatural tampering with the course of God's justice, witchcraft earned its position among the most heinous of all crimes.

Dire though it was, the central threat of witchcraft was its assault on the personalized, hierarchical interactions that characterized Muscovite magic in general. Whether through sorcery or bribery, perversion of justice boiled down to corruption of individual judges, and reflected the same endemic problems of greed and favoritism that plagued the tsarist justice system in its earthly guise. At its imagined worst, sorcery might even lead the tsar himself astray, but the eschatological risks of such a dread development remained largely unexplored, with emphasis instead on this-worldly consequences of a badly advised ruler.[63] Whereas in the diabolical models on offer in Catholic and Protestant Europe, the corruption of individuals could be rolled into visions of a larger conspiracy, a battle of good and evil, in Muscovy even the horrific prospect of derailing the tsar's divine mandate crumbled rapidly into concern with the probity of individual justices.

WITCHCRAFT'S THREAT: THE BONDS OF RECIPROCITY

Like the enchanted salt cast to the winds at crossroads, magic in general operated at the points of intersection among individuals trapped within hierarchy. It functioned at the margins, shoring up and undermining moral expectations, loosing its terrible and terrifying power at the places where moral compact eroded. Where courts were perceived as corrupt, magic was seen to operate. Where masters and serfs clashed in their sense of the limits of acceptable domination and resistance, magic was suspected, and probably deployed. Magical thinking and action encompassed all actors in the moral drama. Wherever corruption, malice, brutality, greed, or desire gnawed at the heart of human relationships, wherever measured interactions were replaced by excess and the normal bounds of oppression were overstepped, thoughts might turn to magic for explanation, rectification, or vengeance.

In his imaginative and perceptive studies of magical spells, Toporkov argues that magic in its essence provided an illicit route toward individual (hence, selfish, uncommunal) wish fulfillment. Spells were performed to serve an individual's sexual urges, or to further other selfish agendas: greed, ambition, cowardice, envy, hatred, vengeance. Hence, spells and magic inherently worked at cross-purposes to the normative goals of the collective. Toporkov suggests that in magical spells and practices, one can detect some of the earliest traces of individualism, or freedom, in Muscovite culture, traces that met with harsh condemnation from the surrounding society.[64] The argument of this book draws on Toporkov's insight but shifts it away from the focus on individualism and freedom, and instead embeds Muscovites' desperate acts of magic in a collective moral economy in which hierarchy locked everyone into a world of harsh constraints. Because Muscovite political and economic order rested on human relationships of patronage, clientage, kinship, and bondage, the morality of power was negotiated at the junctures of those relationships. Covert and overt acts of magic operated at the nodal points in the hierarchical order

Returning to the question with which this chapter opened, what earned for Muscovite witchcraft, with its humble magic of roots and grasses, its unlikely status as one of the three most egregious transgressions imaginable? Perhaps even more terrifying than the venom that witchcraft might inject into the governance of the realm was the insidious way that it could tear apart the moral order and upend the righteous stratification of society at the most intimate and inescapable level. The threat did not assume the contours of a grand eschatological battle engaged by the armies of the Antichrist. Rather, the threat to the social order began and ended at home, or on the road, or in the tsarist court or courtroom, in the structure of human relations. The implications were nonetheless weighty. Whether expressed as effrontery of the lowly toward their betters or brutality of superiors toward their underlings, such assaults on hierarchical order elevated magical crimes into the rarefied air of the truly iniquitous.

The Aftermath

Peter the Great and the Age of Enlightenment

SURPRISINGLY, IT WAS PETER THE GREAT, Russia's renowned modernizer and Westernizer, who brought the satanic pact and an active interest in the idea of satanic magic into the mainstream of Russian jurisprudence.[1] By the early eighteenth century, this line of European thought was distinctly on the wane in its home territories. While Enlightenment thinking and secularization were gradually driving out belief in magic and witchcraft among the relevant legislators, jurists, and judges in Western Europe, Peter was busily framing laws that would introduce the idea of a satanic pact to Russia. In his legal revisions, Peter and his advisers drew heavily on Swedish precedents of the previous century. His main source was the 1683 revision of the military code introduced by Gustavus Adolphus in 1621–22, which in turn drew on earlier European codes, particularly the 1532 *Constitutio criminalis Carolina* of Charles V.[2] Traditional practices did not abruptly vanish, nor did new belief systems suddenly replace older ones. The older model persisted and continued to define the overwhelming majority of cases brought to trial, but through his changes in the law code, Peter brought European ideas about magic resolutely, if tardily, into the conceptual universe of Russian witch belief.[3]

Peter introduced two radically new principles into Russian law, with almost immediate consequences in Russian courtrooms. His Ecclesiastical Regulation of 1721 expressed in law the first elements of *skepticism* toward magic, introducing punishments for charlatans who claimed falsely to be victims of bewitchment. This innovation, the first glimmering of enlightenment secularism, accords with the old, familiar story about Russia's precipitous modernization in the eighteenth century.[4] Peter's introduction of another principle, one more conventionally associated with earlier, pre-Enlightenment thought, is more counterintuitive and requires further consideration. His Military

Statute of 1716 articulated the idea, previously unstated in law, that in addition to inflicting harm, "black magicians" might also be culpable in having had dealings with the Devil.[5]

The legal introduction of the concept of a satanic pact immediately assumed a reality in the courtroom. Whereas earlier judges had confined their leading questions to matters of immediate, this-worldly importance—Who taught you? Whom have you taught? Whom have you bewitched?—eighteenth-century judges expanded their interrogatory repertoire. For instance, interrogators in the consistory court pushed a certain widow, Katerina Ivanova, to admit that she "renounced Christianity and had communication with those devils."[6] Still backed with the persuasive arguments of torture—burning pincers, water torture, beating, and the strapaddo—such questions reliably produced appropriate answers. The numbers of satanic cases remained small, but they became more frequent and more clearly identified with the myth of the pact. E. B. Smilianskaia describes a number of clearly satanic cases in the early eighteenth century: a 1723 renunciation of God, father, and mother; a 1727 case of denying God; a 1740 anti-prayer abjuring God and promising to baptize any future children in the name of "Father Satanail," a name derived from Satan. Moving later in the century, she recounts even more full-fledged, elaborately Western-style cases, including a pact sealed with a kiss on Satan's backside, and a marvelous letter to the "all-generous great prince Satanail" with a discussion of presenting the Devil a stolen communion wafer.[7] As in the European courts of the previous centuries, once confessions had been extracted and publicized, this new model of witchcraft moved off the pages of legal texts and gained some foothold in the popular imagination.

A poignant illustration of the way that the myth inserted itself into the popular consciousness is found in a sad case from 1759, filed by its nineteenth-century archivist under the title "The case of the soldier Semyon Popov, who renounced God and gave his soul to the Devil." The son of a provincial church deacon, Popov distinguished himself at a young age by his skill at writing. According to his lengthy confession, he came to the notice of first the regional archbishop and then the metropolitan, who saw to it that he attended top-notch seminaries and received good positions in their eparchial centers. Unfortunately, Popov gave himself over to drink, and before he knew what was happening, he found himself defrocked, banished from ecclesiastical circles, and enrolled in the dismal ranks of garrison soldiers.

> Semyon thought he could better himself through the Devil (*d'iavol*). He thought he could gain wealth and through wealth get out of military service. For that reason he decided to renounce God and give himself to the Devil and as a token

> of faith to give him a God-denying letter that he deliberately composed. . . . Having cut himself with a knife on his right leg and let the blood form a little bubble, he wrote the God-denying letter as follows:
>
> I, slave Simen, renounce God the Creator and all created by his hand and deny him and give myself to you, Lord Devil, not only in my body but also in my soul. And even at the Coming of Christ who is called the Creator, I will not be faithful to him; instead, I renounce Christianity. I, Simen, signed with my own hand.
>
> And upon writing this letter he, Semyon, went to an empty place to read that letter and to call the Devil to himself in order to get out of military service.

To his chagrin, not only did the Devil not grant him great wealth or help him escape from military service, but he didn't even have the decency to appear at all. This pushed the wretched soldier to repent of his action. The very next day he took his letter, written crudely in his own blood, and turned himself in to a regimental officer at the Kronstadt garrison. From there he was handed over to the St. Petersburg Spiritual Consistory for a hearing. After reviewing the evidence, the consistory, being a merciful and enlightened body, sentenced him to be whipped and sent in chains for re-education. The letter addressed to Lord Devil, crudely scrawled in a faded brown that could well be blood, still sits among the consistory's records of the case.[8]

Aside from its pathos, Popov's odyssey illustrates the disruption of Muscovite beliefs that the new legislation had effected. In his work on fifteenth-century European witchcraft mythologies, Kieckhefer finds that the imposition of new belief systems from above resulted in a disorganized set of targets of witchcraft accusations, since the new beliefs corresponded with no indigenous set of assumptions about who was a likely witch. Similarly chaotic accusations are evident in Russia after the introduction from above of a Western belief system: the eighteenth century witnessed the partial reversal of the seventeenth-century pattern of social superiors' accusing their inferiors or of exchanges of accusations among social equals. In the first half of the eighteenth century, according to A. S. Lavrov, accusations more commonly were lodged up rather than down the social scale, with serfs commonly accusing their masters.[9]

In this newly disordered understanding of witchcraft, the Devil played an increasingly noticeable role, but one still cannot justifiably argue that magic came to be understood as essentially demonic even after the Petrine reforms. The articulation of the law was, itself, ambivalent about the Devil's role. Peter's articles allowed for an interesting looseness in the definition of what constituted magic. Article 1 of the Military Code stated: "The punishment of burning is the usual form of execution for magicians who rely on black books, *if* they have harmed someone through their enchantments (*charodeistvo*), *or have actually (deistvitel'no) come into the service of the Devil.*" Peter's code sustained the possibility that magic might be worked *without* inflicting harm and *without* taking up with the Devil. The statute continued: "But if by his enchantment he has inflicted no harm at all on anyone, according to the contrivance of the matter, such a one should be punished by the other punishments listed above, and in addition should do public religious repentance."[10] Peter's legislators thus interwove various legal sources to create a late-breaking development, combining the possibility of satanic intervention with the equal probability of magic free of satanism and of malice. Throughout the eighteenth century, the ambivalent legacy of this Petrine overlay left its traces in the trials of witches. A lively intermixing of folkloric and fairytale elements softened demonic appearances, and the Western notion that witches bore an antipathy to Christian rites and amulets failed to take hold. Smilianskaia notes that the widow Katerina Ivanov, forced by the consistory to confess to renouncing Christianity, raised no eyebrows when she also insisted that during the ten years she kept company with devils, she also regularly prayed to Jesus Christ Son of God and took holy communion.[11]

MUSCOVITE MAGIC AND THE FRICTIONS OF HIERARCHY

Whether imagined and feared by its targets or employed and deployed by its users, witchcraft left a dangerous imprint on people's lives. The latent pool of quotidian magic—apotropaic spells to ward off evil, protective charms to guard health, healing prayers and teas—rarely yielded formal accusations in court; and even negative outcomes from healers' ministrations generally provoked no formal protest. Where magic was seen to threaten the established order of personal power relationships, law suits were more likely to ensue. When magic was perceived at the critical nodal points in Muscovy's finely tuned system of precedence and seniority, alarms sounded. Through magic, those who were born to obey strove not to overturn or upend the system, but to survive in it. With grandiose audacity, their spells aimed high: "As honey is valued by the powerful people, so may the powerful people value So-and-So." "As the powerful cannot live without bread and salt, so may they be unable to live without So-and-So." "The powerful," *vlasti*, and the strong people, *sil'nye liudi*, constituted a reality, readily recognizable to anyone and everyone in Muscovite society, where everyone was bound to serve and humbly obey someone else. Only one position—that of divinity—demanded no degree of subordination, and only rarely did spells aim so high: "As So-and-So rejoices at the Resurrection of Christ at Easter, so may everyone rejoice at So-and-So."[12]

This, a handy spell, would have resonated for every Muscovite, from the tsar to the lowliest subject. Superiors and their subordinates were united in their understanding of magic as a mode of adjusting a fiercely hierarchical world in which they all were bound.

When witchcraft troubles a society, it tends to coalesce preferentially around the particular raw spots in the social order, thus casting into sharp relief the nature of those featured strains and anxieties. In post-apartheid Soweto, Adam Ashforth finds that people who enjoy economic success beyond their peers are targeted with witchcraft accusations. In his revealingly titled study, *Witches and Neighbors*, Robin Briggs stresses the importance of intimate, face-to-face encounters in generating witchcraft suspicions within early modern villages. In Colonial New England, Carol Karlsen singles out female inheritance or other forms of female challenge to patriarchal order as contributing to suspicions of witchcraft, while Paul Boyer and Stephen Nissenbaum highlight instead the tensions between traditional farmers of Salem Village and the more commercially engaged people of Salem Town. In New Guinea, Raymond C. Kelly finds witchcraft associated with the theft of other people's life force, particular as manifested by the traffic in semen. In his work on Cameroon, Peter Geschiere identifies the legacy of colonial rule, institutional centralization, and the pressures of global capitalism as generative of witchcraft suspicions. Painful shadows of the Atlantic slave trade shape witchcraft imagery in other parts of Africa. Geschiere reports evocative legends of people "being taken away [by witches], their hands tied, toward the ocean, without being able to see their captors' faces."[13]

Although no single explanatory rubric will suffice to contain all the marvelous variety of Russian witchcraft cases, a striking pattern emerges: it was the tensions of hierarchy, excesses of abuse, and violations of expectations of reciprocity that generated the most active uses of witchcraft, and those deemed most pernicious and most actively prosecuted. While Muscovites of all degrees relied on magic to navigate their way through lives fraught with hardship and danger, it was at the fraying seams of the social fabric that everyday practices shaded into fearsome criminal witchcraft.

Appendix A

LIST OF WITCHCRAFT TRIALS

Sorted chronologically, with archival references and publication information as available. When one document lists multiple cases, the citations appear multiple times.

1. 1601 (*Moscow*)	Zguta, "Witchcraft Trials," 1194.
2. 1606 (*Perm*)	*AI*, vol. 2, no. 66, 82.
3. 1606 (*Perm*)	*AI*, vol. 2, no. 66, 82–83.
4. 1611 (*Novgorod*)	RNB, Sobranie Pogodina, no. 1593, l. 1.
5. 1616 (*Moscow*)	Zabelin, *Domashnii byt' russkikh tsarits*, 224–50.
6. 1620s (?)	"Skazanie o tsarstve Tsaria Fedora Ioannovicha," stlb. 758–71.
7. 1622–23 (*Voronezh*)	RGADA, f. 210, Moskovskii stol, stlb. 15, ll. 394–441. In Novombergskii, *Koldovstvo*, no. 1, 3–9.
8. 1624–25 (*Briansk*)	RGADA, f. 210, Prikaznyi stol, stlb. 14, stolpik 1, ll. 110–13, 440–42.
9. 1624–25 (*Kursk*)	RGADA, f. 210, Prikaznyi stol, stlb. 14, stolpik 1, ll. 148–54, 313, 323, 325–29. In Novombergskii, *Slovo i delo*, vol. 1, no. 16, 13–14.
10. 1625 (*Sapozhok*)	RGADA, f. 210, Prikaznyi stol, stlb. 91, ll. 293–302.
11. 1625 (*Verkhotur'e*)	*AI*, vol. 3, no. 137, 224–25.
12. 1626 (*Arzamas*)	RGADA, f. 210, Prikaznyi stol, stlb. 17, stolpik 2, ll. 27–29 (see also stlb. 2725, ll. 16–19).
13. 1626 (*Dedilov*)	RGADA, f. 210, Prikaznyi stol, stlb. 2725, ll. 40–42.
14. 1626 (*Mikhailov*)	RGADA, f. 210, Prikaznyi stol, stlb. 17, stolpik 2, ll. 502–5.

15. 1626 (*Suzdal'*) — RGADA, f. 210, Prikaznyi stol, stlb. 17, ll. 54–61.
16. 1626 (*Toropets*) — RGADA, f. 210, Prikaznyi stol, stlb. 2725, ll. 45–48.
17. 1626 (*Mikhailov*) — RGADA, f. 210, Prikaznyi stol, stlb. 17, stolpik 2, ll. 515–50v.
18. 1626 (*Ustiug*) — *RIB*, 25, no. 10, cols. 11–12.
19. 1627–28 (*Bolkhov*) — RGADA, f. 210, Prikaznyi stol, stlb. 22, stolpik 1, ll. 122–26.
20. 1628 (*Nizhnii Novgorod*) — *AAE*, vol. 3, no. 176, 259.
21. 1628–29 (*Velikie Luki*) — RGADA, f. 210, Prikaznyi stol, stlb. 46, stolpik 1, ll. 247–76, 309–12.
22. 1628–30 (*Galich'*) — RGADA, f. 210, Novgorodskii stol, stlb. 10, ll. 620–24, 643–44. In Novombergskii, *Koldovstvo*, no. 3, 12–14.
23. 1628–30 (*Toropets*) — RGADA, f. 210, Novgorodskii stol, stlb. 10, ll. 7–29, 86–94. Partially reproduced in Novombergskii, *Koldovstvo*, no. 2, 9–12.
24. 1629 (*n. p.*) — RIB, v. 14, no. 304, cols. 677–81 (1894).
25. 1629–30 (*Alatyr', Arzamas*) — RGADA, f. 210, Moskovskii stol, stlb. 54, stolpik 2, ll. 74–80; and Prikaznyi stol, stlb. 33, stolpik 1, ll. 708–19.
26. 1629–30 (*Arzamaz; Nizhegorod*) — RGADA, f. 210, Moskovskii stol, stlb. 54, stolpik 2, ll. 32–42, 195–213. In Novombergskii, *Koldovstvo*, no. 4, 14–25. [See also 1628–32 (*Alatyr'*), RGADA, f. 210, Prikaznyi stol, stlb. 33, stolpik 1, ll. 617–38.]
27. 1629–30 (*Lebedian'*) — RGADA, f. 210, Moskovskii stol, stlb. 54, stolpik 2, ll. 244–63, 327. In Novombergskii, *Koldovstvo*, no. 5, 25–33.
28. 1629–31 (*Mtsensk*) — RGADA, f. 210, Prikaznyi stol, stlb. 50, ll. 13–120.
29. 1630 (Bolkhov) — RGADA, f. 210, Prikaznyi stol, stlb. 36, stolpik 1, ll. 144–50.
30. 1631 (*Kashira*) — RGADA, f. 210, Prikaznyi stol, stlb. 57, ll. 394–401.
31. 1631 (*Mangazeia*) — RGADA, f. 141, no. 40. Spells published in Toporkov, *Russkie zagovory iz rukopisnykh istochnikov*, 313–17.
32. 1631 (*Kolomna*) — RGADA, f. 210, Prikaznyi stol, stlb. 37, ll. 873–79, 889–908.
33. 1631–32 (*Velikii Ustiug*) — RGADA, f. 141, no. 30, ch. 1, ll. 165–72. Spells published in Toporkov, *Russkie zagovory iz rukopisnykh istochnikov*, 318–23.

34. 1631–33 (*Kashira*)	RGADA, f. 210, Prikaznyi stol, stlb. 57, ll. 394–401.
35. 1631–33 (*Ukrainskie goroda*)	RGADA, f. 210, Prikaznyi stol, stlb. 57, ll. 552–61. In *AAE*, vol. 3, no. 197, 83–284.
36. 1632 (*Tobolsk*)	RGADA, Prikaznye dela starykh let, f. 141, no. 71, ch. 1, ll. 123–25; Mordovina and Stanislavskii, "Gadatel'nye knigi," 325.
37. 1635 (*Moscow*)	Kantorovich, *Srednevekovye protsessy o ved'makh*, 168–70; Zabelin, *Domashnii byt' russkikh tsarits*, 419–23.
38. 1635 (*Pskov*)	RGADA, f. 210, Novgorodskii stol, stlb. 68, ll. 273–74.
39. 1635–36 (*Chukhloma, Galich*)	RGADA, f. 210, Prikaznyi stol, stlb. 95, ll. 219–56. Kozlov, "Chukhlomskoe delo 1635–1636 gg.," 445–62.
40. 1635–36 (*Orel*)	RGADA, f. 210, Belgorodskii stol, stlb. 59, ll. 128–30.
41. 1635–36 (*Suzdal'*)	RGADA, f. 210, Belgorodskii stol, stlb. 83, ll. 851–54. In Novombergskii, *Koldovstvo*, no. 7, 34–35.
42. 1636 (*Orel*)	Belgorodskii stol, stlb. 59, ll. 126–28. In Novomberskii, *Koldovstvo*, no. 6, 33.
43. 1637 (*Putivl'*)	RGADA, f. 210, Belgorodskii stol, stlb. 83, ll. 58–62.
44. 1638–41 (*Moscow*)	RGADA, f. 396, op. 1, no. 2904, ll. 1–55ob.; Kotkov, *Moskovskaia delovaia i bytovaia pis'mennost'*, no. 16, 235–50; Kantorovich, *Srednevekovye protsessy o ved'makh*, 170–75; Novomberskii, *Koldovstvo*, no. 33, 112–34.
45. 1639 (*Moscow*)	RGADA, f. 396, op. 1, no. 2940, ll. 1–17ob.; Kotkov, *Moskovskaia delovaia i bytovaia pis'mennost'*, no. 17, 250–54.
46. 1640 (*Efremov*)	RGADA, f. 210, Belgorodskii stol, stlb. 160, ll. 103–15. In Novombergskii, *Koldovstvo*, no. 8, 35–40.
47. 1640 (*Mosal'sk*)	RGADA, f. 210, Vladimirskii stol, stlb. 60, ll. 263–69. In Novombergskii, *Vrachebnoe stroenie*, no. 7, xxviii–xxxi.
48. 1641–42 (*Iablonova*)	RGADA, f. 210, Prikaznyi stol, stlb. 139, ll. 106–10, 944–47.
49. 1642–43 (*Moscow*)	Zguta, "Witchcraft Trials," 1195; Zertsalov, "K materialam o vorozhbe."
50. 1642–43 (*Moscow*)	RGADA, f. 210, Prikaznyi stol, stlb. 139, ll. 1–92. Zertsalov, "K materialam o vorozhbe," 1–38; and Kotkov, *Moskovskaia delovaia i bytovaia pis'mennost'*, no. 18, 254–77.

51. 1644 (*Ryl'sk*)	RGADA, f. 210, Prikaznyi stol, stlb. 275, ll. 200–213.
52. 1645–47 (*Moscow*)	Bakhrushin, "Moskovskoe vosstanie 1648," 63.
53. 1646–47 (*Kozlov*)	RGADA, f. 210, Belgorodskii stol, stlb. 199, ll. 108–9, 115.
54. 1647 (*Beloozero*)	Zabelin, *Domashnii byt' russkikh tsarei*, 248.
55. 1647 (*Beloozero*)	*AAE*, v. 4, no. 18, p. 31.
56. 1647 (*Kozlov, Voronezh*)	RGADA, f. 210, Prikaznyi stol, stlb. 565, ll. 6–21.
57. 1647 (*Moscow*)	Esipov, "Koldovstvo v XVII i XVIII stoletiiakh," 64–66.
58. 1647 (*Moscow*)	Ryan, *Bathhouse at Midnight*, 413; cites RGADA, f. 6, ed. khr. 3.
59. 1647 (*Suzdal'*)	RGADA, f. 210, Prikaznyi stol, stlb. 564, ll. 154–234; Kozlov, "I toiu de vorozhboiu ona," 280–300.
60. 1647 (*Vologda*)	RGADA, f. 210, Prikaznyi stol, stlb. 172, ll. 1–2, 432–37, 482.
61. 1647 (*Sevsk, Moscow*)	RGADA, f. 210, Prikaznyi stol, stlb. 564, ll. 696–705.
62. 1647–48 (*Chern'*)	RGADA, f. 210, Prikaznyi stol, stlb. 567, ll. 539–49. In Novombergskii, *Vrachebnoe stroenie*, no. 20, 157–61.
63. 1647–48 (*Efremov*)	RGADA, f. 210, Prikaznyi stol, stlb. 567, ll. 1–4. In Novombergskii, *Vrachebnoe stroenie*, no. 16, 150–51.
64. 1647–48 (*Kostroma, Bolkhov*)	RGADA, f. 210, Prikaznyi stol, stlb. 569, ll. 197–203. In Novombergskii, *Vrachebnoe stroenie*, no.19, 154–57.
65. 1647–48 (*Mozhaisk*)	RGADA, f. 210, Belgorodskii stol, stlb. 284, ll. 425–47. In Novombergskii, *Koldovstvo*, no. 9, 40–53.
66. 1647–48 (*Shatsk*)	RGADA, f. 210, Belgorodskii stol, stlb. 284, ll. 391–418. In Novombergskii, *Koldovstvo*, no. 11, 63–73.
67. 1647/48 (*Tomsk*)	RGADA, f. 214, stlb. 422; Ogloblin, *Obozrenie stolbtsov i knig*, 370.
68. 1647–49 (*Gorodets*)	RGADA, f. 210, Belgorodskii stol, stlb. 270, ll. 412–16.
69. 1648 (*Belev*)	RGADA, f. 210, Prikaznyi stol, stlb. 567, ll. 202–6. In Novombergskii, *Vrachebnoe stroenie*, no. 18, 152–54.
70. 1648 (*Bezhetskii Verkh*)	RGADA f. 210, Novgorodskii stol, stlb. 96, ll. 316–25. Novombergskii, *Koldovstvo*, no. 12, 73–74 (incorrectly listed as Belgorodskii stol, stlb. 96).

71. 1648 (*Bolhov*)	RGADA, f. 210, Prikaznyi stol, stlb. 567, ll. 190–93, 278–83. In Novombergskii, *Vrachebnoe stroenie*, no. 17, 151–52.
72. 1648 (*Sevsk*)	RGADA, f. 210, Belgorodskii stol, stlb. 284, ll. 351–70. In Novombergskii, *Koldovstvo*, no. 10, 53–63.
73. 1648	Maikov, *Velikorusskie zaklinaniia*, 570; Toporkov and Turilov, *Otrechennoe chtenie*, 30.
74. 1648–49 (*Kursk*)	RGADA, f. 210, Belgorodskii stol, stlb. 288, ll. 29, 200–204.
75. 1648–50 (*Kozlov*)	RGADA, f. 210, Prikaznyi stol, stlb. 268, ll. 155–58.
76. 1648–50 (*Tomsk*)	RGADA, f. 214, stlb. 381.
77. 1649 (*Khotmyshsk*)	RGADA, f. 210, Sevskii stol, stlb. 137, ll. 343–48.
78. 1649 (*Khotmyshsk*)	RGADA, f. 210, Belgorodskii stol, stlb. 877, ll. 159–61. In Novombergskii, *Koldovstvo*, no. 13, 74–75.
79. 1649 (*Moscow*)	RGADA, f. 210, Prikaznyi stol, stlb. 567, ll. 469–74.
80. 1649 (*Narymsk*)	RGADA, f. 214, stlb. 381, Ogloblin, *Obozrenie stolbtsov i knig*, 200; 370–71.
81. 1649 (*n.p*)	Cherepnin, "Iz istorii drevnerusskogo koldovstva," 94; Toporkov, *Zagovory*, 174.
82. 1649–50 (*Alatyr'*)	RGADA, f. 210, Moskovskii stol, stlb. 265, ll. 8–90. In Novombergskii, *Vrachebnoe stroenie*, no. 5, viii–xxvi.
83. 1649–50 (*Kozlov*)	RGADA, f. 210, Prikaznyi stol, stlb. 268, ll. 209–28.
84. 1649–50 (*Sevsk*)	RGADA, f. 210, Belgorodskii stol, stlb. 306. ll. 810–13.
85. 1650 (*Moscow, Tula*)	RGADA, f. 396, op. 1, delo 676/4087, ll. 1–8.
86. 1650 (*Novosil'*)	Novomberskii, *Slovo i delo*, vol. 1, 238.
87. 1650 (*Ostashkov*)	RGADA, f. 210, Moskovskii stol, stlb. 265, ll. 396–417. Partially published in Novombergskii, *Vrachebnoe stroenie*, no. 10, pp. xxxiii–xxxviii (ll. 396–403, 415–17.)
88. 1651 (*Karachaev*)	RGADA, f. 210, Prikaznyi stol, stlb. 275, ll. 19–20.
89. 1651 (*Ostashkov*)	RGADA, f. 210, Belgorodskii stol, stlb. 208, ll. 205–7; Novombergskii, *Vrachebnoe stroenie*, no. 11, xxxviii–xxxix.
90. 1651 (*Kozlov*)	RGADA, f. 210, Prikaznyi stol, stlb. 210, ll. 54–55.
91. 1651 (*Kozlov; Pereslavl'-Zaleskii*)	GADA, f. 210, Prikaznyi stol, stlb. 210, ll. 56–57.
92. 1651 (*Sevsk*)	RGADA, f. 210, Prikaznyi stol, stlb. 186, ll. 984–1001.

93. 1651/52 (*Ilimsk*)	RGADA, f. 214, stlb. 586, ll. 7–15.
94. 1652–53 (*Elets*)	RGADA, f. 210, Prikaznyi stol, stlb. 203, ll. 1–4.
95. 1652–53 (*Sevsk*)	RGADA, f. 210, Prikaznyi stol, stlb. 203, ll. 66–67.
96. 1653 (*Belev, Kaluga*)	RGADA, f. 210, Prikaznyi stol, stlb. 204, l. 16. In Novombergskii, *Vrachebnoe stroenie*, no. 47, lxxxvi–lxxxvii.
97. 1653 (*Moscow*)	RGADA, f. 210, Moskovskii stol, stlb. 294, ll. 336–41. In Novombergskii, *Koldovstvo*, no. 19, 83–85.
98. 1653–54 (*Aleksin*)	RGADA, f. 210, Belgorodskii stol, stlb. 1202, ll. 387–88. In Novombergskii, *Koldovstvo*, no. 15, 77–78.
99. 1653–54 (*Briansk*)	RGADA, f. 210, Belgorodskii stol, stlb. 1202, ll. 378–86.
100. 1654 (*Mtsensk*)	RGADA, f. 210, Belgorodskii stol, stlb. 369, ll. 231–36. In Novombergskii, *Koldovstvo*, no. 18, 80–83.
101. 1654 (*Tot'ma*)	Afanas'ev, *Poeticheskoe vozzrenie slavian na prirodu*, 627.
102. 1655/56 (*Lukh*)	RGADA, f. 210, Bezglasnoi stol, stlb. 216, ll. 3–12.
103. 1656 (Usmon')	RGADA, f. 210, Prikaznyi stol, stlb. 546, ll. 183–86; Novombergskii, *Materialy k istorii meditsiny*, vol. 4, no. 28, 173–74.
104. 1656–57 (*Vologda?*)	RGADA, f. 210, Sevskii stol, stlb. 161, ll. 206–8.
105. 1657 (*Lukh*)	RGADA, f. 210, Prikaznyi stol, stlb. 861, ll. 35–35ob. In Novombergskii, *Vrachebnoe stroenie*, no. 37, 197.
106. 1657–58 (*Ol'shansk*)	RGADA, f. 210, Sevskii stol, stlb. 164, ll. 324–34.
107. 1657–58 (*Murom*)	RGADA, f. 210, Prikaznyi stol, stlb. 861, ll. 1–28. In Novombergskii, *Vrachebnoe stroenie*, no. 35, 190–95.
108. 1658 (*Lukh*)	RGADA, f. 210, Vladimirskii stol, stlb. 142, l. 94 (three cases listed on one page).
109. 1658 (*Lukh*)	RGADA, f. 210, Vladimirskii stol, stlb. 142, l. 94 (three cases listed). In Kotkov, *Pamiatniki delovoi pis'mennosti*, no. 103, 147–48.
110. 1658 (*Lukh*)	RGADA, f. 210, Vladimirskii stol, stlb. 142, l. 94 (three cases listed). In Kotkov, *Pamiatniki delovoi pis'mennosti*, no. 103, 147–48.
111. 1658 (*Lukh*)	RGADA, f. 210, Vladimirskii stol, stlb. 142, l. 95 (five cases listed). In Kotkov, *Pamiatniki delovoi pis'mennosti*, no. 103, 148.
112. 1658 (*Lukh*)	RGADA, f. 210, Vladimirskii stol, stlb. 142, l. 95 (five cases listed). In Kotkov, *Pamiatniki delovoi pis'mennosti*, no. 103, 148.

113. 1658 (*Lukh*)	RGADA, f. 210, Vladimirskii stol, stlb. 142, l. 95 (five cases listed). In Kotkov, *Pamiatniki delovoi pis'mennosti*, no. 103, 148.
114. 1658 (*Lukh*)	RGADA, f. 210, Vladimirskii stol, stlb. 142, l. 95 (five cases listed). In Kotkov, *Pamiatniki delovoi pis'mennosti*, no. 103, 148.
115. 1658 (*Lukh*)	RGADA, f. 210, Vladimirskii stol, stlb. 142, l. 95 (five cases listed on one page). In Kotkov, *Pamiatniki delovoi pis'mennosti*, no. 103, 147–48.
116. 1658 (*Lukh*)	RGADA, f. 210, Vladimirskii stol, stlb. 142, ll. 58–38. In Kotkov, *Pamiatniki delovoi pis'mennosti*, no. 157. (See also Prikaznyi stol, stlb. 300 and 314.)
117. 1658 (*Lukh*)	RGADA, f. 210, Prikaznyi stol, stlb. 861, l. 36. In Novombergskii, *Vrachebnoe stroenie*, no. 38, 197.
118. 1658–59 (*Lukh*)	RGADA, f. 210, Prikaznyi stol, stlb. 300, ll. 1–88.
119. 1658–59 (*Lukh*)	RGADA, f. 210, Prikaznyi stol, stlb. 314, ll. 204–204ob. In Kotkov, *Pamiatniki delovoi pis'mennosti*, no. 156, 181.
120. 1659 (*Lukh*)	RGADA f. 210, Prikaznyi stol, stlb. 314, ll. 159–67, 192–93.
121. 1660 (*Kozlov; Sokol'*)	RGADA, f. 210, Prikaznyi stol, stlb. 595, ll. 599–626.
122. 1660 (*Vologda*)	Maikov, *Velikorusskie zaklinaniia*, no. 351, 151–52.
123. 1661 (*Peremyshl'*)	RGADA, f. 210; Belgorodskii stol, stlb. 441, ll. 149–52.
124. 1663–64 (*Iaroslavl'*)	RGADA, f. 210, Belgorodskii stol, stlb. 658, ll. 299–304. In Novombergskii, *Koldovstvo*, no. 20, 85–88.
125. 1663–64 (*Lukh*)	RGADA, f. 210, Prikaznyi stol, stlb. 653, ll. 20–87; Novombergskii, *Materialy po istorii meditsiny*, vol. 4, nos. 39–40, pp. 197–220.
126. 1663–67 (*Iaroslavl'*)	RGADA f. 1257, op. 1, no. 3, ll. 4–6ob.
127. 1664 (*Dobroe*)	RGADA, f. 210, Prikaznyi stol, stlb. 383, ll. 126–27.
128. 1665–66 (*Sumi*)	RGADA, f. 210, Sevskii stol, stlb. 226, ll. 134–44.
129. 1666 (*Akhtyrka*)	RGADA, f. 210, Sevskii stol, stlb. 215, ll. 54–64.
130. 1666 (*Briansk*)	RGADA, f. 210, Sevskii stol, stlb. 215, ll. 223–35.
131. 1666 (*Gadiach*)	RGADA, f. 210, Belgorodskii stol, stlb. 596, ll. 22–27, 30, 35. In Novombergskii, *Koldovstvo*, no. 24, 94.

132. 1666–67 (*Sumi, Belgorod*)	RGADA, f. 210, Belgorodskii stol, stlb. 597, ll. 135–38. Partially published in Novombergskii, *Koldovstvo*, no. 23, 93–94; see also RGADA f. 210, Belgorodskii stol, stlb. 599, ll. 565–71, 654–55, Novombergskii, *Koldovstvo*, no. 21, 88–90.
133. 1667 (*Shuia*)	Borisov, *Starinnye akty*, no. 99, 180–81.
134. 1668 (*Solikamsk*)	RGADA f. 210, op. 14, Sevskii stol, stlb. 230, ll. 1–4. Kozlov, "Fragment koldovskogo dela XVII veka," 347–53.
135. 1669 (*Shuia*)	Borisov, *Starinnye akty*, no. 109.
136. 1669–70 (*Oboian'*)	RGADA, f. 210, Belgorodskii stol, stlb. 652, ll. 628–35. In Novombergskii, *Koldovstvo*, no. 22, 92–93.
137. 1670 (*Kostroma*)	RGADA, f. 210, Prikaznyi stol, stlb. 861, ll. 29–34. In Novombergskii, *Materialy po istorii meditsiny*, vol. 4, no. 41, 220–24. See also Belgorodskii stol, stlb. 1100, ll. 1–370, esp. 4–6; Prikaznyi stol, stlb. 1006.
138. 1670 (*Moscow*)	Ryan, *Bathhouse at Midnight*, 413; Longworth, *Alexis, Tsar of All the Russias*, 199.
139. 1670 (*Shuia*)	Borisov, *Opisanie goroda Shuia*, no. 45–no. 46, 337–38, 339–34.
140. 1670 (*Temnikovo*)	Shvetsova, *Krest'ianskaia voina pod predvoditel'stvom Stepana Razina*, vol. 2, pt. 1, no. 293, 366–68.
141. 1670 (*Smolensk*)	RGADA, f. 210, Prikaznyi stol, stlb. 426, ll. 76–100.
142. 1670–72 (*Kostroma, Iaroslavl'*)	RGADA, f. 210, Prikaznyi stol, stlb. 1006, ll. 1–54. See also Belgorodskii stol., stlb. 1100, ll. 1–370, esp. 4–6; Prikaznyi stol, stlb. 861, ll. 29–34.
143. 1671 (*Moscow*)	RGADA, f. 210, Prikaznyi stol, stlb. 426, ll. 1–17, 162–63, 170–71, 174–76, 323, 332, 342.
144. 1671 (*Moscow*)	Ryan, *Bathhouse at Midnight*, 413; cites RGADA, f. 6, ed. khr. 7.
145. 1671 (*Smolensk*)	RGADA, f. 210, Prikaznyi stol, stlb. 426, ll. 91–100, 110–13, 128–38, 143–44.
146. 1671 (*Temnikovo*)	Popov, *Materialy dlia istorii vozmushcheniia Stenki Razina*, 107–8.
147. 1671 (*Tula*)	RGADA, f. 210, Prikaznyi stol, stlb. 416, ll. 149–61. In Novombergskii, *Materialy po istorii meditsiny*, vol. 4, no. 43, 226–31.
148. 1671 (*Vologda*)	RGADA, f. 210, Prikaznyi stol, stlb. 426, ll. 100–109, 114–23, 148–53.

149. 1671 (*Vologda*)	RGADA, f. 210, Prikaznyi stol, stlb. 426, ll. 235–41, 246–47, 249–50, 252, 258–66, 269–91, 301–5.
150. 1672 (*Kostroma*)	RGADA, f. 210, Prikaznyi stol, stlb. 679, ll. 283–91.
151. 1672 (*Moscow*)	RGADA, f. 210, Prikaznyi stol, stlb. 434, ll. 4–200.
152. 1672–73 (*Iaroslavl'*)	RGADA, f. 210, Prikaznyi stol, stlb. 672, ll. 54–128.
153. 1672–73 (*Kostroma*)	RGADA, f. 210, Belgorodskii stol, stlb. 1100, ll. 1–370, esp. 4–6. See also Prikaznyi stol, stlb. 861, and stlb. 1006.
154. 1673 (*Dobroe*)	RGADA, f. 210, Prikaznyi stol, stlb. 592, ll. 201–9.
155. 1673 (*Velikie Luki*)	RGADA, f. 210, Prikaznyi stol, stlb. 717, ll. 1–55; Novombergskii, *Materialy po istorii meditsiny*, vol. 4, no. 47, 263–76.
156. 1674 (*Moscow*)	Novombergskii, *Materialy po istorii meditsiny*, vol. 3, 526–30; Levin, "Healers and Witches," 129.
157. 1674 (*Shatsk*)	RGADA, f. 210, Belgorodskii stol, stlb. 768, ll. 47–55; Novombergskii, *Koldovstvo*, no. 25, 94–99.
158. 1674 (*Shuia*)	Borisov, *Opisanie goroda Shuia*, no. 50, 345.
159. 1674 (Torzhok)	RGADA, f. 210, Belgorodskii stol, stlb. 768, ll. 57–68, 93–95.
160. 1674 (*n.p.*)	RGADA, f. 210, Belgorodskii stol, stlb. 768, ll. 135–37.
161. 1674 (*Tot'ma*)	Maksimov, *Nechistaia, nevedomaia, i krestnaia sila*, 100.
162. 1675 (*Kolomna*)	Mordovina and Stanislavskii, "Gadatel'nye knigi," 322; Titov, "Iosif Arkhiepiskop Kolomenskii," 85.
163. 1675 (*Moscow*)	Ryan, *Bathhouse at Midnight*, 413; Longworth, *Alexis, Tsar of All the Russias*, 222.
164. 1675–76 (*Dobroe*)	RGADA, f. 210, Prikaznyi stol, stlb. 721, ll. 121–25, 154–55.
165. 1675–76 (*Galich*)	RGADA, f. 210, Prikaznyi stol, stlb. 721, ll. 260–368, 468–69.
166. 1675–76 (*Dobroe*)	RGADA, f. 210, Belgorodskii stol, stlb. 826, ll. 81–96. In Novombergskii, *Koldovstvo*, no. 26, 99–106.
167. 162. 1676 (*Kashira*)	RGADA, f. 210, Belgorodskii stol, stlb. 925, ll. 98–101. In Novombergskii, *Koldovstvo*, no. 27, 106–7.
168. 1676 (*Moscow, Vologda*)	RGADA, f. 210, Prikaznyi stol, stlb. 734, ll. 115–203. See also stlb. 749, ll. 1–385. Extracts in Kotkov, *Moskovskaia delovaia i bytovaia pis'mennost'*, 213–24
169. 1676 (*Sokol'sk*)	RGADA, f. 210, Belgorodskii stol, stlb. 925, ll. 456–57. In Novombergskii, *Koldovstvo*, no. 28, 107–8.

170. 1676–77 (*Sevsk*)	RGADA, f. 210, Novgorodskii stol, stlb. 272, ll. 143–45.
171. 1677 (*Kurmysh*)	RGADA, f. 210, Moskovskii stol, stlb. 525, ll. 338–41. In Novombergskii, *Koldovstvo*, no. 29, 108–9.
172. 1678/79 (*Surgut*)	RGADA, f. 214, stlb. 333. Ogloblin, *Obozrenie stolbtsov i knig*, 200.
173. 1679 (*Siberia*)	RGADA, f. 214, op. 5, d. 230, l. 3, 85; Kozlov, "Chukhlomskoe delo," 449, note 13.
174. 1679–80 (*Akhtyrka*)	RGADA, f. 210, Belgorodskii stol, stlb. 898, ll. 36–40, 41–60, 129.
175. 1679–80 (*Vologda*)	SPBII RAN, koll. 117, op. 1, no. 1305.
176. 1682 (*Moscow*)	Levin, "Witches and Healers," 124; Esipov, "Koldovstvo v XVII i XVIII stoletiakh," 66–70.
177. 1683–84 (*Efremov*)	RGADA, f. 210, Belgorodskii stol, stlb. 1059, ll. 162–72.
178. 1684 (*Moscow*)	RGADA, f. 210, Belgorodskii stol, stlb. 1195, ll. 5–17. Partially published in Novomberskii, *Koldovstvo*, no. 31, 111.
179. 1684–85 (*Putivl'*)	RGADA, f. 210, Belgorodskii stol, stlb. 1165, ll. 430–35. Also stlb. 1171, l. 112.
180. 1684–87 (*Iakutsk*)	RGADA, f. 214, op. 1, stlb. 1396, l. 366 ob.; f. 1177, op. 3, stlb. 2426, ll. 1–13; f. 210, op. 17, stlb. 26, l. 8. Shashkov, "Iakutskoe delo o koldune Ivane Zheglove," 83–88.
181. 1685 (*Moscow*)	RGADA, f. 210, Belgorodskii stol, stlb. 1195, ll. 228, 255–57.
182. 1685 (*Venev*)	RGADA, f. 210, Prikaznyi stol, stlb. 872, ll. 209–11.
183. 1685 (*Vologda*)	RGADA, f. 210, Belgorodskii stol, stlb. 1195, ll. 228–37, 255–57, 279–81.
184. 1685 (*Vologda*)	RGADA, f. 210, Belgorodskii stol, stlb. 1195, ll. 207–13.
185. 1685 (*Vologda*)	RGADA, f. 210, Belgorodskii stol, stlb. 1195, l. 214–23.
186. 1686 (*Moscow*)	RGADA, f. 210, Belgorodskii stol, stlb. 1195, ll. 694–95, 730–32.
187. 1686/87 (*Turinsk*)	RGADA, f. 214, stlb. 983; Ogloblin, *Obozrenie stolbtsov i knig*, 200.
188. 1687 (*Dobroe*)	RGADA, f. 210, Prikaznyi stol, stlb. 1124, ll. 93–96, 251–251ob.
189. 1688 (Ryl'sk)	RGADA, f. 210, Prikaznyi stol, stlb. 1122, ll. 35–51.

190. 1688–89 (*Borovsk*)	RGADA, f. 210, Prikaznyi stol, stlb. 1133, stolpik 2, ll. 132–99. Spells partially published in Toporkov, *Zagovory*, 366, and in Toporkov, *Russkie zagovory iz rukopisnykh istochnikov*, 330–41.
191. 1689 (*Iarensk, Moscow*)	Truvorov, "Volkhvy i vorozhei," 713; *Rozysknyia dela o Fedore Shaklovitom*, vol. 3, cols. 1235–71.
192. 1689 (*Moscow*)	Ivanits, *Russian Folk Belief*, 88; Afanas'ev, *Poeticheskoe vozzrenie slavian na prirodu*, 648–49.
193. 1689 (*Moscow*)	Truvorov, "Volkhvy i vorozhei," 713.
194. 1689 (*Moscow*)	Truvorov, "Volkhvy i vorozhei," 714.
195. 1689 (*Moscow*)	Truvorov, "Volkhvy i vorozhei," 714–15.
196. 1689 (*Moscow*)	Truvorov, "Volkhvy i vorozhei," 713; *Rozysknyia dela o Fedore Shaklovitom*.
197. 1689 (*Nizhnii Novgorod*)	Truvorov, "Volkhvy i vorozhei," 703–11.
198. 1689–90 (*Kostroma; Zavoloch'ia; Rzhev*)	RGADA, f. 210, Novgorodskii stol, stlb. 150, ll. 731–40; stlb. 210, ll. 161–92, 284–93, 356–57.
199. 1689–90 (*Moscow; Iaroslavets-Malyi*)	RGADA, f. 210, Prikaznyi stol, stlb. 1235, ll. 28–42. In Novombergskii, *Materialy po istorii meditsiny*, vol. 4, no. 55, 375–79.
200. 1689–91 (*Moscow*)	*Rozysknyia dela o Fedore Shakovitom*, vol. 2, 27, 167, 180, 268, 507, 825; Mordovina and Stanislavskii, "Gadatel'nye knigi," 322.
201. 1690 (*Belgorod*)	RGADA, f. 210, Belgorodskii stol, stlb. 1526, ll. 79–83.
202. 1690 (*Belgorod*)	RGADA, f. 210, Belgorodskii stol, stlb. 1526. ll. 500, 502, 557–59; ll. 557–59 in Novombergskii, *Koldovstvo*, no. 32, 111–12.
203. 1690 (*Dobroe*)	RGADA, f. 210, Prikaznyi stol, stlb. 1225, ll. 1–51.
204. 1690 (*Galich*)	RGADA, f. 210, Prikaznyi stol, stlb. 8, ll. 1–130. Also partially in Novombergskii, *Vrachebnoe stroenie*, no. 51, xci–xcviii, incl. ll. 1–15.
205. 1690 (*Kineshma*)	Semevskii, *Istoriko–iuridicheskie akty*, no. vii, 70–71.
206. 1690 (*Vologda*)	Sankt–Peterburgskii institute istorii RAN (SPBII RAN), koll. 117, op. 1, no. 1866, ll. 1–2.
207. 1690–1691 (*Kozlov*)	RGADA, f. 210, Prikaznyi stol, stlb. 2630, ll. 1–70. (See also stolbtsy 2640 and 2646.)
208. 1691 (*Moscow*)	RGADA, f. 371, Preobrazhenskii prikaz, op. 2, no. 723, l. 19, 25, 91, 125; Lavrov, *Koldovstvo i religiia*, 355.
209. 1692 (*Belgorod*)	RGADA, f. 210, Prikaznyi stol, stlb. 1483, ll. 1–6.

210. 1692 (*Novgorod, Arkhangelsk*)	*RGADA*, f. 159, *Prikaznye dela starykh let*, op. 3, no. 4208, ll. 1–13.
211. 1692 (*Kostroma*)	Mordovina and Stanislavskii, "Gadatel'nye knigi," 322.
212. 1692 (*Tot'ma*)	RGADA, f. 159, op. 1, no. 326, ll. 1–5.
213. 1692 (*Vologda*)	SPBII RAN, koll. 117, op. 1, no. 1931, ll. 1–4.
214. 1693 (*Kozlov*)	RGADA, f. 210, Prikaznyi stol, stlb. 679, ll. 297–300.
215. 1694 (*Beloozero*)	RGADA, f. 210, Belgorodskii stol, stlb. 1032, 11–13, 165–94.
216. 1694 (*Beloozero*)	RGADA, f. 210, Prikaznyi stol, stlb. 1677, ll. 1–58.
217. 1695–96 (*Elets*)	RGADA, f. 210, Prikaznyi stol, stlb. 1859, ll. 147–60.
218. 1696 (*Usman'*)	RGADA, f. 210, Prikaznyi stol, stlb. 1385, ll. 99–100.
219. 1697 (*Beloozero*)	RGADA, f. 210, Novgorodskii stol, stlb. 233, ll. 206–7.
220. 1697–98 (*Moscow*)	RGADA, f. 210, Prikaznyi stol, stlb. 2109, ll. 1–36.
221. 1698 (*Iaroslavets–Malyi*)	RGADA, f. 210, Prikaznyi stol, stlb. 2152, ll. 5–17.
222. 1699 (*Moscow*)	RGADA, f. 371, Preobrazhenskii prikaz, op. 2, no. 760, ll. 20–54; Lavrov, *Koldovstvo i religiia*, 111–13, 333.
223. 1699–1700 (*Kolomna*)	RGADA, f. 210, Prikaznyi stol, stlb. 2565, ll. 286–95.
224. 1700 (*Vorotynsk*)	RGADA, f. 210, Prikaznyi stol, stlb. 2679, ll. 34–52.
225. 1700–1701 (*Chernavsk*)	RGADA, f. 210, Prikaznyi stol, stlb. 2565, ll. 458–61.
226. 1700–1701 (*Voronezh*)	RGADA, f. 210, Prikaznyi stol, stlb. 2346, ll. 1–64.
227. 1701 (*Oskol–Staryi*)	RGADA, f. 210, Prikaznyi stol, stlb. 2651, ll. 1–15.

Appendix B

LIST OF LAWS AND DECREES AGAINST WITCHCRAFT AND MAGIC

1551 *(Moscow)*	*AI*, vol. 1, no. 154.
1598 (*various*)	*AAE*, vol. II, no. 10, 57–61 (oath of loyalty to Tsar Boris Godunov).
1605 (various)	*AAE*, vol. II, no. 37, 94–95 (oath of loyalty to Tsar Dmitrii Ivanovich).
1606 (various)	*AAE*, vol. II, no. 44, 100–103 (oath\` of loyalty to Tsar Vasilii Shuiskii).
1647	RGADA f. 381, no. 1584, ll. 1–2.
1647–53 (*Korocha*)	RGADA, f. 210, stolbtsy dopolnitel'nogo stola, stlb. 51, ll. 5–8.
1648 (*Belgorod*)	RGADA, f. 210, Belgorodskii stol, stlb. 288, ll. 82–88. Also in Novombergskii, *Koldovstvo*, no. 14, 75–77.
1648 (*Iur'ev Pol'skii*)	RGADA, f. 210, Belgorodskii stolb, stlb. 298, ll. 377–80.
1648 (*Khotmyshsk*)	RGADA, f. 210, Belgorodskii stol, stlb. 298, ll. 377–80.
1648 (*Korocha, Chern', and various*)	RGADA, f. 210, Belgorodskii stol, stlb. 270, ll. 442–44, 445–51, 452–53, 601–5, 609–12; *AI*, vol. 4, no. 35, 124–26.
1648 (*various*)	RGADA, f. 210, Novgorodskii stol, stlb. 96, ll. 11–12 (*Bezhetskii verkh*), 1–10 (*Dmitrov*), 14

	(*Kashin*), 251–54 (*Kostroma*). [Also received in *Belgorod, Shuia, Tobol'sk*: Kharuzin, "K voprosu o bor'be," 145, 149.]
1649 (*Belgorod*)	RGADA, f. 210, Sevskii stol, stlb. 137, ll. 455–56.
1652 (*Pereslavl'-Zalesskii*)	RGADA, f. 210, Belgorodskii stol, stlb. 337, ll. 142–46.
1653 (*Belev*)	RGADA, f. 210, Belgorodskii stol, stlb. 1260, ll. 1–2.
1653 (*Karpov and various*)	RGADA, f. 210, Belgorodskii stol, stlb. 361, ll. 167–70. In Novomberskii, *Koldovstvo*, no. 16, 78–79; Oparina, "Neizvestnyi ukaz 1648," 91.
1653 (*Kozlov*)	RGADA, f. 210, Prikaznyi stol, stlb. 194, ll. 97–98, 101–3.
1653 (*Lukh*)	RGADA, f. 210, Sevskii stol, stlb. 148, ll. 92–94.
1653 (*Oskol'*)	RGADA, f. 210, Belgorodskii stol, stlb. 362, ll. 165, 244–47. In Novombergskii, *Koldovstvo*, no. 17, 79–80.
1653 (*various*)	RGADA, f. 210, Prikaznyi stol, stlb. 203, ll. 25–27, 406–7, 28–31, 133–36, 224–27, 237–40, 390–95, 396, 403, 397, 404–5, 461–76. Novombergskii, *Vrachebnoe stroenie*, no. 46, lxxxiv–lxxxvi; Oparina, "Neizvestnyi ukaz 1653" (includes ll. 463–65, 466–67).
1653 (*Moscow*)	*Kormchaia kniga* (Moscow, 1653), l. 517; cited in Kozlov, "Chukhlomoskoe delo 1635–1636," 462, note 11.
1654 (*Belev*)	RGADA, f. 210, Belgorodskii stol, stlb. 1202, l. 394 (response to 1653 decree).
1654 (*Moscow*)	RGADA, f. 210, Prikaznyi stol, stlb. 153, l. 384.
1673 (*Kineshma*)	RGADA, f. 210, Moskovskii stol, stlb. 485, ll. 28–33, 639–51.
1673 (*Murom*)	RGADA, f. 210, Moskovskii stol, stlb. 485, ll. 28–33, 639–51, 692–95, 768–78.
1682 (*Moscow*)	Kantorovich, *Srednevekovye protsessy o ved'makh*, 177 (Charter of the Moscow Slavonic–Greco–Latin Academy).

Notes

INTRODUCTION

1. RGADA, f. 210, Prikaznyi stol, stlb. 2725, ll. 40–42.
2. Ibid., l. 42.
3. Ibid., stlb. 565, ll. 6–21.
4. M.V. Korogodina argues for an upsurge of interest in magic with the influx of new translations from the Balkans in the sixteenth century, which correlates with an increase in the number of penitential questions probing related sins. Korogodina, *Ispoved'*, 204–5.
5. I have documentation of 227 trials from the seventeenth century. I cannot claim completeness, but this is certainly an extensive sample of surviving cases, and my findings remain stable as new cases crop up. I can identify the number and gender of 495 individuals in 223 cases. Presuming a single witch per case for the remaining 4 records (involving unspecified numbers of "witches"), we arrive at a minimum of 499 accused individuals.
6. E. B. Smilianskaia examined "almost 200 trials" involving 168 men and 36 women between 1700 and 1760. Smilianskaia, *Volshebniki*, 65, note 1. Elsewhere she mentions 240 cases. Ibid., 75, 143–45. See also Lavrov, *Koldovstvo i religiia*, 116.
7. These figures derive from 87 trials with known outcomes and involved 193 individuals: 74 (38%) exiled; 71 (37%) released with sureties; 27 (14%) executed.
8. "Your slave" was a self-deprecatory formula conventionally used by Muscovite elites in addressing the tsar.
9. RGADA, f. 210, Prikaznyi stol, stlb. 2109, ll. 1–36.
10. Evans-Pritchard, *Witchcraft, Oracles, and Magic*. Richard Kieckhefer notes that the idea originated in sixteenth-century religious polemic, and finds it ultimately "unhelpful in dealing with medieval material": Kieckhefer, *Magic in the Middle Ages*, 14–15. More specifically, it underlay Protestant attacks on Catholic ritual and the priests who performed (magical) sacraments. The distinction found a place in anthropological theory in the late nineteenth and early twentieth centuries.
11. Apparition: RGADA, f. 210, Prikaznyi stol, stlb. 17, ll. 54–61. Evil eye (*uroki*): ibid., stlb. 426, ll. 100–109, 114–23, 148–53; stlb. 564, ll. 154–234; ibid., Belgorodskii stol, stlb. 284, ll. 425–47; Novombergskii, *Koldovstvo*, no. 9, pp. 40–53.
12. Rowlands, "Not 'the Usual Suspects'?" 4; Thomas, *Religion and the Decline of Magic*, 436.
13. N.M. Gal'kovskii agrees that *volkhvy* were non-Russians and perhaps pagan: *Bor'ba khristianstva s ostatkami iazychestva*, v. 1, 131–42; Korogodina disagrees: *Ispoved'*, 206. For analysis of the vocabulary, see Ryan, *Bathhouse at Midnight*, 84–86.

14. On Western medical practice in Muscovy, see Collis, "Magic, Medicine, and Authority"; Dumschat, *Ausländische Mediziner im Moskauer Rußland*; Levin, "Healers and Witches"; Unkovskaya, *Brief Lives*.

15. Schulte, "Men as Accused Witches," 54.

16. Thompson, "Moral Economy of the English Crowd," 78.The only application of this concept to questions of witchcraft that I have found is Austen, "The Moral Economy of Witchcraft," which focuses on economic and theoretical implications.

17. Thompson, "Moral Economy Reviewed," 269.

18. Thompson, "Moral Economy of the English Crowd," 78, 90.

19. By and large, serfs plowed the fields while slaves performed more intimate functions for their masters, serving as domestic laborers, estate overseers and administrators, or military aides.

20. My thanks to Ekaterina Pravilova for drawing my attention to the changing use of language over time. In the seventeenth century the verb "*vladet'*," to have, to own, or to hold, refers primarily to property. In one case, a woman uses it to describe hope of ending her master's ability to "have" her sexually: RGADA, f. 210, Prikaznyi stol, stlb. 1859, ll. 148–49.

21. It is probably no coincidence that studies of witchcraft in colonial Latin America and the Caribbean uncover similar dynamics. Their slave economies created structures not dissimilar to those on the Russian estate. See, for example, Behar, "Sexual Witchcraft, Colonialism, and Women's Powers."

22. Scott, *Weapons of the Weak*; Scott, *Domination and the Arts of Resistance*; Scott, *Moral Economy of the Peasant*.

23. Abu-Lughod, "Romance of Resistance," 42,

24. Russian landlords' suppressed anxieties about their serfs in the next century are the focus of Thomas Newlin's well titled "Rural Ruses: Illusion and Anxiety on the Russian Estate, 1775–1815."

25. Novombergskii, *Koldovstvo*, no. 26, 103.

26. Through the seventeenth century, Western skeptics generally stopped short of questioning the reality of witchcraft per se, which rested on strong biblical foundations.

27. On Maria of Tver: *PSRL*, vol. 6, *Sofiiskaia pervaia letopis'*, 186. On the idiosyncratic nature of this account given by an eyewitness with a particular viewpoint, see Kloss, *Nikonovskii svod i russkie letopisi*. On Sofia: *PSRL*, vol. 6, 279. *Brezhenie* (trans. from Fennell, *Ivan the Great of Moscow*, 337).

28. *PSRL*, vol. 29, *Letopisets nachala tsarstva*, 153.

29. A few high profile trials or inquests took place in the late sixteenth century. See Ryan, *Bathhouse at Midnight*, 410–12. The few early seventeenth-century trials include: 1606, *Akty istoricheskie*, vol. 2, 1598–1613, 82–83, and 1611, RNB, *Sobranie Pogodina*, no. 1593, l. 1 (glued to binding). Thanks to A. S. Lavrov for sharing this case.

30. Lavrov, *Koldovstvo i religiia*; Ryan, *Bathhouse at Midnight*; Smilianskaia, *Volshebniki, bogokhul'niki, eretiki*; Worobec, "Decriminalizing Witchcraft in Pre-Emancipation Russia," unpublished article (with thanks for permission to cite); Worobec; *Possessed*.

31. Marker, personal communication. Toporkov includes a useful index of spells by "functional type," with quite a few seventeenth-century spells concerning livestock but none concerning agriculture: *Russkie zagovory*, 785–90. Lavrov notes the absence of agrarian and weather magic in the eighteenth century as well. Lavrov, *Koldovstvo i religiia*, 94.

32. On the emergence of a modern sense of the political and its connection to magic, see Nun-Ingerflom, "How Old Magic Does the Trick for Modern Politics."

CHAPTER 1

1. Bailey, *Magic and Superstition in Europe*; Collins, *Magic in the Ancient Greek World*; Luck, *Arcana Mundi;* Maguire, *Byzantine Magic*.

2. Scot, *Discoverie of Witchcraft*, bk. 1, 8. In an early instance, Johann Weyer explained in 1563 that women might imagine themselves empowered with witchcraft when "dulled by age, or inconstant by reason of her sex, or unsteady because of her weak-mindedness, or in despair because of a disease of the mind . . . " (Weyer, *Witches, Devils, and Doctors in the Renaissance*, 174). Nadine Kuperty-Tsur finds that already in 1546 Rabelais advanced the argument that the witch was a construct of those observing her ("Comment l'humanisme a-t-il tué les sorcières? La Sybille du Tiers Livre de Rabelais." Talk, University of Michigan, March 2011.). On witchcraft and the scientific revolution, see Easlea, *Witch Hunting, Magic, and the New Philosophy.*

3. Voltaire, *Philosophical Dictionary*, vol. 1, 205; vol. 2, 298.

4. Michelet, *Sorcière*, 5, 9.

5. Murray, *God of the Witches*, 18, 19. Ginzburg, *Night Battles*. See also, Wood, "Reality of Witch Cults Reasserted."

6. Russell, *Witchcraft in the Middle Ages*, 19; Cohn, *Europe's Inner Demons*; Moore, *Formation of a Persecuting Society.* On the linkage of heresy and witchcraft, a useful historiographic review is found in Behringer, "How Waldensians Became Witches," 155–92. Stephens, *Demon Lovers*; Kieckhefer, *European Witch Trials*; Kieckhefer, *Magic in the Middle Ages*; Kieckhefer, "Mythologies of Witchcraft"; and Kieckhefer, "Specific Rationality of Medieval Magic"; Levack, *Witch-Hunt in Early Modern Europe*; Clark, *Thinking with Demons.*

7. Ehrenreich and English, *Witches, Midwives, and Nurses*; critique: Harley, "Historians as Demonologists," 1–26.

8. Daly, *Gyn/Ecology*, chap. 6; Barstow, *Witchcraze*; Dworkin, *Woman Hating*, chap. 7; Willis, *Malevolent Nurture.*

9. Broedel, *Malleus Maleficarum.*

10. Kamensky, *Governing the Tongue*; Karlsen, *Devil in the Shape of a Woman*; Juster, *Disorderly Women*; Reis, "Devil, the Body, and the Feminine Soul."

11. Demos, *Entertaining Satan.*

12. Ferber, *Demonic Possession and Exorcism*; Purkiss, *Witch in History*, 145–78; Robisheaux, *Last Witch of Langenburg*; Roper, "Witchcraft and Fantasy"; Sabean, "Sacred Bond of Unity," 94–112; Watt, *Scourge of Demons*; and earlier, in a different vein, Caro Baroja, *Brujas y su mundo.*

13. Thomas, *Religion and the Decline of Magic*; Macfarlane, *Witchcraft in Tudor and Stuart England*; Karlsen, *Devil in the Shape of a Woman.*

14. Stephens, *Demon Lovers*, 26. For a different interpretation of the preoccupations of demonologists, see Machielsen, "Thinking with Montaigne." Scholarship on the connection between witchcraft and women also points to Galenic views of the female body, seen as porous (hence susceptible to both physical and diabolical penetration) and leaky (hence contaminating and toxic). Caciola, *Discerning Spirits*; Hults, *Witch as Muse*; Maclean, *Renaissance Notion of a Woman*; Roper, *Witch Craze*; Purkiss, *Witch in History*; Simons, *Sex of Men in Premodern Europe*; Stephens, *Demon Lovers*; Sluhovsky, *Believe Not Every Spirit.*

15. Purkiss, *Witch in History*, 91–144; Roper, *Witch Craze*; and Roper, *Oedipus and the Devil.*

16. Noting that the world of early modern intellectual thought did not accurately reflect the realities of the courtroom, Stuart Clark argues that within the categorical binaries of early modern intellectual thought, it was "literally unthinkable, at this level, that witches should be male" (Clark, *Thinking with Demons,* 130; see also Clark, "'Gendering' of Witchcraft"). Other scholars note that many early modern texts employed male or gender-neutral nouns in their discussions of witches.

17. Monter, "Toads and Eucharists," 563–95.

18. On numbers, see Behringer, "Neun Millionen Hexen," 664–85.

19. Midelfort, *Witch Hunting in Southwestern Germany,* 12–63, 179.

20. Apps and Gow, *Male Witches in Early Modern Europe*; Kent, "Masculinity and Male Witches"; Labouvie, "Männer im Hexenprozess"; Schulte, *Man as Witch.*

21. Rowlands provides an unusually useful introduction to the edited volume *Witchcraft and Masculinities*: "Not 'the Usual Suspects'?" Although this is not the place to review each of the

contributions in depth, the book well rewards reading. In particular, see de Blécourt, "The Werewolf, the Witch, and the Warlock"; Briggs, "Male Witches in the Duchy of Lorraine"; Gaskill, "Masculinity and Witchcraft"; and Voltmer, "Witch-Finders, Witch-Hunters, or Kings of the Sabbath?" Katrin Moeller also confirms some of Labouvie's "separate spheres" findings, although with significant overlaps: *Dass Willkür über recht ginge*, 228–31. Robert Walinski-Kiehl discusses connections of ideas of male sexual drive and vulnerability to the Devil, as well as issues of male honor, in "Males, 'Masculine Honor,' and Witch-Hunting."

22. Rowlands, "Not 'the Usual Suspects'?" 24.

23. Ankarloo and Henningsen, *Early Modern European Witchcraft*; and more recently, Mitchell, *Witchcraft and Magic*.

24. Ginzburg, *Ecstasies*; Pócs, *Between the Living and the Dead*. In Finnmark, accused witches and Sami shamans were categorized as one and the same. See Hagen, "Female Witches and Sami Sorcerers"; Hagen, *Shaman of Alta*; and Hagen, "Witch-Hunt in Early Modern Finnmark." Recent critiques call the entire concept of "shamanism" into question, noting that the concept is poorly defined and suggesting that the term itself (found first in a Russian source from the seventeenth century) derives from a Whiggish, Westerncentric hierarchical and social evolutionary categorization of legitimate and "primitive" religion: Francfort and Hamayon, *Concept of Shamanism*; Stuckrad, "Refutation and Desire."

25. I have collected only a few cases from Siberia, but the same distinctions seem to be maintained. Indigenous practitioners are labeled as "shamans" or "sorcerers," while Russians are accused as witches. Witches: RGADA, f. 214, stlb. 586, ll. 7–15 (Ilimsk); stlb. 381 (Tomsk); Shashkov, "Iakutskoe delo o koldune Ivane Zheglove"; Ogloblin, *Obozrenie stolbtsov i knig Sibirskago prikaza*, 200. Shamans: Al'kor and Grekov, *Kolonial'naia politika Moskovskogo gosudarstva v Iakutii*, no. 138; RGADA, f. 1177, no. 2, l. 152; no. 16, ll. 78–80.

26. Laughing and crying men: RGADA f. 210, Prikaznyi stol, stlb. 564, l. 216, ll. 154–234. Red-haired vision: Ibid., stlb. 17, ll. 54–61; quote on l. 55. Shaggy men: Ibid., Moskovskii stol, stlb. 294, ll. 336–41.

27. On the role of wars of religion, see, for instance, Certeau, *Possession at Loudun*. On overseas encounters and witchcraft, see Purkiss, *Witch in History*, 251–76; Cervantes, *Devil in the New World*; de Mello e Souza, *Devil and the Land of the Holy Cross*. On the role of the printing press, particularly in the circulation of images, see Gibson, *Early Modern Witches*; Zika, *Appearance of Witchcraft*.

28. Purkiss, *Witch in History*, 251–76.

29. Kenses, "Some Unexplored Relationships," 179–212; Norton, *In the Devil's Snare*. Charles Halperin argues that medieval "bookmen" confronted the reality of the Mongol conquest of Rus' by refusing to acknowledge their total defeat. This is a very different strategy than attempting to cleanse their own community through targeting witches. Halperin, *Russia and the Golden Horde*.

30. Michels, *At War with the Church*. Lavrov also notes that in the eighteenth century Old Believers are still almost entirely absent from witchcraft trials (*Koldovstvo i religiia*, 131).

31. Apocalypticism: Kamil, *Fortress of the Soul*; Seaver, *Wallington's World*; Wintroub, *Savage Mirror*.

32. Andreev, *Pod znakom*; Flier, "Till the End of Time"; Rowland, "Blessed Host of the Heavenly Tsar"; Rowland, "Moscow—The Third Rome or the New Jerusalem?" But cf. the darker view in Iurganov, *Kategorii russkoi srednevekovoi kul'tury*; Bulychev, *Mezhdu sviatymi i demony*.

33. Purkiss, *Witch in History*, 91–118; Willis, *Malevolent Nurture*.

34. On binaries and anti-behavior, Clark, "'Gendering' of Witchcraft," 426–37; Clark, *Thinking with Demons*, 31–78; Rowland, "'Fantasticall and Devilishe Persons,'" 169; Lotman and Uspenskij, "Role of Dual Models."

35. Ryan, *Bathhouse at Midnight*, 68; Worobec, *Possessed*, e.g., 91–92.

36. Cross worn on back: RGADA, f. 210, Sevskii stol, stlb. 230, l. 1. Spells: Zhuravel, *Siiuzhet o dogovore cheloveka s d'iavolom*, 82; Ryan, *Bathouse at Midnight*, 181, 182; Toporkov, *Russkie zagovory*; Toporkov and Turilov, *Otrechennoe chtenie*.

37. The concept of "pollution," popular in witchcraft studies largely through the important contributions of Mary Douglas, proves difficult to apply to Russian witches. The opprobrium heaped on Muscovite witches was heated, but rarely concentrated on matters of dirt or pollution. Accused witches were not described as personally unclean, and their behavior was not notably impure. Their presence in the community was rarely remarked on as surprising in any way, since they were usually members of the community, fully embedded, and were not condemned for polluting the social body. Douglas, *Purity and Danger*, 95–129.

38. Ryan, *Bathhouse at Midnight*, 413; Kantorovich, *Srednevekovye protsessy o ved'makh*, 170–75; Zabelin, "Sysknye dela o vorozheiakh i koldun'iakh"; Novomberskii, *Koldovstvo*, no. 33, 112–34; RGADA, f. 210, Prikaznyi stol, stlb. 567, ll. 539–49.

39. Ostling, *Between the Devil and the Host*, 124. Raymond Kelly finds the same dynamic at work in the circulation of "life force" in the form of semen among the people he studied in New Guinea ("Witchcraft and Sexual Relations," 36–53).

40. Tavern keepers: RGADA, f. 210, Prikaznyi stol, stlb. 416, ll. 149–61; ibid., Belgorodskii stol, stlb. 59, ll. 128–30.

41. Toporkov, "Gramota no. 521," 240–41.

42. Siegel, *Naming the Witch*, 1.

43. Ibid.

44. Eriksen, *Wayward Puritans*. Another clear statement of a similar position: Ben-Yehuda, "European Witch Craze of the Fourteenth to Seventeenth Centuries"; and "European Witch Craze: Still a Sociologist's Perspective."

45. Briggs, *Witches and Neighbors*; Roper, *Witch Craze*, esp. 181–221. David Warren Sabean also examines a tragic case of self-accusation: "Sacred Bond of Unity," 94–112.

46. On the importance of changes in law and legal structure and process, see Henningsen, *Witches' Advocate*; Henningsen, Tedeschi, and Amiel, *Inquisition in Early Modern Europe*; Hoffer, *Salem Witchcraft Trials*; Konig, *Law and Society*, 136–85; Larner, *Enemies of God*; Larner, *Witchcraft and Religion*; Levack, "State Building and Witch Hunting in Early Modern Europe"; and Levack, "Crime and the Law."

47. Brown, "Muscovite Government Bureaux"; Brown "Bureaucratic Administration"; Kollmann, *Crime and Punishment in Early Modern Russia*; Demidova; *Sluzhilaia biurokratiia*; Zimin, *Rossiia na rubezhe XV–XVI stoletii.*

48. Blécourt, "Werewolf, the Witch, and the Warlock"; Goodare, "Men and the Witch Hunt in Scotland"; Heuser, "Kurkölnischen Hexenprozesse"; Voltmer, "Witch-Finders, Witch-Hunters, or Kings of the Sabbath?" Konig, *Law and Society in Puritan Massachusetts.*

49. On climate and witch-hunting: Behringer, "Weather, Hunger, and Fear"; Behringer, "Climatic Change and Witch-Hunting"; and Pfister, "Climatic Extremes, Recurrent Crises, and Witch Hunts." On religious tensions and witch-hunting: Behringer, *Witchcraft Persecutions in Bavaria.* On German scholarship on witchcraft, see review article by Schwerhoff, "Ot povsednevnykh podozrenii."

50. The idea of "the general crisis of the seventeenth century" was originally formulated in Hobsbawm, "General Crisis of the European Economy"; and Trevor-Roper, "General Crisis of the Seventeenth Century"; and further developed by Goldstone, *Revolution and Rebellion.* For Russia: Crummey, "Muscovy and the 'General Crisis of the Seventeenth Century' "; Dunning, "Does Jack Goldstone's Model of Early Modern State Crises Apply to Russia?" 572; and most recently, by a scholar also interested in magic and witchcraft, Lavrov, "Hovanščina et la crise financière"; and *Koldovstvo i religiia.*

51. Ashforth, *Witchcraft, Violence, and Democracy*, 13.

52. Toporkov, *Russkie zagovory*; Cherepanova, *Mifologicheskie rasskazy;* Ivanits, *Russian Folk Belief*; Ryan, *Bathhouse at Midnight, 40*; Toporkov, *Zagovory v russkoi rukopisnoi traditsii.*

53. Ashforth, *Witchcraft, Violence, and Democracy*, 313.

54. "Zhenshchina," in *Entsiklopedicheskii slovar'*, vol. 11 (St. Petersburg, 1894), 886; quoted in Atkinson, "Society and the Sexes in the Russian Past," 16, note 46. Smirnov, "Baby bogomerzkiia," 217–40. Moreover, in cases involving food preparation, male cooks were accused as frequently as females. Tavern keepers were charged with serving bewitching grog. Townsmen faced trial for offering passersby ladles of enchanted water. Male serfs or slaves worked as cooks in their masters' houses. See also similar claims in Efimenko, "Sud nad ved'mami," and Aristov, "Sud'ba russkoi zhenshchiny v do-petrovskoe vremia," 191–92.

55. Trevor-Roper, "European Witch-Craze," 185.

56. Zguta, "Witchcraft Trials."

57. Catherine the Great, *Siberian Shaman.*

58. Ryan, *Bathhouse at Midnight*; Worobec, *Possessed*; Clay, "Russian Ethnographers in the Service of Empire"; Thomas, "Collecting for the Fatherland"; Knight, "Science, Empire, and Nationality," 108–42.

59. Antonovych, *Koldovstvo*; Afanas'ev, *Mify, pover'ia i sueveriia slavian*; Dal', *O poveriakh, sueveriakh, i predrassudkakh russkogo naroda.* Other significant publications included Maksimov, *Nechistaia, nevedomaia i krestnaia sila*; Kantorovich, *Srednevekovye protsessy o ved'makh.*

60. Toporkov, *Russkie zagovory*, 61.

61. Chistov, *Russkie narodnye sotsial'no-utopicheskie legendy*; Klibanov, *Kritika religioznogo sektanstva.*

62. Florovsky, *Ways of Russian Theology*, vol. 5, p. 3, with translation modified. An earlier view of witchcraft as a symptom of "paganism and superstition" is voiced in Kharuzin, "K voprosu o bor'be," 151.

63. Lotman and Uspenskij, "Role of Dual Models," 7.

64. Rybakov, *Iazychestvo drevnikh slavian,* esp. 597–605. For insightful analysis of the debate, see Chernetsov, "Dvoeverie," 16–19; and Smilianskaia, *Volshebniki,* 7–11.

65. Petrukhin, *Drevniaia Rus'*, 23. See also Klibanov, *Dukhovnaia kul'tura srednevekovoi Rusi*, 42; Sedov and Chernetsov, "Slavianskoe iazychestvo," 76–81; and Zhivov, "Dvoeverie," 54. See also Korogodina, *Ispoved'*, 203, 225–29, on questions about pagan worship addressed by confessional guides.

66. Levin, "Dvoeverie and Popular Religion," 31–52; Rock, *Popular Religion in Russia: "Double Belief" and the Making of an Academic Myth.* Aleksandr B. Strakhov takes an even stronger position on the purely Christian meanings of folk belief and ritual, in *Noch' pered Rozhdestvom.*

67. Smilianskaia, *Volshebniki,* 40.

68. Eve Levin demonstrates that folk prayers also called on Christian saints and teachings in somewhat popularized form to effect their magic. Levin, "Supplicatory Prayers," 96–114.

69. Novombergskii, *Koldovstvo*, vi.

70. Zguta, "Witchcraft Trials," 1205.

71. Ryan, *Bathhouse at Midnight*, 414; Smilianskaia examines 500 trials of "spiritual crimes" dating from 1700–1801 and involving more than 1,500 individuals in the roles of accused, witnesses, officials, judges, and so forth, but her study includes heresy and blasphemy trials as well as trials of accused witches Approximately 240 of her cases involve witchcraft, and the numbers of individuals involved in each case remain small, as they are in the seventeenth-century cases. While it is difficult to derive precise numbers from her study, the case descriptions seem to justify extrapolating numbers similar to those of the previous century, hence something around 400 individuals involved in 240 trials. Smilianskaia, *Volshebniki,* 19–21, 65, note 1 (mentions 200 witchcraft trials heard in central institutions); 75, 143–45 (mention 240 witchcraft trials).

72. The numbers game would be quite entertaining, if it weren't so ghoulish. The often-repeated number of nine million dates back to a creative miscalculation by Gottfried Christian Voigt in the eighteenth century. It was repopularized by suffragist Matilda Joslyn Gage in the nineteenth century, and inflated still further in Benjamin Christensen's 1922 Swedish film,

Häxan. Mary Daly and others cite the number of eight million witches killed (*Gyn/Ecology*, 183), and Dan Brown comes up with the number five million in *The Da Vinci Code*. In the 1980s, more serious counts revealed that these figures were off by more than two orders of magnitude. In his 1987 textbook, Brian Levack puts the number between fifty thousand and one hundred thousand (*Witch-Hunt in Early Modern Europe*, 21–26). More recent works, such as Marko Nenonen's, revises the total number of victims down still more, to below fifty thousand ("Witch Hunts in Europe," 165–86). See also Toivo, "Witch-Craze as Holocaust."

73. Antonovych, *Koldovstvo*; Zguta, "Was There a Witch Craze in Muscovite Russia?" Ryan, "Witchcraft Hysteria," 49–84.

74. Novombergskii, *Koldovstvo*, vi.

CHAPTER 2

1. RGADA, f. 210, Prikaznyi stol, stlb. 314, ll. 161–62.

2. Briansk to Sevsk to Moscow, Razriad: RGADA, f. 210, Sevskii stol, stlb. 215, ll. 223–35.

3. On the issue of judicial autonomy, see Kollmann, "Judicial Autonomy in the Criminal Law."

4. RGADA f. 210, Prikaznyi stol, stlb. 268, ll. 209–28ob., l. 209.

5. This particular case record breaks off with the first report from Kozlov to Moscow, so this response is a reconstruction based on cases with more complete records.

6. Kozlov presents an overview of the contents of these *stolbtsy* in "Chukhlomskoe delo," 446–47, and "I toiu de vorozhboiu," 282–83.

7. "Novoukaznye stat'i," in *PSZ*, art. 100, 796: "If a wife murders her husband or feeds him poison, bury her alive. And even if her children and close relatives beg to have her not executed, execute her without mercy: bury her in the earth and keep her there until she dies (*za to kaznit', zhivu okopat' v zemliu*)." This practice was already in use prior to 1669. Women convicted of witchcraft in Lukh in 1656 were sentenced to live burial: RGADA, f. 210, Bezglasnoi stol, stlb. 216, l. 9.

8. Burning: RGADA, f. 210, Belgorodskii stol, stlb. 925, ll. 456–57; RGADA, f. 210, Prikaznyi stol, stlb. 721, ll. 121–25, 154–55; RGADA f. 210, Belgorodskii stol, stlb. 284, ll. 391–418; Truvorov, "Volkhvy i vorozhei," 709; Shvetsova, Novosel'skii, and Leb, *Krest'ianskaia voina pod predvoditel'stvom Stepana Razina,* 366–68; Borisov, *Starinnye akty,* no. 109. Illegal burning: RGADA f. 210, Belgorodskii stol, stlb. 596, l. 35. Order to burn sorcerer-teachers at the Moscow Slavonic-Greco-Latin Academy: Kantorovich, *Srednevekovye protsessy o ved'makh,* 177.

9. Roper, *Witchcraze*, 44–68, 119–22; Lukin, *Narodnye predstavleniia*, 3–8.

10. Stephens, *Demon Lovers*, 7.

11. Ostling, *Between the Devil and the Host*, 192.

12. Individual trial publications, *AI*, vol. 2, 82–83; vol. 3, 224–25; *AAE*, vol. 3, 259. Major source publications include: Novombergskii, *Koldovstvo*; *Materialy po istorii meditsiny*; *Vrachebnoe stroenie*. Also, Antonovych, *Koldovstvo*; Kotkov, *Moskovskaia delovaia i bytovaia pis'mennost'*, nos. 16–18, 235–76; Toporkov, *Russkie zagovory*; Toporkov and Turilov, *Otrechennye chteniia.*

13. *Opisanie dokumentov i bumag, khraniashchikhsia v Moskovskom arkhive Ministerstva iustitsii* [Description of documents and papers preserved in the Moscow Archive of the Ministry of Justice, henceforth *ODiB*].

14. *ODiB*, vol. 15, stlb. 33; vol. 16, stlb. 1006.

15. The Razriad grew in importance through the seventeenth century and consolidated almost all judicial functions under its control. As Peter B. Brown writes, it was, "in effect, the processor chip of the bureaucracy" ("With All Deliberate Speed," 151). The fact that so many cases involving charges of witchcraft directed against the tsar and members of the royal family were heard by the Razriad weakens any suspicion that more politicized cases might have gone

to the private or secret chancelleries of the tsars. On the chancellery system, see, among others, Bogoiavlenskii, *Prikaznye sud'i XVII veka*; Brown, "How Muscovy Governed," 459–529; Debol'skii, *Istoriia prikaznogo stroia Moskovskogo gosudarstva*; Demidova, *Sluzhilaia biurokratiia v Rossii*; Golombiovskii, "Stoly razriadnogo prikaza v 1668–1670 gg.," 6–7; Ogloblin, *Obozrenie istoriko-geograficheskikh materialov*, esp. 147; Zagoskin, *Stoly Razriadnog prikaza*. On the Secret Chancellery, see Gurliand, *Prikaz velikogo gosudaria tainykh del*; Kozlov, "Prikaz tainykh gosudarevykh del," 106–12.

16. *Chetvert'* case: *AI*, vol. 2, no. 66, 82–83; RGADA, f. 159, Prikaznye dela starykh let, op. 1, stlb. 326, ll. 1–5.

17. For instance, records of a single case survive in three different documents in the main, central repository of the Razriad (RGADA, f. 210, Prikaznyi stol, stlb. 679; stlb. 861; stlb.1006), and in the regional bureau of the frontier fortress town, Belgorod: RGADA, f. 210, Belgorodskii stol, stlb. 1100. Case from Kazan: RGADA f. 210, Belgorodskii stol, stlb. 597, ll. 135–38); stlb. 599, ll. 565–71, 654–55. All of these are in the collection of the Razriad (f. 210) and are listed among the "documents of the bureaus of the Razriad (*stolbtsy razriadnykh stolov*)." Even Siberian cases show up in both Siberian and Razriad documentary caches. For instance, Shashkov cites: RGADA, f. 214, op. 1, stlb. 1396, l. 366 ob.; f. 1177, op. 3, stlb. 2426, ll. 1–13; f. 210, op. 17, stlb. 26, l. 8.

18. RGADA, f. 210, Prikaznyi stol, stlb. 565, ll. 6–21; Moskovskii stol, stlb. 265, ll. 396–417.

19. Ibid., Belgorodskii stol, stlb. 1059, ll. 162–72.

20. Most recently, A. S. Lavrov drew my attention to early cases dating to 1606 and 1611.

21. Zhuravel', *Siuzhet o dogovore cheloveka*, 69. Also, Korogodina, *Ispoved'*, 284–85.

22. RGADA, f. 210, Belgorodskii stol, stlb. 1165, ll. 430–35. Also stlb. 1171, l. 112. Another struggle between ecclesiastical and secular courts, again won by the state: Ibid., Prikaznyi stol, stlb. 1859, ll. 147–60.

23. Monastic personnel and monastic peasants tried in governors' courts: RGADA, f. 210, Prikaznyi stol, stlb. 275, ll. 200–213 (1644); stlb. 33, stolpik 1, ll. 617–38 (1628–32); Prikaznyi stol, stlb. 426, ll. 91–100, 110–13, 128–38, 143–44 (1671); stlb. 426, ll. 76–100; stlb. 721, ll. 260–368, 468–69; Moskovskii stol, stlb. 54, stolpik 2, ll. 32–42, 195–213 (1629–30).

24. *PSZ*, v. 1, art. 442, 800; and "Novoukaznye stat'i," PSZ, v. 1, art. 119, 798.

25. SPb II (RAN), koll. 117, op. 1, no. 1305. Thanks to A. S. Lavrov for his notes on the case.

26. "Sat under guard at the Razriad": RGADA, f. 210, Prikaznyi stol, stlb. 434, l. 86. Priests as defendants in secular courts: Prikaznyi stol, stlb. 434, ll. 4–200; stlb. 564, ll. 696–705; stlb. 734, ll. 115–203; stlb. 749, 3ll. 1–85; stlb. 721, ll. 260–368, 468–69; stlb. 2630, ll. 1–70; stlb. 2679, ll. 1–33; Novgorodskii stol, stlb. 210, ll. 161–63, 284–93, 356–57; stlb. 150; Belgorodskii stol, stlb. 160, ll. 103–15; stlb. 1165, ll. 430–35; stlb. 1171, l. 112. Priests' wives, widows, sons as defendants: RGADA, f. 210, Prikaznyi stol, stlb. 37, ll. 873–79, 889–908; stlb. 426, ll. 1–17, 162–63, 170–71, 174–76, 323, 332, 342; stlb. 2346, ll. 1–64. Deacon: RGADA, f. 210, Prikaznyi stol, stlb. 37, ll. 873–79, 889–908. Sons, wives, grandsons of deacons or igumens: RGADA, f. 210, Prikaznyi stol, stlb. 653, ll. 20–87; Belgorodskii stol, stlb. 306, ll. 810–13; stlb. 369, ll. 231–36. Priests named as sources of magical spells: RGADA, f. 159 (Prikaznye dela starykh let), op. 1, no. 326, ll. 1–5.

27. RGADA, f. 210, Prikaznyi stol, stlb. 2346, l. 5. Poison and bewitchment (*otrava i porcha*) are systematically listed together in this case.

28. Ibid., l. 7. The reference is to a statute of 1689, which repeats the article of the *Novoukaznye stat'i* of 1669: *PSZ*, art. 119, 798–99.

29. RGADA, f. 210, Prikaznyi stol, stlb. 2346, ll. 9–10.

30. Ibid., l. 15.

31. Ecclesiastical/secular cooperation: Ibid., Prikaznyi stol, stlb. 17, stolpik 2, ll. 27–29; and stlb. 2725, ll. 1–19; stlb. 434, ll. 4–200; stlb. 564, ll. 696–705; *AAE*, vol. 3 (1836), no. 176, 259. The *Dvortsovoi prikaz* oversaw cases of ecclesiastics implicated in secular crimes in the early seventeenth century.

32. RGADA, f. 210, Prikaznyi stol, stlb. 8, ll. 1–130.

33. Ibid., Prikaznyi stol, stlb. 1859, ll. 147–60.

34. A. S. Lavrov, personal e-mail communication, July 9, 2010. I am grateful to him for sharing his archival knowledge and general wisdom on the topic of witchcraft.

35. RGADA f. 210, Prikaznyi stol, stlb. 564, l. 182.

36. Once again, A. S. Lavrov's findings support this position. After examining the archives of regional governors' offices, where cases were heard locally and referred up to Moscow, both he and I have concluded that most of these cases are traceable in central as well as local archives. Thanks to him for sharing this finding. For a different assessment of the question of source survival and invisible trials, see Ryan, *Bathhouse at Midnight*, esp. 275, n. 151.

37. For instance, RGADA, f. 210, Belgorodskii stol, stlb. 284, ll. 391–418.

38. Masters vs. own peasants: RGADA, f. 210, Belgorodskii stol, stlb. 96, ll. 316–25; stlb. 284, ll. 391–418; stlb. 658, ll. 299–304; Moskovskii stol, stlb. 265, ll. 8–90; Novgorodskii stol, stlb. 96, ll. 316–25; Prikaznyi stol, stlb. 46, stolpik 1, ll. 247–76, 309–12; stlb. 186, ll. 984–1001; stlb. 204, l. 16; Prikaznyi stol, stlb. 275, ll. 19–20; stlb. 426, ll. 235–41, 246–47, 249–50, 252, 258–66, 269–91, 301–5; stlb. 434, ll. 4–200; stlb. 567, ll. 202–6; Prikaznyi stol, stlb. 734, ll. 115–203; stlb. 749, ll. 1–385; stlb. 1225, ll. 1–51; Prikaznyi stol, stlb. 1859, ll. 147–60; and f. 159, op. 3, n. 4208, ll. 1–13. On the question of manorial jurisdiction, Lavrov, *Koldovstvo i religiia*, 330–31.

39. Frank, *Crime, Cultural Conflict, and Justice*, 243–75; Worobec, "Witchcraft Beliefs and Practices," 180–87. Church courts still could assess small fines and short prison sentences for witchcraft, and did so through the early twentieth century. Orlando Figes describes an instance of imprisonment for sorcery in 1902! Figes, *A People's Tragedy*, 234.

40. Kollmann, "Lynchings and Legality in Early Modern Russia," 91–96. Kollmann discusses a 1636 case involving either unauthorized execution of eight men by the governor or mob lynching of the eight convicts. I have not been able to incorporate fully the findings of Kollmann's important book, *Crime and Punishment*, published in 2012.

41. RGADA, f. 210, Belgorodskii stol, stlb. 284, ll. 391–418; stlb. 652, ll. 628–35.

42. Ibid., stlb. 596, ll. 22–27, 30, 35. The case was reported in 1666. It has no resolution. By the 1660s, the hetman fell under the joint authority of the Military Chancellery and the Foreign Affairs Chancellery: Brown, "With All Deliberate Speed," 151; Ogloblin, *Kievskii stol*, 536–41. Kantorovich discusses a case in which an estate agent casually reported the arrest of a number of witches by his own authority on the estate and the execution of more on another estate. The case comes from the second half of the eighteenth century, and by then serfdom had intensified its hold and serfs had lost much of their claim to public justice as subjects of the tsar. Kantorovich, *Srednevekovye protsessy o ved'makh*, 178. Furthermore, most of his eighteenth-century cases come from Antonovych, *Koldovsto*, and Efimenko, "Sud nad ved'mami," who used Ukrainian rather than Russian material.

43. RGADA, f. 210, Sevskii stol, stlb. 215, l. 61.

CHAPTER 3

1. RGADA, f. 210, Belgorodskii stol, stlb. 826, ll. 81–96.

2. Mathiesen, "Magic in Slavia Orthodoxia," 173. The same position was voiced earlier by Trevor-Roper, "European Witch-Craze," 185.

3. Levack, *Witch-Hunt in Early Modern Europe*, 9. I completely agree with Levack's characterization, although it is worth noting that Peter Geschiere describes strikingly parallel beliefs among the Maka of Cameroon in the late twentieth century. "During the night, when the owl calls," true witches leave their bodies and fly to nocturnal gatherings involving "grand orgies," culminating in "an anthropophagic banquet where the witches eat the hearts of their kin." The absence of Satan still marks a significant distinction. Geschiere, *Modernity of Witchcraft*, 40.

4. Zhuravel', *Siuzhet o dogovore cheloveka*, 3, 7. Tales about pacts with the Devil include "Povest' o Savve Grudtsyne," in *PLDR. XVII vek*, Bk. 1, 41; and "Povest' o nekoem kuptse Grigorii, kako khote ego zhena z zhidovinom umoriti," in ibid., 94. Set in Rome, this story must be based on a foreign import.

5. Worobec, *Possessed*, 44–45.

6. Pervukhin, *Tserkov' Ilii Proroka v Iaroslavle.*

7. "Povest' o Savve Grudtsyne," in *PLDR*, 41; and "Povest' o Savve Grudtsyn," in Skripil', *Russkaia povest'*, 84.

8. Antonov and Maizul's, *Demony i greshniki*; Worobec, *Possessed*, 42–45.

9. On the question of satanism in Muscovite witchcraft, see Kivelson and Shaheen, "Prosaic Witchcraft."

10. RGADA f. 210, Belgorodskii stol, stlb. 826, ll. 81–96.

11. Uspenskii, "Pravo i religiia," esp. 220. Similarly, Kantorovich, *Srednevekovye protsessy o ved'makh*, 161–63; Ivanits, *Russian Folk Belief*, 94–95; Smilianskaia, *Volshebniki*, 42; Zguta, "Witchcraft Trials," 1209.

12. Clark, "Protestant Demonology," 45–82.

13. Ivanits, *Russian Folk Belief*, 121. Michael MacDonald points out that most English people displayed a similar lack of curiosity about the sources of magical power. MacDonald, *Mystical Bedlam*, 199.

14. Zhuravel', *Siuzhet o dogovore cheloveka*, 45.

15. Ryan, *Bathhouse at Midnight*, 40. Belief in many of these colorful spirits cannot be documented until the nineteenth century.

16. Kantorovich, *Srednevekovye protsessy o ved'makh*, 163.

17. *Stoglav*, 136.

18. Ibid., 139–40.

19. *AI*, vol. 1, no. 154.

20. *Stoglav*, 140–41.

21. Ibid., 262–62.

22. Ibid., 267.

23. Ryan, "Witchcraft Hysteria," 49–84.

24. *Stoglav*, chap. 20, 137–38. In 1564, denunciations of "godless (*bezbozhnaia*) Lithuania, loathsome-to-God (*bogomerzkie*) Latins, the most evil (*zleishii*) iconoclasts, pagan Lithuanians, and Islam," use the same terms freely for non-magical enemies: *AAE*, vol. 1, 302.

25. *Stoglav*, chap. 24, 141; chap. 93, 265.

26. Franklin, *Writing, Society, and Culture*, 272. Although Mathiesen says medieval Rus' did not import demonologies from Byzantium ("Magic in Slavia Orthodoxa," 172–73).

27. Pouncy, *Domostroi*, 114; Orlov, *Domostroi*, 22.

28. Pouncy, *Domostroi*, 113; Orlov, *Domostroi*, 22.

29. Only in condemnations of a few very particular behaviors did the *Stoglav* and *Domostroi* apply the label of "demonism" with any consistency: mummery and certain kinds of singing and dancing, and consulting "black" or prohibited books of magic and prophesy, merited consistent labeling as "demonic (besovskoe)" or even "satanic (sotonicheskoie)." Orlov, *Domostroi*, 112–13.

30. Ryan, *Bathhouse at Midnight*, 38.

31. "Novoukaznye stat'i (1669)," in *PSZ*, art. 118, 798; RGADA, f. 210, Moskovskii stol, stlb. 485, ll. 638–39. Boris Uspenskii also notes the strong element of criminality in Muscovite condemnations of witchcraft ("Pravo i religiia," 204–10).

32. *AAE*, vol. 1, no. 244, 267.

33. For example, RGADA, f. 210, Prikaznyi stol, stlb. 416, ll. 149–51; Novombergskii, *Materialy po istorii meditsiny*, vol. 4, no. 28, 173–74. On this perception of witchcraft as crime rather

than sin, see also Uspenskii, "Pravo i religiia," 204–10. With good reason, Iu. A. Kozlov asserts that "witchcraft, in the opinion of the secular authorities, pertained to the category of criminal offences," and "witchcraft was simply a method for carrying out a crime," although the evidence does not support his conclusion that only those witchcraft accusations involving "crimes against the faith" merited the death penalty, where "criminal offenses, '*vorovstvo*,' was punished by other means." Kozlov, "Chukhlomskoe delo," 445, 447.

34. Novombergskii, *Koldovstvo*, 75–80.

35. RGADA, f. 210, Novgorodskii stol, stlb. 96 (1649), ll. 11–12 (Verkha), 1–10 (Dmitrov), 14 (Kashin), 251–54 (Kostroma); Belgorodskii stol. stlb. 298, ll. 377–80 (1648).

36. On the mid-century decrees, see Khuruzin, "K voprosu o bor'be," 143–51; and Oparina, "Neizvestnyi ukaz," 88–91. Several versions of the "unknown" 1653 decree were published in Novombergskii, *Kołdovstvo*, no. 17, 79–80.

37. RGADA, f. 210, Sevskago stola, stlb. 148, ll. 92–94. *Oskol':* Ibid., Belgorodskii stol, stlb. 362, ll. 165, 244–47. Belev: Ibid., stlb. 1202, l. 394 (governor's response; no magic in Belev).

38. Fögen, "Balsamon on Magic," 103.

39. Generic references: RGADA, f. 210, Belgorodskii stol, stlb. 1032, 11–13, 165–94, on 168; Prikaznyi stol, stlb. 2109, l. 3; stlb. 1677, l. 43; stlb. 416, l. 161; stlb. 186, l. 984; Belgorodskii stol, stlb. 1526, l. 82; stlb. 652, ll. 628–35; stlb. 599, l. 565.

40. Ibid., Sevskii stol, stlb. 215, ll. 226–27.

41. Disrespectful sons: RGADA, f. 210, Sevskii stol, stlb. 215, l. 231. Dishonor: RGADA, f. 210, Prikaznyi stol, stlb. 1122, l. 48.

42. Ibid., Prikaznyi stol, op. 13, stlb. 734, l. 196. The same article of the law code is quoted in ibid., Belgorodskii stol, stlb. 1169, l. 750. The cases refer to chapter 1, article 1, "Concerning Blasphemers and Heretics." On the *Ulozhenie*, see Hellie, *Muscovite Law Code*; Hellie, "Ulozhenie Commentary," 202–22; and Hellie, "Commentary on [*Ulozhenie*] Chapters 3 through 6," 65–70.

43. The *gradskii zakon* referred to the Byzantine *Procheros Nomos*. See Kaiser, *Growth of the Law*, 22, n. 71. This passage from the *gradskii zakon* is also quoted in the *Novoukaznye stat'i*, which were issued right at the time when this case took place: "Novoukaznye stat'i," *PSZ*, art. 99, 795.

44. RGADA, f. 210, Razriadnyi prikaz, op. 14, Sevskii stol, stlb. 230, l. 4. This document and its reference to Byzantine law are discussed in Kozlov, "Fragment koldovskogo dela." The other case with an extract of the Byzantine statute along with the *Ulozhenie* is RGADA, f. 159, op. 3, no. 4208 (1692). Ivan IV's 1551 decree against magicians and their craft, issued in response to the Stoglav's recommendations, also points to the *gradskii zakon*, but recommends excommunication as the punishment. *AI*, vol. 1, no. 154.

45. Leading questions: for example RGADA, f. 214, Sibirskii prikaz, stlb. 586, l. 13); Moskovskii stol, stlb. 54, stolpik 2, ll. 74–80; Prikaznyi stol, stlb. 33, stolpik 1, ll. 708–19.

46. "The Trial of Suzann Gaudry (1652)," in Kors and Peters, *Witchcraft in Europe*, 359–67; quotes on 359–62.

47. RGADA, f. 214, stlb. 586, ll. 7, 8, 14–15.

48. On the lack of distinction between spells and prayers: Levin, "Supplicatory Prayers"; Smilianskaia, *Volshebniki*, 77.

49. Ippolitova lists a number of references to *voronets* (*Russkie rukopisnye travniki*, 53, 57, 91, 99, 104, 299, 346–48, 350–54). As its sinister name suggests, Baneberry is a poisonous plant with poisonous berries.

50. RGADA, f. 210, Moskovskii stol, stlb. 54, stolpik 2, ll. 74–80; Prikaznyi stol, st. 33, stolpik 1, ll. 708–19.

51. Ibid.

52. Ibid. On unclean forces, see the classic study by Maksimov, *Nechistaia, nevedomaia i krestnaia sila*.

53. Zhuravel' discusses *kikimora* in *Siuzhet o dogovore cheloveka*, 48: "The pranks of this unclean [spirit] are characteristic of such mythological characters such as *kikimora*, household spirits and courtyard spirits." Also Ryan, *Bathhouse at Midnight*, 62, n. 97.

54. RGADA, f. 210, Prikaznyi stol, stlb. 95, l. 219. This case is published and discussed in Kozlov, "Chukhlomskoe dela."

55. RGADA, f. 210, Prikaznyi stol, stlb. 95, l. 220.

56. Ibid., l. 224. The text says peasant (*krestianskikh*) souls, but the meaning suggests that he meant Christian (*khrest'ianskikh*). In another case where a witness expresses fear that dealings with magic might compromise religious salvation, a widow testified that even when her husband was sick, "they kept their faith in God's help. And they didn't go for any fortune-telling." Ibid., stlb. 564, l. 187.

57. Ibid., stlb. 95, l. 245.

58. Ibid., l. 224.

59. Ibid., stlb. 1225, ll. 151.

60. Ibid., l. 12.

61. Ibid., stlb. 186, l. 992.

62. Ibid., Sevskii stol, stlb. 161, l. 208.

63. Ibid., 206.

64. Ibid., Prikaznyi stol, stlb. 734, l. 139.

65. Novombergskii, *Koldovstvo*, no. 5, 27; RGADA, Moskovskii stol, stlb. 54, ll. 244–63, 327. See also the extensive list of curative roots and grasses in RGADA, f. 159, op. 3, no. 4208, l. 2.

66. Ibid., f. 210, Sevskii stol, stlb. 230, ll. 1–2; Moskovskii stol, stlb. 54, ll. 244–63, 327.

67. Ibid., Prikaznyi stol, stlb. 564, l. 199; Belgorodskii stol, stlb. 826, ll. 81–96.

68. Ippolitova, *Russkie rukopisnye travniki*, 334–44. Gestural stage instructions were included in spells, as in one meant to send woe to young girls: "I lie down not blessing myself; I arise not crossing myself . . ." RGADA, f. 210, Prikaznyi stol, stlb. 1133, l. 184.

69. Novombergskii, *Koldovstvo*, no. 33; Novombergskii, *Vrachebnoe stroenie*, no. 11; Eleonskaia, "Zagovor i koldovstvo na Rusi," 613; Astakhova, "Poetical Image and Elements of Philosophy," 268–69.

70. RGADA, f. 396, stlb. 4087, l. 5.

71. Thanks to Will Ryan for stressing this point in fruitful discussions of the issue. See also Levin, "Witches and Healers," 131; Smilianskaia, *Volshebniki*, 108, with word as mediator.

72. Snow White device of apples as bearers of curses appears in testimony from English witchcraft trials: Purkiss, *Witch in History*, 108, 128, 277. Sleeping Beauty trope, spinning: Ibid., 97, 113, 139.

73. RGADA, f. 210, Belgorodskii stol, stlb. 284, ll. 351–70. Bewitchment following failure to invite to christening in England: Purkiss, *Witch in History*, 98.

74. RGADA, f. 210, Belgorodskii stol, stlb. 284, ll. 351–70.

75. Ibid., Prikaznyi stol, stlb. 564, l. 211.

76. Ibid., stlb. 734, ll. 190, 192.

77. Nineteenth-century material, esp. Belarusian and Ukrainian: Ryan, *Bathhouse at Midnight*, 12, 34, 75–85, 184, 196–99, 427. Destruction of Rye: RGADA, f. 210, Prikaznyi stol, stlb. 717; Novombergskii, *Materialy po istorii meditsiny*, no. 47, 263–76. Destruction of wheat: RGADA, f. 210, Prikaznyi stol, stlb. 426, ll. 76–100.

78. On her late appearance, see Johns, *Baba Yaga*, 255. In spite of the evidence of a story about one of Ivan the Terrible's wives who turned into a magpie, no trace of magical shape shifting enters court transcripts. On the magpie tale, see Perrie, *Image of Ivan the Terrible*, 178–79; Ryan, "Witchcraft Hysteria," 69; Ryan, *Bathhouse at Midnight*, 81. Spells for shape shifting, assuming animal forms, also date to later periods. Nice examples of prosaic goals in Smilianskaia, *Volshebniki*, 70.

79. RGADA, f. 214, stlb. 586, l. 12. A similarly prosaic set of spells is listed in RGADA, f. 210, Prikaznyi stol, stlb. 734, ll. 174–94. Particularly detailed lists of spells: Prikaznyi stol, stlb. 734, ll. 115–203; Sevskii stol, stlb. 230, ll. 1–4; f. 214, stlb. 586, 7–15. In one anomalous case, desperate litigants blamed witches for sending them terrifying visions: f. 210, Moskovskii stol, stlb. 294, ll. 336–41.

80. Crosses under foot: RGADA, f. 210, Prikaznyi stol, stlb. 300, ll. 22, 24; stlb. 139, ll. 944–97. The other case of a cross worn underfoot is the Zheglov case discussed below. Cross worn on back: Sevskii stol, stlb. 230, l. 1. Going without a cross: Prikaznyi stol, stlb. 50, ll. 36, 37. Removing cross: f. 371, Preobrazhenskii prikaz, op. 2, no. 760, l. 27. Penitentials inquire about crosses under foot: Korogodina, *Ispoved'*, 230; also see charming early twentieth-century illustration of this practice (231).

81. RGADA, f. 210, Belgorodskii stol, stlb. 599, ll. 565–71, 654–70 (1663–67); Prikaznyi stol, stlb. 95, l. 220. Gorikhvostov also testified that Khramoi "feared the cross."

82. RGADA, f. 210, Prikaznyi stol, stlb. 129, ll. 1–92; Zertsalov, "K materialam o vorozhbe," 1–38; and Kotkov, *Moskovskaia delovaia i bytovaia pis'mennost'*, no. 18, 254–77.

83. Diabolic apparition: RGADA f. 210, Prikaznyi stol, stlb. 564, ll. 154–234. Satan with the Devil: Prikaznyi stol, stlbs. 653, 1133; discussed in Toporkov, *Zagovory v russkoi rukopisnoi traditsii*, 366.

84. RGADA, f. 210, Prikaznyi stol, stlb. 184.

85. Ibid., stlb. 172, ll. 2, 432; stlb. 861, ll. 29–34 (*otets moi Satana*, l. 33); same case continued in stlb. 1006, ll. 154.

86. Ibid., stlb. 653, ll. 20–87; Novombergskii, *Materialy po istorii meditsiny*, no. 39, 197–220, quotes on 208. Toporkov, *Zagovory v russkoi rukopisnoi traditsii*, 143–44.

87. Shashkov, "Iakutskoe delo o koldune Ivane Zheglove," 86; also discussed in Toporkov, *Zagovory v russkoi rukopisnoi traditsii*, 141.

88. Shashkov, "Iakutskoe delo o koldune Ivane Zheglove," 86, note 14; Zhuravel', *Siuzhet o dogovore cheloveka*, 43, 45.

89. Zhuravel', *Siuzhet o dogovore cheloveka*, 45.

90. The first large-scale assault on schismatic belief was the campaign against what would come to be known as the Old Belief, starting in the second half of the seventeenth century. Earlier "heresies," the mysterious *Strigol'nik* heresy of the fourteenth century and the "Judaizers" of the late fifteenth to early sixteenth centuries, were minute in scale, confined to high court and church circles. On the Old Belief, see esp. Michels, *At War with the Church*. On earlier heresies, see Kazakova and Lur'e, *Antifeodal'nyeereticheskie dvizheniia na Rusi*, esp. 34–71; Goldfrank, "Burn, Baby, Burn," 17–32.

CHAPTER 4

1. The preponderance of men among those charged with witchcraft not only bears out but also surpasses the numbers (forty women, fifty-nine men) found by Russell Zguta in his early work on the subject. Zguta, "Witchcraft Trials," 1196. In her study of witchcraft, 1700–1760, Smilianskaia finds even more skewed figures: 168 males to 36 females (82 percent to 18 percent). Smilianskaia, *Volshebniki*, 65.

2. The Devil generally refrains from same-sex unions in early modern witch lore, although discussions of sodomy also referred to his influence and Sabbath orgies were notorious for pairings of all sorts. See Puff, *Sodomy in Reformation Germany and Switzerland*. On the porosity of female bodies, see Caciola, "Mystics, Demoniacs, and the Physiology of Spirit Possession," 268–306.

3. Strathern, *Gender of the Gift*.

4. Boydston, "Gender as a Question of Historical Analysis," 558, 560, 565; Drawing on Oyewùmí, "Visualizing the Body,"11.

5. Cross and Sherbowitz-Wetzor, *Russian Primary Chronicle*, 153.

6. Korogodina, *Ispoved'*, 207.

7. *Stoglav*, chap. 41, question 22; Pouncy, *Domostroi*, 109–10, 112–20, 131, 182. Decrees forbidding the practice: RGADA, f. 210, Novgorodskoi stol, stlb. 96; Belgorodskoi stol, stlb. 270, stolpik 7, ll. 452–53, 601–5, 609–12; stlb. 298, ll. 377–80; Moskovskii stol, stlb, 485, l. 639; Korogodina, *Ispoved'*, 205–6.

8. *Baba* defined in Sreznevskii, *Slovar' drevnerusskogo iazyka*, vol. 1, 35. *Baba* signifying "witch": RGADA, f. 210, Belgorodskii stol, stlb. 306, ll. 810–13; Moskovskii stol, stlb. 54, stolpik 2, ll. 244–63, 327; Prikaznyi stol, stlb. 46, stolpik 1, ll. 247–76, 309–12; stlb. 57, ll. 552–61; stlb. 186, ll. 984–1001; stlb. 426, ll. 100–109, 114–23, 148–53; stlb. 564, ll.154–234; stlb. 567, ll. 539–49; stlb. 1225, ll. 1–51. Kantorovich, *Srenevekovye protsessy o ved'makh*, 170–75; Novombergskii, *Koldovstvo*, no. 33, 112–34; Truvorov, "Volkhvy i vorozhei," 709.

9. Johns continues: "Certainly Baba Iaga has an origin and a history, but given the lack of solid evidence, these must remain a matter of speculation" ("Baba Iaga and the Russian Mother," 25). The first identifiable images of Baba Iaga date to the early eighteenth century: Rovinskii, *Russkie narodnye kartinki*, nos. 37–38, 133, 134. Ryan notes that in any case she was "maybe more prevalent in Belorussia and the Ukraine, which were under Polish, and thus German and Western influence," than in Russia (*Bathhouse at Midnight*, 79).

10. Larner, *Witchcraft and Religion*, 85.

11. RGADA, f. 210, Prikaznyi stol, stlb. 1133, stolpik 2, ll. 178–79.

12. "The Tale of the Demoniac Solomoniia," translated by Marcia A. Morris. I would like to thank Marcia Morris for allowing me to see and cite her excellent translation. On Solomoniia, see Pigin, *Iz istorii russkoi demonologii XVII veka*; Remizov, *Besnovatye*.

13. See also Devil's unsuccessful deception of Fevroniia in "The Tale of Peter and Fevroniia," in Skripil' and Larin, *Russkie povesti*, 108–15.

14. A woman named Agashka admitted under torture to a spell to make her former lover "love her and pine for her," thus employing the usual language of male sex spells. In preparing the potion, she utilized his "essence (*estestvo*)," presumably semen. RGADA f. 210, Belgorodskii stol, stlb. 284, ll. 391–418. Another woman used the same manly essence (*estestva muzheska*) to increase her husband's ardor (*k iarosti*): RGADA, Prikaznyi stol, stlb. 861, ll. 1–28. Toporkov discusses the gendered nature of love spells in *Zagovory v russkoi rukopisnoi traditsii*, 24–45, 121–52. A medieval female love spell that follows the same patterns as "spells for women" is discussed and reproduced in Toporkov, "Gramota no. 521." Women's love magic relied on ingredients such as honey, roots, knots, sweat, and breast milk which were slipped into food or drink. For example, questions asked of women in confession: Almasov, *Tainaia ispoved'*, I, 408; III, 164, 166, 168,

15. A few examples: RGADA, f. 210, Sevskii stol, ed. khr. 230, ll. 1–4; RGADA, f. 214, ed. khr. 586, 7–15; ibid., f. 210, Prikaznyi stol, stlb. 734, ll. 115–203.

16. RGADA, f. 210, Prikaznyi stol, stlb. 653, l. 29.

17. RGADA f. 210, Prikaznyi stol, stlb. 1133, ll. 184–85; Toporkov, *Zagovory v russkoi rukopisnoi traditsii*, 366.

18. RGADA f. 210, Prikaznyi stol, stlb. 1133, stolpik 2, ll. 132–199.

19. Sketch in ibid., l. 180ob. The *Domostroi* dictates that women should abstain from strong alcohol and never drink in mixed company. Pouncy, *Domostroi*, chap. 36, 138–39; Kollmann discusses women's honor and the insult inherent in knocking off a woman's headgear in *By Honor Bound*, 79. On this image and its violently pornographic content, see also Kivelson, "Caught in the Act."

20. Cases involving causing and/or curing impotence: RGADA, f. 210, Belgorodskii stol, stlb. 284, ll. 425–47, ll. 351–70, ll. 391–418; stlb. 306. ll. 810–13; stlb. 768, ll. 47–55; stlb. 1202, ll. 387–88; stlb. 1202, ll. 387–88; Vladimirskii stol, stlb. 142, ll. 58–38; stlb. 300, ll. 1–88; Truvorov, "Volkhvy i vorozhei," 709, 714; *PSZ*, vol. 3, no. 1362.

21. RGADA, f. 210, Belgorodskii stol, stlb. 284, ll. 425–47.

22. Ibid.

23. Ibid., stlb. 1202, ll. 387–88.

24. RGADA, f. 210, Vladimirskii stol, stlb. 142, l. 118.

25. RGADA, f. 159, op. 3, no. 4208, l. 3. Thanks to A.S. Lavrov for his notes on this case.

26. Oddly, Collins added that the blame was generally placed on "Nuns, whose prime devotion tends that way." Collins, *Present State of Russia*, 20.

27. RGADA, f. 210, Prikaznyi stol., stlb. 268, l. 214.

28. Ibid., l. 217.

29. Ibid., Belgorodskii stol, stlb. 768, ll. 135–37.

30. Ibid., Prikaznyi stol, stlb. 734, l. 192.

31. RGADA, f. 214, stlb. 586, l. 12.

32. RGADA, f. 210, Sevskii stol, stlb. 230, l. 2.

33. Kramer and Sprenger, *Malleus Maleficarum*, 50, 52, 56.

34. Caveats especially strongly posed by Clark, *Thinking with Demons*, 112–16, 129–30.

35. "Judgment on the Witch Walpurga Hausmännin," 107–8.

36. RGADA, f. 210, Sevskii stol, stlb. 230, ll. 1–4, esp. l. 2.

37. Ibid., Prikaznyi stol, stlb. 46, stolpik 1, ll. 247–76, 309–12.

38. Ibid., stlb. 1225, l. 7.

39. Ibid., Moskovskii stol, stlb. 294, ll. 336–41.

40. Ibid., Prikaznyi stol, stlb. 1122, ll. 35–51.

41. Ibid., stlb. 17, stolpik 2, ll. 502–5. Accused female witches also admit to living in sin with male partners: Belgorodskii stol, stlb. 284, ll. 391–418.

42. Ibid., Prikaznyi stol, stlb. 2725, ll. 40–42.

43. Ibid., stlb. 1677, ll. 44–46. See also stlb. 2630, ll. 1–70; stlb. 2640; stlb. 2646; Novgorodskii stol, stlb. 233, ll. 206–7.

44. Ibid., Prikaznyi stol, stlb. 1133, stolpik 2, ll. 132–99.

45. Ibid., stlb. 426, ll. 92, 93.

46. Ibid., Sevskii stol, stlb. 215, ll. 229–30.

47. Ibid., l. 231.

48. "Novoukaznye stat'i," in *PSZ*, vol. 1, arts. 88–90, 795, art. 102, 796. The sixteenth-century *Book of Royal Degrees* (*Stepennaia kniga*) repeats the prohibitions on witchcraft from the medieval Statute of Prince Vladimir, which clump witchcraft (*vedovstvo, potvory, charodeianie, vl'khvovanie, zeleiinichestvo*) together with moral infractions (adultery, lust, sowing discord between husband and wife, prostitution) but also with violations of social hierarchy, especially of sons against fathers, daughters against mothers, or daughters-in-law against mothers-in-law. Both texts claim ecclesiastical jurisdiction for these infractions. Zhivov, "On the Language of *The Book of Degrees*," 146–47.

49. Roper, *Holy Household;* and Roper, "Was There a Crisis in Gender Relations in Sixteenth-Century Germany?" in *Oedipus and the Devil*, 37–52; Ozment, *When Fathers Ruled*.

50. Misogyny is difficult to quantify in relative terms, and it would be hard to find an early modern society that would not demonstrate its effects. For examples of some recent work showing that Muscovite courts took women's claims seriously, see Kaiser, "'He Said, She Said,'" 197–216; Pushkareva, *Women in Russian History*; Thyrêt, *Between God and Tsar*; Weickhardt, "Legal Rights of Women in Russia," 1–23.

51. Lavrov also finds that women's "competence in witchcraft" was limited by the fact that the ranks of horse doctors, millers, soldiers, and so forth, the most common milieus for witchcraft, were closed to them. Lavrov, *Koldovstvo i religiia*, 115. Also Worobec, *Possessed*, 35. Toporkov also notes the way that spells represented overwhelmingly male activities and mentalities, and male "brutality." He observes that priests were big spell-keepers. Toporkov, *Russkie zagovory iz rukopisnykh istochnikakh*, 13.

52. Kollmann, *By Honor Bound*, 65–94. Studying the imperial period, Elise Kimerling Wirschafter finds that gender was more a source of social integration than of differentiation, and she identifies "fun-

damentally different understandings of gender and its role in the organization of social life" than one might expect from a Western model (*Social Identity in Imperial Russia*, 17, 19).

53. Pouncy, *Domostroi*, 124, 143.

54. Bushkovitch argues that humility becomes one of the salient virtues expounded in seventeenth-century texts: *Religion and Society*, 142.

55. For example, Kaiser, "Quotidian Orthodoxy"; Levin, "From Corpse to Cult," 81–103; Chrissidis, "Whoever Does Not Drink to the End"; Kivelson, *Cartographies*; Rowland, "Two Cultures, One Throne Room," 33–58. This assessment of the role of Orthodoxy in Muscovite popular culture still has not gained unanimous support. Kaiser himself remains circumspect about generalizing his findings.

56. Bushkovitch, "Cultural Change among the Russian Boyars"; Chrissidis, "A Jesuit Aristotle"; Flier, "Court Ceremony in an Age of Reform"; Hughes, *Russia in the Age of Peter the Great.* On the influx of Kievan clerics in the second half of the seventeenth and early eighteenth century, see Bushkovitch, *Religion and Society*; Marker, *Imperial Saint*; Marker, "A Saint's Intimate Life"; Plokhy, *Origins of the Slavic Nations.*

57. On the charter of the academy: Kantorovich, *Srednevekovye protsessy o ved'makh*, 177. On the academy: Chrissidis, "A Jesuit Aristotle."

58. Here my reading differs from Isolde Thyrêt's in "Muscovite Miracle Stories," 115–31.

59. This gendered division of affect was expressed in colonial New England as well. Kamensky, *Governing the Tongue.*

60. "Skazanie o tsarstve Tsaria Fedoroa Ioannovicha," 761–62; Challis and Dewey, "Divine Folly in Old Kievan Literature," 255–64; Rowland, "Problem of Advice," 259–83.

61. Levin, *Sex and Society*; and Levin "Sexual Vocabulary in Medieval Russia," 41–52. On the church's pragmatic accommodations to the needs of the flesh, see also Martin, *Bride for the Tsar*, esp. 130–33. A more recent publication on the body is Kabakova and Conte, *Telo v russkoi kul'tury.*

62. Studies of ancient and medieval Christian ideas about the body and sex offer inspiring comparative insights. See, for example, Brown, *Body and Society;* Bynum, *Resurrection of the Body*; Maguire, *Icons of Their Bodies*; Pagels, *Adam, Eve, and the Serpent.*

63. Although Daniel Kaiser finds few Transfiguration icons listed in Muscovite wills. See Kaiser, "Icons and Private Devotion," 130, 132; Kaiser, "Beyond the Pages of the Stepennaia Kniga," 297.

64. Greene, *Bodies Like Bright Stars*; Levin, "From Corpse to Cult," 81–103.

65. Korogodina, *Ispoved'*, 217–43; Kizenko, "Review," 646; Viktor Zhivov, "Sin and Salvation in the History of Russian Spirituality," public lecture, University of Michigan, February 22, 2012.

66. Pokorovskaia, "Neizvestnyi spisok," 288. Whether or not Daniil should be classified as an Orthodox writer, his inspiration here derives from John Chrysostom.

67. "Beseda ottsa s synom o zhenskom zlobe," SKKDR, 3:1, 137–39.

68. Pokorovskaia, "Neizvestnyi spisok," 288. On Daniil Zatochnik, see, among others, Birnbaum and Romanchuk, "Kem byil zagodochnyi Daniil Zatochnik?" 576–602; Likhachev, "Daniil Zatochnik," 112–15.

69. Pokrovskaia, "Neizvestnyi spisok," 287.

70. Antonov and Maizul's, *Demony i greshniki*; Levin, *Sex and Society*, 46–52, 179–80; Worobec, *Possessed*, 42–45.

71. The literature generally assumes that the tale reflects a seventeenth-century urban context. Marcia A. Morris reviews some of the controversies in dating the tale, but concludes that a late seventeenth- rather than early eighteenth-century date is more compelling: "*Tale of Savva Grudcyn* and the Poetics of Transition," 203–4. More recently, Pierre Gonneau dates the tale to the early eighteenth century: "Faust Russe ou 'L'histoire de Savva Grudcyn,'" 423–84.

72. The tale contains numerous traces of Western influence, and so may not accurately reflect a purely Muscovite sexual sensibility. Passages take from versions of the tale in "Povest' o Savve Grudtsyne," in *PLDR*, 41; and "Povest' o Savve Grudtsyne," in Skripil', *Russkaia povest' XVII veka*, 84.

73. "Povest' o Savve Grudtsyne," *PLDR*, 41. The unpleasant "Tale of the Merchant Grigorii and How His Wife and a Jew Wanted to Kill Him" echoes these themes. "Povest' o nekoem kuptse Grigorii, kako khote ego zhena z zhidovinom umoriti," *PLDR*, 94.

74. Stuart Clark argues that the same self-fulfilling methodology is at work in scholarship on European witchcraft that focuses excessively on particularly vituperative misogynistic passages in the *Malleus*. "'Gendering' of Witchcraft in French Demonology," 426–37.

75. On original sin, see Ware, *Orthodox Church*, 222–25; and Meyendorff, *Byzantine Theology*, 143–46.

76. Sergeev, "Dukhovnyi stikh 'Plach Adama' na ikone," 281–82, 284.

77. Chrysostom passage is quoted in ibid., 285.

78. Eve is usually shown with breasts, but the images are decidedly asexual and often it is hard to tell which is Adam and which is Eve without careful inspection. Images of Adam and Eve: Muzei drevnerusskogo iskusstva imeni Andreia Rubleva *(zhertvennik kontsa XVI–nachala XVII veka)*; Alpatov, *Early Russian Icon Painting*, plate 203, "The Symbol of Faith," second half of the seventeenth century, from the Kolomenskoe Museum, Moscow; Popov, *Tver Icons,* plate. 173, Door to a Prothesis, Scenes: "The Expulsion from Paradise," and "The Parable of the Lame Man and the Blind Man," first half of the seventeenth century; Briusova, *Russkaia zhivopis' 17 veka*, no. 52: *Simvol' very,* mid-seventeenth century; color plates 114–15, 130. There are many images reproduced in Sakovich, *Narodnaia gravirovannaia kniga Vasiliia Korenia*, vol. 1.

79. "Povest' o Gore i Zlochastii, kak Gore-Zlochastie dovelo molottsa vo inocheskii chin," in *PLDR*, 28. On "Misery-Luckless-Plight," see Wigzell (Vigzell), "Bludnye synov'ia ili bluzhdaiushchie dushi," 754–62; Vinogradova, "Povest' o Gore-Zlochastii," 622–41.

80. Faith Wigzell identifies the central crime or sin in the tale as the youth's rejection of a righteous, prosperous, and happy life and his willful preference for a bitter and corrupt life. She rejects the reading that the tale concerns conflict between parents and children ("Bludnye synov'ia ili bluzhdaiushchie dushi," 758).

81. "Povest' o Gore i Zlochastii," *PLDR,* 38. Marcia A. Morris notes and analyzes similar unmotivated plot developments in "*The Tale of Savva Grudcyn* and the Poetics of Transition," 202–16.

82. "Povest' ob Uliianii Osor'inoi," in Skripil', *Russkaia povest' XVII veka*, 40. The tale is also reproduced in "Povest' ob Uliianii Osor'inoi," in *PLDR*, 98–104. Bushkovitch remarks on the absence of attention to sexual sin in the tale and stresses its emphasis on charity and humility (*Religion and Society*, 145–49, 227, note 41).

83. Sytova, *Lubok.*

84. Levin, *Sex and Society*; and Levin, "Infanticide in Pre-Petrine Russia."

85. Williams, *Defining Dominion*, 11.

86. To this W. F. Ryan adds that the fact that military chancelleries and military law adjudicated these cases contributed to the predominance of men: "Witchcraft Hysteria," 77. In practice, however, these courts and laws had broad jurisdiction and society-wide application.

87. RGADA, f. 210, Belgorodskii stol, stlb. 83, ll. 217–20, 455–58, 633–39; stlb. 441, ll. 149–52 (maybe); stlb. 767, ll. 47–55; stlb. 768, ll. 47–55; stlb. 877, ll 159–61; stlb. 925, ll. 98–101; stlb. 1526, ll. 500, 502, 557–59; Moskovskii stol, stlb. 54, stolpik 2, ll. 32–42, 195–213; and ll. 74–80 and 244–327; stlb. 265, ll. 8–90, and ll. 396–417; stlb. 294, ll. 336–41; stlb. 525, ll. 338–41; Novgorodskii stol, stlb. 10, ll. 27–29, 86–94; Prikaznyi stol, stlb. 17, ll. 54–61; stlb. 33, stolpik 1, ll. 708–19; stlb. 46, stolpik 1, ll. 247–76, 309–12; stlb. 268, ll. 209–28; stlb. 300, ll. 1–88; stlb. 314, ll. 159–67, 192–93; stlb. 416, ll. 149–61; stlb. 426, ll. 1–17, 162–63, 170–71, 174–76, 323, 332, 342; and ll. 235–41, 246–47, 249–50, 252, 258–66, 269–91, 301–5; stlb. 564, ll. 154–234;

stlb. 734, ll. 115–203; stlb. 749, l. 187; stlb. 1235, ll. 28–42; stlb. 2565, ll. 286–95; stlb. 2727, ll. 45–48; Sevskii stol, stlb. 164, 324–34; stlb. 215, ll. 54–64; Vladimirskii stol, stlb. 142, l. 138 RGADA, f. 214, stlb. 586, ll. 7–15.

88. On townspeople's petitions to limit their own mobility, see *AAE*, vol. 4, nos. 32, 36; Smirnov, *Posadskie liudi i ikh klassovaia bor'ba*; Hellie, "Stratification of Muscovite Society," 119–75. On collective responsibility, see Dewey and Kleimola, "Suretyship and Collective Responsibility."

89. RGADA, f. 210, Prikaznyi stol, stlb. 434, ll. 4–200, quotes on ll. 21, 23, 24, 188, 190.

90. On the ambivalent concept of freedom, see Kivelson, "Bitter Slavery and Pious Servitude."

91. On the explosion of record keeping and its effects on the lives of servitors, see Poe, "Elite Service Registry in Muscovy," 251–88.

92. For example, RGADA, f. 210, Belgorodskii stol, stlb. 11, stolpik 1, ll. 498–506; stlb. 433, ll. 1080–82; stlb. 1195, ll. 582–88, 599–603 (1684–86); Moskovskii stol, stlb. 13, stolpik 1, ll. 209–15, 286; stolpik 2, ll. 55–56, 134, 288–89, 291a, 317–19, 327, "holding suspicious people"; ll. 522–23, "unauthorized presence in Moscow"; stlb. 15, stolpik 1, ll. 47–55, "suspicious man"; stlb. 46, stolpik 1, ll. 122–23; stlb. 68, stolpik 2, ll. 38–40, "capture of wanderer"; Novgorodskii stol, stlb. 351, l. 255 (1697), report by landholders of not holding any "*prishlye,*" "*vol'nye,*" *or* "*guliashchie liudi*" (newly arrived, free, or wandering people). Kleimola, "Duty to Denounce," 778.

93. Michels, *At War with the Church*, 160–61. It was, however, even worse to be considered a "runaway" or "shirker" than a "free" or "wandering" person. See list of Cossacks and *strel'tsy* as "free people" rather than as "runaways": RGADA, f. 210, Belgorodskii stol, stlb. 270, stolpik 7, ll. 759–61.

94. RGADA f. 210, Prikaznyi stol, stlb. 300, ll. 26, 27.

95. RGADA, f. 210, Belgorodskii stol, stlb. 284, ll. 391–418 (Tatars?); stlb. 441, ll. 149–52 (Pole, Lithuanian, or Serb?); stlb. 599, ll. 565–71, 654–60 (Cherkassians); stlb. 658, ll. 299–304 (Tatars?); stlb. 768, ll. 47–55 (Poles); stlb. 1526, ll. 50, 502, 557–59 (Cherkassians); Moskovskii stol, stlb. 54, stolpik 2, ll. 32–42, 195–213 (Mordvin); ll. 244–63, 327 (Tatarka); stlb. 265, ll. 8–90 (Mordvin); Prikaznyi stol, stlb. 33, stolpik 1, ll. 617–38 (Cheremis); ll. 708–19; (also Moskovskii stol, stlb. 54, stolpik 2, ll. 74–80) (Mordvin and Cherkass); Prikaznyi stol, stlb. 46, stolpik 1, ll. 247–76, 309–12 (treasonous Lithuanian border crossing); stlb. 57, ll. 394–401 (Tatarin); ll. 552–61 (Polish-Lithuanian plot to bewitch hops); ll. 562–72 (Pole); stlb. 152, ll. 57–78, 79–83 (Armenian); stlb. 186, ll. 984–1001 (Gypsy teacher); stlb. 275, ll. 200–213 (Lithuanian connection); stlb. 567, ll. 539–49 (Kazachka); stlb. 656, ll. 6–21; stlb. 717, ll. 1–55 (Latvian); stlb. 861, ll. 1–28 (Mordvin); stlb. 1483, ll. 1–6 (Cherkass); SPBII RAN, koll. 117, op. 1, no. 1931, l. 4 (Cherkass); Novombergskii, *Vrachebnoe stroenie*, no. 35, p. 191 (Mordvins); Sevskii stol, stlb. 215, ll. 54–56 (Cherkass); stlb. 226, ll. 134–44 (Cherkass); Novombergskii, *Materialy po istorii meditsiny*, vol. 3, no. 47, 263–76 (Latvian teacher), 526–30 (Greek); Truvorov, "Volkhvy i vorozhei," 713 (Tatars). Again, more than the identifiable 13 percent of the suspects may have been non-Russian, but the surviving documents do not label them as such.

96. Truvorov, "Volkhvy i vorozhei," 713. This punishment appears to consist of placing the forbidden texts on the culprits back and setting the pages on fire.

97. In the 1660s, two Cherkassians were accused of bewitching communion bread, an accusation that looks like a symptom of Russian ethno-religious anxiety. RGADA, f. 210, Sevskii stol, stlb. 215, ll. 54–64.

98. Ibid., Prikaznyi stol, stlb. 33, stolpik 1, ll. 708–19; stlb. 54, stolpik 2, ll. 74–80 (1628).

99. Luehrmann, "Magic of Others." Romaniello finds that Russian peasants used witchcraft accusations to drive Mordvins off their land in the Nizhnii Novgorod region in the seventeenth century: *Elusive Empire*, 164–65.

100. Demos, *Enemy Within*, chap. 2.

101. Healers: RGADA, f. 210, Belgorodskii stol, stlb. 83, ll. 851–54; stlb. 96, ll. 316–25; stlb. 208, ll. 205–7; stlb. 284, ll. 425–47; stlb. 925, ll. 98–101; stlb.1195, ll. 694–95, 730–32; stlb.1202, ll. 387–88; stlb. 1526, ll. 500, 502, 557–59; Moskovskii stol, stlb. 54, stolpik 2, ll. 74–80, 32–42,

195–213, 244–63, 327 (cases also appear in Prikaznyi stol, stlb. 33, stolpik 1, ll. 708–19; 617–38); stlb. 265, ll. 396–417; Novgorodskii stol, stlb. 10, ll. 27–29, 86–94; Prikaznyi stol, stlb. 8, ll. 1–30; stlb. 33, ll. 617–38; stlb. 46, stolpik 1, ll. 247–76, 309–12; stlb. 50, ll. 13–120; stlb.95, ll. 219–56; stlb.186, ll. 984–1001; stlb. 268, ll. 209–28; stlb. 300, ll. 1–89 ob. stlb. 314, ll. 159–67, 192–93; stlb. 416, ll. 149–61; stlb. 426, ll. 76–80, 99–109, 114–20, 123, 148–53; stlb. 567, ll. 538–49; stlb. 569, ll. 197–203; stlb. 595, ll. 599–626; stlb. 861, l. 35 (and stlb. 1006, l. 54, and Belgorodskii stol, stlb. 1100); stlb. 1138, ll. 11–18; stlb. 1225, ll. 1–51; stlb. 1235, ll. 28–42; stlb. 1385, ll. 99–100; stlb. 1483, ll. 1–6; stlb. 2152, ll. 5–17; stlb. 2346, ll. 1–64; stlb. 2565, ll. 286–95; Sevskii stol, stlb. 161, ll. 206–8; RGADA, f. 159, op. 3, no. 4208, ll. 1–13; Vladimirskii stol, stlb. 142, ll. 115–18, 135–38; Kantorovich, *Srenevekovye protsessy o ved'makh*, 173, 174; Truvorov, "Volkhvy i vorozhei," 709; *Rozysknyia dela o Fedore Shaklovitom*, vol. 3, cols. 1235–71. On witches and healers: Levin, "Healers and Witches," 105–33.

102. RGADA, f. 210, Prikaznyi stol, stlb. 300, l. 63.

103. Cherepnin asserts that most healers were itinerants ("Iz istorii drevnerusskogo koldovstva," 90). Eve Levin is currently working on healing in Muscovy, and has published some of her preliminary findings. See, for example, "Healers and Witches."

104. Novombergskii, *Koldovstvo*, no. 25, 96.

105. Ibid., no. 20, 86. The particular healing sought in this case concerned relationships rather than health.

106. RGADA, f. 159, op. 3, no. 4208, ll. 2–3.

107. Novombergskii thought that those who sought magical services were just as much at risk as those who administered them (*Koldovstvo*, xxvii–xxix). Lavrov distinguishes between the two (*Koldovstvo i religiia*, 99–102, 107–15). My findings suggest that the onus lay more heavily on the purveyor, but the person who used the charm could also be harshly punished.

108. Healing professions: Lavrov, *Koldovstvo i religiia*, 115; Military, clergy, and politics: Ryan, "Witchcraft Hysteria," 73–74.

109. For example: RGADA, f. 210, Belgorodskii stol, stlb. 1202, ll. 387–88; Moskovskii stol, stlb. 54, stolpik 2, ll. 32–42, 195–213; Prikaznyi stol, stlb. 33, stolpik 1, ll. 617–38; stlb. 416, ll. 149–61; stlb. 2152, ll. 5–17.

110. Ibid., Novgorodskii stol, stlb. 10, ll. 620–24, 643–44.

111. Ibid., Prikaznyi stol, stlb. 595, ll. 599, 606.

112. Ibid., Belgoroskii stol, stlb. 1526, ll. 500, 502, 557–59.

113. Ibid., Moskovskii stol, stlb. 54, stolpik 2, ll. 32–42, 195–213.

114. Ibid., Prikaznyi stol, stlb. 95, l. 250; Kantorovich, *Srednevekovye protsessy o ved'makh*, 172.

115. RGADA, f. 210, Prikaznyi stol, stlb. 2725, l. 17.

116. Ibid., Belgorodskii stol, stlb. 284, ll. 351–70 (published in Novombergskii, *Koldovstvo*, no. 10, 56). Also: "And whether Stepan's horse died from his medicine (*lekarstvo*) or died naturally, that he doesn't know." RGADA, f. 210, Prikaznyi stol, stlb. 1385, ll. 99–100.

117. RGADA, f. 210, Prikaznyi stol, stlb. 564, l. 187.

118. Cherepnin, "Iz istorii drevnerusskogo koldovstva," 97, 99; Novombergskii, *Koldovstvo*, nos. 24–26; RGADA, f. 210, Prikaznyi stol, stlb. 300, l. 10; stlb. 1225, ll. 6–7. Chapter 6 develops this theme further.

119. RGADA, f. 210, Prikaznyi stol, stlb. 567, l. 203 (1648). Karlsen on lack of deference to men as a contributing factor in New England: *Devil in the Shape of a Woman*, 150.

120. RGADA, f. 210, Prikaznyi stol, stlb. 300, ll. 6–7.

121. Ippolitova, *Ispoved'*, 205–32, 284–88. On their reluctance to consider themselves witches, see Smillianskaia, *Volshebniki*, 53–55.

122. Ryan discusses prediction by thunder, but not magic to affect weather: *Bathhouse at Midnight*, 378–90.

123. Thanks to Christine Worobec for raising this point. See discussion of gendered spheres of magic in chapter 5.

124. MacDonald, *Witchcraft and Hysteria in England*, liii.

125. In the volumes cataloguing the documents of the Razriadnyi prikaz, fond 210, I identified 274 non-witchcraft cases involving vagrants (*guliashchie, vol'nye, 'priezhie liudi, brodiagi*). Since these documents derive from the Ministry of Military Affairs, there may be some over-representation of males in the cases. Nonetheless, when the archival guide lists only 3 out of 274 cases as involving female itinerants, the imbalance seems powerfully demonstrated. *ODiB*, vols. 10–20. See, for example, RGADA, f. 210, Belgorodskii stol, stlb. 11, stolpik 3, ll. 211–56; stlb. 338, ch. 1, ll. 180–82; stlb. 395, ll. 124–25, 435–46; stlb. 523, ll. 26–29, 60–65, 132–33, 601–2. Hellie discusses several cases of runaway female slaves, who of necessity adopted lives of vagrancy before their recapture, in *Slavery in Russia*, 244, 269, 486.

126. RGADA, f. 210, Prikaznyi stol, stlb. 679, l. 287; stlb. 861, l. 29; Belgorodskii stol, stlb. 284, ll. 391–418; Novombergskii, *Koldovstvo*, no. 11, 66.

127. RGADA, f. 210, Belgorodskii stol, stlb. 898, l. 129. The dots represented the sides of dice.

128. Karlsen, *Devil in the Shape of a Woman*, 22–23. Jonathan Durrant finds the same pattern in the Bavarian prince-bishopric of Eichstätt: although under torture the accused named up to 70 percent male accomplices, judges chose not to follow up on these leads. Durrant also concludes, provocatively, that although it mattered deeply to judges, "gender was not significant in popular conceptions of the 'witch', either in Eichstätt, or much of the rest of Europe" ("Why Some Men and Not Others?" 105, 101). Monter shows that in Normandy, almost the opposite was true: it was harder to make charges stick to a woman than to a man ("Toads and Eucharists").

129. Women are slightly over-representation among the small number executed. Executions are recorded for something in the range of seventeen or more men and nine women, meaning that about 65 percent of those executed were male, as opposed to 73 percent of the accused.

CHAPTER 5

1. Broedel, *Malleus Maleficarum*, 174; Labouvie, "Männer im Hexenprozess," 59–67. Other studies of specialized male magic: Monter, "Toads and Eucharists"; LeRoy Ladurie, "Aiguillette"; Kent, "Masculinity and Male Witches."

2. RGADA, f. 210, Prikaznyi stol, stlb. 416, ll. 149–61; Novombergskii, *Materialy po istorii meditsiny*, 226; Kotkov, *Pamiatniki delovoi pis'mennosti*, no. 157; RGADA, f. 210, Prikaznyi stol, stlb. 653, ll. 20–87; stlb. 2346, l. 64. Further, witnesses charged that the healer had falsely accused another woman of witchcraft because her brother had refused to pay him a five-ruble bribe as protection.

3. RGADA, f. 210, Moskovskii stol, stlb. 54, stolpik 2, ll. 244–63, 327.

4. Ibid., Sevskii stol, stlb. 215, l. 58.

5. Ibid., Prikaznyi stol, stlb. 416, ll. 149–61.

6. Ibid., Belgorodskii stol, stlb. 59, ll. 126–28.

7. Kantorovich, *Srednevekovye protsessy o ved'makh*, 173–74; Novomberskii, *Koldovstvo*, no. 33, 112–34.

8. Roper, "Witchcraft and Fantasy," 199–225; Roper, *Witch Craze*, 140–59; Purkiss, *Witch in History*, 91–118.

9. Levin, "Childbirth in Pre-Petrine Russia," 44–59. Birthing mothers were housed in the bathhouse, a site strongly associated, according to later tradition, with magic and spirits. Ryan, *Bathhouse at Midnight*, 49–52.

10. Korogodina, *Ispoved'*, 209.

11. RGADA, f. 210, Prikaznyi stol, stlb. 186, l. 986; Belgorodskii stol, stlb. 596, ll. 22–27, 30, 35; Prikaznyi stol, stlb. 46, stolpik 1, ll. 247–76, 309–12. Cursing/bewitching children to death (along with the rest of their families): Belgorodskii stol, stlb. 768, ll. 47–55; stlb. 826, ll. 81–96; Prikaznyi stol, stlb. 426, ll. 91–100, 110–13, 128–38, 143–44; stlb. 721, ll. 121–25,

154–55; stlb. 1225, ll. 1–51; stlb. 2109, ll. 1–36 ; stlb. 2346, ll. 1–64. Healing: Prikaznyi stol, stlb. 426, ll. 100–109, 114–23, 148–53; stlb. 679, ll. 283–91; stlb. 861, ll. 35–35ob.

12. Ibid., Prikaznyi stol, stlb. 734, ll. 190, 191. See also stlb. 749, ll. 1–385.

13. Ibid., stlb. 434, l. 191.

14. Ibid., Moskovskii stol, stlb. 54, stolpik 2, ll. 74–75; see also Prikaznyi stol, stlb. 33, stolpik 1, ll. 708–19.

15. Ibid., Prikaznyi stol, stlb. 1225, l. 7.

16. Karlsen, *Devil in the Shape of a Woman*, 117–52.

17. RGADA f. 210, Belgorodskii stol, stlb. 284, ll. 351–70. See also stlb. 306, ll. 810–13.

18. Ibid., stlb. 284, ll. 351–70. "Eating" was a form of magically induced wasting.

19. Ibid., Prikaznyi stol, stlb. 595, ll. 605, 606, 622.

20. Kamensky, *Governing the Tongue*, 161. RGADA, f. 210, Belgorodskii stol, stlb. 284, ll. 391–418; Novombergskii, *Koldovstvo*, no. 11, 67.

21. Curses: RGADA, f. 210, Prikaznyi stol, stlb. 426, l. 98; stlb. 268, l. 214; stlb. 595, l. 600; Novgorodskii stol, stlb. 10, ll. 620–24, 643–44; stlb. 272, ll. 143–45; Vladimirskii stol, stlb. 60, l. 265.

22. Kamensky, *Governing the Tongue*, 160, quote from Favret-Saada, *Deadly Words*, 144, 113.

23. Kamensky, *Governing the Tongue*, 158–59. Envy and vanity, other characterological traits frequently associated with witchcraft in the West, went essentially unremarked in Muscovite cases.

24. Williams, *Defining Dominion*, 11.

25. RGADA, f. 210, Prikaznyi stol, stlb. 2565, l. 288.

26. Ibid., l. 286.

27. Ibid., l. 288.

28. Ibid., l. 287.

29. Keane, "Religious Language," 47–71; Robson, "Signs of Power," 130–169; Gaster, "Amulets and Talismans,"145–47; Tambiah, "Magical Power of Words," 177–206. Examples of magical writing at the Kelsey Museum, University of Michigan: "Traditions of Magic in Late Antiquity: Protective Magic: Babylonian Demon Bowls," http://www.lib.umich.edu/traditions-magic-late-antiquity/def2.display.html (accessed March 5, 2010).

30. Marker, "Literacy and Literacy Texts," 89. Carol Belkin Stevens and Christoph Witzenrath find significantly higher rates among (male) Cossacks and frontier servitors: Stevens, "Belgorod," and Witzenrath, "Literacy and Orality."

31. Ryan describes a case from 1722 in which: "The record notes a fact that was evidently thought significant, that some of these documents [spell books and texts of prognostication, such as *The Gates of Aristotle*] were in cursive but some were in semi-uncial with rubrication (i.e., had an ecclesiastical appearance)." Ryan, *Bathhouse at Midnight*, 419. See also Toporkov, *Russkie zagovory iz rukopisnykh istochnikov*, 21. On the religious connotations of writing in early Rus', see Franklin, *Writing, Society, and Culture*, 259, 275. On the importance of the visual presentation of writing, see Franklin, "Mapping the Graphosphere," 531–60.

32. RGADA, f. 210, Prikaznyi stol, stlb. 8, ll. 1–130.

33. Ibid., stlb. 721, l. 260.

34. Ibid., stlb. 2725, ll. 45–48 (1629).

35. Eleonskaia, *K izucheniiu zagovora i koldovstva*, 15; quoted and translated in Ivanits, *Russian Folk Belief*, 89.

36. RGADA, f. 210, Belgorodskii stol, stlb. 1032, 11–13, 165–94.

37. Ibid, ll. 166, 168a.

38. Mordovina and Stanislavskii, "Gadatel'naia kniga," 336. Men sometimes named women as their teachers in telling fortunes, but most fortune-telling did not rely on written texts (323). The strip of letters doesn't quite fit the pattern, since the letters run higher in the alphanumeric scale, too high to represent normal dice, and appear in pairs as well as triplets. Cherepnin

describes a woman telling fortunes with forty-one bones; perhaps they came in high denominations. Cherepnin, "Iz istorii drevnerusskogo koldovstva," 102.

39. RGADA, f. 210, Belgorodskii stol, stlb. 1032, l. 170.

40. The possibility of female literacy also occurred to the judges in a case brought against a female healer in Vologda in 1672. Ibid., Prikaznyi stol, stlb. 426, l. 103. Andrei Bezobrazov's wife purportedly made use of writing in her spells: *Rozysknyia dela o Fedore Shaklovitom*, 2:11–12. Among witchcraft suspects in the early eighteenth century, Lavrov finds 64 percent of 113 men were demonstrably literate, and not a single one of the 16 woman showed evidence of literacy: *Koldovstvo i religiia*, 119.

41. RGADA f. 210, Belgorodskii stol, stlb. 1032; ll. 11–13, 165–94.

42. Ibid., l. 169.

43. Ibid., ll. 11–13, 165–83.

44. "Novoukaznye stat'i," in *PSZ*, art. 120, no. 431, 799.

45. RGADA, f. 210, Prikaznyi stol, stlb. 734, ll. 117, 179. See also stlb. 749, ll. 1–385. Extracts from this case are published in Kotkov, *Moskovskaia delovaia i bytovaia pis'mennost'*, 213–24.

46. RGADA,f. 210, Prikaznyi stol, stlb. 734, ll. 120, 121.

47. Ibid, ll. 182–85. Another chain of men, including two peasants and a priest, involved in copying and dictating spells: RGADA, f. 159 (Prikaznye dela starykh let), op. 1, no. 326, l. 1.

48. RGADA, f. 210, Prikaznyi stol, stlb. 734, l. 120.

49. Ibid., stlb. 749, l. 186.

50. Ibid., ll. 189–90.

51. RGADA, f. 214, stlb. 586, ll. 7–15; l. 8.

52. RGADA, f. 210, Belgorodskii stol, stlb. 1032, l. 166. Another case where a clerk doesn't dare read the documents: Ibid., Prikaznyi stol, stlb. 2651, l. 14.

53. RGADA, f. 210, Prikaznyi stol, stlb. 734, l. 116.

54. RGADA, f. 210, Prikaznyi stol (ODB 16), no. 679, ll. 297–300. Thanks to Nancy Kollmann for sharing her notes with me.

55. Ibid., l. 298.

56. Ibid., stlb. 734, l. 198; stlb. 749; stlb. 567, ll. 202–6; Truvorov, "Volkhvy i vorozhei," 709. Another case of burning texts on back: RGADA, f. 210, Prikaznyi stol, stlb. 2565, ll. 458–61.On branding as communicative punishment, see Kollmann, "Marking the Body," 557–65.

57. RGADA, f. 210, Prikaznyi stol, stlb. 565, ll. 9–10.

58. Ibid., l. 11.

59. Ibid., l. 10.

60. Ibid., l. 19.

61. Ibid., ll. 20–21ob.

62. Ibid., Sevskii stol, stlb. 148, ll. 92–94; Prikaznyi stol, stlb. 203, ll. 30, 390–91; Belgorodskii stol, stlb. 361, ll. 167–70; Novombergskii, *Koldovstvo*, no. 16, 78–79.

63. Pouncy, *Domostroi*, 112–13. See discussion in Ryan, *Bathhouse at Midnight*, 21, 226–27.

64. Ippolitova, *Ispoved'*, 287.

65. Rewriting these books through independent exegesis "might criminally defile the apostles, prophets, or Church fathers." In Kotoshikhin, *O Rossii v tsarstvovanie Alekseia Mikhailovicha*, 95. A deacon convicted of possessing *Rafli*: *AAE*, vol. 3, no. 176, 259.

66. RGADA, f. 210, Belgorodskii stol, stlb. 768, ll. 93–94; Prikaznyi stol, stlb. 91, ll. 293–302; stlb. 672, ll. 54–128; stlb. 734, ll. 115–203; also in stlb. 749; stlb.1677, l. 58; stlb. 2630, l. 70 (and in stolbtsy 2640 and 2646).

67. Ibid., Prikaznyi stol, stlb. 749, l. 189.

68. On Artamon Matveev, see Bushkovitch, *Peter the Great*, 45–124, esp. 90–97. Quotes from Gabel in Bushkovitch, 91–92.

69. Fuhrmann, *Tsar Alexis*, 221. On foreign writing and magic, see Oparina, "'Chuzhie' pis'mena v russkoi magii," 53–62; Toporkov, *Russkie zagovory iz rukopisnykh istochnikov*, 54.

70. RGADA, f. 210, Prikaznyi stol, stlb. 749, l. 165; and stlb. 734, ll. 115–17.

71. Ibid., stlb. 734, ll. 117–18.

72. Franklin, *Writing, Society, and Culture*, 276–79.

73. RGADA, f. 210, Prikaznyi stol, stlb. 565, ll. 6–21.

74. Ibid., stlb. 734, l. 349.

75. Broedel, *Malleus Maleficarum*, 174; Williams, *Defining Dominion*, 11–12.

76. On the "Printing Office poets," see Bushkovitch, *Religion and Society*, 134–49. On private letters, see Morozov, "Chastnoe pis'mo," 287–90; Stefanovich and Morozov, *Roman Vilimovich v gostiakh u Petra Ignat'evicha*.

77. RGADA, f. 210, Belgorodskii stol, stlb. 298, ll. 377–80.

78. Possession cases: Ibid., Belgorodskii stol, stlb. 270 (symptoms like possession, but the term is not used in the text); stlb. 1100; Bezglasnoi stol, stlb. 216, ll. 3–12; Moskovskii stol, stlb. 525, ll. 338–41; Novgorodskii stol, stlb. 10, ll. 620–24, 643–44; Prikaznyi stol, stlb. 50, ll. 13–120 (symptoms similar to possession, but the term is not used in the text.); stlb. 95, ll. 219–56; stlb. 300, ll. 1–88; stlb. 314, ll. 159–67, 192–93; stlb. 416, ll. 149–61; stlb. 595, ll. 599–626; stlb. 653, ll. 20–87; stlb. 679, ll. 283–91; stlb. 861, ll. 29–34; stlb. 1006, l. 54; Kotkov, *Pamiatniki delovoi pis'mennosti*, no. 157, ll. 115–18; ll. 135, 139; Borisov, *Opisanie goroda Shui*, No. 45, 337–38; No. 46, 339–40; *AI*, vol. 2, no. 66, 82–83; RGADA, f. 159, Prikaznye dela starykh let, op. 1, no. 326, ll. 1–5; Shashkov, "Iakutskoe delo," 87; Lavrov, *Koldovstvo i religiia*, 355 (RGADA, f. 371, Preobrazhenskii prikaz, op. 2, no. 723, l. 19, 25, 91, 125); Lavrov, *Koldovstvo i religiia*, 414. Avvakum writes of exorcizing demons through prayer and application holy oil from several people. He does not identify them by sex, but describes them only as "three or four mad people (*cheloveka tri chetyre beshenykh*) who were brought to me." Avvakum, *Zhitie*, 41.

79. *Oderzhimye*: Borisov, *Opisanie goroda Shui*, No. 45, 337–38, 1670; RGADA, f. 210, Prikaznyi stol, stlb. 95, l. 250; Prikazny stol, stlb. 300, l. 1. Three terms (*porchenye, klikushi, and oderzhimye*) are used in court documents. The term *besnovaty* may appear only in religious texts.

80. RGADA, f. 210, Prikaznyi stol, stlb. 679, l. 287.

81. On the distinction between witches' voluntary submission to the Devil and the unwilling subjugation of the possessed: Sluhovsky, *Believe Not Every Spirit*; Worobec, *Possessed*, 51, 66–67, 76; Levin, "Healers and Witches," 113.

82. RGADA, f. 210, Sevskii stol, stlb. 148, ll. 92–94.

83. Ibid., Prikaznyi stol, stlb. 314, ll. 204–204ob. Lukh cases: Bezglasnoi stol, stlb. 216, ll. 3–12; Prikaznyi stol, stlb. 300, ll. 1–88; stlb. 314, ll. 159–67, 192–93; stlb. 653, ll. 20–87; Prikaznyi stol, stlb. 861, ll. 35–36; Vladimirskii stol, stlb. 142, ll. 92–95.

84. Ibid., Prikaznyi stol, no. 300, l. 3.

85. Ibid., Bezglasnoi stol, stlb. 216, ll. 7, 8–10.

86. Vodarskii, *Naselenie Rossii*, 204.

87. RGADA, f. 210, Prikaznyi stol, no. 300, l. 16.

88. Ibid., ll. 24–25.

89. Ibid., l. 32.

90. Ibid., Prikaznyi stol, no. 314, l. 160.

91. Ibid., Bezglasnoi stol, stlb. 216, ll. 3–12. Three townswomen's names were mentioned, but only one was held by the authorities.

92. Ibid., Vladimirskii stol, stlb. 142, l. 137.

93. Ibid., Prikaznyi stol, stlb. 314, l. 192.

94. Kotkov, *Pamiatniki delovoi pis'mennosti*, nos. 157–59, 181.

95. Ibid., no. 157, p. 183.

96. Ibid., no. 157.

97. *AI*, vol. 2, no. 66, 82–83.

98. RGADA, f. 210, Novgorodskii stol, stlb. 10, ll. 620–24, 643–44.

99. Ibid., Prikaznyi stol, stlb. 416, l. 150.

100. RGADA, f. 159 (Prikaznye dela starykh let), op. 1, no. 326, l. 1.

101. Borisov, *Opisanie goroda Shui*, No. 45, 337–38.

102. RGADA, f. 210, Moskovskii stol, stlb. 525, ll. 338–41.

103. Ibid., Prikaznyi stol, stlb. 595, ll. 605, 606. In a 1629 case from Mtsensk, a man complains of bewitchment and "*lomota,*" aching. While aching is characteristic of possession, in this case the ache seems literal rather than the more elaborate symptoms of possession. RGADA, f. 210, Prikaznyi stol, stlb. 50, l. 33.

104. Ibid., Belgorodskii stol, stlb. 270, ll. 412–16; quote l. 413.

105. Lavrov finds the same ratio among *klikushi* between 1700 and 1740. He identifies forty-two shriekers, of which four were men. Three-quarters were young married women. *Koldovstvo i religiia*, 385–86. On trials as a theater in which to air claims in public, see Smail, *Consumption of Justice.*

106. Worobec, *Possessed*, 45. Avvakum described an encounter with a "*klikusha,*" a female shrieker, who, when "the Devil (*bes*) fell upon her, began to bark like a dog and bleat like a goat and cuckoo like a cuckoo bird." Avvakum, *Zhitie*, 41.

107. Zhitie prepodobnogo i bogonosnogo ottsa nashego igumena Sergiia Chudotvortsa, napisannoe Epifaniem Premudriem (po izdaniiu 1646 goda), chap. 7, "O prognanii besov molitvami sviatogo," http://www.stsl.ru/lib/book2/chap_e2-7.htm#ch_e7 (accessed November 14, 2006). An earlier case in Worobec, *Possessed*, 47–48.

108. Romaniello, *Elusive Empire*, 132–33.

109. Ekaterina Mel'nikova confirms the skew toward men sufferers in iconographic depictions of healing the demon-possessed. Of six such scenes she lists in her notes, one appears to depict a woman ("Otchityvanie besnovatykh," 231–33).

110. On the requirement that women postpone their desire to devote themselves to God while they fulfilled their familial obligations, see Meehan, *Holy Women of Russia*; Iuliana Osorina, discussed in chapter 4.

111. Thyrêt, "Muscovite Miracle Stories," 115–31.

112. On demographics of European possession, see Ferber, "Possession and the Sexes," 219–23.

113. Certeau, *Possession at Loudun*; Ferber, *Demonic Possession and Exorcism;* Hall, "A Servant Possessed," 197–212; Hallett, *Witchcraft, Exorcism and the Politics of Possession*; Niau, *History of the Devils of Loudun*; Watt, *Scourge of Demons.*

114. Lewis, "Structural Approach to Witchcraft," 296.

115. RGADA, f. 210, Prikaznyi stol, no. 300, ll. 20, 21.

116. Ibid., l. 20. The same phrase used by another of the possessed: l. 19.

117. Macdonald, *Witchcraft and Hysteria in Elizabethan England*, xxxiii–xxxiv, xxxvi–xxxviii. James Sharpe argues that possession gave voice to oppressed young women in patriarchal households in England: "Disruption in the Well-Ordered Household," 187–212.

118. Paul Johnson offers a highly original, intellectual history of the rise of paired notions of possession and the impenetrable, "contract-worthy individual" in the thought of early modern Europeans in his "Atlantic Genealogy of Spirit Possession." On modern subjectivity, see Hellbeck, *Revolution on My Mind.*

119. Macdonald, *Witchcraft and Hysteria in Elizabethan England,* xl.

120. Diane Purkiss, *Witch in History*, 91–144; and Holmes, "Women: Witches and Witnesses," 303–22. On Jeanne des Anges and the role of male mediation, see Goldsmith, *Publishing Women's Life Stories*, 42–72. Sarah Ferber invokes "a gender economy of exorcism," in "Possession and the Sexes," 218.

121. Truvorov, "Volkhvy i vorozhei," 703.

CHAPTER 6

1. Novombergskii, *Koldovstvo*, no. 20, 85–86.

2. Ibid., 87.

3. Thompson, "Moral Economy of the English Crowd," 78.

4. Novombergskii notes this pattern in *Koldovstvo*, xxix. Kateryna Dysa finds patterns similar to the ones discussed here in her analysis of early modern Ukrainian trials, "Orthodox Demonology and the Perception of Witchcraft," and in unpublished work that she kindly allowed me to read. In his study of early eighteenth-century Russia, A. L. Lavrov finds the *inverse* pattern: superiors accused of using magic by their subordinates: *Koldovstvo i religiia*, 333–36.

5. RGADA, f. 210, Prikaznyi stol, stlb. 565, ll. 6–21; quotes on ll. 17–18.

6. Ibid., l. 21ob.

7. Bushkovitch, *Religion and Society*, 142–43; Flier, "Golden Hall Iconography"; Kollmann, "Quality of Mercy"; Rowland, "Problem of Advice."

8. Levin, "A Kansas Apocalypse," 193.

9. "Nakaz Vladimirtsev vybrannomu imi iz svoei sredy dvorianinu. . . ." (June 28, 1648), SPb II (RAN), sobranie A. M. Artem'eva, no. 2.

10. For the initial formulation of the "hypertrophic state" formulation, see Hellie, "Structure of Modern Russian History," 13.

11. RGADA, f. 159 (Prikaznye dela starykh let), op. 1, no. 326, l. 1.

12. RGADA, f. 210, Prikaznyi stol, stlb. 434, ll. 4–200; stlb. 734, ll. 115–203; Toporkov, *Zagovory v russkoi rukopisnoi traditsii*, 389; Maikov, *Velikorusskie zaklinaniia*, no. 351, 151–52. A. B. Ippolitova classifies such spells as "social" spells, aimed at influencing relations in the social realm, and, along with E. B. Smilianskaia, differentiates spells directed toward authorities and officials from spells directed toward those within the more intimate field of household and family. Ippolitova, *Russkie rukopisnye travniki*, 326–64; Smililianskaia, *Volshebniki, bogokhul'niki, eretiki*, 142–86.

13. Toporkov, *Zagovory v russkoi rukopisnoi traditsii*, 66.

14. Ibid., 389–400.

15. Ibid., 197–200; Smilianskaia, *Volshebniki, bogokhul'niki, eretiki*, 75, 143–45. On "the powerful people" as an identifiable sociological phenomenon: Andreev, "'Sil'nye liudi,'" 77–88.

16. RGADA, f. 396, op. 1, delo 676/4087, l. 5.

17. Lavrov observes that the arms of the Petrine state were too short to reach into villages in the countryside (*Koldovstvo i religiia*, 110). This may be true as well. The outreach of the early modern Russian state—a strong-weak state—was undeniably erratic.

18. *Stoglav*, chap. 17, 136–37.

19. Afanas'ev, *Poeticheskiia vozzreniia slavian na prirodu*, 2: 275.

20. RGADA, f. 210, Prikaznyi stol, stlb. 564, ll. 696, 698.

21. Ibid, stlb. 567, ll. 471–73.

22. Truvorov, "Volkhvy i vorozhei," 706.

23. Ibid.

24. Ibid., 707.

25. Ibid., 709.

26. Ibid., 703. This is the sole case in which the court documents show a woman using written magic, but even here, she has her husband perform the actual writing.

27. Ibid., 709. Another major case involving charges of sorcery directed against the tsar and his family was the infamous Shaklovityi case, but in that case the charge was that magic was used to harm rather than to win the hearts of the royal family: RGADA, f. 210, Prikaznyi stol, stlb. 1235, ll. 28–42. Another case, in 1694, also involved charges of attempts to bewitch the tsar and family "to death" (stlb. 1677, l. 58).

28. On these embroidered cloths, see Thyrêt, "Blessed is the Tsaritsa's Womb."

29. Kotkov, *Moskovskaia delovaia i bytovaia pis'mennost'*, 239–40; and similar case, 250–77. On these cases, see Perrie, "Tsaritsa, the Needlewomen, and the Witches." Tampering with the sovereign's footprints was specifically banned in the loyalty oaths administered to subjects at the time of the coronation of rulers from Boris Godunov on. See *AAE*, vol. 2, no. 10, 58 (Boris Godunov, 1598); no. 37, 94–95 (Dmitrii Ivanovich); no. 44, 100–103 (Vasilii Shuiskii, 1606).

30. Kotkov, *Moskovskaia delovaia i bytovaia pis'mennost'*, 239, 245, 247–48.

31. Ibid., 238–39, 243, 246.

32. Ibid., 240. During the trial it came out that Dar'ia had a lover, which would have exacerbated her desperate domestic situation. One of her friends, Ovdot'ia Iaryshkina, purportedly provided her brothers with women, Dar'ia among them (238).

33. Kaiser, "He Said, She Said"; Kollmann, "Extremes of Patriarchy"; Weickhardt, "Legal Rights of Women."

34. Kotkov, *Moskovskaia delovaia i bytovaia pis'mennost'*, 238.

35. Kantorovich, *Srednevekovye protessy o ved'makh*, 168–70.

36. In 1647 in Suzdal' an elderly fortune-teller recalled that the wife of a chancellery servitor had asked her to make her son-in-law love her daughter, his wife. The defendant explained that she was a specialist; she had not obliged the anxious mother "because she doesn't know how to do anything other than look at salt and tell fortunes." RGADA f. 210, Prikaznyi stol, stlb. 564, ll. 183–84.

37. Novombergskii, *Koldovstvo*, no. 1, 3–9; RGADA, f. 210, Moskovskii stol, stlb. 15, ll. 394–401.

38. Pouncy, *Domostroi*, 143. On domestic relations in Muscovy, see Poe, "Sexual Life of Muscovites."

39. Kollmann, "Limits of Patriarchal Abuse."

40. RGADA, f. 210, Prikaznyi stol, stlb. 861, l. 9.

41. Kateryna Dysa, "Dangerous Proximity," unpublished manuscript, with thanks for permission to cite.

42. RGADA, f. 210, Prikaznyi stol, stlb. 567, ll. 202–3. The oppressed in many societies turn to magic to "lessen the rigors of enslavement." Lawrence Levine finds that American slaves used magic to "cool [their master's] angry passion" and protect themselves from beatings and whippings. Levine, *Black Culture and Black Consciousness*, 68–73.

43. Truvorov, "Volkhvy i vorozhei," 708.

44. Novosel'skii, *Votchinnik i ego khoziaistvo*.

45. Hellie, *Slavery in Russia*, 505. Hellie makes this point forcefully, in connection with another scandal involving Bezobrazov, and also in the colorful case of Danilka "Big Beard," who sued and presumably won against his purported master, G. V. Lodygin, 504–52. Hellie also notes, however, that in other circumstances masters seem to have been able to get away with anything, even murder, of slaves (e.g., 482).

46. Pouncy, *Domostroi*, 124, 143.

47. RGADA, f. 210, Prikaznyi stol, stlb. 434, ll. 7, 18ob., 190. In 1658 a peasant woman named Oniutka strewed enchanted salt at the gates of the estate bailiff's house, "to take away [the bailiff's] heart and to free her husband," who was being wrongfully held in irons and tortured by the bailiff in the master's house. Ibid., stlb. 300, l. 10. Magic "of the heart (*po serdtsu*)" could work both ways: malevolent spells could harden an overseer's heart "so that my husband would be put in prison." Ibid., l. 38.

48. Ibid., stlb. 46, l. 250. As best I can tell, water-pepper is *Polygonaceae* or knotweed, and *strekil'* is *Badiga fluviatilis,* a sponge that grows by riverbanks. But I hesitate to overly systematize pre-Linnean plant names.

49. RGADA, f. 210, Prikaznyi stol, stlb. 46, l. 256.

50. Ibid. Toporkov says "magic inscribed itself in the context of social psychology and functioned as a means (however fictitious) on which the oppressed might place their hopes." Toporkov, *Russkie zagovory iz rukopisnykh istochnikov*, 19.

51. *AIu*, no. 407, 428.

52. Levin, *Sex and Society*, 101; Daniel Kaiser finds active church oversight of marriage in the Muscovite north, where serfdom was less entrenched. Kaiser, "Church Control Over Marriage," 567–85.

53. RGADA, f. 210, Prikaznyi stol, stlb. 46, ll. 270, 275.

54. Women cursing their masters and mistresses: Cherepnin, "Iz istorii drevnerusskogo koldovstva," 97, 99; RGADA, f. 210, Prikaznyi stol, stlb. 300, l. 10; stlb. 1225, ll. 6–7.

55. On food and magic: Morozova, "Obychai, verovaniia, magiia, sviazannye s nachalom i zaversheniem trapezy," 16–35; and Valentsova, "Magicheskie funktsii edy," 202–15.

56. Newlin, "Rural Ruses," offers relevant insights into the anxieties of the serf-owning estate in the eighteenth century.

57. RGADA, f. 210, Prikaznyi stol, stb. 1859, l. 149.

58. Ibid., ll. 148–49.

59. Ibid., stlb. 861, ll. 25–26. In the case of the tsaritsa's craftswomen, the decrepit elderly women who had provided the magical wherewithal received far harsher penalties: the ones who were lucky enough to survive torture were exiled with their husbands to various Siberian cities.

60. Ibid., stlb. 186, ll. 984–1001.

61. Ibid., stlb. 46, l. 274.

62. Thomas, *Religion and the Decline of Magic*, 502–69; Macfarlane, *Witchcraft in Tudor and Stuart England*, 147–57, 196–97.

63. RGADA, f. 210, Prikaznyi stol, stlb. 426, l. 258.

64. Ibid., ll. 275, 283, 303. Some of the male suspects broke down and confessed under torture and even incriminated one another, but none would incriminate the women.

65. Ibid., ll. 289, 301–2.

66. Ibid., stlb. 1859, ll. 151, 160.

67. Ibid., ll. 151–52.

68. Ibid., l. 152.

69. Ibid., stlb. 186, ll. 984–1001; stlb. 1225, ll. 1–51.

70. In that particular case, failure to appear seems to have been involuntary: the husband, it turned out, had been imprisoned and not released to attend his confrontation. Afterward, he had been reduced to serfdom, from his previous status as provincial clerk in Poshekhon'e, and his wife along with him. Ibid., stlb. 2630, ll. 31, 32.

71. Men excusing themselves through drunkenness, youth, or stupidity are common. A few examples: RGADA, f. 214, stlb. 586, l. 15; RGADA, Moskovskoi oruzheinoi, f. 396, ed. khr. 4087, l. 6. RGADA, f. 210, Belgorodskii stol, stlb. 1169, l. 747; stlb. 1195, ll. 694–95, 730–32; stlb. 1202, ll. 387–88; Prikaznyi stol, stlb. 565, l. 17; stlb. 734, ll. 115–203; stlb. 749, ll. 117, 175, 189, 193, 198, 199.

72. Smail, *Consumption of Justice*. See also Davis, *Fiction in the Archives*.

73. Smilianskaia, *Volshebniki, bogokhul'niki, eretiki*, 144.

74. Ibid., 144–45; also Ippolitova, *Russkie rukopisnye travniki*, 329.

75. Kollmann, "Law and Society."

76. Uspenskii, "Pravo i religiia," 201. The laws place witches in the same category as prostitutes for purposes of dishonor calculations: "And to prostitutes and witches dishonor compensation of two *den'gi* according to their trade *(A bliadiam i vedun'iam besschchest'ia dve dengi po ikh promyslom)*": "1589 Sudebnik," *PRP* 4 (1956): 421, art. 70. On the 1605 *Sudebnik*, see Kollmann, *By Honor Bound*, 54; Hellie, "The Law," 376.

77. On "hierarchies of protection," see Chrissidis, "Whoever Does Not Drink to the End," 121–22.

CHAPTER 7

1. RGADA, f. 210, Prikaznyi stol, stlb. 653, ll. 79–80. E. B. Anisimov describes a process of breaking ribs with red-hot pincers, from Kotoshkin. The application of fire was considered more extreme than other forms of torture, but it was routinely used in witchcraft cases. Anisimov, *Dyba i knut*, 410–12. On regimes of punishment, exile, and torture, see, among others: Gentes, *Exile to Siberia*; Schrader, *Languages of the Lash*.

2. "In the torture chamber": RGADA, f. 210, Belgorodskii stol, stlb. 1195, l. 694; *Rozysknyia dela o Fedore Shakovitom i ego soobshchnikakh,* vol. 2, 323; Olearius, *Travels of Olearius*, 229.

3. Kollmann, "Torture in Early Modern Russia," 161.

4. For example, Novombergskii, *Koldovstvo,* no. 11, 63 (though elsewhere the record specifies "harsh torture" with fire).

5. RGADA, f. 210, Sevskii stol, stlb. 215, ll. 54–64, quote on l. 62.

6. Ibid., Prikaznyi stol, stlb. 565, l. 12. On water torture, see Anisimov, *Dyba i knut,* 415. Russians do not seem to have used the now infamous water-boarding, popular with European courts. Instead, water torture involved dripping water, drop by drop, on a shaved head. This torture was administered to the late seventeenth-century rebel, Stenka Razin.

7. RGADA, f. 210, Belgorodskii stol, stlb. 1032, l. 184.

8. *Sobornoe Ulozhenie,* chap. 25, art. 15.

9. Anisimov, *Dyba i knut,* 395–96.

10. Dershowitz, "Tortured Reasoning," 257–80. In the context of the Algerian War, General Paul Aussaresses justifies the use of torture as a necessary weapon of war: *Battle of the Casbah.*

11. Scarry, *Body in Pain,* 28–38; quotes on 29, 36, 38.

12. For example, *Sobornoe Ulozhenie,* chap. 21, art. 90.

13. Ibid., chap. 10, art. 161.

14. *Sobornoe Ulozhenie,* chap. 9, art. 14. Also *Sobornoe Ulozhenie,* chap. 9, art. 13; chap. 25, art. 15. Torture is still mandated in the *Novoukaznye stat'i* of 1669, reputedly a more humane law code: *PSZ,* vol. 2, art. 99, 795.

15. RGADA, f. 210, Prikaznyi stol, stlb. 565, l. 51.

16. Ibid., stlb. 426, ll. 274, 281.

17. "Skazanie o tsarstve Tsaria Feodora Ioannovicha," 764.

18. Ibid., stlb. 275, ll. 200–213ob.

19. Kollmann, "Torture in Early Modern Russia," 162, 164.

20. Ibid., 169.

21. Borisov, *Opisanie goroda Shuia,* Nos. 45–46, 337–44; RGADA, f. 210, Belgorodskii stol, stlb. 597, ll. 135–38; stlb. 599, ll. 565–71, 654–55; Prikaznyi stol, stlb. 95, ll. 219–56.

22. Peters, *Torture,* 69.

23. RGADA, f. 210, Belgorodskii stol, stlb. 652, ll. 628–35.

24. Ibid., Prikaznyi stol, stlb. 861, ll. 29–34. See also Belgorodskii stol., stlb. 1100; Prikaznyi stol, stlb. 653, ll. 20–87; stlb. 1006; *AI,* vol. 2, 82–83.

25. RGADA, f. 210, Belgorodskii stol, stlb. 59, l. 121.

26. RGADA, f. 210, Prikaznyi stol, stlb. 567, ll. 539–49. The name "Rotagaia Baba" (horned witch or horned old woman) is intriguing. M. P. Alekseev examines uses of the word in late seventeenth- and eighteenth-century literary texts, but these elegant allegorical uses are not relevant to our *baba*: "'Proroche rogatyi' Feofana Prokopovicha," 17–43. Thanks to Aleksandr Lavrov for this reference.

27. RGADA, f. 210, Prikaznyi stol, stlb. 861, ll. 1–28. On the herb *uzhevnik,* see Ippolitova, *Russkie rukopisnye travniki,* 484.

28. For instance, "He, Iudka, learned [spells] in his village of Kalustino from someone else's peasant and not from his own, but I don't remember the name of that peasant. . . . Now they say that peasant died" (RGADA, f. 210, Prikaznyi stol, stlb. 1235, l. 29). Or, "Her mother Marinka taught her all that but she herself taught no one. . . . Her mother died four years ago" (stlb. 426, l. 103). Other examples: stlb. 33, stolpik 1, ll. 708–19; stlb. 426, l. 270; Moskovskii stol, stlb. 54, stolpik 2, ll. 74–80.

29. RGADA, f. 210, Prikaznyi stol, stlb. 653, l. 83.

30. Novombergskii, *Koldovstvo,* no. 4, 20.

31. Ibid., no. 11, 66.

32. RGADA, f. 210, Prikaznyi stol, stlb. 861, l. 12. In 1644, Grishka Titov, in a case discussed above, retracted his confession, saying that he had confessed only because he was "unable to endure the pain of torture." RGADA, f. 210, Prikaznyi stol, stlb. 275, l. 208.

33. Novombergskii, *Koldovstvo*, no. 4, 19.

34. "Spell against torture": RGADA, f. 210, Prikaznyi stol, stlb. 734, ll. 117–18.

35. Ibid., stlb. 565, ll. 6–6ob.

36. Mayer, "Annals of Justice"; Miller, "Torture." Thanks to Amon Burton ("The Torturous Road from Nuremberg to Guantanamo Bay: Human Rights and the War on Terror") and Brian Levack ("Torture Then and Now") for insights raised in papers at "The Midnight Sun Witchcraft Conference" in Vardo, Norway, June 28 to July 1, 2007.

37. De Pee, "Cases of the New Terrace," 49. On early modern Europe, see also Hanson, "Torture and Truth in Renaissance England," 53–84; Peters, *Torture*, 40–73.

38. Silverman, *Tortured Subjects*, 9, 22.

39. On contested ideas about truth in Muscovite courts, see Kaiser, "He Said, She Said," 197–216.

40. Silverman, *Tortured Subjects*, 3, 22.

41. Keane, "Ecrire l'au-delà."

42. Greene, *Bodies Like Bright Stars.*

43. Mitchell Merback offers a rich exploration of the resonances between sacred martyrdom and corporal punishment in theaters of execution and in devotional practice in Western Europe. Merback, *Thief, the Cross, and the Wheel.*

44. Halperin, "Culture of Ivan IV's Court," 105.

45. RGADA, f. 210, Prikaznyi stol, stlb. 1133, stolpik 2, ll. 177, 179.

46. Ibid.; Toporkov, *Zagovory*, 366.

47. RGADA, f. 210, Prikaznyi stol, stlb. 300, ll. 16–25, 32, 160; stlb. 314, ll. 159–67, 192–93 (misery overtook her).

48. See chapter 4 on these tales.

49. Cut off hand: RGADA, f. 210, Prikaznyi stol, stlb. 420, ll. 106–7. Burn text on back: ibid., stlb. 734, l. 198; ibid, ll. 115–203. See also stlb. 749; stlb. 567, ll. 202–6; stlb. 2565, l. 451.

50. Kollmann, "Punishment and the Law," 559, 560.

51. Keane, "Ecrire l'au-delà."

52. Kollmann, "Torture in Early Modern Russia"; *Sobornoe Ulozhenie,* chap. 21, art. 88. Prohibition on private torture is reiterated in *Novoukaznye stat'i.*

53. RGADA, f. 210, Prikaznyi stol, stlb. 434, ll. 21, 23, 24, 188, 190.

54. Anisimov explains that "*rosprosa s pristrastiem*" meant exposure to the implements of torture with the intent of scaring the accused into a confession. Transcripts also record testimony *pri*, *u*, and *posle* (at [the sight of], during, and after torture). Anisimov, *Dyba i knut*, 391, 428.

55. RGADA, f. 210, Prikaznyi stol, stlb. 1225, 1–7, 41–42, 45, 46.

56. Ibid., stlb. 186, ll. 985, 1000. A similar case involving witchcraft allegations, wrongful enslavement, and holding in chains without an official order was investigated in Ostashkov in 1650. The victim in this case was a man, and the tormentor the local governor: ibid., Moskovskii stol, stlb. 265; ll. 396–417; Novombergskii, *Vrachebnoe stroenie.* no. 10, xxxiii–xxxviii.

57. RGADA, f. 210, Prikaznyi stol, stlb. 2346, ll. 6, 38, 39, 43.

58. Ibid., stlb. 861, ll. 1–21.

59. Ibid., Moskovskii stol, stlb. 15, ll. 394–41 (1622–23).

60. Ibid.

61. Ibid., Prikaznyi stol, stlb. 46, stolpik 1, ll. 247–76, 309–12.

62. Ibid., Prikaznyi stol, stlb. 679, ll. 284, 285, 290.

63. Kors and Peters, *Witchcraft in Europe*, 352.

64. Ibid., 351.

65. Alleg, *Question*, 43, 41.

66. Ibid., 47.

67. For instance, see the victims' testimony published in Danner, *Torture and Truth.*

68. Sartre, "Preface," xxix.

69. Ibid., xxxii.

70. Ibid., xxxix.

71. Ibid., xxxviii.

CHAPTER 8

1. Kollmann, "Torture in Early Modern Russia," 165–66; 100 blows: Novombergskii, *Slovo i delo*, vol. 1, nos. 33 and 38 (1627).

2. Kors and Peters, *Witchcraft in Europe*, 246.

3. Ibid., 269–70.

4. In popular parlance in later eras, either heretic or vampire could denote witch. The usage in these trials suggests that the same was true in the seventeenth century, although it doesn't come up much. Ryan, *Bathhouse at Midnight*, 40–41; Oinas, "Heretics as Vampires and Demons in Russia," 433–41.

5. Mentions of heresy: RGADA, f. 210, Belgorodskii stol, stlb. 1195, ll. 228–37, 255–57; stlb. 1198, ll. 228–35, 255–57, 279–81; Moskovskii stol, stlb. 525, ll. 228–37, 255–57; Prikaznyi stol, stlb. 50, ll. 13–120; stlb. 91, ll. 293–302; stlb. 426, ll. 76–100; stlb. 567, ll. 469–74; stlb. 721, ll. 121–25, 154–44; stlb. 861, ll. 1–28; stlb. 1006, ll. 1–54; stlb. 1859, ll. 147–60; stlb. 2630, ll. 1–70; stlb. 2651, ll. 1–15; Sevskii stol, stlb. 137, ll. 343–48; f. 159, op. 1, no. 326, ll. 1–5; Semevskii, *Istoriko-iuridicheskie akty*, no. vii, 70–71; Shevtsova, Novosel'skii, and Lebedev, *Krest'ianskaia voina pod predvotditel'stvom Stepana Razina*, vol. 2, pt. 1, no. 293, 366–41; Novombergskii, *Koldovstvo*, no. 29, 108–9.

6. Semevskii, *Istoriko-iuridicheskie akty*, no. vii, 70–71.

7. Novombergskii, *Koldovstvo*, no. 29, 108–9. Heresy and witchcraft could function as synonyms. For example, RGADA, f. 210, Prikaznyi stol, stlb. 1124.

8. Shevtsova, Novosel'skii, and Lebedev, *Krest'ianskaia voina pod Predvoditel'stvom Stepana Razina*, vol. 2, pt. 1, no. 293, 366–68.

9. RGADA, f. 210, Prikaznyi stol, stlb. 91, ll. 293–302; stlb. 2630, l. 70 (also stolbtsy 2640 and 2646); stlb. 721, ll. 121–25, 154–55.

10. A nuanced treatment of this question is in Smilianskaia, *Volshebniki, bogokhul'niki, eretiki*, 120–22.

11. Novombergskii, *Koldovstvo.*

12. Ryan, "Witchcraft Hysteria," 72, 76, 77, 81.

13. Weickhardt, "Due Process and Equal Justice."

14. Her confession eerily matches that attributed to the "sly woman, lackey of the Enemy, and bride of Satan," Varvara, who foretold Boris Godunov's ascent to the throne and seven-year rule in "Skazanie o tsarstve Tsaria Fedora Ioannovicha," 759. The relationship between the two remains to be explored. Godunov seems to have feared witchcraft; he introduced the ban on sorcery directed toward his person into the oath of loyalty administered to Muscovite subjects on his ascension to the throne in 1598. *AAE*, vol. 2, no. 10, 58.

15. RGADA, f. 210, Prikaznyi stol, stlb. 564, ll. 154–234.

16. Zabelin, *Domashnii byt' russkikh tsarits*, 224–50. Russell Martin discusses the politics of these failed royal marriages but avoids the innuendos of sorcery. Martin, *Bride for the Tsar*, 169–85. The assumption that Ivan IV's wives succumbed to bewitchment are expressed in the church deliberations on the possibility of an uncanonical fourth marriage: *AAE*, vol.1, no. 284, 329 (1572).

17. Matveev: RGADA f. 159, op. 3, no. 4208 (1692); Lithuanian border crossing: RGADA, f. 210, Belgorodskii stol, stlb. 284, ll. 425–47; Prikaznyi stol, stlb. 46, stolpik 1, ll. 247–76, 309–12; stlb. 275, ll. 200–213. Plots against the sovereign's health or of his bride or other family members (or to win their love): RGADA, f. 210, Sevskii stol, stlb. 161, ll. 206–8; Kantorovich, *Srednevekovye protsessy o ved'makh*, 170–75; Novomberskii, *Koldovstvo*, no. 33, 112–34; Zertsalov, *K materialam o vorozhbe v drevnei Rusi*; Esipov, "Koldovstvo v XVII i XVIII stoletiiakh," 64–66; Ivanits, *Russian Folk Belief*, 88; Ryan, *Bathhouse at Midnight*, 413; Longworth, *Alexis*, 199, 222; *Rozysknyia dela o Fedore Shaklovitom*, vol. 3, cols. 1235–71. Assault on governor: RGADA, f. 210, Belgorodskii stol, stlb. 160, ll. 103–15; Prikaznyi stol, stlb. 2109, l. 36. Rebellion: Sevskii stol, stlb. 161, ll. 206–8; Belgorodskii stol, stlb. 768, ll. 57–68, 93–95; Prikaznyi stol, stlb. 672, ll. 54–128; Shvetsova, Novosel'skii, and Lebedev, *Krest'ianskaia voina pod predvoditel'stvom Stepana Razina*, vol. 2, pt. 1, no. 293, 366–68. Political predictions: RGADA f. 210, Prikaznyi stol, stlb. 564, ll. 154–234. Anonymous letters: Belgorodskii stol, stlb. 1032, 11–13, 165–94; Prikaznyi stol, stlb. 1677, 58 ll.; Novgorodskii stol, stlb. 233, ll. 206–7; Sevskii stol, stlb. 161, ll. 206–8. *Prikaz* personnel: Belgorodskii stol, stlb. 898, ll. 36–40, 41–60, 129; Prikaznyi stol, stlb. 139, ll. 106–10, 944–47; stlb. 749, l. 385; stlb. 734, ll. 115–203. Sovereign's word or deed: Belgorodskii stol, stlb. 284, ll. 425–47; Prikaznyi stol, stlb. 14, stolpik 1. 148–54; stlb. 275, ll. 200–213; stlb. 434, l. 190 (and hiding conscripts, l. 192); stlb. 564, ll. 696–705; stlb. 567, ll. 469–74; stlb. 569, ll. 197–203; Novomberskii, *Slovo i delo*, vol. 1, 238; Zguta, "Witchcraft Trials," 1195.

18. Lavrov, *Koldovstvo i religiia*, 331–32.

19. RGADA, f. 210, Novgorodskii stol, stlb. 233, ll. 206–7; Prikaznyi stol, stlb. 1235, ll. 28–42;

stlb. 16.

20. RGADA, f. 210, Prikaznyi stol, stlb. 1677, l. 58. Peter was estranged from his tsaritsa, Evdokiia Lopukhina, at the time and was cracking down on the Lopukhin clan. Bushkovitch, *Peter the Great*, 197–98.

21. *Rozysknyia dela o Fedore Shaklovitom*; RGADA, f. 210, Prikaznyi stol, stlb. 1235, ll. 28–42.

22. RGADA, f. 210, Prikaznyi stol, stlb. 1235, l. 29.

23. Ibid., l. 30. In the same spirit, Prince V. V. Golitsyn was suspected of treasonously keeping "a koldun (witch) in his bathhouse to make magic love spells to attract the Regent Sofia" and a Polish wizard to predict whether he would marry her. Ryan, *Bathhouse at Midnight*, 51, 416.

24. RGADA, f. 210, Prikaznyi stol, stlb. 595, l. 617.

25. Ibid., stlb. 314, l. 159.

26. The last document in the record, written in Moscow on July 7, 1623, leaves the case unresolved. Ibid., Moskovskii stol, stlb. 15, ll. 394–41.

27. Ibid., Prikaznyi stol, stlb. 861, l. 3.

28. Cf. Lavrov, *Koldovstvo i religiia*, 110–11.

29. Levin, "Healers and Witches," 132.

30. On liturgical society, that is, a society bound at every level in service; Mousnier, *Social Hierarchies*, 115; Davies, *State Power and Community*, 183.

31. RGADA, f. 210, Prikaznyi stol, stlb. 1235, l. 30.

32. Kollmann, *Kinship and Politics*; Kollmann, *By Honor Bound*.

33. Scholars of the West also point to difficulties in defining "political magic": Kieckhefer, *Magic in the Middle Ages*, 97.

34. "Skazanie o tsarstve Tsaria Fedoroa Ioannovicha," 758–59.

35. Ryan, *Bathhouse at Midnight*, 39; "Chronograph of 1617": "Iz Khronografa 1617 goda," in *PDRL XVI–XVII vv.*, 328, 332; Massa, *A Short History*, 118, 138, 146–50, 157–58. *AAE* 2: 38, 58–59; Margeret, *Russian Empire and the Grand Duchy of Muscovy*, 60, 73; Dunning, "Who Was Tsar Dmitrii?" 705–29; Bussow, *Disturbed State of the Russian Realm*, 78; *RIB* 13: cols. 55–56, 656–57, 818–20.

36. "Anonimnoe shvedskoe sochinenie o vosstanii v Moskve v 1648 g.," in Bazilevich, *Gorodskie vosstaniia*, 55–56.

37. *PSRL* 31: 188–203 (*Letopisets 1619–91).* Special thanks to Nancy Kollmann for her help with this section and for generously sharing her translations of chronicle sources. On the seventeenth-century rebellions, see Buganov, *Moskovskie vosstaniia kontsa XVII veka*; Buganov, *Vosstanie v Moskve 1682 g.*; Lavrov, *Regentstvo tsarevny Sof'i Alekseevny.*

38. PSRL 31: 174–76 (*Mazurinskii letopisets*).

39. PSRL 31: 188–203 (*Letopisets 1619–91*).

40. PSRL, 31: 174–76 (*Mazurinskii letopisets*), 174–76. Naryshkin, a victim of mob anger, had earlier accused Sophia's favorite, Prince V. V. Golitsyn, of "bewitching the tsar to gain favor." Bushkovitch, *Peter the Great*, 210.

41. Jerome Horsey, "Travels," in Berry and Crummey, *Rude and Barbarous Kingdom*, 274, 279. Zimin, "Doktor Nikolai Bulev," 78–86. On foreign doctors, see Levin, "Healers and Witches," 128–29; and Unkovskaya, *Brief Lives.*

42. Kogorodina, *Ispoved'*, 304.

43. For example, "Povest' o Shemiakinom sude," in Adrianova-Peretts, *Russkaia demokraticheskaia satira XVII veka*, 17–25.

44. Shakhmatov, "Chelobitnaia 'mira,'" 18

45. Davies, *State Power and Community*, 175–76.

46. Dewey, "Judges and the Evidence in Muscovite Law," 194; Kleimola, "Justice in Medieval Russia," 91; Weickhardt, "Due Process and Equal Justice," Kollmann, "Law and Society."

47. Olearius writes that whoever petitioned first tended to win a case. I would add that whoever petitioned first *in any particular round of appeal* tended to win. *Travels of Olearius*, 229.

48. The petitions submitted during the 1648 riots express precisely this conception of authority. Shakhmatov, "Chelobitnaia 'mira,'" 14. See also Lukin, *Narodnye predstavleniia o gosudarstvennoi vlasti*, 45–47.

49. On judicial duels, cf. Dewey, "Trial by Combat in Muscovite Russia," 26; Weickhardt, "Muscovite Judicial Duels as a Legal Fiction," 713–32. On cross kissing, Kleimola, "Duty to Denounce in Muscovite Russia," 759–79. On "God's Justice," Kleimola, "Justice in Medieval Russia," 58–68.

50. Shakhmatov, "Chelobitnaia 'mira,'" 14.

51. Davies, *State Power and Community*, 220.

52. *Stoglav*, chap. 41, question 22.

53. *AI*, vol. 1, no. 154. In spite of the *Stoglav*'s recommendation, execution for sorcery entered the law only in the middle of the seventeenth century.

54. *Stoglav*, chap. 41, question 17, 86; Kollmann, "Moscow *Stoglav*," 546.

55. *Stoglav*, chap. 41, question 17, 86.

56. *PSRL*, vol. 29 (*Letopisets nachala tsarstva*), 153.

57. *AAE*, vol. 1, no. 284, 329. Given his fear of witchcraft, it is interesting that according to foreign contemporaries (Staden, Taube, and Kruse) Ivan the Terrible had his henchmen, the *oprichniki*, take an oath that combined the power of a god-denying oath with the language of a love spell (renouncing food, drink, mother, father, clan and tribe, and adhering only to him). Staden, *Land and Government of Muscovy*, 30; Taube and Kruse, discussed in Pavlov and Perrie, *Ivan the Terrible*, 112.

58. On the rise of concern with witchcraft in this era, see Korogodina, *Ispoved'*, 205. On Ivan's concern with witchcraft and questions of authenticity, see among many others, Brian Boeck, "Eyewitness or False Witness," 161–77.

59. Rzhiga, *I. S. Peresvetov*, 65. On Peresvetov, see also Lur'e, "Peresvetov, Ivan Semenovich."

60. Rzhiga, *I. S. Peresvetov*, 63.

61. Ibid., 66.

62. RGADA, f. 210, Prikaznyi stol, stlb. 564, ll. 696–705.

63. See Rowland, "Problem of Advice."

64. Toporkov, "Gramota no. 521," 230–41. On individualism in Muscovy: Kollmann, "Society, Identity, and Modernity," 417–32; Kaiser, "Discovering Individualism among the Deceased," 433–60; Hellie, "Great Paradox of the Seventeenth Century," 116–28.

THE AFTERMATH

1. On eighteenth-century witchcraft and magic, see Lavrov, *Koldovstvo i religiia*; Pokrovskii, "Ispoved' altaiskogo krest'ianina," and "Tetrad' zagovorov 1734 goda," 239–65; Smilianskaia, *Volshebniki, bogokhul'niki, eretiki*; Worobec, *Possessed*, 54–62.

2. Ryan, *Bathhouse at Midnight*, 416–17.

3. On the surprisingly easy and common conjunctures of modernity and witchcraft, see Ashforth *Witchcraft, Violence, and Democracy*; Geschiere, *Modernity of Witchcraft*; and Siegel, *Naming the Witch*.

4. On Peter's laws on possession, see Worobec, "Decriminalizing Witchcraft in Pre-Emancipation Russia." Thanks to her for permission to read and cite this stimulating paper.

5. "Voinskikh artikulov (Military articles, chap. 1—Of the Fear of God, arts. 1–2)," in Sofronenko, *Zakonodatel'nye akty Petra I*, 321–23; Ryan, "Witchcraft Hysteria," 65.

6. Smilianskaia, *Volshebniki, bogokhul'niki, eretiki*, 96.

7. Ibid., 84–86, 129, 134–35. W. F. Ryan catalogues over two-dozen cases with demonic elements from the eighteenth century, ranging from 1722 to 1770 (*Bathhouse at Midnight*, 419–23).

8. RGADA, f. 7, Preobrazhenskii prikaz, op. 1, ed. khr. 1917, l. 16.

9. Lavrov, *Koldovstvo i religiia*.

10. "Voinskikh artikulov," 321–23.

11. Smilianskaia, *Volshebniki, bogokhul'niki, eretiki*, 94.

12. Toporkov, *Russkie zagovory iz rukopisnykh istochnikov*, 66; Andreev, " 'Sil'nye liudi.' "

13. Ashforth, *Madumo;* Briggs, *Witches and Neighbors;* Karlsen, *Devil in the Shape of a Woman*; Boyer and Nissenbaum, *Salem Possessed*; Kelly, "Witchcraft and Sexual Relations"; Geschiere, *Modernity of Witchcraft*, 157. Geschiere's more recent work explores the tensions within the family as a source of witchcraft anxiety: "Witchcraft, Intimacy, and Trust: Africa in Comparison." Lecture presented at the Africa Workshop Series, University of Michigan, Ann Arbor, Michigan, April 14, 2010.

Bibliography

Abu-Lughod, Lila. "The Romance of Resistance: Tracing Transformations of Power through Bedouin Women." *American Ethnologist* 17, no. 1 (1990): 41–55.

Adrianova-Peretts, V. P., ed. *Russkaia demokraticheskaia satira XVII veka*. Moscow: Nauka, 1977.

Afanas'ev, A. N. *Mify, pover'ia i sueveriia slavian: Poeticheskie vozzreniia slavian na prirody*. Edited by K. Korolev. 3 vols. 1865–1869. Reprint. Moscow: EKSMO, 2002.

———. *Poeticheskiia vozzreniia slavian na prirodu*. Vol. 2. *Opyt sravnitel'nago izucheniia slavianskikh predanii i verovanii, v sviazi s mificheskimi skazaniiami drugikh rodstvennykh narodov*. 1868. Slavistic Printings and Reprintings 214. The Hague: Mouton, 1969.

Akty istoricheskie (AI). 5 vols. St. Petersburg: Tip. Ekspeditsii zagotovleniia gosudarstvennykh bumag, 1841.

Akty iuridicheskie, ili sobranie form starinnogo deloproizvodstva (AIu). St. Petersburg: Tip. 2 Otdeleniia sobstvennoi E. I. V. Kantseliarii, 1838.

Akty, sobrannye v bibliotekakh i arkhivakh rossiiskoi imperii arkheograficheskoiu ekspeditsieiu. dopolneny i izdany vysochaishe uchrezhdennoiu kommissieiu (AAE). Vol. 1, *1294–1598*. Vol. 2, *1598–1613*. Vol. 3, *1613–1645*. Vol. 4, *1645–1700*. St. Petersburg: Tip. 2 Otdeleniia sobstvennoi E. I. V. Kantseliarii, 1836. http://babel.hathitrust.org/cgi/pt?id=inu.32000006268645.

Alekseev, A. I. *Pod znakom kontsa vremen: Ocherki russkoi religioznosti kontsa XIV–nachala XVI vekov*. St. Peterburg: Aleteiia, 2002.

Alekseev, M. P. "'Proroche rogatyi' Feofana Prokopovicha." In *Iz istorii russkikh literaturnykh otnoshenii XVIII–XX vekov*, edited by S. V. Katorskii, 17–43. Moscow-Leningrad: Izd-vo Akademii nauk SSSR, 1959.

Al'kor, Ia. P., and B. D. Grekov, eds. *Kolonial'naia politika Moskovskogo gosudarstva v Iakutii*. Leningrad: Institut narodov Severa TsIK SSSR, 1936.

Alleg, Henri. *The Question*. Translated by John Calder. Lincoln: University of Nebraska Press, 2006.

Almazov, A. I. *Tainaia ispoved' v Pravoslavnoi vostochnoi tserkvi: opyt vneshnei istorii*. 3 vols. Odessa: Tip. Shtaba odesskago voennago okruga, 1894.

Alpatov, M. V. *Early Russian Icon Painting*. 3rd ed. Moscow: Iskusstvo, 1984.

Andreev, I. L. "'Sil'nye liudi' Moskovskogo gosudarstva i bor'ba dvorian s nimi v 20–40-e gody XVII veka." *Istoriia SSSR*, no. 5 (1990): 77–88.

Anisimov, E. V. *Dyba i knut: Politicheskii sysk i russkoe obshchestvo v XVIII veke*. Moscow: Novoe literaturnoe obozrenie, 1999.

Ankarloo, Bengt, and Gustav Henningsen, eds. *Early Modern European Witchcraft: Centres and Peripheries*. Oxford: Clarendon Press, 1990.

Antonov, Dmitrii Igorevich. *Smuta v kul'ture srednevekovoi Rusi: Evoliutsiia drevnerusskikh mifologem v knizhnosti nachala XVII veka*. Moscow: RGGU, 2009.

Antonov, Dmitrii Igorevich, and Mikhail Romanovich Maizul's. *Demony i greshniki v drevnerusskoi ikonografii: Semiotika obraza*. Moscow: Indrik, 2011.

Antonovych, V. *Koldovstvo: Dokumenty–protsessy–izsledovanie*. Peterburg: Tip. V. Kirshbauma, 1877.

Apps, Lara, and Andrew Gow. *Male Witches in Early Modern Europe*. New York: Palgrave, 2003.

Aristov, I. Ia. "Sud'ba russkoi zhenshchiny v do-petrovskoe vremia." *Zaria*. 1871, no. 3, 191–2.

Ashforth, Adam. *Madumo, a Man Bewitched*. Chicago: University of Chicago Press, 2000.

———. *Witchcraft, Violence, and Democracy in South Africa*. Chicago: University of Chicago Press, 2005.

Astakhova, A. M. "The Poetical Image and Elements of Philosophy in Russian Exorcisms." In *Sed'moi Mezhdunarodnyi kongress antropologicheskikh i etnograficheskikh nauk, 3–10 Avgusta 1964 g*. Vol. 6, 268–69. Moscow:Nauka, 1969.

Atkinson, Dorothy. "Society and the Sexes in the Russian Past." In *Women in Russia*, edited by Atkinson, Dorothy, Alexander Dallin, and Gail W. Lapidus. Stanford: Stanford University Press, 1977, 3–38.

Aussaresses, Paul. *The Battle of the Casbah: Terrorism and Counter-Terrorism in Algeria, 1955–1957*. Translated by Robert L. Miller. New York: Enigma Books, 2002.

Austen, Ralph A. "The Moral Economy of Witchcraft: An Essay in Comparative History." In *Modernity and its Malcontents: Ritual and Power in Postcolonial Africa*, edited by Jean Comaroff and John L. Comaroff, 89–110. Chicago: University of Chicago Press, 1993.

Avvakum, Archpriest. *Zhitie Protopopa Avvakuma im samim napisanoe.* Edited by N. S. Tikhonravov. St. Petersburg: Obshchestvennaia pol'za, 1861.

Bailey, Michael David. *Battling Demons: Witchcraft, Heresy, and Reform in the Late Middle Ages.* University Park: Pennsylvania State University Press, 2003.

———. *Heresy, Witchcraft, and Reform: Johannes Nider and the Religious World of the Late Middle Ages.* University Park: Pennsylvania State University Press, 1998.

———. *Magic and Superstition in Europe: A Concise History from Antiquity to the Present.* Lanham, Md.: Rowman & Littlefield, 2007.

Bakhrushin, S. V. "Moskovskoe vosstanie 1648." In *S. V. Bakhrushin: Nauchnye Trudy,* vol. 2. 46–91. Moscow: AN SSSR, 1954.

Baron, Samuel H., and Nancy Shields Kollmann, eds. *Religion and Culture in Early Modern Russia and Ukraine.* DeKalb: Northern Illinois University Press, 1997.

Barry, Jonathan, and Owen Davies, eds. *Palgrave Advances in Witchcraft Historiography.* New York: Palgrave Macmillan, 2007.

Barry, Jonathan, Marianne Hester, and Gareth Roberts, eds. *Witchcraft in Early Modern Europe: Studies in Culture and Belief.* Cambridge: Cambridge University Press, 1996.

Barstow, Anne L. *Witchcraze: A New History of the European Witch Hunts.* San Francisco: Pandora, 1994.

Bazilevich, K. V., ed. *Gorodskie vosstaniia v Moskovskom gosudarstve XVII veka: Sbornik dokumentov.* Moscow: Gosudarstvennoe sotsial'no-ekonomicheskoe izdatel'stvo, 1936.

Behar, Ruth. "Sexual Witchcraft, Colonialism, and Women's Powers: Views from the Mexican Inquisition." In *Sexuality and Marriage in Colonial Latin America,* edited by Asunción Lavrín, 178–206. Lincoln: University of Nebraska Press, 1989.

Behringer, Wolfgang. "Climatic Change and Witch-Hunting: The Impact of the Little Ice Age on Mentalities." *Climatic Change* 43, no. 1 (1999): 335–51.

———. "How Waldensians Became Witches: Heretics and Their Journey to the Other World." In *Communicating with the Spirits,* vol. 1 of *Demons, Spirits, Witches,* edited by Éva Pócs and Gábor Klaniczay. 155–92. Budapest: Central European University Press, 2005.

———. "Neun Millionen Hexen: Entstehung, Tradition und Kritik eines populären Mythos." *Geschichte in Wissenschaft und Unterricht* 49 (1998): 664–85.

———. "Weather, Hunger, and Fear: Origins of the European Witch-Hunts in Climate, Society, and Mentality." *German History* 13, no. 1 (1995): 1–27.

———. *Witches and Witch-Hunts: A Global History.* Themes in History. Malden, MA: Polity Press, 2004.

Behringer, Wolfgang. *Witchcraft Persecutions in Bavaria: Popular Magic, Religious Zealotry, and Reason of State in Early Modern Europe.* Translated by J. C. Grayson and David Lederer. Cambridge: Cambridge University Press, 1997.

Ben-Yehuda, Nachman. "The European Witch Craze of the Fourteenth to Seventeenth Centuries: A Sociologist's Perspective." *American Journal of Sociology* 86, no. 1 (1980): 1–31.

———. "The European Witch Craze: Still a Sociologist's Perspective." *American Journal of Sociology* 88, no. 6 (1983): 1275–79.

Berry, Lloyd E., and Robert O. Crummey, eds. *Rude and Barbarous Kingdom: Russia in the Accounts of Sixteenth-Century English Voyagers.* Madison: University of Wisconsin Press, 1968.

Birnbaum, H., and R. Romanchuk. "Kem byil zagodochnyi Daniil Zatochnik? (K voprosu o kul'ture chteniia v Drevnei Rusi)." *TODRL* 50 (1996): 576–602.

Blécourt, Willem de. "The Werewolf, the Witch, and the Warlock: Aspects of Gender in the Early Modern Period." In Rowlands, *Witchcraft and Masculinities in Early Modern Europe*, 191–213.

Boeck, Brian J. "Eyewitness or False Witness: Two Lives of Metropolitan Filipp of Moscow." *Jahrbücher für Geschichte Osteuropas* 55, no. 2 (2007): 161–77.

Bogoiavlenskii, S. K. *Prikaznye sud'i XVII veka.* Moscow: Izd-vo Akademii nauk SSSR, 1946.

Borisov, Vladimir, ed. *Opisanie goroda Shui i ego okrestnostei, s prilozheniem starinnykh aktov.* Moscow: Tip. Ved. Mosk. gorod. Politsii, 1851.

———. *Starinnye akty, sluzhashchie preimushchestvo dopolneniem k opisaniiu g. Shui i ego okrestnostei.* Moscow: Tip. V. Got'e, 1853.

Boydston, Jeanne. "Gender as a Question of Historical Analysis." *Gender & History* 20, no. 3 (2008): 558–83.

Boyer, Paul S, and Stephen Nissenbaum. *Salem Possessed: The Social Origins of Witchcraft.* Cambridge: Harvard University Press, 1974.

Briggs, Robin. "Male Witches in the Duchy of Lorraine." In Rowlands, *Witchcraft and Masculinities in Early Modern Europe*, 31–51.

———. *Witches and Neighbors: The Social and Cultural Context of European Witchcraft.* New York: Viking Penguin, 1996.

Briusova, V. G. *Russkaia zhivopis' 17 veka.* Moscow: Iskusstvo, 1984.

Broedel, Hans Peter. *The Malleus Maleficarum and the Construction of Witchcraft: Theology and Popular Belief.* Manchester: Manchester University Press, 2003.

Brown, Peter. *The Body and Society: Men, Women, and Sexual Renunciation in Early Christianity.* New York: Columbia University Press, 1988.

Brown, Peter B. "Bureaucratic Administration in Seventeenth-Century Russia." In Kotilaine and Poe, *Modernizing Muscovy*, 54–75.

———. "How Muscovy Governed: Seventeenth-Century Russian Central Administration." *Russian History* 36 (2009): 459–529.

———. "Muscovite Government Bureaux." *Russian History* 10 (1983): 269–330.

———. "With All Deliberate Speed: The Officialdom and Departments of the Seventeenth-Century Muscovite Military Chancellery (*Razriad*)." *Russian History* 28, nos. 1–4 (2001): 137–52.

Buganov, V. I. *Moskovskie vosstaniia kontsa XVII veka.* Moscow: Nauka, 1969.

———. *Vosstanie v Moskve 1682 g.: Sbornik dokumentov.* Moscow: Nauka, 1976.

Bulychev, A. A. *Mezhdu sviatymi i demonami: Zametki o posmertnoi sud'be opal'nykh Tsaria Ivana Groznogo.* Moscow: Znak, 2005.

Burbank, Jane, and David L. Ransel, eds. *Imperial Russia: New Histories for the Empire.* Bloomington: Indiana University Press, 1998.

Bushkovitch, Paul. "Cultural Change among the Russian Boyars, 1650–1680: New Sources and Old Problems." *Forschungen zur Osteuropäischen Geschichte* 36 (2000): 91–112.

———. *Peter the Great: The Struggle for Power, 1671–1725.* Cambridge: Cambridge University Press, 2001.

———. *Religion and Society in Russia: The Sixteenth and Seventeenth Centuries.* New York: Oxford University Press, 1992.

Bussow, Conrad. *The Disturbed State of the Russian Realm.* Edited by G. Edward Orchard. Montréal: McGill-Queen's University Press, 1994.

Bynum, Caroline Walker. *The Resurrection of the Body in Western Christianity, 200–1336.* New York: Columbia University Press, 1995.

Caciola, Nancy. *Discerning Spirits: Divine and Demonic Possession in the Middle Ages.* Ithaca: Cornell University Press, 2003.

———. "Mystics, Demoniacs, and the Physiology of Spirit Possession in Medieval Europe." *Comparative Studies in Society and History* 42, no. 2 (2000): 268–306.

Caro Baroja, Julio. *Las brujas y su mundo.* Biblioteca 30 aniversario. Madrid: Alianza, 1997.

Catherine the Great. *Two Comedies by Catherine the Great, Empress of Russia: "Oh, These Times!" and "The Siberian Shaman."* Edited by Lurana Donnels O'Malley. London: Routledge, 1998.

Certeau, Michel de. *The Possession at Loudun.* Translated by Michael B. Smith. Chicago: University of Chicago Press, 2000.

Cervantes, Fernando. *The Devil in the New World: The Impact of Diabolism in New Spain.* New Haven: Yale University Press, 1994.

Challis, Natalie, and Horace W. Dewey. "Divine Folly in Old Kievan Literature: The Tale of Isaac the Cave Dweller." *Slavic and East European Journal* 22, no. 3 (1978): 255–64.

Cherepanova, O. A., ed. *Mifologicheskie rasskazy i legendy russkogo severa.* St. Petersburg: Izd-vo S.-Peterburgskogo universiteta, 1996.

Cherepnin, L. V. "Iz istorii drevnerusskogo koldovstva XVII veka." *Etnografiia,* no. 2 (1929): 86–109.

Cherepnin, L. V., and K. A. Sofronenko, eds. *Pamiatniki russkogo prava (PRP).* 4 vols. Moscow: Gosudarstvennoe izd. iuridicheskoi literatury, 1955.

Chernetsov, A. V. "Dvoeverie: Mirazh ili real'nost'?" *Zhivaia starina* 4 (1994): 16–19.

Chistov, Kirill Vasil'evich. *Russkie narodnye sotsial'no-utopicheskie legendy.* Moscow: Nauka, 1967.

Chrissidis, Nikolaos. "A Jesuit-Aristotle in Seventeenth-Century Russia: Cosmology and the Planetary System in the Slavo-Greco-Latin Academy." In Kotilaine and Poe, *Modernizing Muscovy,* 380–405.

———. "Whoever Does Not Drink to the End, He Wishes Evil: Ritual Drinking and Politics in Early Modern Russia." In Kivelson, Petrone, Kollmann, and Flier, *New Muscovite Cultural History,* 107–24.

Christensen, Benjamin. *Häxan: Witchcraft Through the Ages,* 1922. Film.

Chteniia v Imperatorskom obshchestve istorii i drevnostei rossiiskikh, pri Moskovskom universitete (ChOIDR). 264 vols. Moscow: Universitetskaia tipografiia, 1846–1918.

Clark, Stuart. "The 'Gendering' of Witchcraft in French Demonology: Misogyny or Polarity?" *French History* 5, no. 4 (1991): 426–37.

———. "Protestant Demonology: Sin, Superstition, and Society (c. 1520–c. 1630)." In Ankarloo and Henningsen, *Early Modern European Witchcraft,* 45–82.

———. *Thinking with Demons: The Idea of Witchcraft in Early Modern Europe.* Oxford: Oxford University Press, 1997.

Clay, Catherine B. "Russian Ethnographers in the Service of Empire, 1856–1862." *Slavic Review* 54, no. 1 (1995): 45–61.

Cohn, Norman Rufus Colin. *Europe's Inner Demons: The Demonization of Christians in Medieval Christendom.* Rev. ed. London: Pimlico, 1993.

Collins, Derek. *Magic in the Ancient Greek World.* Malden, Mass.: Blackwell, 2008.

Collins, Samuel. *The Present State of Russia in a Letter to a Friend at London.* London: Printed by John Winter for Dorman Newman, 1671. http://wwwlib.umi.com/eebo/image/52932.

Collis, Robert. "Magic, Medicine, and Authority in Mid-Seventeenth-Century Muscovy: Andreas Engelhardt (d. 1683) and the Role of the Western Physician at the Court of Tsar Aleksei Mikhailovich, 1656–1666." *Russian History* (forthcoming).

Cracraft, James, and Daniel B. Rowland, eds. *Architectures of Russian Identity: 1500 to the Present.* Ithaca: Cornell University Press, 2003.

Cross, Samuel H., and Olgerd P Sherbowitz-Wetzor, eds. *The Russian Primary Chronicle: Laurentian Text.* Cambridge, Mass.: Mediaeval Academy of America, 1953.

Crummey, Robert O. "Ecclesiastical Elites and Popular Belief and Practice in Seventeenth-Century Russia." In Tracy and Ragnow, *Religion and the Early Modern State,* 52–79.

———. "Muscovy and the 'General Crisis of the Seventeenth Century.'" *Journal of Early Modern History* 2, no. 2 (1998): 156–80.

———. "Old Belief as Popular Religion: New Approaches." *Slavic Review* 52, no. 4 (1993): 700–712.

———. "Popular Orthodoxy and Resistance: Guest Editor's Introduction." *Russian Studies in History* 49, no. 3 (Winter 2010–11): 3–7.

———. "Religious Radicalism in Seventeenth-Century Russia: Reexamining the Kapiton Movement." *Forschungen zur Osteuropäischen Geschichte* 46 (1992): 171–86.

Dal', Vladimir Ivanovich. *O poveriiakh, sueveriiakh, i predrassudkakh russkogo naroda: Materialy po russkoi demonologii.* Edited by A. Kharitonov and D. N. Sadovnikov. 1880. Reprint. St. Petersburg: Izd-vo Litera, 1994.

Daly, Mary. *Gyn/Ecology: The Metaethics of Radical Feminism.* Boston: Beacon Press, 1978.

Danner, Mark. *Torture and Truth: America, Abu Ghraib, and the War on Terror.* New York: New York Review Books, 2004.

Davies, Brian L. *State Power and Community in Early Modern Russia: The Case of Kozlov, 1635–1649.* New York: Palgrave Macmillan, 2004.

Davis, Natalie Zemon. *Fiction in the Archives: Pardon Tales and Their Tellers in Sixteenth-Century France.* Stanford: Stanford University Press, 1987.

Debol'skii, N. N. *Istoriia prikaznago stroia Moskovskago gosudarstva.* St. Peterburg: Klimkovskii, 1900.

De Mello e Souza, Laura. *The Devil and the Land of the Holy Cross: Witchcraft, Slavery, and Popular Religion in Colonial Brazil.* Translated by Diane Grosklaus Whitty. Austin: University of Texas Press, 2004.

Demidova, N. F. *Sluzhilaia biurokratiia v Rossii XVII veka i ee rol' v formirovanii absoliutizma.* Moscow: Nauka, 1987.

Demos, John. *The Enemy Within: Two Thousand Years of Witch-Hunting in the Western World.* New York: Viking, 2008.

———. *Entertaining Satan: Witchcraft and the Culture of Early New England.* New York: Oxford University Press, 1982.

Dershowitz, Alan. "Tortured Reasoning." In *Torture: A Collection,* edited by Sanford Levinson, 257–80. Oxford: Oxford University Press, 2004.

Dewey, Horace W. "Judges and the Evidence in Muscovite Law." *Slavonic and East European Review* 36, no. 86 (1957): 189–94.

———. "The White Lake Charter: A Mediaeval Russian Administrative Statute." *Speculum* 32, no. 1 (1957): 74–83.

———. "Trial by Combat in Muscovite Russia." *Oxford Slavonic Papers* 9 (1959): 21–31.

Dewey, Horace W., and Ann M. Kleimola. "Suretyship and Collective Responsibility in Pre-Petrine Russia." *Jahrbücher für Geschichte Osteuropas* 18, no. 3 (1970): 337–54.

Di Simplicio, Oscar. "Giandomenico Fei, the Only Male Witch: A Tuscan or an Italian Anomaly?" In Rowlands, *Witchcraft and Masculinities in Early Modern Europe,* 121–49.

Douglas, Mary. *Purity and Danger: An Analysis of Concepts of Pollution and Taboo.* New York: Praeger, 1966.

Dumschat, Sabine. *Ausländische Mediziner im Moskauer Russland.* Stuttgart: Steiner, 2006.

Dunning, Chester. "Does Jack Goldstone's Model of Early Modern State Crises Apply to Russia?" *Comparative Studies in Society and History* 39, no. 3 (1997): 572–92.

———. "Who Was Tsar Dmitrii?" *Slavic Review* 60, no. 4 (2001): 705–29.

Dunning, Chester S. L., Russell Martin, and Daniel B. Rowland, eds. *Rude and Barbarous Kingdom Revisited: Essays in Russian History and Culture in Honor of Robert O. Crummey.* Bloomington, Ind.: Slavica, 2008.

Durrant, Jonathan. "Why Some Men and Not Others? The Male Witches of Eichstätt." In Rowlands, *Witchcraft and Masculinities in Early Modern Europe,* 100–120.

Dworkin, Andrea. *Woman Hating.* New York: Dutton, 1974.

Dysa, Kateryna. "Orthodox Demonology and the Perception of Witchcraft in Early Modern Ukraine." In *Friars, Nobles and Burghers—Sermons, Images and Prints: Studies of Culture and Society in Early-Modern Europe. In Memoriam István György Tóth,* edited by Jaroslav Miller and László Kontler. Budapest: CEU Press, 2010, 341–60.

Easlea, Brian. *Witch Hunting, Magic, and the New Philosophy: An Introduction to Debates of the Scientific Revolution, 1450–1750.* Atlantic Highlands, N.J: Humanities Press, 1980.

Efimenko, P. I. "Sud nad ved'mami." *Kievskaia starina* 7 (1883): 374–401.

Ehrenreich, Barbara, and Deirdre English. *Witches, Midwives, and Nurses: A History of Women Healers.* Old Westbury, N.Y.: The Feminist Press, 1973.

Eleonskaia, Elena Nikolaevna. *K izucheniiu zagovora i koldovstva v Rossii.* Moscow: Izdanie Kommissii po narodnoi slovesnosti pri Etnograficheskom otdelie I.O.L.E.A.iE, 1917.

———. *Skazka, zagovor, i koldovstvo v Rossii: Sbornik trudov.* Edited by L. N Vinogradova. Traditsionnaia dukhovnaia kul'tura slavian. Moscow: Izd-vo Indrik, 1994.

———. "Zagovor i koldovstvo na Rusi v XVII i XVIII stoletiiakh." *Russkii arkhiv* 4 (1912): 611–24.

Erikson, Kai T. *Wayward Puritans: A Study in the Sociology of Deviance.* New York: Wiley, 1966.

Esipov, G. "Koldovstvo v XVII i XVIII stoletiiakh." *Drevniaia i novaia Rossiia,* no. 4 (1878): 64–70, 157–64.

Evans-Pritchard, E. E. *Witchcraft, Oracles, and Magic among the Azande.* Edited by Eva Gillies. Abridged with an introduction by Eva Gillies. Oxford: Clarendon Press, 1976.

Favret-Saada, Jeanne. *Deadly Words: Witchcraft in the Bocage.* Translated by Catherine Cullen. Cambridge: Cambridge University Press, 1980.

Fennell, John Lister Illingworth. *Ivan the Great of Moscow.* New York: Macmillan, 1962.

Ferber, Sarah. *Demonic Possession and Exorcism in Early Modern France.* London: Routledge, 2004.

———. "Possession and the Sexes." In Rowlands, *Witchcraft and Masculinities in Early Modern Europe,* 214–38.

Figes, Orlando. *A People's Tragedy: The Russian Revolution, 1891–1924.* London: J. Cape, 1996.

Flier, Michael S. "Court Ceremony in an Age of Reform: Patriarch Nikon and the Palm Sunday Ritual." In Baron and Kollmann, *Religion and Culture in Early Modern Russia and Ukraine*, 73–95.

———. "Filling in the Blanks: The Church of the Intercession and the Architectonics of Medieval Muscovite Ritual." *Harvard Ukrainian Studies* 19, nos. 1–4 (1995): 120–37.

———. "Golden Hall Iconography and the Makarian Initiative." In Kivelson, Petrone, Kollmann, and Flier, *New Muscovite Cultural History*, 63–76.

———. "Till the End of Time: The Apocalypse in Russian Historical Experience Before 1500." In Kivelson and Greene, *Orthodox Russia*, 127–58.

Flier, Michael S., and Daniel B. Rowland, eds. *Medieval Russian Culture.* Vol. 2. Berkeley: University of California Press, 1994.

Florovsky, Georges. *Ways of Russian Theology, Pt. 1.* Translated by Robert L. Nichols. Vol. 5 of the *Collected Works of Georges Florovsky.* Belmont, Mass.: Nordland, 1979.

Fögen, Marie Theres. "Balsamon on Magic: From Roman Secular Law to Byzantine Canon Law." In Maguire, *Byzantine Magic*, 99–115.

Forrester, Sibelan. "Russian Village Magic in the Late Soviet Period: One Woman's Repertoire of Zagovory." *Russian History* (forthcoming).

Francfort, Henri Paul, and Roberte Hamayon, eds. *The Concept of Shamanism: Uses and Abuses*. Budapest: Akadémiai Kiadó, 2001.

Frank, Stephen. *Crime, Cultural Conflict, and Justice in Rural Russia, 1856–1914.* Berkeley: University of California Press, 1999.

Franklin, Simon. "Mapping the Graphosphere Cultures of Writing in Early Nineteenth-Century Russia (and Before)." *Kritika—Explorations in Russian and Eurasian History* 12, no. 3 (2011): 531–60.

———. *Writing, Society, and Culture in Early Rus', c. 950–1300.* Cambridge: Cambridge University Press, 2002.

Fuhrmann, Joseph T. *Tsar Alexis: His Reign and His Russia.* Gulf Breeze, Flor.: Academic International Press, 1981.

Gaskill, Malcolm. "Masculinity and Witchcraft in Seventeenth-Century England." In Rowlands, *Witchcraft and Masculinities in Early Modern Europe*, 171–90.

Gaster, Theodore H. "Amulets and Talismans." In *Hidden Truths: Magic, Alchemy, and the Occult*, edited by Lawrence Eugene Sullivan, 145–50. New York: Macmillan, 1989.

Gentes, Andrew Armand. *Exile to Siberia, 1590–1822.* New York: Palgrave Macmillan, 2008.

Geschiere, Peter. *The Modernity of Witchcraft: Politics and the Occult in Postcolonial Africa.* Translated by Janet Roitman. Charlottesville: University Press of Virginia, 1997.

Gibson, Marion, ed. *Early Modern Witches: Witchcraft Cases in Contemporary Writing.* London: Routledge, 2000.

Ginzburg, Carlo. *Ecstasies: Deciphering the Witches' Sabbath*. Translated by Raymond Rosenthal. New York: Pantheon Books, 1991.

———. *The Night Battles: Witchcraft and Agrarian Cults in the Sixteenth and Seventeenth Centuries*. Translated by Jonn and Anne Tedeschi. New York: Penguin Books, 1985.

Girard, René. *The Scapegoat*. Baltimore: Johns Hopkins University Press, 1986.

Godbeer, Richard. *The Devil's Dominion: Magic and Religion in Early New England*. Cambridge: Cambridge University Press, 1992.

Goldfrank, David M. "Burn, Baby, Burn: Popular Culture and Heresy in Late Medieval Russia." *Journal of Popular Culture* 31, no. 4 (1998): 17–32.

Goldsmith, Elizabeth C. *Publishing Women's Life Stories in France, 1647–1720: From Voice to Print*. Aldershot: Ashgate, 2001.

Goldstone, Jack A. *Revolution and Rebellion in the Early Modern World*. Berkeley: University of California Press, 1991.

Golombiovskii, A. A. "Stoly razriadnogo prikaza v 1668–1670 gg." *Zhurnal ministerstva narodnogo prosveshcheniia* 270 (August 1890): 1–17.

Golombiovskii, A. A., and N. N. Ardashev. "Prikaznye, zemskie, tamozhnye, gubnye, sudovye izby Moskovskogo gosudarstva: Obzor dokumentov XVI–XVII vekakh v delakh XVIII veka, peredannykh v Moskovskii arkhiv Ministerstva iustitsii iz uprazdnennykh v 1864 g. uchrezhdenii." *Zapiski Moskovskogo Arkheologicheskogo Instituta* 4 (1909): 1–86.

Gonneau, Pierre. "Le Faust Russe ou 'L'histoire de Savva Grudcyn.'" *Journal des savants* 2, no. 1 (2004): 423–84.

Goodare, Julian. "Men and the Witch-Hunt in Scotland." In Rowlands, *Witchcraft and Masculinities in Early Modern Europe*, 149–70.

Greene, Robert H. *Bodies Like Bright Stars: Saints and Relics in Orthodox Russia*. DeKalb: Northern Illinois University Press, 2010.

Gurliand, I. Ia. *Prikaz velikago gosudaria tainykh del*. Iaroslavl': Tipografiia gubernskago pravleniia, 1902.

Hagen, Rune Blix. "Female Witches and Sami Sorcerers in the Witch Trials of Arctic Norway (1593–1695)." *Arv: Nordic Yearbook of Folklore* 62 (2006): 123–42.

———. *The Shaman of Alta: The 1627 Witch Trial of Quiwe Baarsen*. Tromsø: R. Hagen, 2002.

———. "The Witch-Hunt in Early Modern Finnmark." *Acta borealia* 16, no. 1 (1999): 43–62.

Hall, David D., ed. "A Servant Possessed (1671–1672)." In *Witch-Hunting in Seventeenth-Century New England: A Documentary History, 1638–1692*, 197–212. Boston: Northeastern University Press, 1991.

Hallett, Nicky. *Witchcraft, Exorcism and the Politics of Possession in a Seventeenth-century Convent: "How Sister Ursula Was Once Bewiched and Sister Margaret Twice,"* Burlington: Ashgate, 2007.

Halperin, Charles J. "The Culture of Ivan IV's Court: The Religious Beliefs of Bureaucrats." In Kivelson, Petrone, Kollmann, and Flier, *New Muscovite Cultural History*, 93–106.

———. *Russia and the Golden Horde: The Mongol Impact on Medieval Russian History.* Bloomington: Indiana University Press, 1985.

Hanson, Elizabeth. "Torture and Truth in Renaissance England." *Representations*, no. 34 (1991): 53–84.

Harley, David. "Historians as Demonologists: The Myth of the Midwife-Witch." *Social History of Medicine* 3, no. 1 (1990): 1–26.

Hellbeck, Jochen. *Revolution on My Mind: Writing a Diary Under Stalin.* Cambridge, MA: Harvard University Press, 2006.

Hellie, Richard. "Commentary [*Ulozhenie*] on Chapters 3 through 6." *Russian History* 17 (1990): 65–78.

———. "The Great Paradox of the Seventeenth Century: The Stratification of Muscovite Society and the 'Individualization' of Its High Culture, Especially Literature." In *O Rus!: Studia litteraria slavica in honorem Hugh McLean*, edited by Simon Karlinsky, James L. Rice, and Barry P. Scherr, 116–28. Oakland, Calif.: Berkeley Slavic Specialties, 1995.

———. "The Law." In Perrie, *From Early Rus' to 1689*, 360–86.

———. *Slavery in Russia, 1450–1725.* Chicago: University of Chicago Press, 1982.

———. "The Stratification of Muscovite Society: The Townsmen." *Russian History* 5, nos. 1–2 (1978): 119–75.

———. "The Structure of Modern Russian History: Toward a Dynamic Model." *Russian History* 4, nos. 1–2 (1977): 1–22.

———. "*Ulozhenie* Commentary: Preamble and Chapters 1–2." *Russian History* 15 (1988): 155–224.

———, ed. *The Muscovite Law Code (Ulozhenie) of 1649.* Vol. 3 of *The Laws of Russia.* Irvine, Calif.: C. Schlacks Jr., 1988.

Henningsen, Gustav. *The Witches' Advocate: Basque Witchcraft and the Spanish Inquisition, 1609–1614.* Reno: University of Nevada Press, 1980.

Henningsen, Gustav, John A Tedeschi, and Charles Amiel, eds. *The Inquisition in Early Modern Europe: Studies on Sources and Methods.* Dekalb: Northern Illinois University Press, 1986.

Herberstein, Sigmund. *Description of Moscow and Muscovy, 1557.* Edited by Bertold Picard. London: Dent, 1969.

Hester, Marianne. *Lewd Women and Wicked Witches: A Study of the Dynamics of Male Domination.* New York : Routledge, 1992.

Heuser, Peter Arnold. "Die kurkölnischen Hexenprozesse des 16. und 17. Jahrhunderts in geschlechtergeschichtlicher Perspektive." In *Geschlecht, Magie und Hexenverfolgung,* edited by Ingrid Ahrendt-Schulte, 133–74. *Hexenforschung* 7. Bielefeld: Verlag für Regionalgeschichte, 2002.

Hobsbawm, Eric. "Discussion of H. R. Trevor-Roper: 'The General Crisis of the Seventeenth Century,' II." *Past & Present* 18, no. 1 (1960): 12–14.

———. "The General Crisis of the European Economy in the Seventeenth Century." *Past & Present* 5, no. 1 (1954): 33–53.

Hoffer, Peter Charles. *The Salem Witchcraft Trials: A Legal History*. Lawrence: University Press of Kansas, 1997.

Holmes, Clive. "Women: Witches and Witnesses." In *The Witchcraft Reader*, edited by Darren Oldridge, 303–22. London: Routledge, 2001.

Hughes, Lindsey. *Russia in the Age of Peter the Great*. New Haven: Yale University Press, 1998.

Hults, Linda C. *The Witch as Muse: Art, Gender, and Power in Early Modern Europe*. Philadelphia: University of Pennsylvania Press, 2011.

Ippolitova, Aleksandra Borisovna. *Russkie rukopisnye travniki XVII–XVIII vekov: Issledovanie fol'klora i etnobotaniki*. Traditsionnaia dukhovnaia kul'tura slavian. Sovremennye issledovaniia. Moscow: Indrik, 2008.

Iurganov, A. L. *Kategorii russkoi srednevekovoi kul'tury*. Moscow: In-t "Otkrytoe ob-vo," 1998.

Ivanits, Linda J. *Russian Folk Belief*. Armonk, N.Y.: M. E. Sharpe, 1989.

"Iz Khronografa 1617 goda." In *PLDR. Konets XVI-nachala XVII vekov*, 318–57.

Johansen, Jens Christian V. "Denmark: The Sociology of Accusations." In Ankarloo and Henningsen, *Early Modern European Witchcraft*, 339–65.

Johns, Andreas. *Baba Iaga: The Ambiguous Mother and Witch of the Russian Folktale*. New York: Peter Lang, 2004.

———. "Baba Iaga and the Russian Mother." *Slavic and East European Journal* 42, no. 1 (1998): 21–36.

Johnson, Paul Christopher. "An Atlantic Genealogy of 'Spirit Possession.'" *Comparative Studies in Society and History* 53, no. 2 (2011): 393–425.

"Judgment on the Witch Walpurga Hausmännin." In *The Fugger News-letters: Being a Selection of Letters from the Unpublished Correspondents of the House of Fugger during the Years 1568–1605*, edited by Victor von Klarwill. Translated by Pauline de Chary, 107–14. New York: G. P. Putnam's Sons, 1925.

Juster, Susan. "Demogogues or Mystagogues?: Gender and the Language of Prophecy in the Age of Democratic Revolutions." *American Historical Review* 104, no. 5 (1999): 1560–81.

———. *Disorderly Women: Sexual Politics and Evangelicalism in Revolutionary New England*. Ithaca: Cornell University Press, 1994.

Kabakova, G. I., and Francis Conte, eds. *Telo v russkoi kul'ture: Sbornik statei*. Moscow: Novoe literaturnoe obozrenie, 2005.

Kaiser, Daniel H. "Beyond the Pages of the *Stepennaia Kniga*: Icon Veneration in 16th-Century Muscovy." In Lenhoff and Kleimola, The Book of Royal Degrees *and the Genesis of Russian Historical Consciousness*, 287–301.

———. "Church Control Over Marriage in Seventeenth-Century Russia." *Russian Review* 65 (2006): 567–85.

———. "Discovering Individualism among the Deceased: Gravestones in Early Modern Russia." In Kotilaine and Poe, *Modernizing Muscovy*, 433–60.

———. *The Growth of the Law in Medieval Russia.* Princeton: Princeton University Press, 1980.

———. "'He Said, She Said': Rape and Gender Discourse in Early Modern Russia." *Kritika: Explorations in Russian and Eurasian History* 3, no. 2 (2002): 197–216.

———. "Icons and Private Devotion among Eighteenth-Century Moscow Townsfolk." *Journal of Social History* 45, no. 1 (2011): 125–47.

———. "Quotidian Orthodoxy: Domestic Life in Early Modern Russia." In Kivelson and Greene, *Orthodox Russia*, 179–92.

Kamensky, Jane. *Governing the Tongue: The Politics of Speech in Early New England.* New York: Oxford University Press, 1997.

Kamil, Neil. *Fortress of the Soul: Violence, Metaphysics, and Material Life in the Huguenots' New World, 1517–1751.* Baltimore: Johns Hopkins University Press, 2005.

Kantorovich, Ia. A. *Srednevekovye protsessy o ved'makh: Reprintnoe vosproizvedenie izdaniia 1899 goda.* Moscow: Kniga, 1990.

Karlsen, Carol F. *The Devil in the Shape of a Woman: Witchcraft in Colonial New England.* New York: Norton, 1987.

Kazakova, N. A., and Ia. S Lur'e. *Antifeodal'nye ereticheskie dvizheniia na Rusi XIV–nachala XVI veka.* Moscow: Izd-vo Akademii nauk SSSR, 1955.

Keane, Webb. "Ecrire l'au-delà: les pouvoirs de la synethésie sémiotique." *Intellectica* 3, no. 50 (2008): 73–91.

———. "Religious Language." *Annual Review of Anthropology* 26 (1997): 47–71.

Keenan, Edward L. *The Kurbskii-Groznyi Apocrypha: The Seventeenth-Century Genesis of the "Correspondence" Attributed to Prince A. M. Kurbskii and Tsar Ivan IV.* Cambridge: Harvard University Press, 1971.

———. "Putting Kurbskij in His Place, or: Observations and Suggestions Concerning the Place of the History of the Grand Prince of Muscovy in the History of Muscovite Literary Culture." *Forschungen zur Osteuropäischen Geschichte* 24 (1978): 131–61.

Kelly, Raymond C. "Witchcraft and Sexual Relations: An Exploration in the Social and Semantic Implications of the Structure of Belief." In *Man and Woman in the New Guinea Highlands*, edited by Paula Brown, Georgeda Buchbinder, and David Maybury-Lewis, 36–53. Washington: American Anthropological Association, 1976.

Kenses, James E. "Some Unexplored Relationships of Essex County Witchcraft and the Indian Wars of 1675 and 1689." *Essex Institute Historical Collections* 120 (1984): 179–212.

Kent, E. J. "Masculinity and Male Witches in Old and New England, 1593–1680." *History Workshop Journal* 60, no. 1 (2005): 69–92.

Kharuzin, N. "K voprosu o bor'be Moskovskogo pravitel'stva s narodnymi iazycheskimi obriadami i sueveriiami v polovine XVII veka." *Etnograficheskoe obozrenie*, no. 1 (1897): 143–51.

Kieckhefer, Richard. *European Witch Trials: Their Foundations in Popular and Learned Culture, 1300–1500*. Berkeley: University of California Press, 1976.

———. *Magic in the Middle Ages*. Cambridge Medieval Textbooks. Cambridge: Cambridge University Press, 1990.

———. "Mythologies of Witchcraft in the Fifteenth Century." *Magic, Ritual, and Witchcraft* 1, no. 1 (2006): 79–108.

———. "The Specific Rationality of Medieval Magic." *American Historical Review* 99, no. 3 (1994): 813–36.

Kivelson, Valerie A. *Autocracy in the Provinces: The Muscovite Gentry and Political Culture in the Seventeenth Century*. Stanford: Stanford University Press, 1996.

———. "Bitter Slavery and Pious Servitude: Freedom and Its Critics in Muscovite Russia." *Forschungen zur Osteuropäischen Geschichte* 58 (2001): 109–19.

———. *Cartographies of Tsardom: The Land and Its Meanings in Seventeenth-Century Russia*. Ithaca: Cornell University Press, 2006.

———. "Caught in the Act: An Illustration of Erotic Magic at Work." In *Dubitando: Studies in History and Culture in Honor of Donald Ostrowski*, edited by Brian Boeck, Russell E. Martin, and Daniel Rowland, 1–17. Bloomington, Ind.: Slavica Publishers, 2012.

———. "Muscovite 'Citizenship': Rights Without Freedom." *Journal of Modern History* 74, no. 3 (2002): 465–89.

———. "What Was *Chernoknizhestvo*?: Black Books and Foreign Writings in Muscovite Magic." In Dunning, Martin, and Rowland, *Rude and Barbarous Kingdom Revisited*, 1–15.

———. "Witchcraft Trials in Russia: History and Historiography." In *Oxford Handbook of Witchcraft*, edited by Brian P. Levack, 355–74. Oxford: Oxford University Press, 2013.

Kivelson, Valerie A., and Robert H. Greene, eds. *Orthodox Russia: Belief and Practice under the Tsars*. University Park: The Pennsylvania State University Press, 2003.

Kivelson, Valerie A., and Joan Neuberger, eds. *Picturing Russia: Explorations in Visual Culture*. New Haven: Yale University Press, 2008.

Kivelson, Valerie A., Karen Petrone, Nancy Shields Kollmann, and Michael S. Flier, eds. *The New Muscovite Cultural History: A Collection in Honor of Daniel B. Rowland.* Bloomington, Ind.: Slavica Publishers, 2009.

Kivelson, Valerie A., and Jonathan Shaheen. "Prosaic Witchcraft and Semiotic Totalitarianism: Muscovite Magic Reconsidered." *Slavic Review* 70, no. 1 (2011): 23–44.

Kizenko, Nadieszda. "Review: *Letters from Heaven: Popular Religion in Russia and Ukraine,* and *Ispoved' v Rossii v XIV–XIX vekakh: Issledovanie i teksty.*" *Kritika: Explorations in Russian and Eurasian History* 9, no. 3 (2008): 641–54.

Kleimola, Ann M. "The Duty to Denounce in Muscovite Russia." *Slavic Review* 31, no. 4 (1972): 759–79.

———. "Justice in Medieval Russia: Muscovite Judgment Charters (*Pravye Gramoty*) of the Fifteenth and Sixteenth Centuries." *Transactions of the American Philosophical Society* 65, no. 6. New Series (1975): 1–93.

Kliaus, V. L. *Siuzhetika zagovornykh tekstov slavian v sravnitel'nom izuchenii: K postanovke problemy.* Moscow: IMLI RAN "Nasledie," 2000.

———. *Ukazatel' siuzhetov i siuzhetnykh situatsii zagovornykh tekstov vostochnykh i iuzhnykh slavian.* Moscow: Nasledie, 1997.

Klibanov, A. I. *Dukhovnaia kul'tura srednevekovoi Rusi.* Moscow: Aspekt Press, 1996.

———, ed. *Kritika religioznogo sektantstva (Opyt izucheniia religioznogo sektantstva v 20-kh–nachale 30-kh godov).* Nauchno-ateisticheskaia biblioteka. Moscow: Izd-vo Mysl', 1974.

Kloss, Boris Mikhailovich. *Nikonovskii svod i russkie letopisi XVI–XVII vekov.* Moscow: Nauka, 1980.

Knight, Nathaniel. "Science, Empire, and Nationality: Ethnography in the Russian Geographical Society, 1845–1855." In Burbank and Ransel, *Imperial Russia,* 108–42.

Kollmann, Jack. "The Moscow *Stoglav* ('Hundred Chapters') Church Council of 1551." PhD diss., University of Michigan, 1978.

Kollmann, Nancy Shields. *By Honor Bound: State and Society in Early Modern Russia.* Ithaca: Cornell University Press, 1999.

———. *Crime and Punishment in Early Modern Russia.* Cambridge University Press, 2012.

———. "The Extremes of Patriarchy: Spousal Abuse and Murder in Early Modern Russia." *Russian History* 25, nos. 1–4 (1998): 133–40.

———. "Judicial Autonomy in the Criminal Law: Beloozero and Arzamas." In *Die Geschichte Russlands im 16. und 17. Jahrhundert: Aus der Perspektive seiner Regionen,* edited by Andreas Kappeler, 252–68. Forschungen zur Osteuropäischen Geschichte. Wiesbaden: Harrassowitz, 2004.

———. *Kinship and Politics: The Making of the Muscovite Political System, 1345–1547.* Stanford: Stanford University Press, 1987.

———. "Law and Society." In Perrie, *From Early Rus'to 1689*, 559–78.

———. "Lynchings and Legality in Early Modern Russia." *Forschungen zur Osteuropäischen Geschichte* 56 (2002): 91–96.

———. "Marking the Body in Early Modern Judicial Punishment." *Harvard Ukrainian Studies* 28, nos. 1–4 (2006): 557–65.

———. "The Quality of Mercy in Early Modern Legal Practice." *Kritika—Explorations in Russian and Eurasian History* 7, no. 1 (2006): 5–22.

———. "Society, Identity, and Modernity in Seventeenth-Century Russia." In Kotilaine and Poe, *Modernizing Muscovy*, 417–32.

———. "Torture in Early Modern Russia." In Kivelson, Petrone, Kollmann, and Flier, *New Muscovite Cultural History*, 159–70.

Konig, David Thomas. *Law and Society in Puritan Massachusetts: Essex County, 1629–1692*. Chapel Hill: University of North Carolina Press, 1979.

Kormina, Zh. V., A. A. Panchenko, and S. A. Shtyrkov, eds. *Sny Bogoroditsy: Issledovaniia po antropologii religii*. St. Petersburg: Evropeiskii universitet v Sankt-Peterburge, 2006.

Korogodina, M. V. *Ispoved' v Rossii v xiv–xix vekakh: Issledovanie i teksty*. St. Petersburg: Dmitrii Bulanin, 2006.

Kors, Alan Charles, and Edward Peters, eds. *Witchcraft in Europe, 1100–1700: A Documentary History*. Philadelphia: University of Pennsylvania Press, 1972.

Kostina, A. V., and Liubov' Mironikhina, eds. *Traditsionnoe russkoe zastol'e: Sbornik statei*. Moscow: Gos. respublikanskii tsentr russkogo fol'klora, 2008.

Kostsova, A. S., A. G. Pobedinskaia, and M. B. Piotrovskii, eds. *Russkie zhitiinye ikony: XVI–nachala XX veka*. St. Petersburg: Slaviia, 1999.

Kotilaine, Jarmo, and Marshall Poe, eds. *Modernizing Muscovy: Reform and Social Change in Seventeenth-Century Russia*. London: Routledge, 2004.

Kotkov, Sergei Ivanovich, ed. *Pamiatniki delovoi pis'mennosti XVII veka: Vladimirskii krai*. Moscow: Nauka, 1984.

Kotkov, Sergei Ivanovich, A. S. Oreshnikov, and I. S. Filippova, eds. *Moskovskaia delovaia i bytovaia pis'mennost' XVII veka*. Moscow: Nauka, 1968.

Kotkov, Sergei Ivanovich, and N. P. Pankratova, eds. *Istoriia russkogo iazyka: Pamiatniki XI–XVIII vekakh*. Moscow: AN SSSR, 1982.

Kotoshikhin, Grigorii. *O Rossii v tsarstvovanie Alekseia Mikhailovicha. Sovremennoe sochinenie Grigoriia Kotoshikhina*, 2nd ed. St. Petersburg: Tip. Eduarda Pratsa, 1859.

Kozlov, Iu. A. "Chukhlomskoe delo 1635–1636 gg. 'pushchago veduna' Mitroshka Khromogo." In *Na pereskrestkakh epokh i traditsii*, vol. 5 of *Problemy istorii Rossii*, edited by A. T. Shashkov, 445–62. Ekaterinburg: Volot, 2003.

———. "Fragment koldovskogo dela XVII veka s tsitatami iz Kormchei knigi 1653 g." In *Novgorodskaia Rus': Istoricheskoe prostranstvo i kul'turnoe nasledie*, vol. 3 of *Problemy istorii Rossii*, edited by A. T. Shashkov, Ekaterinburg: Volot, 2000. www.vostlit.info/Texts/Dokumenty/Russ/XVII/1660–1680/Kold_delo_1669/text.htm.

———. "'I toiu de vorozhboiu ona, Dar'itsa, vorozhila mnogoe vremia . . .' (Odin iz moskovskikh koldovskikh protsessov XVII v.)." In *Opyt gosudarstvennogo stroitel'stva XV-XX vv.: sbornik nauchnykh trudov*, vol. 2 of *Problemy istorii Rossii*, edited by A. T. Shashkov, 280–300. Ekaterinburg: Ural'skii gos. universitet, 1998. http://elar.urfu.ru/bitstream/1234.56789/2752/1/pristr-02-18.pdf.

Kozlov, O. F. "Prikaz tainykh gosudarevykh del." *Voprosy istorii* (1982): 106–12.

Kramer, Heinrich, and James Sprenger. *Malleus Maleficarum*. Edited by Montague Summers. Lawrence, Kans.: Digireads.com Publishing, 2010.

Kurbskii, Andrei Mikhailovich. *The Correspondence between Prince A. M. Kurbsky and Tsar Ivan IV of Russia, 1564–1579*. Edited by J. L. I. Fennell. Cambridge: University Press, 1955.

———. *Prince A. M. Kurbsky's History of Ivan IV*. Edited by John Lister Illingworth Fennell. Cambridge: University Press, 1965.

Kuznetsova, O. B., and A. V. Fedorchuk, eds. *Ikony Iaroslavlia 16–19 vekov: Katalog vystavki Iaroslavskogo khudozhestvennogo muzeia*. Moscow: Severnyi palomnik, 2002.

Labouvie, Eva. "Männer im Hexenprozess: Zur Sozialanthropologie eines, 'männlichen' Verständnisses von Magie und Hexerei." *Geschichte und Gesellschaft* 16, no. 1 (1990): 56–78.

Larner, Christina. *Enemies of God: The Witch-Hunt in Scotland*. London: Chatto & Windus, 1981.

———. *Witchcraft and Religion: The Politics of Popular Belief*. New York: Blackwell, 1984.

Lavrov, A. S. "La Hovanščina et la crise financière de la Russie Moscovite." *Cahiers du monde russe* 50, nos. 2–3 (2009): 533–55.

———. *Koldovstvo i religiia v Rossii, 1700–1740 gg*. Moscow: Drevlekhranilishche, 2000.

———. *Regentstvo tsarevny Sof'i Alekseevny: Sluzhiloe obshchestvo i bor'ba za vlast' v verkhakh russkogo gosudarstva v 1682–1689 gg*. Moscow: Arkheograficheskii tsentr, 1999.

Lenhoff, Gail, and Ann Kleimola, eds. The Book of Royal Degrees *and the Genesis of Russian Historical Consciousness*. Bloomington: Slavica, 2011.

LeRoy Ladurie, Emmanuel. "The Aiguillette: Castration by Magic." In *The Mind and Method of the Historian*, translated by Sian and Ben Reynolds, 64–95. Brighton, Sussex: Harvester Press, 1981.

Levack, Brian P. "Crime and the Law." In Barry and Davies, *Palgrave Advances in Witchcraft Historiography*, 293–310.

———. "State Building and Witch Hunting in Early Modern Europe." In Barry, Hester, and Roberts, *Witchcraft in Early Modern Europe*, 96–115.

———. *The Witch-Hunt in Early Modern Europe*. 2nd ed. New York: Longman/Pearson, 1995.

Levin, Eve. "Childbirth in Pre-Petrine Russia: Canon Law and Popular Traditions." In *Russia's Women: Accommodation, Resistance, Transformation*, edited by Barbara Evans

Clements, Barbara Alpern Engel, Christine D. Worobec, Berkeley: University of California Press, 1991, 44–59.

———. "Dvoeverie and Popular Religion." In *Seeking God: The Recovery of Religious Identity in Orthodox Russia, Ukraine, and Georgia*, edited by Stephen K. Batalden, 31–52. DeKalb: Northern Illinois University Press, 1993.

———. "False Miracles and Unattested Dead Bodies: Investigations into Popular Cults in Early Modern Russia." In Tracy and Ragnow, *Religion and the Early Modern State*, 253–83.

———. "From Corpse to Cult in Early Moden Russia." In Kivelson and Greene, *Orthodox Russia*, 81–103.

———. "Healers and Witches in Early Modern Russia." In *Saluting Aron Gurevich: Essays in History, Literature, and Other Related Subjects*, edited by Yelena Mazour-Matusevich and Alexandra Shecket Korros. Leiden: Brill, 2010.

———. "Infanticide in Pre-Petrine Russia." *Jahrbücher für Geschichte Osteuropas* 34, no. 2 (1986): 215–24.

———. "A Kansas Apocalypse: A Russian Manuscript and Its Vision of the Last Days." In Kivelson, Petrone, Kollmann, and Flier, *New Muscovite Cultural History*, 187–206.

———. *Sex and Society in the World of the Orthodox Slavs, 900–1700*. Ithaca: Cornell University Press, 1989.

———. "Sexual Vocabulary in Medieval Russia." In *Sexuality and the Body in Russian Culture*, edited by Jane T. Costlow, Stephanie Sandler, and Judith Vowles, 41–52. Stanford: Stanford University Press, 1993.

———. "Supplicatory Prayers as a Source for Popular Religious Culture in Muscovite Russia." In Baron and Kollmann, *Religion and Culture in Early Modern Russia and Ukraine*, 96–114.

Levine, Lawrence W. *Black Culture and Black Consciousness: Afro-American Folk Thought from Slavery to Freedom*. New York: Oxford University Press, 1977.

Levitt, Marcus C., and A. L. Toporkov, eds. *Eros and Pornography in Russian Culture*. Moscow: Ladomir, 1999.

Lewis, I. M. "A Structural Approach to Witchcraft and Spirit-Possession." In *Witchcraft Confessions and Accusations*, edited by Mary Douglas and E. E. Evans-Pritchard, 293–310. London: Tavistock, 1970.

Likhachev, Dmitrii Sergeevich. "Daniil Zatochnik." In *SKKDR*, vol. 1, *XI–pervaia polovina XIV veka*, edited by D. S. Likhachev, 112–15. Leningrad: Nauka, 1987.

———. *Slovar' knizhnikov i knizhnosti Drevnei Rusi (SKKDR)*. 3 in 8 parts vols. Leningrad: "Nauka," Leningradskoe otd-nie, 1987.

Likhachev, Dmitrii Sergeevich, and Lev Aleksandrovich Dmitriev, eds. *Pamiatniki literatury Drevnei Rusi (PLDR)*. 12 vols. Moscow: Khudozh. literatura, 1978–1994.

Lindquist, Galina. *Conjuring Hope: Magic and Healing in Contemporary Russia*. New York: Berghahn Books, 2006.

Longworth, Philip. *Alexis, Tsar of All the Russias.* London: Secker & Warburg, 1984.

Lotman, Iu. M., and Uspenskij, B.A. "The Role of Dual Models in the Dynamics of Russian Culture (Up to the End of the Eighteenth Century)." In *The Semiotics of Russian Culture,* edited by Ann Shukman, Iu. M. Lotman, and B. A. Uspenskij, 3–35. Ann Arbor: Michigan Slavic Publications, 1984.

Luck, Georg, ed. *Arcana Mundi: Magic and the Occult in the Greek and Roman Worlds: A Collection of Ancient Texts.* Baltimore: Johns Hopkins University Press, 1985.

Luehrmann, Sonja. "The Magic of Others: Mari Witchcraft Reputations and Interethnic Relations in the Volga Region." *Russian History/Histoire Russe* (forthcoming).

Lukin, P.V. *Narodnye predstavleniia o gosudarstvennoi vlasti v Rossii XVII veka.* Moscow: Nauka, 2000.

Lur'e, Ia. S. "Peresvetov, Ivan Semenovich." In *SKKDR,* vol. 2, *Vtoraia polovina XIV–XVI vekov,* 112–15. Leningrad: Nauka, 1987.

MacDonald, Michael. *Mystical Bedlam: Madness, Anxiety, and Healing in Seventeenth-century England.* Cambridge: Cambridge University Press, 1981.

———, ed. *Witchcraft and Hysteria in Elizabethan England: Edward Jorden and the Mary Glover Case.* London: Routledge, 1991.

Macfarlane, Alan. *Witchcraft in Tudor and Stuart England: A Regional and Comparative Study.* London: Routledge & Kegan Paul, 1970.

Machielsen, Jan. "Thinking with Montaigne: Evidence, Scepticism, and Meaning in Early Modern Demonology." *French History* 25, no. 4 (2011): 427–52.

Maclean, Ian. *The Renaissance Notion of Woman: A Study in the Fortunes of Scholasticism and Medical Science in European Intellectual Life.* Cambridge: Cambridge University Press, 1980.

Maguire, Henry, ed. *Byzantine Magic.* Washington, D.C.: Dumbarton Oaks Research Library and Collection, 1995.

———. *The Icons of Their Bodies: Saints and Their Images in Byzantium.* Princeton: Princeton University Press, 1996.

Maikov, L. *Velikorusskie zaklinaniia: Sbornik L. N. Maikova.* 1869. Reprint, edited by A. K. Baiburin. St. Petersburg: Izd-vo Evropeiskogo doma, 1994.

Maksimov, S.V. *Nechistaia, nevedomaia, i krestnaia sila: Sbornik.* 1903. Reprint, Moscow: EKSMO, 2007.

Margeret, Jacques. *The Russian Empire and Grand Duchy of Muscovy: A Seventeenth-Century French Account.* Edited by Chester S. L. Dunning. Pittsburgh: University of Pittsburgh Press, 1983.

Marker, Gary. "A Saint's Intimate Life: The Diariusz of Dimitrii Rostovskii." In *Everyday Life in Russian History: Quotidian Studies in Honor of Daniel Kaiser,* edited by Gary Marker, Marshall Poe, Susan Zayer Rupp, and Joan Neuberger, 127–44. Bloomington, Ind.: Slavica, 2010.

———. *Imperial Saint: The Cult of St. Catherine and the Dawn of Female Rule in Russia.* DeKalb: Northern Illinois University Press, 2007.

———. "Literacy and Literacy Texts in Muscovy: A Reconsideration." *Slavic Review* 49, no. 1 (1990): 74–89.

Martin, Russell E. *A Bride for the Tsar: Bride-Shows and Marriage Politics in Early Modern Russia.* DeKalb: Northern Illinois University Press, 2012.

Mary, Mother, and Archimandrite Kallistos Ware, trans. *The Lenten Triodion.* London: Faber and Faber, 1984.

Massa, Isaac. *A Short History of the Beginnings and Origins of These Present Wars in Moscow under the Reign of Various Sovereigns down to the Year 1610.* Translated by G. Edward Orchard. Toronto: University of Toronto Press, 1982.

Mathiesen, Robert. "Magic in Slavia Orthodoxa: The Written Tradition." In Maguire, *Byzantine Magic*, 155–77.

Mayer, Jane. "Annals of Justice: Outsourcing Torture: The Secret History of America's 'Extraordinary Rendition' Program." *The New Yorker*, February 14, 2005. http://www.newyorker.com/archive/2005/02/14/050214fa_fact6.

Meehan, Brenda. *Holy Women of Russia: The Lives of Five Orthodox Women Offer Spiritual Guidance for Today.* San Francisco: HarperSanFrancisco, 1993.

Mel'nik, A. G., ed. *Ikonografiia rostovskikh sviatykh: Katalog vystavki.* Rostov: Gos. muzei-zapovednik "Rostovskii Kreml'," 1998.

Mel'nikova, Ekaterina. "Otchityvanie besnovatykh: Praktiki i diskursy." *Antropologicheskii Forum*, no. 4 (2006): 220–63. http://anthropologie.kunstkamera.ru/files/pdf/004/04_08_melnikova.pdf.

Merback, Mitchell B. *The Thief, the Cross, and the Wheel: Pain and the Spectacle of Punishment in Medieval and Renaissance Europe.* Chicago: University of Chicago Press, 1999.

Meyendorff, John. *Byzantine Theology: Historical Trends and Doctrinal Themes.* New York: Fordham University Press, 1974.

Michelet, Jules. *La Sorcière: The Witch of the Middle Ages.* Translated by Lionel J. Trotter. London: Simpkin, Marshall, 1863.

Michell, Robert, and Nevill Forbes, trans. *The Chronicle of Novgorod, 1016–1471.* New York: AMS Press, 1970.

Michels, Georg Bernhard. *At War with the Church: Religious Dissent in Seventeenth-Century Russia.* Stanford: Stanford University Press, 1999.

Midelfort, H. C. Erik. *Witch Hunting in Southwestern Germany, 1562–1684: The Social and Intellectual Foundations.* Stanford: Stanford University Press, 1972.

Miller, Seumas. "Torture." In *The Stanford Encyclopedia of Philosophy*, edited by Edward N. Zalta, Summer 2011 edition. http://plato.stanford.edu/archives/sum2011/entries/torture/.

Mitchell, Stephen A. *Witchcraft and Magic in the Nordic Middle Ages*. Philadelphia: University of Pennsylvania Press, 2011.

Moeller, Katrin. *Dass Willkür über recht ginge: Hexenverfolgung in Mecklenburg im 16. und 17. Jahrhundert*. Bielefeld: Verlag für Regionalgeschichte, 2007.

Monter, E. William. "Scandinavian Witchcraft in Anglo-American Perspective." In Ankarloo and Henningsen, *Early Modern European Witchcraft*, 425–42.

———. "Toads and Eucharists: The Male Witches of Normandy, 1564–1660." *French Historical Studies* 20, no. 4 (1997): 563–95.

Moore, R.I. *The Formation of a Persecuting Society: Power and Deviance in Western Europe, 950–1250*. Oxford: Blackwell, 1987.

Mordovina, S. P., and A. L. Stanislavskii. "Gadatel'naia kniga XVII veka kholopa Pimena Kalinina." In Kotkov and Pankratova, *Istoriia russkogo iazyka*, 321–36.

Morozov, B. N. "Chastnoe pis'mo nachala XVII veka." In Kotkov and Pankratova, *Istoriia russkogo iazyka*, 287–90.

Morozova, I. A. "Obychai, verovaniia, magiia, sviazannye s nachalom i zavershenie trapezy." In Kostina and Mironikhina, *Traditsionnoe russkoe zastol'e*, 16–35.

Morris, Marcia A. "*The Tale of Savva Grudcyn* and the Poetics of Transition." *Slavic and East European Journal* 36, no. 2 (1992): 202–16.

Mousnier, Roland. *Social Hierarchies: 1450 to the Present*. London: Croom Helm, 1973.

Muchembled, Robert. "Satanic Myths and Cultural Reality." In Ankarloo and Henningsen, *Early Modern European Witchcraft*, 139–60.

Murray, Margaret Alice. *The God of the Witches*. Oxford: Oxford University Press, 1970.

Nenonen, Marko. "Culture Wars: State, Religion, and Popular Culture." In Barry and Davies, *Palgrave Advances in Witchcraft Historiography*, 108–24.

———. "Witch Hunts in Europe: A New Geography." In *ARV—Nordic Yearbook of Folklore 2006*, vol. 62. Oslo, 2007: 165–86.

Newlin, Thomas. "Rural Ruses: Illusion and Anxiety on the Russian Estate, 1775–1815." *Slavic Review* 57, no. 2 (1998): 295–319.

Niau, Des. *The History of the Devils of Loudun: The Alleged Possession of the Ursuline Nuns, and the Trial and Execution of Urbain Grandier. Told By an Eye-witness*. Translated and edited by Edmund Goldsmid, F.R.H.S. Privately printed, Edinburgh, 1887.

Norton, Mary Beth. *In the Devil's Snare: The Salem Witchcraft Crisis of 1692*. New York: Alfred A. Knopf, 2002.

Novombergskii, N. Ia. *Koldovstvo v Moskovskoi Rusi XVII veka*. St. Petersburg: Tipografiia Al'tshler, 1906.

———. *Materialy po istorii meditsiny v Rossii*. 4 vols. St. Petersburg: Tip. M. M. Stasiulevicha, 1905.

———. *Slovo i delo gosudarevy*. Istoriia russkoi kul'tury. 2 vols. Moscow: Iazyki slavianskoi kul'tury, 2004.

———. *Vrachebnoe stroenie v do-Petrovskoi Rusi: Materialy po istorii meditsiny v Rossii.* Vol. 4. Tomsk, 1907.

Novosel'skii, A. A. *Votchinnik i ego khoziaistvo v XVII veke.* Moscow: Gos. izd-vo, 1929.

Nun-Ingerflom, Claudio Sergio. "How Old Magic Does the Trick for Modern Politics." *Russian History* (forthcoming).

Ogloblin, N. N. *Kievskii stol Razriadnogo prikaza.* Kiev, 1886.

———. *Obozrenie istoriko-geograficheskikh materialov XVII i nachala XVIII vekakh: Zakliuchaiushchikhsia v knigakh Razriadnago prikaza.* Moscow: Tip. L. F. Snegireva, 1884.

———. *Obozrenie stolbtsov i knig Sibirskago prikaza (1592–1768 gg.)*, ch. 1, *Dokumenty voevodskago upravleniia.* Moscow: Universitetskaia tipografiia, 1895.

Oinas, Felix J. "Heretics as Vampires and Demons in Russia." *Slavic and East European Journal* 22, no. 4 (1978): 433–41.

Olearius, Adam. *The Travels of Olearius in Seventeenth-Century Russia.* Edited by Samuel Haskell Baron. Stanford: Stanford University Press, 1967.

Oparina, Tat'iana A. "'Chuzhie' pis'mena v russkoi magii." *Studia Slavica Academiae Scientiarum Hungaricae* 41, nos. 1–2 (2004): 53–62.

———. "Neizvestnyi ukaz 1653 g. o zapreshchenii koldovstva." *Drevniaia Rus': Voprosy medievistiki* 3, no. 9 (2002): 88–91.

Opisanie dokumentov i bumag, khraniashchikhsia v Moskovskom arkhive Ministerstva iustitsii (ODiB). 21 vols. Moscow: Tipo-lit. T-va I. N. Kushnerev, 1869.

Orlov, A. S., ed. *Domostroi po konshinskomu spisku i podobnym.* Moscow: Sinodal'naia Tipografiia, 1908.

Ostling, Michael. *Between the Devil and the Host: Imagining Witchcraft in Early Modern Poland.* Oxford: Oxford University Press, 2011.

Ovsiannikov, Iu., ed. *The Lubok: Seventeenth- to Eighteenth-Century Russian Broadsides.* Moscow: Sov. khudozhnik, 1968.

Oyewùmí, Oyèrónkẹ́. "Visualizing the Body: Western Theories and African Subjects." In *African Gender Studies: A Reader*, edited by Oyèrónkẹ́ Oyewùmí, 3–22. New York: Palgrave Macmillan, 2005.

Ozment, Steven E. *When Fathers Ruled: Family Life in Reformation Europe.* Studies in Cultural History. Cambridge: Harvard University Press, 1983.

Pagels, Elaine H. *Adam, Eve, and the Serpent.* New York: Random House, 1988.

Pamiatniki russkogo prava (PRP). Edited by S. V. Iushkov and L. V. Cherepnin. 8 vols. Moscow: Gosudarstvennoe izd. Iuridicheskoi literatury, 1952–1963.

Pavlov, A. P., and Maureen Perrie. *Ivan the Terrible.* London: Pearson/Longman, 2003.

Pee, Christian de. "Cases of the New Terrace: Canon and Law in Three Southern Song Verdicts." *Journal of Sung-Yuan Studies* 27 (1997): 27–61.

Perrie, Maureen. *The Image of Ivan the Terrible in Russian Folklore.* Cambridge: Cambridge University Press, 1987.

———. "The Tsaritsa, the Needlewomen, and the Witches: Magic in Moscow in the 1630s." *Russian History* (forthcoming).

———, ed. *From Early Rus'to 1689.* Vol. 1 of *The Cambridge History of Russia.* Cambridge: Cambridge University Press, 2006.

Pervukhin, N. G. *Tserkov'Ilii Proroka v Iaroslavle.* Moscow: K. F. Nekrasova, 1915.

Peters, Edward. *Torture.* Expanded ed. Philadelphia: University of Pennsylvania Press, 1996.

Petrukhin, V. Ia. *Drevniaia Rus': IX v.–1263 g.* Moscow: Astrel', 2005.

Pfister, Christian. "Climatic Extremes, Recurrent Crises, and Witch Hunts: Strategies of European Societies in Coping with Exogenous Shocks in the Late Sixteenth and Early Seventeenth Centuries." *Medieval History Journal* 10, nos. 1–2 (2007): 33–73.

Pigin, A. V. *Iz istorii russkoi demonologii XVII veka: Povest' o besnovatoi zhene Solomonii: Issledovanie i teksty.* St. Peterburg: Dmitrii Bulanin, 1998.

———. *Videniia potustoronnego mira v russkoi rukopisnoi knizhnosti.* St. Peterburg: Dmitrii Bulanin, 2006.

Plokhy, Serhii. *The Origins of the Slavic Nations: Premodern Identities in Russia, Ukraine, and Belarus.* Cambridge: Cambridge University Press, 2006.

Pócs, Éva. *Between the Living and the Dead: A Perspective on Witches and Seers in the Early Modern Age.* Translated by Szilvia Rédey and Michael Webb. Budapest: Central European University Press, 1999.

Poe, Marshall. *A People Born to Slavery: Russia in Early Modern European Ethnography, 1476–1748.* Ithaca: Cornell University Press, 2000.

———. "The Sexual Life of Muscovites: Evidence from the Foreign Accounts." *Russian History/Histoire Russe* 35, nos. 3–4 (2008): 409–27.

———. "Elite Service Registry in Muscovy, 1500–1700." *Russian History* 21, nos. 1–4 (1994): 251–88.

———. "What Did Russians Mean When They Called Themselves 'Slaves of the Tsar'?" *Slavic Review* 57, no. 3 (1998): 585–608.

Pokrovskaia, V. F. "Neizvestnyi spisok 'slova' Daniila Zatochnika." *TODRL* 10 (1954): 287–88.

Pokrovskii, N. N. "Ispoved' altaiskogo krest'ianina." In *Pamiatniki kul'tury: Novye otkrytiia: Ezhegodnik 1978*, 49–57. Leningrad: Nauka, 1979.

———. "Materialy po istorii magicheskikh verovanii sibiriakov XVII–XVIII vv." In *Iz istorii sem'i i byta sibirskogo krest'ianstva v XVI–nachale XX v.: sbornik nauchnykh trudov*, edited by M. M. Gromyko and N. A. Minenko, 113–15. Novosibirsk: Novosibirskii gos. universitet, 1975.

———. "Tetrad' zagovorov 1734 goda." In *Nauchnyi ateizm, religiia i sovremennost'*, edited by Aleksei Trofimovich Moskalenko, 239–65. Novosibirsk: Nauka, Sibirskoe otdnie, 1987.

Polnoe sobranie russkikh letopisei (PSRL), 43 vols. to date. St. Petersburg and Moscow: various publishers, 1841–.

Polnoe sobranie zakonov rossiiskoi imperii (PSZ). Series 1, 1649–1825, 45 vols. St. Petersburg: Otdelenie sobstvennoi Ego Imperatorskago Velichestva kantseliarii, 1830.

Popov, G. V. *Tver Icons: Thirteenth to Seventeenth Centuries*. St. Petersburg: Aurora Art Publishers, 1993.

Popov, A. N., ed., *Materialy dlia istorii vozmushcheniia Stenki Razina*. Moscow: L. Stepanova, 1857.

Popov, N. A., ed. *Akty Moskovskago gosudarstva: Razriadnyi prikaz, Moskovskii stol, 1571–1664*. Vol. 1, *1571–1634*. Vol. 2, *1635–1659*. Vol. 3, *1660–1664*. St. Petersburg: Tip. Imperatorskoi akademii nauk, 1890.

Pouncy, Carolyn, ed. *The "Domostroi": Rules for Russian Households in the Time of Ivan the Terrible*. Ithaca: Cornell University Press, 1994.

Puff, Helmut. *Sodomy in Reformation Germany and Switzerland, 1400–1600*. Chicago: University of Chicago Press, 2003.

Purkiss, Diane. *The Witch in History: Early Modern and Twentieth-Century Representations*. London: Routledge, 1996.

Pushkareva, Natal'ia L'vovna. *Women in Russian History: From the Tenth to the Twentieth Century*. Translated by Eve Levin. Armonk, N.Y.: M. E. Sharpe, 1997.

Reis, Elizabeth. "The Devil, the Body, and the Feminine Soul in Puritan New England." *Journal of American History* 82, no. 1 (1995): 15–36.

Remizov, Aleksei. *Besnovatye: Savva Grudtsin i Solomoniia*. Paris: Opleshnik, 1951.

Robisheaux, Thomas Willard. *The Last Witch of Langenburg: Murder in a German Village*. New York: W. W. Norton, 2009.

Robson, James. "Signs of Power: Talismanic Writing in Chinese Buddhism." *History of Religions* 48, no. 2 (2008): 130–69.

Rock, Stella. *Popular Religion in Russia: "Double Belief" and the Making of an Academic Myth*. London: Routledge, 2007.

Romaniello, Matthew P. *The Elusive Empire: Kazan and the Creation of Russia, 1552–1671*. Madison: University of Wisconsin Press, 2012.

Roper, Lyndal. *The Holy Household: Women and Morals in Reformation Augsburg*. New York: Oxford University Press, 1989.

———. *Oedipus and the Devil*. New York: Routledge, 1994.

———. "Witchcraft and Fantasy in Early Modern Germany." In Roper, *Oedipus and the Devil*, 199–225.

———. *Witch Craze: Terror and Fantasy in Baroque Germany*. New Haven: Yale University Press, 2004.

Rovinskii, D. A., ed. *Russkiia narodnyia kartinki*. Vol. 1. Moscow, 1881.

Rowland, Daniel B. "The Blessed Host of the Heavenly Tsar: Biblical Military Imagery in Muscovy." In Flier and Rowland, *Medieval Russian Culture*, 182–212.

———. "Blessed Is the Host of the Heavenly Tsar: An Icon from the Dormition Cathedral of the Moscow Kremlin." In Kivelson and Neuberger, *Picturing Russia*, 33–37.

———. "Boris Godunov's Uses of Architecture." In Cracraft and Rowland, *Architectures of Russian Identity*, 34–47.

———. "Moscow—The Third Rome or the New Israel?" *Russian Review* 55, no. 4 (1996): 591–614.

———. "The Problem of Advice in Muscovite Tales about the Time of Troubles." *Russian History* 6, nos. 1–2 (1979): 259–83.

———. "Two Cultures, One Throne Room: Secular Courtiers and Orthodox Culture in the Golden Hall of the Moscow Kremlin." In Kivelson and Greene, *Orthodox Russia*, 33–58.

Rowland, Robert. "'Fantasticall and Devilishe Persons': European Witch-Beliefs in Comparative Perspective." In Ankarloo and Henningsen, *Early Modern European Witchcraft*, 161–90.

Rowlands, Alison. "Not 'the Usual Suspects?': Male Witches, Witchcraft, and Masculinities in Early Modern Europe." In Rowlands, *Witchcraft and Masculinities in Early Modern Europe*, 1–30.

———, ed. *Witchcraft and Masculinities in Early Modern Europe*. New York: Palgrave Macmillan, 2009.

Rozysknyia dela o Fedore Shaklovitom i ego soobshchnikakh. 4 vols. St. Petersburg: Izd. Arkheograficheskoi kommissii, 1884.

Russell, Jeffrey Burton. *Witchcraft in the Middle Ages*. Ithaca: Cornell University Press, 1972.

Russkaia Istoricheskaia Biblioteka (RIB). 39 vols. St. Petersburg: Petrograd, Leningrad: various publishers, 1872–1927.

Ryan, W. F. *The Bathhouse at Midnight: An Historical Survey of Magic and Divination in Russia*. University Park: The Pennsylvania State University Press, 1999.

———. "Solomon, SATOR, Acrostics, and Leo the Wise in Russia." *Oxford Slavonic Papers* 19 (1986): 46–61.

———. "The Witchcraft Hysteria in Early Modern Europe: Was Russia an Exception?" *Slavonic and East European Review* 76, no. 1 (1998): 49–84.

Rybakov, Boris Aleksandrovich. *Iazychestvo drevnikh slavian*. Moscow: Nauka, 1981.

Rzhiga, V. F. *I. S. Peresvetov: Publitsist XVI veka*. Vol. 1, pt. 2. *ChOIDR*. Moscow: Sinodal'naia Tipografiia, 1908.

Sabean, David Warren. "The Sacred Bond of Unity: Community through the Eyes of a Thirteen-Year-Old Witch (1683)." In *Power in the Blood: Popular Culture and Village Discourse in Early Modern Germany*, 94–112. Cambridge: Cambridge University Press, 1984.

Sakovich, A. G. *Narodnaia gravirovannaia kniga Vasiliia Korenia, 1692–1696*. 2 vols. Moscow: Iskusstvo, 1983.

Sartre, Jean-Paul. "Preface." In Alleg, *The Question*, xxvii–xliv.

Scarry, Elaine. *The Body in Pain: The Making and Unmaking of the World.* New York: Oxford University Press, 1985.

Schrader, Abby M. *Languages of the Lash: Corporal Punishment and Identity in Imperial Russia.* DeKalb: Northern Illinois University Press, 2002.

Schulte, Rolf. *Man as Witch: Male Witches in Central Europe.* New York: Palgrave Macmillan, 2009.

———. "Men as Accused Witches in the Holy Roman Empire." In Rowlands, *Witchcraft and Masculinities in Early Modern Europe*, 52–73.

Schwerhoff, Gerd. "Ot povsednevnykh podozrenii k massovym goneniiam: Noveiskie germanskie issledovaniia po istorii vedovstva v nachale Novogo vremeni." Translated by K. A. Levinson. *Odissei: Chelovek v istorii, 1996* (1996): 306–30.

Scot, Reginald. *The Discoverie of Witchcraft.* Mineola, NY: Dover Publications, 1989.

Scott, James C. *Domination and the Arts of Resistance: Hidden Transcripts.* New Haven: Yale University Press, 1990.

———. *The Moral Economy of the Peasant: Rebellion and Subsistence in Southeast Asia.* New Haven: Yale University Press, 1976.

———. *Weapons of the Weak: Everyday Forms of Peasant Resistance.* New Haven: Yale University Press, 1985.

Seaver, Paul S. *Wallington's World: A Puritan Artisan in Seventeenth-Century London.* Stanford: Stanford University Press, 1985.

Sedov, V. V., and A. V. Chernetsov. "Slavianskoe iazychestvo kak problem mezhdistsiplinarnogo izucheniia." *Vestnik AN SSSR* (1981): 76–81.

Semevskii, M., ed. *Istoriko-iuridicheskie akty XVI i XVII vekov.* St. Petersburg: Tip. V. Balasheva, 1892.

Sergeev, V. N. "Dukhovnyi stikh 'Plach Adama' na ikone." *TODRL* 26 (1971): 280–86.

Ševčenko, Ihor. "Remarks on the Diffusion of Byzantine Scientific and Pseudo-Scientific Literature among the Orthodox Slavs." *Slavonic and East European Review* 59, no. 3 (1981): 321–45.

Shakhmatov, M. V. "Chelobitnaia 'mira' Moskovskago Tsariu Alekseiu Mikhailovichu, 10 iunia 1648 g." In *Vestnik královské českē společnosti nauk: Třída filosoficko-historicko. Rodnik 1933*, 1–23. Prague: Královské českē společnosti nauk, 1934.

Sharpe, J. A. "Disruption in the Well-Ordered Household: Age, Authority, and Possessed Young People." In *The Experience of Authority in Early Modern England*, edited by Paul Griffiths, Adam Fox, and Steve Hindle, 187–212. Basingstoke: Macmillan, 1996.

———. *Instruments of Darkness: Witchcraft in Early Modern England.* Philadelphia: University of Pennsylvania Press, 1996.

Shashkov, A. T. "Iakutskoe delo o koldune Ivane Zheglove." In *Obshchestvennoe soznanie, knizhnost', literatura perioda feodalizma*, edited by D. S. Likhachev and N. N. Pokrovskii. 83–88. Novosibirsk: Nauka, Sibirskoe otdelenie, 1990.

———, ed. *Problemy istorii Rossii.* 6 volumes to date. Ekaterinburg: Ural'skii gos. universitet, 1996–2005.

Shvetsova, E.A., A.A. Novosel'skii, and V.I. Lebedev, eds. *Krest'ianskaia voina pod predvoditel'stvom Stepana Razina: Sbornik dokumentov.* Vol. 2, pt. 1. Moscow: Izd-vo Akademii Nauk SSSR, 1957.

Siegel, James T. *Naming the Witch.* Cultural Memory in the Present. Stanford: Stanford University Press, 2006.

Silverman, Lisa. *Tortured Subjects: Pain, Truth, and the Body in Early Modern France.* Chicago: University of Chicago Press, 2001.

Simons, Patricia. *The Sex of Men in Premodern Europe: A Cultural History.* Cambridge: Cambridge University Press, 2011.

"Skazanie o tsarstve Tsaria Fedoroa Ioannovicha." In *Pamiatniki drevnei russkoi pis'mennosti, otnosiashchiesia k Smutnomu vremeni,* cols. 755–80. Hildesheim: Olms, 1909.

Skripil', Mikhail Osipovich. *Russkaia povest' XVII veka.* Leningrad: Gos. izd-vo khudozh. lit-ry, 1954.

Sluhovsky, Moshe. *Believe Not Every Spirit: Possession, Mysticism, and Discernment in Early Modern Catholicism.* Chicago: University of Chicago Press, 2007.

Smail, Daniel Lord. *The Consumption of Justice: Emotions, Publicity, and Legal Culture in Marseille, 1264–1423.* Ithaca: Cornell University Press, 2003.

Smilianskaia, E. B. *Volshebniki, bogokhul'niki, eretiki: Narodnaia religioznost' i "dukhovnye prestupleniia" v Rossii XVIII veke.* Moscow: Indrik, 2003.

Smirnov, Pavel Petrovich. *Posadskie liudi i ikh klassovaia bor'ba do serediny XVII veka.* Vol. 2. Moscow: Izd-vo Akademii nauk SSSR, 1947.

Smirnov, S. "Baby bogomerzkiia." In *Sbornik statei, posviashchennykh Vasiliiu Osipovichu Kliuchevskomu: Ego uchenikami, druz'iami, i pochitateliami ko dniu tridtsatilietiia ego professorskoi dieiatel'nosti v Moskovskom universitetie, 5 dekabria 1879–5 dekabria 1909 goda,* 217–40. Moscow: T-vo Pechatnaia S. P. Iakovleva, 1909.

Sobornoe Ulozhenie 1649 goda. Edited by M. H. Tikhomirov and P. P. Epifanov. Moscow: Izd-vo Moskovskogo universiteta, 1961. http://hist.msu.ru/ER/Etext/1649.htm.

Sofronenko, K.A., ed. *Zakonodatel'nye akty Petra I: Pervaia chetvert' XVIII veka.* Vol. 8, *PRP.* Moscow: Gosudarstvenna izd. Iuridicheskoi literatury, 1961.

Sreznevskii, I. I. *Slovar' drevnerusskogo iazyka.* 3 vols. in 6 vols. Reprint. Moscow: Kniga, 1989.

Staden, Heinrich von. *The Land and Government of Muscovy: A Sixteenth-Century Account.* Translated by Thomas Esper. Stanford: Stanford University Press, 1967.

Stefanovich, P. S., and B. N. Morozov. *Roman Vilimovich v gostiakh u Petra Ignat'evicha: Pskovskii arkhiv angliiskogo kuptsa 1680-kh godov.* Moscow: Indrik, 2009.

Stephens, Walter. *Demon Lovers: Witchcraft, Sex, and the Crisis of Belief.* Chicago: University of Chicago Press, 2002.

Sterligov, M., ed. *Russkoe koldovstvo, vedovstvo, znakharstvo.* St. Petersburg: Izd-vo "Litera," 1994.

Stevens, Carol B. "Belgorod: Notes on Literacy and Language in the Seventeenth-Century Russian Army." *Russian History* 7, nos. 1–2 (1980): 113–24.

Stoglav. Rarity Reprints 17. 1863. Reprint, Letchworth: Bradda Books, 1971.

Strakhov, Aleksandr Borisovich. *Noch' pered Rozhdestvom: Narodnoe khristianstvo i rozhdestvenskaia obriadnost' na zapade i u slavian.* Cambridge, Mass.: Palaeoslavica, 2003.

Strathern, Marilyn. *The Gender of the Gift: Problems with Women and Problems with Society in Melanesia.* Berkeley: University of California Press, 1988.

Stuckrad, Kocku von. "Refutation and Desire: European Perceptions of Shamanism in the Late Eighteenth Century." *Journal of Religion in Europe* 5, no. 1 (2012): 100–121.

Sytova, Alla, ed. *The Lubok: Russian Folk Pictures, Seventeenth to Nineteenth Century.* Translated by Alex Miller. Leningrad: Aurora Art Publishers, 1984.

Tambiah, Stanley J. "The Magical Power of Words." *Man* 3 (1968): 177–206.

Thomas, Keith. *Religion and the Decline of Magic.* New York: Scribner, 1971.

Thomas, Kevin Tyner. "Collecting for the Fatherland: Early Nineteenth-Century Proposals for a Russian National Museum." In Burbank and Ransel, *Imperial Russia,* 91–107.

Thompson, E. P. "The Moral Economy of the English Crowd in the Eighteenth Century." *Past and Present* 50, no. 1 (1971): 76–136.

———. "The Moral Economy Reviewed." In E. P. Thompson, *Customs in Common,* 259–351. New York: The New Press, 1991.

Thyrêt, Isolde. *Between God and Tsar: Religious Symbolism and the Royal Women of Muscovite Russia.* DeKalb: Northern Illinois University Press, 2001.

———. "'Blessed Is the Tsaritsa's Womb': The Myth of Miraculous Birth and Royal Motherhood in Muscovite Russia." *Russian Review* 53, no. 4 (1994): 479–96.

———. "Muscovite Miracle Stories as Sources for Gender-Specific Religious Experience." In Baron and Kollmann, *Religion and Culture in Early Modern Russia and Ukraine,* 115–31.

Titov, A. A. "Iosif Arkhiepiskop Kolomenskii (Delo o nem, 1675–1676 gg.)." *ChOIDR,* bk. 3, pt. 1 (1911): 1–160.

Titov, V. V. *Lozhnye i otrechennye knigi slavianskoi i russkoi stariny: Teksty-pervoistochniki XV–XVIII vekov. s primechaniiami, kommentariiami, i chastichnym perevodom.* Moscow: Gos. publichnaia istoricheskaia biblioteka Rossii, 1999.

Titova, L. V. "Beseda ottsa s synom o zhenskoi zlobe." In *SKKDR,* vol. 3, *XVII,* pt. 1, 137–39.

Toivo, Raisa Maria. "The Witch-Craze as Holocaust: The Rise of Persecuting Societies." In Barry and Davies, *Palgrave Advances in Witchcraft Historiography,* 90–107.

Toporkov, A. L. "Gramota no. 521: Zagovor ili liubovnaia zapiska?" In *Slovo i kul'tura,* edited by T. A. Agapkina, et al., vol. 2, 230–41. Moscow: Indrik, 1998.

———. *Zagovory v russkoi rukopisnoi traditsii XV–XIX veka: Istoriia, simvolika, poetika.* Moscow: Indrik, 2005.

———, ed. *Russkie zagovory iz rukopisnykh istochnikov XVII–pervoi poloviny XIX veka.* Moscow: Indrik, 2010.

Toporkov, A. L., and A. A. Turilov, eds. *Otrechennoe chtenie v Rossii XVII–XVIII vekov: Publikatsiia tekstov.* Moscow: Indrik, 2002.

Tracy, James D., and Marguerite Ragnow, eds. *Religion and the Early Modern State: Views from China, Russia, and the West.* Cambridge: Cambridge University, 2004.

Trevor-Roper, H. R. "The European Witch-Craze of the Sixteenth and Seventeenth Centuries." In *The European Witch-Craze of the Sixteenth and Seventeenth Centuries, and Other Essays*, 90–192. New York: Harper & Row, 1969.

———. "The General Crisis of the Seventeenth Century." *Past & Present* 16, no. 1 (1959): 31–64.

Trudy Otdela drevnerusskoi literatury (TODRL). Leningrad-St. Petersburg: Nauka, 1934–.

Truvorov, A. N. "Volkhvy i vorozhei na Rusi v kontse XVII veka." *Istoricheskii vestnik* 36, no. 6 (1889): 701–15.

Turilov, A. A., and A. V. Chernetsov. "Novoe imia v istorii russkoi kul'tury." *Priroda* 9 (1985): 88–97.

———. "Otrechennaia kniga Rafli." In *TODRL*, 40: 260–344.

Unkovskaya, Maria V. *Brief Lives: A Handbook of Medical Practitioners in Muscovy, 1620–1701.* London: Wellcome Trust, 1999.

Uspenskii, Boris Aleksandrovich. "Pravo i religiia v Moskovskoi Rusi." In *Rossica/Rusistika/Rossijevedenije*, edited by E. I. Pivovar, et al., 194–286. Moscow: Rossiiskii gosudarstvennyi gumanitarnyi universitet, 2010.

Valentsova, M. M. "Magicheskie funktsii edy." In Kostina and Mironikhina, *Traditsionnoe russkoe zastol'e*, 202–15.

Vinogradova, V. L. "Povest' o Gore-Zlochastii." *TODRL* 12 (1956): 622–41.

Vladimirskii-Budanov, M. F. *Obzor istorii russkago prava.* St. Petersburg: Izd. N. Ia. Ogloblina, 1909.

Vodarskii, Ia. E. *Naselenie Rossii v kontse XVII–nachale XVIII veka: Chislennost', soslovno-klassovyi sostav, razmeshchenie.* Moscow: Nauka, 1977.

Voltaire, François-Marie Arouet de. *A Philosophical Dictionary.* Boston: J. P. Mendum, 1852.

Voltmer, Rita. "Witch-Finders, Witch-Hunters, or Kings of the Sabbath?: The Prominent Role of Men in the Mass Persecutions of the Rhine-Meuse Area (Sixteenth–Seventeenth Centuries)." In Rowlands, *Witchcraft and Masculinities in Early Modern Europe*, 74–99.

Walinski-Kiehl, Robert. "Males, 'Masculine Honor,' and Witch-Hunting in Seventeenth-Century Germany." *Men and Masculinities* 6, no. 3 (2004): 254–71.

Ware, Archimandrite Kallistos. *The Orthodox Church.* Harmondsworth: Penguin Books, 1975.

Watt, Jeffrey R. *The Scourge of Demons: Possession, Lust, and Witchcraft in a Seventeenth-Century Italian Convent*. Rochester: University of Rochester Press, 2009.

Weickhardt, George G. "Due Process and Equal Justice in the Muscovite Codes." *Russian Review* 51, no. 4 (1992): 463–80.

———. "Legal Rights of Women in Russia, 1100–1750." *Slavic Review* 55, no. 1 (1996): 1–23.

———. "Muscovite Judicial Duels as a Legal Fiction." *Kritika: Explorations in Russian and Eurasian History* 7, no. 4 (2006): 713–32.

Weyer, Johann. *Witches, Devils, and Doctors in the Renaissance: Johann Weyer, De Praestigiis Daemonum*. Edited by George Mora and Benjamin G. Kohl. Translated by John Shea. Binghamton, N.Y.: Medieval and Renaissance Texts and Studies, 1991.

Wigzell, Faith. "Bludnye synov'ia ili bluzhdaiushchie dushi: 'Povest' o Gore-Zlochastii' i 'Ocharovannyi strannik' Leskova." *TODRL* 50 (1997): 754–62.

———. "Conceptions of Time in East Slavonic Popular Visions and Dreams about Visiting Heaven and Hell." *New Zealand Slavonic Journal* 36 (n.d.): 289–302.

———. "Traditional Magic or European Occultism?: Commercial Fortune-Telling and Magic in Post-Soviet Russia and Their Relationship to Russian Tradition." *Journal of the Slavic and East European Folklore Association*, no. 14 (2009): 57–90.

Williams, Gerhild Scholz. *Defining Dominion: The Discourses of Magic and Witchcraft in Early Modern France and Germany*. Ann Arbor: University of Michigan Press, 1995.

Willis, Deborah. *Malevolent Nurture: Witch-hunting and Maternal Power in Early Modern England.* Ithaca, NY: Cornell University Press, 1995.

Wintroub, Michael. *A Savage Mirror: Power, Identity, and Knowledge in Early Modern France*. Stanford: Stanford University Press, 2006.

Wirtschafter, Elise Kimerling. *Social Identity in Imperial Russia*. DeKalb: Northern Illinois University Press, 1997.

Witzenrath, Christoph. "Literacy and Orality in the Eurasian Frontier: Imperial Culture and Space in Seventeenth-Century Siberia and Russia." *Slavonic and East European Review* 87, no. 1 (2009): 53–77.

Wood, Juliette. "The Reality of Witch Cults Reasserted: Fertility and Satanism." In Barry and Davies, *Palgrave Advances in Witchcraft Historiography*, 69–89.

Worobec, Christine D. "Decriminalizing Witchcraft in Pre-Emancipation Russia." In *Späte Hexenprozesse*, edited by Wolfgang Behringer. Gütersloh: Verlag für Regionalgeschichte, 2013 (forthcoming).

———. *Possessed: Women, Witches, and Demons in Imperial Russia*. DeKalb: Northern Illinois University Press, 2001.

———. "Witchcraft Beliefs and Practices in Prerevolutionary Russian and Ukrainian Villages." *Russian Review* 54, no. 2 (1995): 165–87.

Wyporska, Wanda. *Witchcraft in Early Modern Poland, 1500–1800*. Palgrave Macmillan, (forthcoming).

Zabelin, Ivan E. *Domashnii byt' russkikh tsarits v XVI i XVII stoletiiakh.* 1915. Reprint, Novosibirsk: Nauka, 1992.

———. "Sysknye dela o vorozheiakh i koldun'iakh pri Tsare Mikhaile Fedoroviche." In *Kometa: Uchebno-literaturnyi almanakh*, edited by N. M. Shchepkin, 471–92. St. Petersburg: Iu. V. Gol'dberg, 1851.

Zagoskin, N. P. *Stoly Razriadnogo prikaza, po khraniashchimsia v Moskovskom arkhive Ministerstva iustitsii knigam ikh: Otchet o zaniatiakh v arkhive oseniu 1878 goda.* Kazan': Tip. Imp. Kazanskogo universiteta, 1878.

Zenbitskii, P. "Zagovory (kontsa XVII veka)." *Zhivaia starina*, no. 1 (1907): 1–6.

Zertsalov, A. N. "K materialam o vorozhbe v drevnei Rusi: Sysknoe delo 1642–1643 gg. o namerenii isportit' Tsaritsu Evdokiiu Luk'ianovnu." *ChOIDR* 3 (1895): 1–38.

Zguta, Russell. "The Ordeal by Water (Swimming of Witches) in the East Slavic World." *Slavic Review* 36, no. 2 (1977): 220–30.

———. "Was There a Witch Craze in Muscovite Russia?" *Southern Folklore Quarterly* 41 (1977): 119–28.

———. "Witchcraft and Medicine in Pre-Petrine Russia." *Russian Review* 37, no. 4 (1978): 438–48.

———. "Witchcraft Trials in Seventeenth-Century Russia." *American Historical Review* 82, no. 5 (1977): 1187–1207.

Zhivov, V. M. "Dvoeverie i osobyi kharakter russkoi kul'turnoi istorii." In *Philologia Slavica: K 70-letiiu akademika N. I. Tolstogo*, edited by V. N. Toporov, 50–59. Moscow: Nauka, 1993.

———. "On the Language of *The Book of Degrees of the Royal Genealogy*." In Lenhoff and Kleimola, The Book of Royal Degrees *and the Genesis of Russian Historical Consciousness*, 141–56.

Zhuravel', O. D. *Siiuzhet o dogovore cheloveka s d'iavolom v drevnerusskoi literature.* Novosibirsk: Sibirskii khronograf, 1996.

Zika, Charles. *The Appearance of Witchcraft: Print and Visual Culture in Sixteenth-Century Europe*. London: Routledge, 2007.

———, ed. *Exorcising Our Demons: Magic, Witchcraft, and Visual Culture in Early Modern Europe.* Leiden: Brill, 2003.

Zimin, A. A. "Doktor Nikolai Bulev—publitsist i uchenyi medik." In *Issledovaniia i materialy po drevnerusskoi literature*, edited by V. D. Kuz'mina. Moscow: AN SSSR, 1961, 78–86.

———. *Rossiia na rubezhe XV–XVI stoletii: Ocherki sotsial'no-politicheskoi istorii*. Moscow: Mysl', 1982.

Index

Note: Page numbers in *italics* indicate illustrations. Page numbers followed by *t* indicate tables.